Bake Something Great!

400
Bars, Squares & Cookies

Jill Snider

Robert
ROSE

Bake Something Great!
Text copyright © 2011 Jill Snider
Photographs copyright © 2011 Robert Rose Inc.
Cover and text design copyright © 2011 Robert Rose Inc.

The recipes in this book were previously published in *Bars & Squares*, published in 2006 by Robert Rose Inc., and in *Cookies*, published in 2007 by Robert Rose Inc.

No part of this publication may be reproduced, stored in a retrieval system or transmitted, in any form or by any means, without the prior written consent of the publisher or a license from the Canadian Copyright Licensing Agency (Access Copyright). For an Access Copyright license, visit www.accesscopyright.ca or call toll-free: 1-800-893-5777.

For complete cataloguing information, see page 480.

Disclaimer

The recipes in this book have been carefully tested by our kitchen and our tasters. To the best of our knowledge, they are safe and nutritious for ordinary use and users. For those people with food or other allergies, or who have special food requirements or health issues, please read the suggested contents of each recipe carefully and determine whether or not they may create a problem for you. All recipes are used at the risk of the consumer.

We cannot be responsible for any hazards, loss or damage that may occur as a result of any recipe use.

For those with special needs, allergies, requirements or health problems, in the event of any doubt, please contact your medical adviser prior to the use of any recipe.

Design and Production: Kevin Cockburn/PageWave Graphics Inc.
Editor: Judith Finlayson
Copy editors: Julia Armstrong and Eleanor Gasparik
Recipe editor and tester: Jennifer MacKenzie
Proofreader: Kelly Jones
Indexer: Gillian Watts
Photographer: Colin Erricson
Associate Photographer: Matt Johannsson
Food Stylists: Kathryn Robertson, Kate Bush and Jill Snider
Prop Stylist: Charlene Erricson

Cover image: Double Fudge Brownies (page 18)
Page 4: Caramel Honey Pecan Bars (page 154) and Praline Bars (page 72)

We acknowledge the financial support of the Government of Canada through the Book Publishing Industry Development Program (BPIDP) for our publishing activities.

Published by Robert Rose Inc.
120 Eglinton Avenue East, Suite 800, Toronto, Ontario, Canada M4P 1E2
Tel: (416) 322-6552 Fax: (416) 322-6936
www.robertrose.ca

Printed and bound in China

1 2 3 4 5 6 7 8 9 PPLS 19 18 17 16 15 14 13 12 11

Contents

Part 1: Bars and Squares

Part 2: Cookies

Acknowledgments

I'd like to thank the many talented people who helped make this cookbook a reality: my publisher, Bob Dees, who firmly believes that bars, squares and cookies are both delicious and easy to make; the team at PageWave Graphics (Andrew Smith, Joseph Gisini, Kevin Cockburn and Daniella Zanchetta), who worked through editorial, design, layouts and production to put it all together; Brenda Venedam and Laurie Andrechuk, who accurately input the recipes; Judith Finlayson, Eleanor Gasparik, Jennifer MacKenzie and Julia Armstrong for their editorial support; Kate Bush and Kathryn Robertson for their amazing food styling; Charlene Erricson for prop styling; and Colin Erricson for his outstanding photographs, which make everything jump off the page.

I'd also like to thank my wonderful mother, Teddy. Although she is no longer with me, I know she would have loved seeing some of her favorite recipes in my book, especially the chapter on nuts. Her baking gave me a love and appreciation for homemade.

Thanks also to my sister, Judie, and nieces, Jennie and Susie, for serving recipes from my previous books at every possible occasion and showing my books to everyone they know. And to all my friends and neighbors who tasted and commented on the recipes — and generously offered to take all those extra bars, squares and cookies off my hands after the testing was done.

Introduction

The enticing aroma of home baking wafting from the kitchen usually brings back pleasant memories of everyday events, as well as special occasions. As the ultimate comfort food, homemade cookies are probably remembered most warmly — everyone loves them and they are welcome any time of year. Put them in lunch boxes, savor them with a mug of steaming coffee or a glass of cold milk, or pack them in fancy wrapping for an always-valued gift.

The fact that cookies don't take very long to bake — about 10 minutes for most — means you don't have to spend a long time in the kitchen to experience gratification. And you don't need any special equipment — just some good cookie sheets.

But bar cookies, such as brownies and other kinds of squares, are an expedient way to produce similar results. Nothing is easier to make; you just spread the batter in the pan, bake and cut. Bars usually contain relatively few ingredients, and the ones with multiple layers are likely to be simpler than they appear. The short baking time means you don't need to spend a lot of time in the kitchen.

Bars and squares are also extremely versatile. A luscious bar is just the thing for coffee breaks and snacks, picnic lunches and cookie swaps. With the addition of ice cream, a sundae sauce or fruit purée, they're easily transformed into a delicious dessert. Sometimes an addition as simple as a chocolate drizzle or a dusting of confectioners' (icing) sugar is all it takes to dress them up for a special occasion. You can also cut them into diamonds or triangles to vary the look.

It's usually just as easy to make a big batch of bars, squares and cookies as a small one, so one recipe can produce a large quantity, which is great for potlucks and bake sales. And bars, squares and cookies can be stored at room temperature, sometimes for as long as a week. Some also freeze well, which means you can bake when it's convenient, getting a head start on special occasions and holiday baking.

Whether you are an experienced or novice baker, this book will help you to appreciate how easy and satisfying baking bars, squares and cookies can be. Baking is a great way to get the whole family into the kitchen to enjoy time together. Whatever your tastes, whatever the occasion and whatever your timeframe, I'm sure you'll find recipes in this book that will inspire you to bake. Some recipes, perhaps those that qualify as family favorites, will bring back treasured memories. Others may seem new and — I hope — will inspire you to experiment. Whether you are baking for everyday or for a special occasion, I sincerely hope you have fun and enjoy the experience.

Happy baking and happy eating!

— Jill Snider

Baking for Success

Baking bars, squares and cookies is relatively quick and easy compared to other types of baking. To achieve success, you need only the basics: reliable, easy-to-follow recipes, good equipment, quality ingredients and attention to detail. The following information will help you achieve the best results every time you bake.

Know Your Oven

Oven temperature plays a critical role in baking. If your oven is too hot, your baked goods will be overly brown on the surface and may not be completely cooked through. If it is not hot enough, you'll end up overcooking the interior to achieve the desirable degree of browning. Ideally, the temperature you set determines how hot the oven will be once it's finished preheating. The problem is, most ovens are 25°F (10°C) hotter or cooler than their setting. Using your oven and observing how quickly or slowly it cooks in relation to the recipes you use will give you a general sense of whether it's hotter or cooler than the setting. A more accurate solution, which I recommend, is to purchase a reliable oven thermometer. This simple, inexpensive device will tell you the exact temperature your oven cooks at, allowing you to adjust the setting accordingly.

Convection Ovens

Convection ovens cook differently than traditional ones. If you're using a convection oven to bake the recipes in this book, check your manual and follow the instructions. Because convection ovens are more energy-efficient than traditional models, you can either reduce the baking time by about 25% or lower the oven temperature by 25°F (10°C). As a rule of thumb, when baking anything for less than 15 minutes, reduce the oven temperature rather than the baking time. Convection ovens, like traditional ones, need to be preheated to the desired temperature when baking.

Use the Right Equipment

Having good-quality equipment makes a big difference when baking. You don't need to invest a lot of money — often the most expensive pans and utensils aren't the best. But take time to ensure that you have what you need and that it works well for you.

Baking Pans

The quality of your pan can make a big difference to the end result of your bars and squares, so it's worth doing research before buying. Ask for advice at a good kitchen supply store or read cooking magazines that test and rate equipment, such as *Cook's Illustrated*. Good-quality, shiny metal pans are a great investment because they bake evenly and do not rust. The recipes in Part 1 of this book have been tested using metal pans; however, glass baking dishes also work well. Some pans cook more quickly than others. If using glass baking dishes or nonstick pans, especially dark ones, lower the oven temperature by 25°F (10°C).

The bars and squares recipes in this book call for one of five pan sizes: an 8-inch (2 L) square; a 9-inch (2.5 L) square; a 13- by 9-inch (3 L) rectangle; a 15- by 10- by 1-inch (2 L) jelly roll pan; or a 17- by 11- by 1-inch (3 L) jelly roll pan. A 9-inch (2.5 L) square pan will yield the same number of pieces as an 8-inch (2 L) square pan, but the pieces will be slightly larger.

For optimum results, use the pan size recommended in the recipe. A different size will affect the baking time and likely change the final result. If your pan is too small, it may overflow or produce underbaked, sunken, doughy bars. If it's too large, you'll end up with dry, overdone bars.

Bowls

Every kitchen needs a variety of bowls in different sizes for combining and mixing ingredients. Metal or glass bowls are preferable. Plastic does not work well for beating egg whites, as it retains oils, which can hamper results. Invest in a few bowls of each size: small, medium and large.

Cookie Cutters

Have a set of round cutters in graduated sizes, as well as a selection of your favorite shapes and characters. Small aspic or canapé cutters are handy for sandwich cookies that have a small cutout on top through which the filling peeps. Cutters with a thin, sharp edge work best.

Cookie Press

Fancy pressed cookies are created when dough is pressed through a cookie press. A cookie press pushes dough down a cylinder and through decorative perforated plates. These devices are available in kitchen supply and cake decorating stores. A pastry bag and tip may be used instead if the dough is soft, such as that used to make meringues and macaroons. A press is needed for stiffer dough, such as that used for spritz cookies.

Cookie Sheets

In most cases, the only pan you will need to bake cookies is a cookie sheet. I like to have at least four without sides because the absence of sides allows the air to circulate properly. I prefer regular metal pans over nonstick because nonstick surfaces are easy to ruin. Also, nonstick surfaces that are dark cause cookies to bake more quickly. If you're using these, decrease your oven temperature by 25°F (10°C).

Electric Mixer

An electric mixer is advantageous for creaming butter-and-sugar mixtures to a light and creamy texture, for beating in whole eggs, for mixing dense ingredients such as cream cheese or for beating egg whites to stiff peaks. It's also useful for achieving a smooth, creamy texture when making frostings. You can use either an electric countertop (stand) mixer or a good-quality hand mixer. If you do a lot of baking, the countertop model is much more efficient and easier to use. When making cookies, it can also handle a stiffer dough.

Food Processor

A food processor is a valuable kitchen tool that performs many tasks that can make cookie preparation faster and easier. It quickly chops, grinds and purées mixtures such as fruit and nuts. Some doughs, such as the Almond and Pine Nut Macaroons (page 281), are prepared completely in a food processor.

Ice Cream Scoops

Using ice cream scoops with a wire release to drop the batter on your cookie sheet will give you uniform size and nicely shaped cookies. The small scoop holds about 1 tbsp (15 mL) of dough and is about $1\frac{1}{2}$ inches (4 cm) in diameter. For monster cookies, you can use a $\frac{1}{4}$-cup (60 mL) scoop, about $2\frac{1}{4}$ inches (5.5 cm) in diameter, or a dry measuring cup.

Measuring Cups and Spoons

You will need glass or clear plastic measuring cups for liquid ingredients, a set of graduated dry ingredient measures and a set of measuring spoons.

Parchment Paper and Silicone Sheets

To ensure that your cookies will be easy to remove from the sheets, invest in parchment paper. It is available in large sheets and rolls and is heatproof. Lining cookie sheets with parchment paper prevents cookies from sticking to and scratching the sheet. It's also convenient. If your cookie sheets have no sides, it's easy to slide the parchment paper on and off the sheet. While one batch of cookies is baking, you can be placing dough on another sheet of parchment paper so it's ready to be transferred to a cookie sheet that has come out of the oven and cooled. Washable silicone sheets also work well in place of parchment paper.

Pastry Blender

For some cookies, such as those made with shortbread or pastry-like dough, or for layered bars that have a shortbread or cookie crust, I like to use a pastry blender to cut cold butter into the flour-sugar mixture. You can also use two knives, your fingers, a food processor or a mixer to achieve the desired crumble mixture. The butter should be cold and cubed, except when you're mixing by hand or using a mixer to prepare crusts, in which case it should be soft. No matter the method, the crumbled mixture usually requires further mixing with your hands to achieve a smooth dough.

Rolling Pin

A rolling pin is essential for making cutout cookies, as the dough must be rolled first.

Spatulas

A couple of rubber spatulas are useful for folding in ingredients and scraping down the side of a mixing bowl. Silicone spatulas are a great asset when you're working with hot mixtures — for instance, the no-bake cookies that are made from ingredients melted on top of the stove. Offset spatulas, which have a bend in the metal spreader, are also useful for spreading mixtures evenly into a pan, flattening cookies and applying frosting. I like to have both a small and a medium one in my kitchen. They're also handy for removing baked cookies and cut bars from the cookie sheet or pan.

Wire Racks

Wire racks are essential for cooling baked goods. Setting the cookie sheet or baking pan on a wire rack allows circulating air to cool the bottom. It's a good idea to have a variety of sizes and shapes (square, rectangular) to suit whatever you're making. I recommend stainless-steel racks, as they last a long time and won't rust.

Wire Whisks

Even if you use an electric mixer, you should have a couple of all-purpose wire whisks, in particular small and medium. These are useful for beating eggs before adding them to batters and for blending eggs and sugar and other mixtures that don't require much beating.

Wooden Spoons

These are great for mixing (although many doughs and batters can be mixed by hand) because the handles are sturdy and comfortable to hold.

Tips for Success

Although bars, squares and cookies are among the simplest treats to bake, here are some helpful tips to make yours even better:

- Stick to the recipe or the variations. Do not use margarine identified as diet, liquid, soft or whipped. These contain added water, and their soft texture will produce unsatisfactory results. Unsalted and salted butter are interchangeable. For the best results and flavor, I prefer butter, but margarine that is 80% fat will also work well in these recipes.
- Altering cookie recipes to make them healthier may sound like a great idea, but it often doesn't work out as planned. Any change in the proportion of ingredients also changes the result. In addition to adding flavor, sugar and fat make cookies crisp and tender. Reducing sugar and fat makes them softer and more cake-like. That said, here are some steps you can take to make bars, squares and cookies more nutritious:
  - Substitute whole wheat flour for half of the white flour to increase the range of nutrients and the amount of fiber.
  - Add dried fruits such as raisins, dates, apricots, figs and cranberries or some fresh chopped apple or grated carrot to up the nutrients and fiber.
  - Replace a whole egg with 2 egg whites if you're concerned about the cholesterol in food.
  - Use mini semisweet chocolate chips in place of the regular-size ones, but use half the amount. It gives the appearance that there is lots of chocolate and you'll still taste chocolate in every bite.
- Have all your ingredients at room temperature before you start. This makes for easy blending.
- Although many recipes call for an electric mixer, when you're beating ingredients such as butter, sugar and eggs, you can also use a wooden spoon. It just takes more work. It is essential that the butter be soft when you start. By either method, beat until smoothly blended, about 3 minutes.
- I prefer regular metal pans over nonstick ones because I like to cut my bars right in the pan. It wouldn't take long to ruin a nonstick surface that way. If your pans are nonstick, consider lining them with parchment paper or greased foil.
- If you choose to grease your cookie sheets rather than use parchment paper, use cooking spray or a light coating of shortening.

Over-greasing causes cookies to spread excessively and brown too quickly around the edges. It isn't necessary to regrease sheets between batches. Follow the instructions in your recipe as to whether the sheet should be left ungreased.

- Be sure to preheat your oven for at least 15 minutes before you're ready to bake so it is at the proper temperature before you put the cookies in.
- When making rolled and cutout cookies, dip your cutter in flour to keep it from sticking to the dough. Cut the cookies as close together as you can. You can reroll the scraps, but the less you handle the dough, the more tender your cookies will be.
- Place cookies about 2 inches (5 cm) apart on the cookie sheet to allow for spreading. If the dough is one that doesn't spread too much, such as shortbread, 1 inch (2.5 cm) apart is usually enough. This placement will be indicated in the recipe.
- When baking, place your cookie sheet on the middle oven rack, making sure it doesn't touch the sides of the oven. This ensures that the heat can circulate properly. For best results, bake only one sheet at a time. If you do bake two at a time, reverse the position of the sheets halfway through baking.
- Most cookies bake quickly, so pay attention to the timing. An extra minute can make a big difference. Always aim to underbake rather than overbake because cookies continue to bake after they come out of the oven. Since oven temperatures vary, check a few minutes before the recommended minimum baking time.
- If you prefer soft, chewy cookies, remove them from the oven about 2 minutes before they are done. If you like them crisp, bake for 2 minutes longer.
- If you've mixed a batch of dough and aren't baking it immediately, be sure to store it in the refrigerator, as any eggs and dairy products will spoil at room temperature.

Cooling and Cutting
Bars and Squares

Most bar cookies should be cooled completely in the pan on a rack before you cut them. There are two exceptions: plain shortbreads and crisp bars are often given a preliminary cut while they're warm, then are cut again after they have cooled completely. If they're not precut, they tend to shatter. If the bar has a sticky filling, it's a good idea to loosen the edges from the pan by running a knife around the edges while the bar is warm. All the recipes indicate when to cut the bars.

Most bars and squares are best cut with a sharp knife. For optimum results, use a sturdy plastic knife to cut brownies and sticky or particularly moist bars or those baked in a nonstick pan. Use a wet knife to cut meringue-topped or cheesecake bars, wiping the crumbs and filling off after each cut. To keep the pan stationary while cutting, place a damp paper towel, dishcloth or computer mouse pad under it.

To prevent the pan from scratching and to make it easy to remove bars, line it with parchment paper or greased foil. Leave a substantial overhang to serve as a handle. Once the bar is cooled, you can lift the entire piece out of the pan and transfer it to a cutting board for easy cutting. Sometimes chilling firms up the bar, making it easier to remove in one piece.

Cookies

Most baked cookies are left on the sheet for about 5 minutes, then transferred to a rack to cool completely. If they seem fragile, leave them on the sheet for another few minutes to firm up before moving them. However, there are always exceptions. Some cookies, like meringues, are left on the sheet to cool completely. Specific cooling directions are indicated in each recipe.

Bars and Squares Cutting Guide

Bar cookies can be cut in a variety of shapes and sizes. Whether you cut them into bars or squares is usually a matter of choice. We have specified cutting into bars or squares in the recipes, but in most cases either is fine. Bar cookies can also be cut into slender sticks, diamonds and triangles to add interest to any cookie platter.

Use a ruler to mark the lines evenly. It's easier to keep the lines straight if you start from the middle of the pan or the middle of the side with an even number of rows. This works for all yields except when cutting 77 squares in a 17- by 11- by 1-inch (3 L) jelly roll pan. In this case, cut parallel lines approximately 1½ inches (4 cm) apart. When you cut squares in a rectangular pan, they won't be perfectly square, but will be close enough to fool most eyes.

Here's a guide to make cutting bars and squares easier:

SIZE OF PAN	DESIRED NUMBER OF BARS	NUMBER OF ROWS
8- by 8-inch (2 L) or 9- by 9-inch (2.5 L) pan	16 squares	4 rows by 4 rows
8- by 8-inch (2 L) or 9- by 9-inch (2.5 L) pan	18 bars	6 rows by 3 rows
8- by 8-inch (2 L) or 9- by 9-inch (2.5 L) pan	20 bars	4 rows by 5 rows
8- by 8-inch (2 L) or 9- by 9-inch (2.5 L) pan	24 bars	6 rows by 4 rows
8- by 8-inch (2 L) or 9- by 9-inch (2.5 L) pan	25 squares	5 rows by 5 rows
8- by 8-inch (2 L) or 9- by 9-inch (2.5 L) pan	32 bars	4 rows by 8 rows
8- by 8-inch (2 L) or 9- by 9-inch (2.5 L) pan	36 squares	6 rows by 6 rows
8- by 8-inch (2 L) or 9- by 9-inch (2.5 L) pan	48 bars	8 rows by 6 rows
13- by 9-inch (3 L) pan	20 bars	4 rows by 5 rows
13- by 9-inch (3 L) pan	24 squares	6 rows by 4 rows
13- by 9-inch (3 L) pan	32 bars	8 rows by 4 rows
13- by 9-inch (3 L) pan	36 bars	6 rows by 6 rows
13- by 9-inch (3 L) pan	48 bars	8 rows by 6 rows
13- by 9-inch (3 L) pan	54 bars	6 rows by 9 rows
15- by 10- by 1-inch (2 L) jelly roll pan	24 squares	6 rows by 4 rows
15- by 10- by 1-inch (2 L) jelly roll pan	36 squares	6 rows by 6 rows
15- by 10- by 1-inch (2 L) jelly roll pan	40 bars	10 rows by 4 rows
15- by 10- by 1-inch (2 L) jelly roll pan	48 squares	8 rows by 6 rows
15- by 10- by 1-inch (2 L) jelly roll pan	48 bars	12 rows by 4 rows
15- by 10- by 1-inch (2 L) jelly roll pan	54 squares	9 rows by 6 rows
15- by 10- by 1-inch (2 L) jelly roll pan	60 squares	10 rows by 6 rows
17- by 11- by 1-inch (3 L) jelly roll pan	24 squares	6 rows by 4 rows
17- by 11- by 1-inch (3 L) jelly roll pan	36 bars	6 rows by 6 rows
17- by 11- by 1-inch (3 L) jelly roll pan	40 bars	10 rows by 4 rows
17- by 11- by 1-inch (3 L) jelly roll pan	48 bars	12 rows by 4 rows
17- by 11- by 1-inch (3 L) jelly roll pan	54 squares	9 rows by 6 rows
17- by 11- by 1-inch (3 L) jelly roll pan	60 bars	12 rows by 5 rows
17- by 11- by 1-inch (3 L) jelly roll pan	66 bars	11 rows by 6 rows
17- by 11- by 1-inch (3 L) jelly roll pan	77 squares	11 rows by 7 rows

Cutting Triangles

To cut triangle shapes, cut squares in half diagonally.

Cutting Diamonds

Diamond shapes work best in rectangular pans. To cut diamond shapes, cut 2 diagonal lines from corner to corner to meet in the middle. Then cut a series of parallel lines 1 or 1½ inches (2.5 or 4 cm) apart. The odd-shaped pieces in the corners and at the ends of the pan are samples for the cook. They're also great to mix into or crumble on top of ice cream.

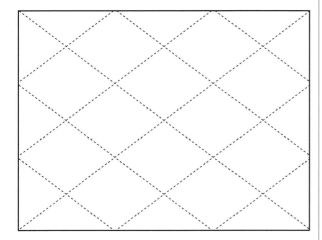

Storing
Storing Bars and Squares

To store bars and squares, layer them in an airtight container, with waxed paper between the layers. Or, if you prefer, wrap them individually in plastic wrap, then stack them in a container. Fragile or frosted bars are better stored in a single layer. They'll keep nicely at room temperature, unless the recipe specifies otherwise, for a few days. Do not store crisp and soft, moist bars together in the same container. The moisture in the soft bars will make the crisp ones soft.

Storing Cookies

Cool cookies completely before storing. Pack them in single layers in an airtight container, with waxed paper between the layers to prevent sticking. Do not store crisp and soft cookies together in the same container. The moisture from the soft cookies will soften the crisp ones.

Freezing
Freezing Bars and Squares

Almost all bars and squares can be frozen with excellent results, even those with a glaze or frosting on top. (I've indicated on each recipe if freezing is not recommended or if it is excellent.) However, if they have fresh fruit in the topping, like the Raspberry Truffle Brownies (page 28), and you plan to freeze them, do not add the fruit before baking. Instead, it can be added as a garnish when the bars are served.

There are several ways to freeze bars, depending on how you plan to use them. If you want to serve the whole pan at once, then freeze it in a single piece. In this case, line the pan with parchment paper or greased foil and let it cool completely after baking. Once cool, lift the bar out of the pan, remove the paper, wrap the entire piece tightly in plastic wrap and freeze. If you prefer to use just a few pieces at a time, cut the cooled bars into pieces and freeze them individually wrapped or in small groups (up to a dozen). If they have a frosting or a glaze that's a bit soft, freeze them unwrapped for about 1 hour to firm up the frosting, then wrap tightly. Write the date on the package so you know when it was frozen. Frozen bars and squares will keep fresh for about 3 months.

Defrost bars at room temperature in their wrappings. Some bars are even delicious eaten directly from the freezer or semi-frozen.

Freezing Cookies

Most cookies can be frozen, even those with a glaze or frosting on top. (If the frosting is a bit soft, freeze the cookies unwrapped for about 1 hour to firm up the frosting.) Pack them in sealed plastic containers or freezer bags. They will keep frozen for up to 6 months. If your recipe calls for a dusting of confectioners' (icing) sugar or a chocolate dip, freeze the cookies while still plain, then decorate them before serving.

I prefer to freeze cookies after they are baked, but most cookie doughs can be made ahead, stored in a tightly covered container and frozen for up to 6 months, or refrigerated for up to 1 week. When you want to use the frozen dough, thaw it overnight in the refrigerator or for 1 hour at room temperature before baking.

Ingredient Equivalents

INGREDIENT	WEIGHT OR QUANTITY	QUANTITY
Apricots (dried)	1 lb (500 g)	3 cups (750 mL)
Butter, margarine	1 lb (500 g)	2 cups (500 mL)
Cherries, maraschino	about 33	10-oz (284 mL) jar
Chocolate, baking	8-oz (225 g) package	8 squares
Chocolate chips	6-oz (175 g) bag	1 cup (250 mL)
Cocoa powder, unsweetened	8-oz (250 g) container	about 3 cups (750 mL)
Coconut, shredded or flaked	7-oz (225 g) bag	$2\frac{2}{3}$ cups (650 mL)
Cranberries, dried	8-oz (250 g) bag	about $2\frac{2}{3}$ cups (650 mL)
Cranberries, fresh or frozen	12-oz (340 g) bag	3 cups (750 mL)
Cream cheese	8-oz (250 g) package	1 cup (250 mL)
Dates (pitted), chopped	1 lb (500 g)	$2\frac{1}{2}$ cups (625 mL)
Egg product substitute	$\frac{1}{4}$ cup (60 mL)	1 whole large egg
Figs (dried), chopped	1 lb (500 g)	$2\frac{2}{3}$ cups (650 mL)
Flour, all-purpose	1 lb (500 g)	$3\frac{1}{3}$ cups (825 mL)
Flour, whole wheat	1 lb (500 g)	$3\frac{1}{2}$ cups (875 mL)
Honey	16-oz (500 g) jar	about $1\frac{1}{4}$ cups (300 mL)
Marshmallows, large	10-oz (300 g) bag 5 marshmallows 1 large marshmallow	40 marshmallows $\frac{1}{2}$ cup (125 mL) 10 miniature
Marshmallows, miniature	$10\frac{1}{2}$-oz (320 g) bag $\frac{1}{2}$ cup (125 mL) 10 miniature	5 cups (1.25 L) 45 marshmallows 1 large marshmallow
Milk, evaporated	14-oz (388 mL) can	$1\frac{1}{2}$ cups (375 mL)
Nuts, shelled		
Almonds (whole)	1 lb (500 g)	$3\frac{1}{2}$ cups (875 mL)
Peanuts (whole)	1 lb (500 g)	3 cups (750 mL)
Pecans (halves)	1 lb (500 g)	4 cups (1 L)
Walnuts (halves)	1 lb (500 g)	$6\frac{1}{4}$ cups (1.55 L)
Peanut butter	18-oz (550 g) jar	2 cups (500 mL)
Raisins	1 lb (500 g)	$2\frac{3}{4}$ cups (675 mL)
Sour cream	8-oz (250 g) container	1 cup (250 mL)
Sugar, brown	2 lb (1 kg)	about 5 cups (1.25 L) packed
Sugar, granulated	1 lb (500 g)	$2\frac{1}{4}$ cups (550 mL)
Sugar, confectioners' (icing)	2 lb (1 kg)	about $7\frac{1}{2}$ cups (1.875 L)

Fresh Fruit Yields

Recipes often call for a volume of fruit, such as 1 cup (250 mL) mashed banana. To make your baking easier, here are some measured yields for commonly used fresh fruits.

- *Apples:* One pound (500 g), or 3 medium, yields about 2 cups (500 mL) sliced.
- *Bananas:* One pound (500 g), or 2 to 3 large, yields about 1 cup (250 mL) mashed.
- *Lemons:* One medium lemon yields about 3 tbsp (45 mL) juice and 1 tbsp (15 mL) grated zest.
- *Limes:* One lime yields 1 to 2 tbsp (15 to 30 mL) juice and 1 tsp (5 mL) grated zest.

- *Oranges:* One orange yields about $\frac{1}{3}$ cup (75 mL) juice and 4 tsp (20 mL) grated zest.
- *Raspberries:* One pound (500 g) contains about 4 cups (1 L) whole or $1\frac{3}{4}$ to 2 cups (425 to 500 mL) crushed.
- *Strawberries:* One pound (500 g) contains about $2\frac{2}{3}$ cups (650 mL) whole, 2 to $2\frac{1}{3}$ cups (500 to 575 mL) sliced or $1\frac{2}{3}$ cups (400 mL) crushed.

Emergency Substitutions

It's always best to use ingredients the recipe calls for, as that reflects how they were tested. But in a pinch, here are some substitutions you can use to avoid a last-minute trip to the store.

Leavenings

1 tsp (5 mL) baking powder = $\frac{1}{4}$ tsp (1 mL) baking soda plus $\frac{1}{2}$ tsp (2 mL) cream of tartar

Flour

1 cup (250 mL) all-purpose flour, unsifted = 1 cup (250 mL) plus 2 tbsp (30 mL) cake and pastry flour, unsifted

1 cup (250 mL) cake and pastry flour, unsifted = 1 cup (250 mL) minus 2 tbsp (30 mL) all-purpose flour, unsifted

1 cup (250 mL) whole wheat flour = 1 cup (250 mL) all-purpose flour

Unbleached all-purpose flour and all-purpose flour can be used interchangeably.

Sweeteners

1 cup (250 mL) granulated sugar = 1 cup (250 mL) packed brown sugar

1 cup (250 mL) packed brown sugar = 1 cup (250 mL) granulated sugar mixed with 2 tbsp (30 mL) molasses

Corn syrup = Equal amount of maple syrup

1 cup (250 mL) honey = $1\frac{1}{4}$ cups (300 mL) granulated sugar plus $\frac{1}{4}$ cup (60 mL) liquid

Chocolate

1 square (1 oz/28 g) unsweetened chocolate = 3 tbsp (45 mL) cocoa powder plus 1 tbsp (15 mL) shortening, butter or margarine

1 cup (250 mL) semisweet chocolate chips = 6 squares (1 oz/28 g each) semisweet chocolate, chopped

Dairy Products

1 cup (250 mL) butter = 1 cup (250 mL) hard margarine **or** in a pinch 1 cup (250 mL) shortening plus 2 tbsp (30 mL) water

1 cup (250 mL) buttermilk or soured milk = 1 tbsp (15 mL) lemon juice or white vinegar plus milk to make 1 cup (250 mL) (let stand for 5 minutes, then stir before using)

1 cup (250 mL) whole milk = 1 cup (250 mL) 2% milk **or** $\frac{1}{2}$ cup (125 mL) evaporated milk plus $\frac{1}{2}$ cup (125 mL) water **or** 1 cup (250 mL) skim milk plus 2 tbsp (30 mL) butter

1 cup (250 mL) sour cream = $\frac{7}{8}$ cup (225 mL) buttermilk or plain yogurt plus 3 tbsp (45 mL) butter

1 cup (250 mL) whipping (35%) cream (for use in cooking, not for whipping) = $\frac{3}{4}$ cup (175 mL) whole milk plus $\frac{1}{3}$ cup (75 mL) butter

Egg

1 whole egg = 2 egg whites or 2 egg yolks plus 1 tbsp (15 mL) water **or** $\frac{1}{4}$ cup (60 mL) egg substitute product

Spices

1 tsp (5 mL) ground cinnamon = 1 tsp (5 mL) pumpkin pie spice

1 tsp (5 mL) ground allspice = $\frac{1}{2}$ tsp (2 mL) ground cinnamon plus pinch ground cloves

1 tbsp (15 mL) chopped gingerroot = 1 tsp (5 mL) ground dried ginger **or** 1 tbsp (15 mL) minced candied ginger with sugar washed off

Miscellaneous

$\frac{1}{2}$ cup (125 mL) raisins = $\frac{1}{2}$ cup (125 mL) dried cranberries, dried cherries or dried blueberries or chopped pitted prunes, apricots or dates

Nuts (any amount)

Almonds, hazelnuts, pecans, walnuts and peanuts are interchangeable in any of the recipes in this book.

Part 1
Bars and Squares

Double Fudge Brownies

Brownies

In my opinion, brownies are the ultimate square. Brownie lovers are divided into two camps: those who like a brownie that is rich, chewy, moist and fudge-like and those who prefer a tender, lighter version that resembles a cake in texture. You'll find plenty of both kinds here. You will also find blond brownies, or blondies, which have the same dense, moist, chewy texture as their chocolate cousins but are a golden color and taste of butterscotch rather than chocolate.

Brownies are ultra-easy to make and very forgiving. Often they're a one-bowl recipe, mixed with a whisk or wooden spoon rather than an electric mixer. Depending on your mood and the availability of ingredients, you can make them plain and simple or load them up with all the trappings to add flavors and texture. Better still, any brownie or blondie can quickly become a sundae. Just add ice cream and sundae sauce.

Brownies keep well at room temperature for approximately a week and can be frozen for up to 3 months. When freezing, I prefer to cut them into individual pieces, wrap well in plastic wrap and store them in airtight freezer bags. If you plan to serve the entire bar at once, line the baking pan with parchment paper or greased aluminum foil, which overhangs the sides. After baking, allow the bar to cool completely in the pan. Using the overhanging paper or foil as a handle, lift it out in one big piece, remove the paper and wrap tightly in plastic wrap for freezing.

Double Fudge Brownies

This brownie looks like a relatively plain two-layer one, but it's actually an intensely flavored chocolate base topped with a rich creamy filling.

MAKES 20 TO 54 BARS OR SQUARES
(see Cutting Guide, page 10)

- **Preparation: 35 minutes**
- **Baking: 30 minutes**
- **Cooling: 4 hours**
- **Freezing: excellent**

TIPS

Rather than combine the dry ingredients in a bowl (Step 2), place a large piece of waxed paper on the counter. Spread the flour on the paper. Fill a fine sieve with the cocoa powder, baking powder and salt and tap until all have sifted through to the flour. Using the paper as a funnel, transfer the dry ingredients to the chocolate mixture.

If you don't have a mixer, you can make the frosting using a large wooden spoon. You may need a bit more cream to achieve a spreadable consistency. This frosting, like most, freezes well.

- **Preheat oven to 325°F (160°C)**
- **13- by 9-inch (3 L) cake pan, greased**

BROWNIE

1 cup	butter	250 mL
4	squares (1 oz/28 g each) unsweetened chocolate, chopped	4
2	eggs	2
2 cups	granulated sugar	500 mL
2 tsp	vanilla	10 mL
1 1/4 cups	all-purpose flour	300 mL
3 tbsp	unsweetened cocoa powder, sifted	45 mL
1/4 tsp	baking powder	1 mL
1/4 tsp	salt	1 mL

CHOCOLATE FROSTING

1/2 cup	butter	125 mL
2	squares (1 oz/28 g each) unsweetened chocolate, chopped	2
4 cups	confectioners' (icing) sugar, sifted	1 L
5 to 6 tbsp	half-and-half (10%) cream	75 to 90 mL
1 tsp	vanilla	5 mL

1. *Brownie:* In a saucepan over low heat, melt butter and chocolate, stirring constantly, until smooth. Remove from heat and let cool slightly.

2. In a bowl, whisk eggs until blended. Whisk in sugar and vanilla until combined. Whisk in chocolate mixture. Combine flour, cocoa, baking powder and salt. Add to chocolate mixture and mix well. Spread evenly in prepared pan.

3. Bake in preheated oven until set, 25 to 30 minutes. Let cool for 5 minutes in pan on rack.

4. *Chocolate Frosting:* Meanwhile, in a small saucepan over low heat, melt butter and chocolate, stirring until smooth. Remove from heat and let cool slightly. In a bowl, combine confectioners' sugar, melted chocolate mixture, 5 tbsp (75 mL) of the cream and vanilla. Using a mixer, beat on low speed until smooth, adding a little more cream, if necessary, to make a spreadable consistency.

5. Drop frosting by spoonfuls onto the hot base, then spread gently to cover. Let cool for 4 hours in pan on rack to completely set. Cut into bars or squares.

Moist 'n' Chewy Chocolate Brownies

These brownies contain a little less chocolate than some of the more luscious ones, but they still have rich chocolate flavor. Their texture is pleasantly moist and chewy.

MAKES 16 TO 48 BARS OR SQUARES
(see Cutting Guide, page 10)

- **Preparation: 15 minutes**
- **Baking: 30 minutes**
- **Freezing: excellent**

TIPS

These brownies are quite dense and chewy. If you prefer them more cake-like, add an egg.

Instead of greasing pans, line them with parchment paper, extending up the sides and over the edges so you can lift out the brownies in a block. Spraying the pan lightly with cooking spray or greasing it lightly before adding the parchment helps the paper to stick, preventing it from shifting.

- **Preheat oven to 375°F (190°C)**
- **9-inch (2.5 L) square cake pan, greased**

1/2 cup	butter	125 mL
3	squares (1 oz/28 g each) unsweetened chocolate, chopped	3
1 1/4 cups	granulated sugar	300 mL
1 1/2 tsp	vanilla	7 mL
3	eggs	3
2/3 cup	all-purpose flour	150 mL
1/2 tsp	baking powder	2 mL
1/4 tsp	salt	1 mL

1. In a saucepan over low heat, melt butter and chocolate, stirring constantly, until smooth. Remove from heat. Stir in sugar and vanilla, mixing well. Whisk in eggs, one at a time, beating lightly after each addition.

2. In a bowl, combine flour, baking powder and salt. Stir into chocolate mixture until well blended. Spread evenly in prepared pan.

3. Bake in preheated oven just until set, 25 to 30 minutes. Let cool completely in pan on rack. Cut into bars or squares.

Variations

Add 1/2 cup (125 mL) chopped nuts after the chocolate and dry mixtures have been combined.

Frost with a chocolate frosting. Chocolate Frosting (see recipe, page 18) and Cocoa Frosting (see recipe, page 20) both work well with this brownie.

Chunky Chocolate Walnut Brownies

You can't go wrong with this — a great plain chocolate brownie with lots of nuts. If you're feeling in the mood for a little excess, add the yummy Cocoa Frosting. Either way, these are a winner.

MAKES 16 TO 48 BARS OR SQUARES
(see Cutting Guide, page 10)

- **Preparation: 15 minutes**
- **Baking: 35 minutes**
- **Freezing: excellent without frosting**

TIPS

If you're using a stand mixer with a large bowl to mix this brownie, whisk the eggs until frothy before adding them. There is not enough volume in the eggs to achieve this result with the mixer. Then continue with Step 2.

In this recipe, beating the eggs and sugar thoroughly produces brownies with a soft, light texture. If you beat the mixture less, or by hand using a wooden spoon, you'll have a firmer brownie.

- **Preheat oven to 350°F (180°C)**
- **9-inch (2.5 L) square cake pan, greased**

BROWNIE

5	squares (1 oz/28 g each) unsweetened chocolate, chopped	5
⅔ cup	butter	150 mL
3	eggs	3
1⅔ cups	granulated sugar	400 mL
1½ tsp	vanilla	7 mL
1 cup	all-purpose flour	250 mL
1 cup	coarsely chopped walnuts	250 mL

COCOA FROSTING, OPTIONAL

3½ cups	confectioners' (icing) sugar	875 mL
½ cup	unsweetened cocoa powder	125 mL
½ cup	butter, softened	125 mL
5 to 6 tbsp	half-and-half (10%) cream	75 to 90 mL

1. *Brownie:* In a saucepan over low heat, melt chocolate and butter, stirring constantly, until smooth. Remove from heat. Set aside.

2. In a large bowl, using an electric mixer on high speed, beat eggs until frothy. Gradually add sugar, beating until thick and creamy, about 5 minutes. Stir in chocolate mixture and vanilla. Stir in flour, mixing well. Stir in walnuts. Spread evenly in prepared pan.

3. Bake in preheated oven just until set, 30 to 35 minutes. Let cool completely in pan on rack. Frost, if desired. Cut into bars or squares.

4. *Cocoa Frosting (if using):* Sift together confectioners' sugar and cocoa powder. In a bowl, using an electric mixer on medium speed, beat butter and half of the sugar mixture. Add 5 tbsp (75 mL) of the cream, beating until smooth. Gradually add remaining confectioners' sugar and cocoa mixture, beating until smooth and adding more cream, as necessary, to make a spreadable consistency.

Variation

Replace walnuts with pecans.

Decadent Mocha Brownies

With these delicious brownies you can have your coffee and eat it, too. The espresso adds amazing flavor.

MAKES 16 TO 48 BARS OR SQUARES
(see Cutting Guide, page 10)

- **Preparation: 15 minutes**
- **Baking: 30 minutes**
- **Freezing: excellent**

TIPS

If you prefer a more intense chocolate flavor, use bittersweet chocolate in place of semisweet.

Instant espresso coffee powder is usually sold in specialty coffee stores, such as Starbucks. If you don't have it, substitute 2 tbsp (30 mL) instant coffee powder in this recipe.

These brownies have a wonderful texture. The key is to not overbeat the batter and to not overbake them. They should still be a little soft in the center when you remove them from the oven. They'll firm up when cooling.

For a fabulous dessert, try these with a scoop of ice cream and warm chocolate sauce.

- **Preheat oven to 350°F (180°C)**
- **8-inch (2 L) square cake pan, greased**

8	squares (1 oz/28 g each) semisweet chocolate, chopped	8
1/4 cup	butter	60 mL
2	eggs	2
3/4 cup	packed brown sugar	175 mL
1 1/2 tsp	vanilla	7 mL
3/4 cup	all-purpose flour	175 mL
1 tbsp	instant espresso coffee powder (see Tips, left)	15 mL
1 tsp	baking powder	5 mL
2/3 cup	semisweet chocolate chips	150 mL

1. In a saucepan over low heat, melt chocolate and butter, stirring constantly, until smooth. Remove from heat. Set aside.

2. In a large bowl, whisk eggs, brown sugar and vanilla just until blended. Stir in chocolate mixture. Stir in flour, coffee powder and baking powder, mixing well. Stir in chocolate chips. Spread evenly in prepared pan.

3. Bake in preheated oven until almost set and still a little soft in the center, 25 to 30 minutes. Let cool completely in pan on rack. Cut into bars or squares.

Variations

Reduce the chocolate chips to 1/3 cup (75 mL) and add 1/3 cup (75 mL) chopped pecans or walnuts.

Omit the coffee powder. You'll still have a wonderful plain brownie.

Brownie Overload

This is the ultimate brownie. It's a real hit at bake sales. You couldn't stir any more ingredients into the batter if you tried.

MAKES 20 TO 54 BARS OR SQUARES
(see **Cutting Guide, page 10**)

- **Preparation: 20 minutes**
- **Baking: 35 minutes**
- **Freezing: excellent**

TIPS

To ease cleanup, rather than combining the dry ingredients in a bowl, place a large piece of waxed paper on the counter. Spread the flour on the paper. Fill a fine sieve with the cocoa powder, baking soda and salt and tap until all have sifted through to the flour. Using the paper as a funnel, transfer the dry ingredients to the chocolate mixture. That way, there's one less bowl to wash.

When baking, always have eggs at room temperature to obtain the best volume.

This method differs from some brownies in that the eggs are beaten thoroughly, resulting in a beautiful, shiny top.

- **Preheat oven to 350°F (180°C)**
- **13- by 9-inch (3 L) cake pan, greased**

1 cup	butter	250 mL
2½ cups	coarsely chopped bittersweet chocolate, divided	625 mL
2 cups	all-purpose flour	500 mL
½ cup	unsweetened cocoa powder, sifted (see Tips, page 30)	125 mL
1 tsp	baking soda	5 mL
½ tsp	salt	2 mL
4	eggs	4
1 cup	granulated sugar	250 mL
1 cup	packed brown sugar	250 mL
2 tsp	vanilla	10 mL
2 cups	coarsely chopped deluxe mixed nuts (no peanuts, about 8 oz/250 g)	500 mL
1 cup	dried cranberries	250 mL

1. In a saucepan over low heat, melt butter and 1½ cups (375 mL) of the chocolate, stirring constantly, until smooth. Remove from heat. Let cool for 10 minutes.

2. Combine flour, cocoa, baking soda and salt. Mix well.

3. In a bowl, using an electric mixer on medium speed, beat eggs, granulated and brown sugars and vanilla until thick and creamy, about 2 minutes. Add melted chocolate mixture and mix on low speed until blended. Stir in flour mixture, mixing just to combine. Stir in nuts, remaining 1 cup (250 mL) chocolate and cranberries and mix well (the batter will be very thick). Spread evenly in prepared pan.

4. Bake in preheated oven until set, 30 to 35 minutes. Let cool completely in pan on rack. Cut into bars or squares.

Variations

Replace dried cranberries with dried cherries or raisins.

Substitute an equal quantity of good-quality chocolate chips for the chopped chocolate.

Toffee Brownies

◆

Keep this recipe in mind for those days when you want to bake but don't have much time. It's extra easy to make, with no sacrifice on taste.

**MAKES 16 TO
48 BARS OR SQUARES
(see Cutting Guide,
page 10)**

- **Preparation: 15 minutes**
- **Baking: 30 minutes**
- **Freezing: excellent**

TIPS

For best results, always have your ingredients at room temperature before you start to bake. This is especially important if you're adding eggs to a warm mixture.

Don't overbeat brownie batter or it will rise too high and then collapse.

My favorite brand of toffee bits is Skor, and I buy them in bulk. Others, such as Heath bits, are also available in bulk, but I don't recommend being over-inventoried on this product. If toffee bits become stale, they take longer to soften.

- **Preheat oven to 350°F (180°C)**
- **8-inch (2 L) square cake pan, greased**

2	squares (1 oz/28 g each) unsweetened chocolate, chopped	2
1/2 cup	butter	125 mL
1 cup	granulated sugar	250 mL
2	eggs	2
1 tsp	vanilla	5 mL
3/4 cup	all-purpose flour	175 mL
3/4 cup	toffee bits	175 mL
2/3 cup	miniature semisweet chocolate chips	150 mL

1. In a saucepan over low heat, melt chocolate and butter, stirring constantly, until smooth. Remove from heat. Stir in sugar, mixing until smooth. Whisk in eggs, one at a time, mixing lightly after each addition. Stir in vanilla and flour, mixing well.

2. Combine toffee bits and chocolate chips. Set aside 1/3 cup (75 mL) for topping. Stir remainder into batter. Spread evenly in prepared pan. Sprinkle reserved toffee-chocolate mixture evenly on top.

3. Bake in preheated oven until set, 25 to 30 minutes. Let cool completely in pan on rack. Cut into bars or squares.

Variations

Replace toffee bits and chocolate chips with 1 1/4 cups (300 mL) chopped chocolate toffee bar. Reserve 1/3 cup (75 mL) for topping.

Add 1/3 cup (75 mL) chopped almonds to the batter along with the chocolate chips.

Chocolate Toffee Bar Brownies

Crunchy toffee bars add flourish to this fabulous version.

MAKES 20 TO 54 BARS OR SQUARES
(see **Cutting Guide**, page 10)

- **Preparation: 20 minutes**
- **Cooling: 30 minutes**
- **Baking: 30 minutes**
- **Freezing: excellent**

TIPS

If you prefer a brownie with a lighter texture, beat eggs, sugar and flavorings, such as almond extract, separately until thick and creamy. Stir chocolate mixture then dry ingredients into egg mixture.

Rather than dirty a bowl when combining the dry ingredients (Step 2), place a large piece of waxed paper on the counter. Spread the flour on the paper. Sprinkle with the baking soda and salt. Using the paper as a funnel, transfer the dry ingredients to the chocolate mixture.

- **Preheat oven to 350°F (180°C)**
- **13- by 9-inch (3 L) cake pan, greased**

3½	squares (1 oz/28 g each) unsweetened chocolate, chopped	3½
¾ cup	butter	175 mL
1⅔ cups	granulated sugar	400 mL
3	eggs	3
½ tsp	almond extract	2 mL
¾ cup	all-purpose flour	175 mL
¼ tsp	baking soda	1 mL
¼ tsp	salt	1 mL
1 cup	coarsely chopped almonds	250 mL
4	crunchy chocolate-covered toffee bars (1.4 oz/39 g each), chopped	4

1. In a saucepan over low heat, melt chocolate and butter, stirring constantly, until smooth. Remove from heat. Let cool to lukewarm, about 30 minutes.

2. Whisk in sugar until well blended. Add eggs, one at a time, whisking lightly after each addition. Stir in almond extract. Combine flour, baking soda and salt. Stir into chocolate mixture, mixing until smooth. Stir in almonds. Spread evenly in prepared pan.

3. Bake in preheated oven until set, 25 to 30 minutes. Immediately sprinkle chopped chocolate bars on top. Let cool completely in pan on rack. Cut into bars or squares.

Variation

Replace almonds with hazelnuts and almond extract with 1 tsp (5 mL) vanilla.

Caramel Brownies

The name doesn't capture the amount of flavor packed in just one square. Rich, chewy and loaded with gooey caramel, chocolate chips and crunchy pecans, these brownies are sensational.

MAKES 20 TO 54 BARS OR SQUARES
(see Cutting Guide, page 10)

- **Preparation: 25 minutes**
- **Baking: 42 minutes**
- **Freezing: excellent**

TIPS

A reliable kitchen scale is a good investment. Having a scale allows you to purchase ingredients in bulk, then weigh out exactly what you need.

Because oven temperatures vary, I recommend that you treat all recipe times as guidelines and begin checking what you're baking well before the minimum recommended time.

- **Preheat oven to 350°F (180°C)**
- **13- by 9-inch (3 L) cake pan, greased**

2 cups	granulated sugar	500 mL
2/3 cup	unsweetened cocoa powder, sifted	150 mL
1 cup	vegetable oil	250 mL
4	eggs	4
1/4 cup	milk	60 mL
1 1/2 cups	all-purpose flour	375 mL
1 tsp	baking powder	5 mL
1/2 tsp	salt	2 mL
1 cup	semisweet chocolate chips	250 mL
1 cup	chopped pecans, divided	250 mL
14 oz	soft caramels, unwrapped (about 50)	400 g
1	can (10 oz/300 mL) sweetened condensed milk	1

1. In a large bowl, whisk sugar, cocoa, oil, eggs and milk until smooth. Combine flour, baking powder and salt. Stir into cocoa mixture, mixing well. Stir in chocolate chips and 1/2 cup (125 mL) of the pecans. Spread two-thirds of the batter evenly in prepared pan. Bake in preheated oven for 12 minutes.

2. Meanwhile, in a heavy saucepan over low heat, heat caramels and sweetened condensed milk, stirring constantly, until caramels are melted and mixture is smooth. Pour over partially baked brownie layer. Sprinkle remaining pecans on top. Drop remaining chocolate batter by spoonfuls over caramel layer. Spread gently, then swirl with the tip of a knife to marbleize the uncooked chocolate batter and caramel layers.

3. Bake in preheated oven just until set, 25 to 30 minutes. Let cool completely in pan on rack. Cut into bars or squares.

Variation
Replace pecans with peanuts or walnuts.

Raspberry Truffle Brownies

Make these luscious brownies for any occasion — I guarantee success.

MAKES 16 TO 48 BARS OR SQUARES
(see Cutting Guide, page 10)

- **Preparation: 20 minutes**
- **Baking: 30 minutes**
- **Freezing: excellent without berries**

TIPS

You can use regular raspberry jam, with seeds, in place of the seedless, but it will have less raspberry flavor.

If you prefer more raspberry flavor and a hint of pink, add 2 tbsp (30 mL) regular raspberry jam to the topping. The seedless version doesn't work as well because the red color isn't as intense.

If you plan to freeze these brownies, don't add the raspberries until serving.

White chocolate has become a popular ingredient in baking. However, it's not really chocolate at all but rather a blend of sugar, cocoa butter, milk solids and vanilla. Because it doesn't melt as easily as regular chocolate, it's particularly important to use low heat and stir it constantly.

- **Preheat oven to 350°F (180°C)**
- **8-inch (2 L) square cake pan, greased**

BROWNIE

3	squares (1 oz/28 g each) unsweetened chocolate	3
1/3 cup	butter	75 mL
1/4 cup	seedless raspberry jam (see Tips, left)	60 mL
2	eggs	2
1 cup	granulated sugar	250 mL
1/2 cup	all-purpose flour	125 mL

TOPPING

2 tbsp	whipping (35%) cream	30 mL
2 tbsp	butter	30 mL
4	squares (1 oz/28 g each) white chocolate, chopped	4
1 1/4 cups	fresh raspberries	300 mL

1. *Brownie:* In a saucepan over low heat, melt unsweetened chocolate, butter and jam, stirring constantly, until smooth. Remove from heat.
2. In a bowl, whisk eggs and sugar until frothy. Whisk in chocolate mixture, then flour, mixing until smooth. Spread evenly in prepared pan.
3. Bake in preheated oven until set, 25 to 30 minutes. Let cool completely in pan on rack.
4. *Topping:* In a small saucepan over low heat, heat cream, butter and white chocolate, stirring until smooth. Let cool for 30 minutes. Spread evenly over brownie. Top with raspberries and chill until cold. Cut into bars or squares.

Variation

If you prefer an intensely chocolate brownie, replace the white chocolate in the topping with semisweet chocolate.

Raspberry Cheesecake Brownies

The slightly tart taste of raspberries in a creamy cheesecake topping, coupled with a dense, moist chocolate base, is a sensational combination.

MAKES 16 TO 48 BARS OR SQUARES
(see **Cutting Guide, page 10**)

- **Preparation: 25 minutes**
- **Baking: 45 minutes**
- **Chilling: overnight**
- **Freezing: excellent without raspberries on top (see Tips, below)**

TIPS

When beating this topping, and others with comparable small volumes, use a hand mixer and a small bowl, or beat with a wooden spoon. The volume is insufficient to work in a stand mixer with a large bowl.

If you plan to freeze these brownies, omit the raspberries before baking and add them as a garnish when serving.

If using frozen raspberries, scatter them over the topping in their frozen state so they'll hold their shape better.

- **Preheat oven to 350°F (180°C)**
- **9-inch (2.5 L) square cake pan, greased**

BROWNIE

4	squares (1 oz/28 g each) unsweetened chocolate, chopped	4
½ cup	butter	125 mL
2 tbsp	unsweetened cocoa powder, sifted (see Tips, page 30)	30 mL
1 tbsp	instant coffee granules	15 mL
1 ⅓ cups	granulated sugar	325 mL
1 tsp	vanilla	5 mL
¼ tsp	salt	1 mL
3	eggs	3
1 cup	all-purpose flour	250 mL

TOPPING

4 oz	cream cheese, softened	125 g
¼ cup	granulated sugar	60 mL
1	egg	1
1 tbsp	grated lemon zest	15 mL
1 tbsp	freshly squeezed lemon juice	15 mL
1 ¼ cups	fresh or individually frozen raspberries (see Tips, left)	300 mL

1. *Brownie:* In a saucepan over low heat, combine chocolate, butter, cocoa and coffee granules, stirring constantly, until chocolate is melted and mixture is smooth. Remove from heat. Stir in sugar, vanilla and salt. Whisk in eggs, one at a time, mixing well after each addition. Stir in flour, mixing until smooth. Spread evenly in prepared pan. Set aside.

2. *Topping:* In a bowl, using an electric mixer on medium speed, beat cream cheese, sugar, egg, lemon zest and juice until smooth. Spread evenly over unbaked base. Scatter raspberries over top.

3. Bake in preheated oven just until set, 40 to 45 minutes. Let cool completely in pan on rack. Chill overnight. Cut into bars or squares.

Chocolate Chunk Banana Brownies

This very chocolaty brownie is flavored with mashed bananas and filled with chunks of chocolate and walnuts.

MAKES 20 TO 54 BARS OR SQUARES
(see Cutting Guide, page 10)

- **Preparation: 20 minutes**
- **Baking: 30 minutes**
- **Freezing: excellent**

TIPS

These brownies are nice plain, dusted with confectioners' (icing) sugar or topped with a chocolate frosting (see recipes, pages 18 and 20).

For recipes calling for chopped chocolate, I like to buy large bittersweet chocolate bars and chop them to the size of chips.

Always sift cocoa before using to get rid of any lumps that have formed during storage.

- **Preheat oven to 350°F (180°C)**
- **13- by 9-inch (3 L) cake pan, greased**

1 cup	granulated sugar	250 mL
1/3 cup	vegetable oil	75 mL
2	eggs	2
1 cup	mashed ripe banana (2 large bananas)	250 mL
3/4 cup	unsweetened cocoa powder, sifted (see Tips, left)	175 mL
1 cup	all-purpose flour	250 mL
1 tsp	baking powder	5 mL
1/2 tsp	baking soda	2 mL
1/4 tsp	salt	1 mL
1 1/2 cups	chopped semisweet chocolate	375 mL
1 1/3 cups	coarsely chopped walnuts	325 mL

1. In a large bowl, using an electric mixer on medium speed, beat sugar, oil and eggs until thick and light, about 2 minutes. Add banana and cocoa and beat on low speed.
2. Combine flour, baking powder, baking soda and salt. Add to cocoa mixture, beating on low speed just to blend. Stir in chopped chocolate and walnuts. Spread evenly in prepared pan.
3. Bake in preheated oven just until set, 25 to 30 minutes. Let cool completely in pan on rack. Cut into bars or squares.

Variations

Replace chocolate chunks with chocolate chips.

Substitute peanut butter chips for the chopped chocolate and coarsely chopped peanuts for the walnuts.

Amazing Amaretto Brownies

◆

Slightly chewy and a little sweet, these have a delicious almond flavor.

MAKES 20 TO 54 BARS OR SQUARES (see Cutting Guide, page 10)

- **Preparation: 25 minutes**
- **Baking: 25 minutes**
- **Freezing: excellent**

TIPS

To ease cleanup, rather than combining the dry ingredients in a bowl, place a large piece of waxed paper on the counter. After measuring, combine the flour, baking powder, salt and ground almonds on the paper. Use the paper as a funnel to transfer the dry ingredients to the chocolate mixture.

Amaretto is the most common almond liqueur. If you prefer, substitute a mixture of almond extract and water for the liqueur. When making the frosting, replace the 1 tbsp (15 mL) almond liqueur with ¼ tsp (1 mL) almond extract mixed with 1 tbsp (15 mL) water. Use ½ tsp (2 mL) almond extract mixed with 2 tbsp (30 mL) water in the batter.

- **Preheat oven to 350°F (180°C)**
- **13- by 9-inch (3 L) cake pan, greased**

BROWNIE

1 cup	sliced almonds, toasted, divided	250 mL
8	squares (1 oz/28 g each) semisweet chocolate, chopped	8
⅓ cup	butter	75 mL
1 cup	granulated sugar	250 mL
2	eggs	2
2 tbsp	almond liqueur	30 mL
1 ¼ cups	all-purpose flour	300 mL
1 tsp	baking powder	5 mL
¼ tsp	salt	1 mL

FROSTING

¼ cup	butter, softened	60 mL
3 cups	confectioners' (icing) sugar, sifted	750 mL
2 tbsp	milk	30 mL
1 tbsp	almond liqueur	15 mL

1. *Brownie:* In a food processor, process ⅓ cup (75 mL) of the almonds until ground. Chop remaining almonds. Set aside.

2. In a saucepan over low heat, melt chocolate and butter, stirring constantly, until smooth. Remove from heat. Stir in sugar, mixing until smooth. Add eggs, one at a time, whisking lightly after each addition. Stir in liqueur.

3. Combine flour, baking powder, salt and ground almonds. Stir into chocolate mixture, mixing until smooth. Spread evenly in prepared pan.

4. Bake in preheated oven just until set, 20 to 25 minutes. Let cool completely in pan on rack.

5. *Frosting:* In a bowl, using an electric mixer on medium speed, beat butter, confectioners' sugar, milk and liqueur until smooth and creamy. Spread over brownie. Sprinkle with reserved chopped almonds. Cut into bars or squares.

Variation

Fold the chopped almonds into the batter after the chocolate mixture has been blended in, instead of sprinkling them on top.

Cappuccino Brownies

I love to pair these flavorful brownies with a steaming mug of cappuccino.

MAKES 16 TO 48 BARS OR SQUARES
(see Cutting Guide, page 10)

- **Preparation: 25 minutes**
- **Baking: 35 minutes**
- **Chilling: 1 hour**
- **Freezing: excellent**

TIPS

Instant espresso powder is usually sold in specialty coffee stores, such as Starbucks. If you don't have it, substitute 2 tbsp (30 mL) instant coffee granules in the brownie and 1 tbsp (15 mL) in the frosting. Crush the granules with the back of a spoon before adding to the recipe.

When freezing brownies, I recommend cutting and wrapping individual squares. They thaw quickly, and you can take out only as many as you need.

Brownies usually rise during baking then collapse slightly on cooling. This is what creates that dense, moist, chewy texture.

- **Preheat oven to 350°F (180°C)**
- **8-inch (2 L) square cake pan, greased**

BROWNIE

1 cup	semisweet chocolate chips	250 mL
½ cup	butter	125 mL
1 cup	granulated sugar	250 mL
1 tsp	vanilla	5 mL
2	eggs	2
1 cup	all-purpose flour	250 mL
1 tbsp	instant espresso coffee powder	15 mL
½ tsp	baking powder	2 mL
¼ tsp	salt	1 mL

FROSTING

1½ tsp	instant espresso coffee powder	7 mL
1 to 2 tbsp	milk or cream	15 to 30 mL
2 cups	confectioners' (icing) sugar, sifted	500 mL
¼ cup	butter, softened	60 mL

GLAZE

1 cup	semisweet chocolate chips	250 mL
⅓ cup	whipping (35%) cream	75 mL

1. *Brownie:* In a saucepan over low heat, melt chocolate chips and butter, stirring constantly, until smooth. Whisk in sugar and vanilla, mixing well. Add eggs, one at a time, whisking lightly after each addition.

2. Combine flour, espresso powder, baking powder and salt. Stir into chocolate mixture, mixing well. Spread evenly in prepared pan.

3. Bake in preheated oven just until set, 30 to 35 minutes. Let cool completely in pan on rack.

4. *Frosting:* In a bowl, combine espresso powder and 1 tbsp (15 mL) milk, stirring to dissolve. Add confectioners' sugar and butter. Using an electric mixer, beat on low speed to blend then on medium speed until creamy, adding more milk, if necessary, to make a smooth, spreadable consistency. Spread evenly over brownie. Chill to harden, about 1 hour.

5. *Glaze:* In a saucepan over low heat, combine chocolate chips and whipping cream, stirring constantly, until melted and smooth. Let cool to lukewarm. Spread over frosting. Chill until chocolate is set, about 1 hour. Cut into bars or squares.

Coconut Marshmallow Brownies

A line of white marshmallows between two layers of dark chocolate makes this attractive and tasty.

MAKES 16 TO 48 BARS OR SQUARES
(**see** Cutting Guide, page 10)

- **Preparation: 25 minutes**
- **Baking: 32 minutes**
- **Freezing: excellent**

TIPS

Make sure your marshmallows are fresh and soft. Stale ones don't soften properly.

I have specified sweetened coconut because it seems to be more readily available than the unsweetened variety. But sweetened and unsweetened coconut can be used interchangeably in any recipe to suit your preference.

- **Preheat oven to 375°F (190°C)**
- **8-inch (2 L) square cake pan, greased**

BROWNIE

1	square (1 oz/28 g) unsweetened chocolate, chopped	1
2 tbsp	butter	30 mL
¾ cup	all-purpose flour	175 mL
1 tsp	baking powder	5 mL
¼ tsp	salt	1 mL
2	eggs	2
1¼ cups	packed brown sugar	300 mL
½ cup	flaked sweetened coconut (see Tips, left)	125 mL
⅓ cup	chopped walnuts	75 mL
20	marshmallows	20

TOPPING

2	squares (1 oz/28 g each) unsweetened chocolate, chopped	2
2 tbsp	butter	30 mL
1 cup	confectioners' (icing) sugar, sifted	250 mL
1 tsp	vanilla	5 mL
1 to 2 tbsp	whipping (35%) cream	15 to 30 mL

1. *Brownie:* In a saucepan over low heat, melt chocolate and butter, stirring constantly, until smooth. Remove from heat. Set aside.

2. Combine flour, baking powder and salt. In a bowl, using an electric mixer on high speed, beat eggs and brown sugar until light and creamy. Stir in flour mixture, mixing well. Divide batter in half. Stir coconut into one half of the batter. Stir chocolate mixture and walnuts into the other half. Spread coconut batter in prepared pan. Drop chocolate batter by spoonfuls over top. Spread evenly.

3. Bake in preheated oven just until set, 25 to 30 minutes. Cut marshmallows in half. Place on hot brownie. Bake for 2 minutes longer to soften. Let cool completely in pan on rack.

4. *Topping:* In a small saucepan over low heat, melt chocolate and butter, stirring constantly, until smooth. Remove from heat and let cool for 10 minutes. Whisk in confectioners' sugar, vanilla and just enough cream to make a smooth, spreadable consistency. Spread quickly over marshmallows. Let cool. Cut into bars or squares.

Rocky Road Brownies

Any chapter on brownies should include some form of this classic chewy version. In this recipe, the marshmallows disappear during baking; in other versions, you can actually see a marshmallow layer.

MAKES 16 TO 48 BARS OR SQUARES
(see **Cutting Guide,** page 10)

- **Preparation: 20 minutes**
- **Baking: 40 minutes**
- **Freezing: excellent**

TIPS

I recommend that you use pure vanilla extract in all your baking. Nothing else will give you the same burst of flavor.

You will always get the best results when you use the pan size recommended in a recipe. But if you need to substitute an 8-inch (2 L) square cake pan when baking these rocky roads, add 5 to 10 minutes to the baking time.

Not only do brownies freeze well, but it's also hard to resist them right from the freezer.

- **Preheat oven to 325°F (160°C)**
- **9-inch (2.5 L) square cake pan, greased (see Tips, left)**

BROWNIE

3	squares (1 oz/28 g each) unsweetened chocolate, chopped	3
3/4 cup	butter	175 mL
1 1/2 cups	granulated sugar	375 mL
1 tsp	vanilla	5 mL
3	eggs	3
1 cup	all-purpose flour	250 mL
3/4 tsp	baking powder	3 mL
1 1/2 cups	miniature marshmallows	375 mL
1 1/2 cups	peanuts	375 mL

CHOCOLATE GLAZE, OPTIONAL

4	squares (1 oz/28 g each) semisweet chocolate, chopped	4
2 tbsp	whipping (35%) cream	30 mL

1. *Brownie:* In a saucepan over low heat, melt chocolate and butter, stirring constantly, until smooth. Remove from heat. Add sugar and vanilla and mix well. Add eggs, one at a time, whisking lightly after each addition.

2. Combine flour and baking powder. Stir into chocolate mixture, mixing well. Stir in marshmallows and peanuts. Spread evenly in prepared pan.

3. Bake in preheated oven just until set, 35 to 40 minutes. Let cool completely in pan on rack.

4. *Chocolate Glaze (if using):* In a small saucepan over low heat, combine chocolate and whipping cream, stirring until chocolate is melted and mixture is smooth. Let cool for 20 minutes. Spread over brownie. Chill until chocolate is set. Cut into bars or squares.

Variation

Although your brownies won't qualify as rocky road, you can substitute an equal quantity of any other nut for the peanuts.

Chocolate Peanut Butter Brownies

This triple-layer bar is a delicious combination of flavors. The mild chocolate complements the creamy peanut butter.

MAKES 16 TO 48 BARS OR SQUARES (see Cutting Guide, page 10)

- **Preparation: 30 minutes**
- **Baking: 30 minutes**
- **Freezing: excellent**

TIPS

Dry-roasted peanuts have great taste and a crunchy texture that works well in brownies.

Peanuts, like all nuts, tend to go rancid quickly because of their high fat content. Store them in the freezer to retain freshness.

Most ovens have "hot spots," which result in unevenly baked goods. Prevent uneven baking by placing the pans in the center of the oven and rotating them halfway through the baking time, if necessary. Use just one oven rack — don't stack.

- **Preheat oven to 350°F (180°C)**
- **9-inch (2.5 L) square cake pan, greased**

CRUST

1 1/4 cups	graham wafer crumbs	300 mL
1/4 cup	granulated sugar	60 mL
1/3 cup	finely chopped peanuts	75 mL
1/2 cup	butter, melted	125 mL

BROWNIE FILLING

2	squares (1 oz/28 g each) unsweetened chocolate, chopped	2
1/2 cup	butter	125 mL
1 cup	granulated sugar	250 mL
2	eggs	2
1 tsp	vanilla	5 mL
2/3 cup	all-purpose flour	150 mL
2/3 cup	chopped peanuts	150 mL

PEANUT BUTTER FROSTING

1/4 cup	butter, softened	60 mL
2 tbsp	creamy peanut butter	30 mL
2 cups	confectioners' (icing) sugar, sifted	500 mL
1 to 3 tbsp	milk	15 to 45 mL

1. *Crust:* In a bowl, combine graham wafer crumbs, sugar, peanuts and butter. Mix until crumbs are thoroughly moistened. Press evenly in prepared pan. Set aside.

2. *Brownie Filling:* In a saucepan over low heat, melt chocolate and butter, stirring constantly, until smooth. Remove from heat. Stir in sugar and mix until smooth. Add eggs, one at a time, whisking lightly after each addition. Stir in vanilla. Stir in flour and peanuts, mixing well. Spread evenly in prepared pan.

3. Bake in preheated oven just until set, 25 to 30 minutes. Let cool completely in pan on rack.

4. *Peanut Butter Frosting:* In a bowl, using an electric mixer on low speed, beat butter and peanut butter until blended. Alternately add confectioners' sugar and milk, using just enough milk to make a smooth, spreadable consistency. Spread evenly over brownie. Cut into bars or squares.

Milk Chocolate Pecan Brownies

◆

This pairing of chunks of milk chocolate and pecans in a dark chocolate brownie is one of my favorites.

MAKES 20 TO 54 BARS OR SQUARES (see Cutting Guide, page 10)

- **Preparation: 20 minutes**
- **Baking: 30 minutes**
- **Freezing: excellent**

TIPS

To ease cleanup, rather than combining the dry ingredients in a bowl (Step 2), place a large piece of waxed paper on the counter. After measuring, combine the flour, baking powder and salt on the paper. Using the paper as a funnel, transfer the dry ingredients to the chocolate mixture.

If you like the pairing of coffee and chocolate, try adding 1 tbsp (15 mL) instant espresso coffee powder to the flour mixture. Instant espresso coffee is usually sold in specialty coffee stores.

- Preheat oven to 350°F (180°C)
- 13- by 9-inch (3 L) cake pan, greased

7	squares (1 oz/28 g each) unsweetened chocolate, chopped	7
3	squares (1 oz/28 g each) semisweet chocolate, chopped	3
1 cup	butter	250 mL
2 cups	packed brown sugar	500 mL
4	eggs	4
1 cup	all-purpose flour	250 mL
3/4 tsp	baking powder	3 mL
1/2 tsp	salt	2 mL
1 cup	milk chocolate chips	250 mL
1 1/4 cups	coarsely chopped pecans	300 mL

1. In a saucepan over low heat, melt unsweetened and semisweet chocolate and butter, stirring constantly, until smooth. Remove from heat. Whisk in brown sugar until smooth. Add eggs, one at a time, whisking lightly after each addition.

2. Combine flour, baking powder and salt. Stir into chocolate mixture, mixing well. Stir in milk chocolate chips and pecans. Spread evenly in prepared pan.

3. Bake in preheated oven just until set, 25 to 30 minutes. Let cool completely in pan on rack. Cut into bars or squares.

Variations

Use whatever nuts your family likes.

If you prefer a stronger chocolate flavor, replace the milk chocolate chips with chopped bittersweet chocolate or semisweet chocolate chips.

White Chocolate Cranberry Hazelnut Brownies

I'm sure this creamy white chocolate brownie, loaded with hazelnuts and cranberries, will become one of your favorites.

MAKES 16 TO 48 BARS OR SQUARES (see Cutting Guide, page 10)

- **Preparation: 20 minutes**
- **Baking: 30 minutes**
- **Freezing: excellent**

TIPS

These make a nice holiday gift. Pack them in a decorative airtight cookie tin or box, tie with a festive ribbon and add the recipe with your gift tag.

If you can find orange-flavored dried cranberries, try them in this recipe. They taste particularly delicious in this brownie.

- **Preheat oven to 375°F (190°C)**
- **8-inch (2 L) square cake pan, greased**

6	squares (1 oz/28 g each) white chocolate, chopped	6
¾ cup	granulated sugar	175 mL
2	eggs	2
⅓ cup	butter, melted	75 mL
1 tsp	vanilla	5 mL
1¼ cups	all-purpose flour	300 mL
¾ tsp	baking powder	3 mL
¾ cup	coarsely chopped hazelnuts	175 mL
⅓ cup	dried cranberries	75 mL

1. In a small saucepan over low heat, melt white chocolate, stirring constantly, until smooth. Remove from heat and set aside.

2. In a bowl, whisk sugar and eggs until blended. Whisk in melted butter and vanilla. Combine flour and baking powder. Stir into egg mixture alternately with melted chocolate, making 2 additions of each and mixing until smooth. Stir in hazelnuts and cranberries. Spread evenly in prepared pan.

3. Bake in preheated oven just until set and golden, 25 to 30 minutes. Let cool completely in pan on rack. Cut into bars or squares.

White Chocolate Apricot Brownies

Here's a golden brownie that's moist and chewy yet cake-like. I love the flavor of apricots and almonds.

MAKES 16 TO 48 BARS OR SQUARES (see Cutting Guide, page 10)

- Preparation: 20 minutes
- Baking: 30 minutes
- Freezing: excellent

TIPS

To ease cleanup, rather than combining the dry ingredients in a bowl (Step 2), place a large piece of waxed paper on the counter. After measuring, combine the flour, baking powder and salt on the paper. Using the paper as a funnel, transfer the dry ingredients to the chocolate mixture.

The easiest way to chop dried apricots is with a pair of kitchen shears. Spray the blades with cooking spray or brush them lightly with oil to prevent sticking.

If you prefer a sweeter taste, dust the brownie with confectioners' (icing) sugar after it's cooled.

- **Preheat oven to 350°F (180°C)**
- **9-inch (2.5 L) square cake pan, greased**

4	squares (1 oz/28 g each) white chocolate, chopped	4
1/3 cup	butter	75 mL
1/2 cup	granulated sugar	125 mL
2	eggs	2
2 tsp	grated orange zest	10 mL
3/4 cup	all-purpose flour	175 mL
1/2 tsp	baking powder	2 mL
1/4 tsp	salt	1 mL
1 cup	chopped dried apricots (see Tips, left)	250 mL
2/3 cup	slivered almonds	150 mL

1. In a large saucepan over low heat, melt white chocolate and butter, stirring constantly, until smooth. Remove from heat and stir in sugar. Add eggs, one at a time, whisking lightly after each addition. Stir in orange zest.

2. Combine flour, baking powder and salt. Stir into chocolate mixture, mixing well. Stir in apricots and almonds. Spread evenly in prepared pan.

3. Bake in preheated oven just until set, 25 to 30 minutes. Let cool completely in pan on rack. Cut into bars or squares.

Variations

Omit orange zest. Add 1/2 tsp (2 mL) almond extract or 1 tsp (5 mL) vanilla.

Replace apricots with dried cranberries.

White Chocolate Macadamia Brownies

This rich, buttery brownie has a chewy texture and lots of crunchy macadamia nuts.

MAKES 20 TO 54 BARS OR SQUARES
(see Cutting Guide, page 10)

- **Preparation: 20 minutes**
- **Baking: 25 minutes**
- **Freezing: excellent**

TIPS

I prefer to use butter in baking because it has the best flavor of all the fats.

For a great dessert, cut these brownies into larger squares and serve them slightly warm with a generous drizzle of hot fudge sauce and a sprinkling of chopped macadamia nuts.

For the best taste, store and serve these bars at room temperature. If you're keeping them for longer than 3 days, freeze them.

- **Preheat oven to 350°F (180°C)**
- **13- by 9-inch (3 L) cake pan, greased**

12	squares (1 oz/28 g each) white chocolate, chopped and divided	12
½ cup	butter	125 mL
2	eggs	2
½ cup	granulated sugar	125 mL
1 tsp	vanilla	5 mL
1 cup	all-purpose flour	250 mL
¼ tsp	salt	1 mL
1 cup	chopped toasted macadamia nuts	250 mL

1. In a saucepan over low heat, melt 7 squares of the white chocolate with the butter, stirring constantly, until smooth. Remove from heat and set aside.

2. In a large bowl, using an electric mixer on high speed, beat eggs until frothy. Gradually add sugar, beating until thick and creamy. Stir in chocolate mixture and vanilla. Stir in flour and salt, mixing well. Stir in nuts and remaining white chocolate. Spread evenly in prepared pan.

3. Bake in preheated oven just until set, about 25 minutes. Let cool completely in pan on rack. Cut into bars or squares.

Variations

Replace the white chocolate with milk chocolate.

Replace macadamia nuts with slivered almonds or chopped cashews.

Chocolate Macadamia Blondies

Here's an all-time favorite that's very easy to make.

**MAKES 20 TO
54 BARS OR SQUARES
(see Cutting Guide,
page 10)**

- **Preparation: 20 minutes**
- **Baking: 35 minutes**
- **Freezing: excellent**

TIPS

Macadamia nuts are expensive, which makes these bars quite special. If you're making them for a kids' party, you may prefer to try them with almonds. I'm sure there'll be no complaints and no bars leftover either.

Chop macadamia nuts by hand with a sharp chef's knife. Because they're softer than most nuts, they don't chop well in a food processor.

- **Preheat oven to 325°F (160°C)**
- **13- by 9-inch (3 L) cake pan, greased**

1 cup	butter, softened	250 mL
2¼ cups	packed brown sugar	550 mL
2	eggs	2
1½ tsp	vanilla	7 mL
2 cups	all-purpose flour	500 mL
2 tsp	baking powder	10 mL
1 cup	milk chocolate chips	250 mL
1 cup	white chocolate chips	250 mL
1⅓ cups	coarsely chopped macadamia nuts, divided	325 mL

1. In a large bowl, using an electric mixer on medium speed, beat butter and brown sugar until light and creamy, about 5 minutes. Add eggs and vanilla, beating until smooth.

2. Combine flour and baking powder. Beat into butter mixture on low speed, mixing well. Stir in milk chocolate and white chocolate chips and 1 cup (250 mL) of the macadamia nuts. Spread evenly in prepared pan. Sprinkle remaining nuts on top and press lightly into batter.

3. Bake in preheated oven just until set, 30 to 35 minutes. Let cool completely in pan on rack. Cut into bars or squares.

Variations

Replace milk chocolate chips with semisweet chocolate chips.

Replace white chocolate chips with semisweet chocolate chips to make a brownie.

Substitute white chocolate chunks for both types of chips.

Cherry Almond Blondies

◆

This moist, cake-like bar has a wonderful almond flavor and dried cherries throughout.

MAKES 20 TO 54 BARS OR SQUARES
(see Cutting Guide, page 10)

- **Preparation: 25 minutes**
- **Baking: 45 minutes**
- **Freezing: excellent**

TIPS

To ease cleanup, rather than combining the dry ingredients in a bowl (Step 2), place a large piece of waxed paper on the counter. Spread the flour on the paper. Sprinkle the ground almonds, baking powder and salt over top. Using the paper as a funnel, transfer the dry ingredients to the batter.

Serve these bars as an alternative to, or along with, fruitcake. Add some white shortbread and you have a very attractive Christmas platter or gift box.

- **Preheat oven to 350°F (180°C)**
- **13- by 9-inch (3 L) cake pan, greased**

¼ cup	almond liqueur	60 mL
1 cup	dried cherries	250 mL
2½ cups	all-purpose flour	625 mL
½ cup	ground almonds	125 mL
2 tsp	baking powder	10 mL
¼ tsp	salt	1 mL
1 cup	butter, softened	250 mL
1¾ cups	granulated sugar	425 mL
4	eggs	4
1 tbsp	grated orange zest	15 mL
1 cup	sliced almonds	250 mL
7 oz	almond paste, diced	210 g

1. In a saucepan over medium heat, bring almond liqueur and cherries to boil. Remove from heat. Let cool for 30 minutes.
2. Combine flour, ground almonds, baking powder and salt.
3. In a bowl, using an electric mixer on medium speed, beat butter and sugar until smooth and creamy, about 3 minutes. Add eggs, one at a time, beating well after each addition. Beat in orange zest. Stir in dry ingredients, mixing just until combined. Stir in sliced almonds, almond paste and cherry mixture. Spread evenly in prepared pan.
4. Bake in preheated oven until a toothpick inserted in center comes out clean, 40 to 45 minutes. Let cool completely in pan on rack. Cut into bars or squares.

Variations

Replace dried cherries with snipped dried apricots.

Replace almond liqueur with orange juice.

Apple Blondies with Brown Sugar Frosting

I'm not sure whether I like the frosting or the apple blondie the best. Both components are scrumptious. You'll have to decide for yourself.

MAKES 20 TO 54 BARS OR SQUARES (see Cutting Guide, page 10)

- **Preparation: 25 minutes**
- **Baking: 30 minutes**
- **Freezing: excellent**

TIPS

This frosting is very soft when first mixed, which makes it very nice to spread. It firms up on cooling.

Choose apples that are crisp, tart and not too moist. Granny Smith, Golden Delicious and Spartans are good choices for this recipe.

- **Preheat oven to 350°F (180°C)**
- **13- by 9-inch (3 L) cake pan, greased**

BLONDIE

2/3 cup	butter, softened	150 mL
2 cups	packed brown sugar	500 mL
2	eggs	2
1 tsp	vanilla	2 mL
2 cups	all-purpose flour	500 mL
2 tsp	baking powder	10 mL
1/4 tsp	salt	1 mL
1 cup	chopped peeled apples	250 mL
3/4 cup	chopped walnuts	175 mL

BROWN SUGAR FROSTING

1/2 cup	butter	125 mL
1 cup	packed brown sugar	250 mL
1/4 cup	milk or cream	60 mL
2 cups	confectioners' (icing) sugar, sifted	500 mL

1. *Blondie:* In a large bowl, using an electric mixer on medium speed, beat butter, brown sugar, eggs and vanilla until thick and smooth, about 3 minutes. Combine flour, baking powder and salt. Add to butter mixture on low speed, mixing until blended. Stir in apples and nuts, mixing well. Spread evenly in prepared pan.

2. Bake in preheated oven until set and golden, 25 to 30 minutes. Let cool completely in pan on rack.

3. *Brown Sugar Frosting:* In a small saucepan over low heat, melt butter. Stir in brown sugar and milk. Bring mixture just to a boil then remove from heat and let cool to lukewarm. Stir in confectioners' sugar, mixing until smooth. Spread evenly over bar. Let stand until frosting is firm enough to cut. Cut into bars or squares.

Variations

Omit the frosting if you prefer a plain apple walnut blondie. If you're not a fan of nuts, omit the walnuts.

Two-Tone Dream Bars

Chocolate Bars and Squares

Bars that feature chocolate range from ooey, gooey, moist and chewy to crisp and crunchy. They are easy to make for spur-of-the-moment company, yet delicious enough for elegant entertaining. There is nothing like a rich chocolate dessert to impress your guests. If you have chocoholics among your relatives and friends, a gift of homemade chocolate cookie bars is so much nicer and more personal than a box of store-bought chocolates. Although the recipes in this chapter also feature fruit, nuts, coconut, caramel and other great ingredients, the ruling flavor is chocolate. Enjoy.

Two-Tone Dream Bars

Although these look and sound quite decadent they're actually fairly light in texture — the perfect solution for any midnight cravings.

MAKES 20 TO 54 BARS (see Cutting Guide, page 10)

- **Preparation: 25 minutes**
- **Baking: 32 minutes**
- **Freezing: excellent**

TIPS

A small offset spatula makes spreading easy, especially on small areas such as the top of bars. It's also good at getting into corners.

To store bars, refrigerate them in an airtight container or leave at room temperature, depending on the type of bar. If you plan to freeze them, wrap tightly in plastic wrap and freeze for up to 3 months. I like to cut them into bars before freezing so I can remove the required number whenever I need them rather than having to thaw or cut the entire piece.

- **Preheat oven to 350°F (180°C)**
- **13- by 9-inch (3 L) cake pan, greased**

CRUST

1 cup	all-purpose flour	250 mL
⅓ cup	granulated sugar	75 mL
⅓ cup	butter, softened	75 mL

FILLING

1 cup	graham wafer crumbs	250 mL
1 cup	semisweet chocolate chips	250 mL
⅔ cup	coarsely chopped walnuts	150 mL
1	can (10 oz/300 mL) sweetened condensed milk	1

TOPPING

8	squares (1 oz/28 g each) white chocolate, chopped	8
2 tbsp	butter	30 mL

1. *Crust:* In a bowl, combine flour, sugar and butter. Using an electric mixer on low speed, beat until crumbly. Press evenly into prepared pan. Bake in preheated oven until golden around the edges, 10 to 12 minutes.

2. *Filling:* In a bowl, combine graham wafer crumbs, chocolate chips, walnuts and condensed milk, mixing until well blended. Drop mixture by spoonfuls over warm base. Spread evenly. Return to oven and bake until top is lightly browned, about 20 minutes. Let cool completely in pan on rack.

3. *Topping:* In a saucepan over low heat, melt white chocolate and butter, stirring constantly, until smooth. Spread evenly over bars. Chill until chocolate sets, about 10 minutes. Cut into bars.

Variations

Use your favorite kind of chocolate chip for the filling in this recipe. White and milk chocolate chips are especially nice.

Replace the graham wafer crumbs with vanilla wafer crumbs.

One-Bite Chocolate Cheesecake Bars

These bars are sumptuous. The almond crust and the creamy, not-too-rich chocolate cheesecake top are a marriage made in heaven.

MAKES 18 TO 48 BARS
(see Cutting Guide, page 10)

- **Preparation: 25 minutes**
- **Baking: 47 minutes**
- **Freezing: excellent**

TIPS

There are a number of ways to melt chocolate chips. You can place them in a double boiler over hot, not boiling, water or in a small saucepan over low heat. In both cases, stir frequently until smooth. Or melt them in a microwave oven on Medium power until softened (about 1 minute for ¼ cup/60 mL), then stir until smooth.

If you prefer, use a food processor rather than a mixer to prepare the base and the topping. It's actually quicker. When mixing the base in a food processor, use cold butter, cubed.

- **Preheat oven to 350°F (180°C)**
- **8-inch (2 L) square cake pan, greased**

BASE

1 cup	all-purpose flour	250 mL
¼ cup	granulated sugar	60 mL
½ cup	ground almonds	125 mL
½ cup	butter, softened	125 mL

TOPPING

1	package (8 oz/250 g) cream cheese, softened	1
⅔ cup	semisweet chocolate chips, melted (see Tips, left)	150 mL
⅔ cup	granulated sugar	150 mL
2	eggs	2
⅔ cup	table (18%) cream	150 mL
½ tsp	almond extract	2 mL

1. *Base:* In a bowl, combine flour, sugar and ground almonds. Using an electric mixer on low speed, beat in butter until crumbly. Press evenly into prepared pan. Bake in preheated oven until golden around the edges, 10 to 12 minutes.

2. *Topping:* In a large bowl, using an electric mixer on low speed, beat cream cheese until smooth. Add melted chocolate, sugar and eggs, beating on low speed until blended. Gradually add cream and almond extract, mixing until smooth. Spread over base.

3. Return to oven and bake until top is just set, 25 to 35 minutes. Let cool completely in pan on rack, then refrigerate until firm for easy cutting. Cut into bars.

Variations

Replace almond extract with 1 tbsp (15 mL) instant espresso coffee powder.

Replace the ground almonds with ¼ cup (60 mL) flaked sweetened coconut and the almond extract with an equal quantity of vanilla.

Caramel Peanut Ripple Bars

◆

With several different layers, these bars are particularly attractive. Even so, they're surprisingly easy to make.

MAKES 20 TO 54 BARS (see Cutting Guide, page 10)

- **Preparation: 35 minutes**
- **Baking: 30 minutes**
- **Freezing: excellent**

TIPS

When lining a pan with parchment, leave an overhang at the sides. When the bar is completely cool, you can lift it right out of the pan and transfer to a cutting board for easy slicing.

To store, place cooled bars in a single layer in an airtight container. Store at room temperature for 4 days or freeze for up to 4 months.

- **Preheat oven to 350°F (180°C)**
- **13- by 9-inch (3 L) cake pan, greased and lined with parchment**

½ cup + 2 tbsp	butter, softened, divided	155 mL
1 cup	packed brown sugar	250 mL
1	egg	1
1 tsp	vanilla	5 mL
1¼ cups	all-purpose flour	300 mL
½ tsp	baking soda	2 mL
1½ cups	quick-cooking rolled oats	375 mL
6 oz	soft caramels, unwrapped (about 20)	175 g
2 tbsp	milk	30 mL
2¾ cups	miniature marshmallows, divided	675 mL
1⅓ cups	peanuts, divided	325 mL
1½ cups	semisweet chocolate chips	375 mL
1	can (10 oz/300 mL) sweetened condensed milk	1

1. In a large bowl, using an electric mixer on low speed, beat ½ cup (125 mL) butter and brown sugar until creamy. Add egg and vanilla, beating until smooth. Beat in flour and baking soda, mixing well. Stir in oats until blended. Reserve ⅔ cup (150 mL) of the oat mixture for the top. Press remaining mixture firmly into prepared pan. Set aside.

2. In a saucepan over low heat, combine caramels and milk. Heat, stirring, until caramels have melted and mixture is smooth. Carefully spread over base. Sprinkle 2 cups (500 mL) of the marshmallows and 1 cup (250 mL) of the peanuts on top.

3. In a small saucepan, combine chocolate chips, sweetened condensed milk and remaining 2 tbsp (30 mL) of the butter. Heat over low heat, stirring constantly, until chocolate is melted and mixture is smooth. Pour evenly over marshmallows and peanut layer. Using your fingertips, scatter reserved oat mixture on top. Sprinkle with remaining marshmallows and peanuts.

4. Bake in preheated oven until golden, 25 to 30 minutes. Let cool completely in pan on rack. Cut into bars.

Chocolate Marshmallow Crisps

You can't go wrong with this combination of chocolate, peanut butter and crisp rice cereal. It's always a favorite.

MAKES 24 TO 60 BARS OR SQUARES
(see Cutting Guide, page 10)

- **Preparation: 25 minutes**
- **Baking: 23 minutes**
- **Freezing: excellent**

TIPS

Mini candy-coated chocolate pieces, such as M&M's, can be purchased in bulk stores. They're nice to have on hand as an easy decorating tool for baking with kids. If you prefer a more adult look, leave them out.

So long as peanut allergies aren't a concern, these bars make a great treat for kids' lunch boxes.

- **Preheat oven to 350°F (180°C)**
- **15- by 10- by 1-inch (2 L) jelly roll pan, greased**

BASE

¾ cup	butter, softened	175 mL
1½ cups	granulated sugar	375 mL
3	eggs	3
1⅓ cups	all-purpose flour	325 mL
⅓ cup	unsweetened cocoa powder, sifted	75 mL
½ tsp	baking powder	2 mL
¼ tsp	salt	1 mL
¾ cup	chopped peanuts	175 mL
4 cups	miniature marshmallows	1 L

TOPPING

1½ cups	semisweet chocolate chips	375 mL
1 cup	creamy peanut butter	250 mL
3 tbsp	butter	45 mL
2 cups	crisp rice cereal	500 mL
1 cup	miniature candy-coated chocolate pieces, optional (see Tips, left)	250 mL

1. *Base:* In a large bowl, using an electric mixer on medium speed, beat butter, sugar and eggs until light and creamy.
2. Combine flour, cocoa, baking powder and salt. On low speed, beat into creamed mixture, mixing well. Stir in peanuts. Spread evenly in prepared pan.
3. Bake in preheated oven just until set, 15 to 20 minutes. Sprinkle marshmallows in single layer over top. Return to oven until marshmallows are puffed, 2 to 3 minutes. Let cool completely in pan on rack.
4. *Topping:* In a saucepan, combine chocolate chips, peanut butter and butter. Heat over low heat, stirring constantly, until chocolate is melted and mixture is smooth. Stir in cereal and candy. Spread immediately over base. Chill to set topping. Cut into bars or squares.

Variation

If you prefer a milder chocolate taste, substitute milk chocolate chips for the semisweet.

Chocolate Buttercrunch Bars

These bars have everything. They're moist, chewy, crunchy and delicious all in one bite. You can tell from the batter (a bit of dough holding lots of fabulous ingredients together) that they'll be amazing.

MAKES 18 TO 48 BARS (see Cutting Guide, page 10)

- **Preparation: 20 minutes**
- **Baking: 30 minutes**
- **Freezing: excellent**

TIPS

Skor or Heath bars work well in this recipe.

Chill the candy bars before chopping. Put them in a heavy plastic bag and smash with a meat mallet for easy crushing. You'll end up with a mixture of large and small pieces, which is nice.

- **Preheat oven to 350°F (180°C)**
- **9-inch (2.5 L) square cake pan, greased**

½ cup	butter, melted	125 mL
¾ cup	packed brown sugar	175 mL
¼ cup	granulated sugar	60 mL
1	egg	1
1 tsp	vanilla	5 mL
¾ tsp	almond extract	3 mL
¾ cup	all-purpose flour	175 mL
¼ tsp	baking soda	1 mL
¼ tsp	ground cinnamon	1 mL
4	crunchy chocolate-covered toffee bars (1.4 oz/39 g each), chopped (see Tips, left)	4
¾ cup	coarsely chopped unblanched almonds, toasted	175 mL
⅔ cup	semisweet chocolate chips	150 mL

1. In a bowl, whisk melted butter, brown and granulated sugars, egg, vanilla and almond extract until smoothly blended. Stir in flour, baking soda and cinnamon, mixing well. Stir in candy bars, almonds and chocolate chips. Mix well. Spread evenly in prepared pan.

2. Bake in preheated oven just until set, 25 to 30 minutes. Let cool completely in pan on rack. Cut into bars.

Variations

Omit the almond extract if it isn't a favorite flavor.

Replace the almonds with roasted peanuts.

Substitute Crispy Crunch for the toffee bars.

Chewy Chocolate Almond Bars

◆

These bars are great for entertaining and make a superb addition to any potluck. They're easy to make and one of my favorites.

MAKES 18 TO 48 BARS (see Cutting Guide, page 10)

- **Preparation: 20 minutes**
- **Baking: 42 minutes**
- **Freezing: excellent**

TIPS

To measure dry ingredients, use nesting-type dry measures that are level on top. Lightly spoon ingredients into the measure, then level off with a knife or spatula.

Measure ingredients like corn syrup in liquid measuring cups that have a spout. Liquid measures are usually glass or clear plastic.

If using glass baking dishes in place of metal pans, decrease the oven temperature by 25°F (10°C).

- **Preheat oven to 350°F (180°C)**
- **9-inch (2.5 L) square cake pan, greased**

CRUST

1 cup	all-purpose flour	250 mL
½ cup	ground almonds	125 mL
¼ cup	packed brown sugar	60 mL
½ cup	cold butter, cubed	125 mL

TOPPING

2	eggs	2
½ cup	granulated sugar	125 mL
½ cup	corn syrup	125 mL
2 tbsp	butter, melted	30 mL
½ tsp	almond extract	2 mL
1 cup	milk chocolate chips	250 mL
¾ cup	slivered almonds	175 mL

1. *Crust:* In a bowl, combine flour, ground almonds and brown sugar. Using a pastry blender, 2 knives or your fingers, cut in butter until mixture resembles coarse crumbs. Press evenly into prepared pan. Bake in preheated oven until golden around the edges, 10 to 12 minutes.

2. *Topping:* In a bowl, whisk eggs, sugar, syrup, melted butter and almond extract until well blended. Stir in chocolate chips and almonds. Pour evenly over crust.

3. Return to oven and bake until set and golden, 25 to 30 minutes. Let cool completely in pan on rack. Cut into bars.

Variations

If you prefer, substitute an equal quantity of white chocolate chips for milk chocolate chips in this recipe.

Replace almonds with pecans, walnuts, cashews or peanuts.

Chocolate Caramel Oat Squares

A chocolate bar–like filling nestles between layers of a crumble cookie crust.

MAKES 24 TO 60 SQUARES
(see **Cutting Guide**, page 10)

- **Preparation: 20 minutes**
- **Baking: 25 minutes**
- **Freezing: excellent**

TIPS

If you prefer, bake these squares in two 9-inch (2.5 L) square pans for the same amount of time.

Chilling caramels makes them easier to unwrap. Of course, the easiest way is to let the kids help with this job. Be sure to have a few extra caramels on hand to replace the ones that disappear.

The fresher the caramels the more easily they melt.

- **Preheat oven to 350°F (180°C)**
- **15- by 10- by 1-inch (2 L) jelly roll pan, greased**

CRUST

2 cups	all-purpose flour	500 mL
2 cups	quick-cooking rolled oats	500 mL
1 ⅓ cups	packed brown sugar	325 mL
1 tsp	baking soda	5 mL
¼ tsp	salt	1 mL
1 ½ cups	cold butter, cubed	375 mL

FILLING

1 lb	soft caramels, unwrapped (about 60)	500 g
1 cup	evaporated milk	250 mL
2 cups	semisweet chocolate chips	500 mL
1 cup	chopped walnuts	250 mL

1. *Crust:* In a bowl, combine flour, oats, brown sugar, baking soda and salt. Using a pastry blender, 2 knives or your fingers, cut in butter until mixture resembles coarse crumbs. Press half of mixture evenly into prepared pan. Bake in preheated oven just until starting to brown around the edges, about 5 minutes. Set remainder aside.

2. *Filling:* In a heavy saucepan, combine caramels and evaporated milk. Heat over low heat, stirring until caramels are melted and mixture is smooth. Remove from heat and set aside.

3. Sprinkle chocolate chips and walnuts over hot crust. Pour caramel mixture evenly over top. Sprinkle with remaining crust mixture.

4. Return to oven and bake until golden, 15 to 20 minutes. Let cool completely in pan on rack. Cut into squares.

Variation

Replace semisweet chocolate chips with milk chocolate, white or butterscotch chips.

Crunchy Toffee Chocolate Bars

These squares are crunchy, creamy and chocolaty in one delicious mouthful.

MAKES 20 TO 54 BARS (see Cutting Guide, page 10)

- **Preparation: 30 minutes**
- **Baking: 42 minutes**
- **Cooking: 10 minutes**
- **Freezing: excellent**

TIPS

If you prefer, use a large wooden spoon to mix the crust instead of an electric mixer.

Toffee bits are available in bags. They're broken pieces of the toffee part of Heath or Skor bars (no chocolate).

Be sure to use fresh, pure chocolate chips. When chocolate chips get older or are made from imitation chocolate, they don't melt as easily, making spreading difficult. Store chocolate in a cool, dry place, not in the freezer or refrigerator.

- **Preheat oven to 350°F (180°C)**
- **13- by 9-inch (3 L) cake pan, greased**

CRUST

¾ cup	butter, softened	175 mL
¾ cup	packed brown sugar	175 mL
1½ cups	all-purpose flour	375 mL
½ cup	quick-cooking rolled oats	125 mL

FILLING

1	can (10 oz/300 mL) sweetened condensed milk	1
2 tbsp	butter	30 mL
½ tsp	almond extract	2 mL
2 cups	semisweet chocolate chips	500 mL
1 cup	toffee bits (see Tips, left)	250 mL
½ cup	finely chopped almonds	125 mL

1. *Crust:* In a bowl, combine butter, brown sugar, flour and rolled oats. Using an electric mixer on low speed, mix until well blended and mixture comes together. Press evenly into prepared pan. Bake in preheated oven until light golden, 20 to 25 minutes. Let cool in pan on rack while preparing filling.

2. *Filling:* In a small heavy saucepan over medium heat, combine sweetened condensed milk, butter and almond extract. Heat, stirring constantly, until thickened, 5 to 10 minutes. Spread over cooled base.

3. Return to oven and bake until top is golden, 12 to 15 minutes. Sprinkle chocolate chips evenly over top. Return to oven and bake until chocolate is shiny and soft, about 2 minutes. Remove from oven. Spread chocolate evenly. Sprinkle toffee bits and almonds on top, pressing lightly into the chocolate layer. Let cool completely in pan on rack. If necessary, refrigerate just to set chocolate before cutting into bars. Store at room temperature.

Double Deluxe Bars

Two layers make up one delicious bar. A tender cookie-like base holds a dense fruit and nut topping with lots of chocolate chips scattered throughout.

MAKES 20 TO 54 BARS (see Cutting Guide, page 10)

- **Preparation: 20 minutes**
- **Baking: 40 minutes**
- **Freezing: excellent**

TIPS

Dried fruits dry out during storage. To restore some of the lost moisture, plump them in boiling water for a few minutes. Drain well and pat dry before using.

Due to its high moisture content, brown sugar tends to lump during storage. It should be stored in an airtight container or heavy plastic bag in a cool, dry place. If it hardens and becomes lumpy, put it in a plastic bag with a slice of apple. Seal tightly and leave a few days to soften.

- **Preheat oven to 350°F (180°C)**
- **13- by 9-inch (3 L) cake pan, greased**

CRUST

2 cups	all-purpose flour	500 mL
½ cup	packed brown sugar	125 mL
¾ cup	cold butter, cubed	175 mL

TOPPING

¼ cup	all-purpose flour	60 mL
½ tsp	baking powder	2 mL
¼ tsp	salt	1 mL
2	eggs	2
1½ cups	packed brown sugar	375 mL
1 tsp	vanilla	5 mL
1½ cups	semisweet chocolate chips	375 mL
1 cup	dried cranberries	250 mL
¾ cup	flaked coconut	175 mL
¾ cup	chopped pecans	175 mL

1. *Crust:* In a bowl, combine flour and brown sugar. Using a pastry blender, 2 knives or your fingers, cut in butter until mixture resembles coarse crumbs. Press evenly into prepared pan. Bake in preheated oven until golden around the edges, 12 to 15 minutes.

2. *Topping:* Combine flour, baking powder and salt. Set aside. In a bowl, whisk eggs, brown sugar and vanilla until frothy. Whisk in flour mixture, mixing well. Stir in chocolate chips, cranberries, coconut and pecans, mixing until ingredients are moistened. Spread over crust.

3. Return to oven and bake until topping is set and golden, 20 to 25 minutes. Let cool completely in pan on rack. Cut into bars.

Variations

Replace dried cranberries with raisins.

Use your favorite nut in place of pecans.

Chocolate Pecan Squares

These squares remind me of bite-size pieces of pecan pie enhanced with chocolate. Because they are so rich, I like to cut them in small pieces. Triangles are a pretty shape.

MAKES 16 TO 36 SQUARES (see Cutting Guide, page 10)

- **Preparation: 20 minutes**
- **Baking: 45 minutes**
- **Freezing: excellent**

TIPS

Most recipes in this book call for butter, melted, which means you measure the butter, then melt it. If the recipe calls for melted butter, then it's melted before measuring.

If you've run out of chocolate chips, chop up a chocolate bar or chocolate squares.

- **Preheat oven to 350°F (180°C)**
- **9-inch (2.5 L) square cake pan, greased**

CRUST

1 cup	all-purpose flour	250 mL
¼ cup	granulated sugar	60 mL
⅓ cup	butter, softened	75 mL

TOPPING

2	eggs	2
½ cup	granulated sugar	125 mL
½ cup	corn syrup	125 mL
2 tbsp	butter, melted	30 mL
1 cup	semisweet chocolate chips	250 mL
¾ cup	chopped pecans	175 mL

1. *Crust:* In a bowl, combine flour, sugar and butter. Using an electric mixer on low speed, beat until crumbly. Press evenly into prepared pan. Bake in preheated oven until edges are lightly browned, 12 to 15 minutes.

2. *Topping:* In a bowl, whisk eggs, sugar, corn syrup and melted butter until blended. Stir in chocolate chips and pecans. Pour evenly over crust.

3. Return to oven and bake until set and golden, 25 to 30 minutes. Let cool completely in pan on rack. Cut into squares.

Variation

Try walnuts or almonds instead of the pecans for a nice flavor change.

Chocolate Cherry Nut Bars

I love the combination of flavors in these chunky colorful bars. Enjoy with caution — they can quickly become addictive.

MAKES 20 TO 54 BARS (see Cutting Guide, page 10)

- **Preparation: 20 minutes**
- **Baking: 37 minutes**
- **Freezing: excellent**

TIPS

Candied (glacé) cherries darken with age. Look for ones that are a bright color.

Get a head start on your holiday baking. Make an extra pan of these and freeze them.

- **Preheat oven to 350°F (180°C)**
- **13- by 9-inch (3 L) cake pan, greased**

CRUST

1 1/4 cups	all-purpose flour	300 mL
1/2 cup	packed brown sugar	125 mL
3/4 cup	cold butter, cubed	175 mL

TOPPING

2	eggs	2
2/3 cup	packed brown sugar	150 mL
1 1/2 cups	deluxe salted mixed nuts (no peanuts)	375 mL
1 1/2 cups	halved red and green candied (glacé) cherries	375 mL
1 cup	semisweet chocolate chips	250 mL

1. *Crust:* In a bowl, combine flour and brown sugar. Using a pastry blender, 2 knives or your fingers, cut in butter until mixture resembles coarse crumbs. Press evenly into prepared pan. Bake in preheated oven until golden around the edges, 10 to 12 minutes.

2. *Topping:* In a bowl, whisk eggs and brown sugar until blended. Stir in nuts, cherries and chocolate chips, mixing well. Spread evenly over crust.

3. Return to oven and bake until topping is set, 20 to 25 minutes. Let cool completely in pan on rack. Cut into bars.

Variations

Replace semisweet chocolate chips with white chocolate chips.

Use all red cherries instead of the red and green mixture.

Replace 1/2 cup (125 mL) of the cherries with candied (glacé) pineapple.

Add a drizzle of melted white chocolate on cooled bars. It shows off the color nicely.

Chocolate Marshmallow Meringue Bars

A layer of chocolate, nuts and marshmallows hides under a beautiful golden meringue and sits on a soft, buttery crust — delicious, but they won't make a dieter's list.

MAKES 20 TO 54 BARS (see Cutting Guide, page 10)

- **Preparation: 25 minutes**
- **Baking: 30 minutes**
- **Freezing: excellent**

TIPS

Although it's always important to have all your ingredients at room temperature for baking, this is particularly true when making meringue. Otherwise, you won't get the desired volume.

Don't be surprised if your meringue thins out a bit when folding in the brown sugar. Because of the high amount of sugar, it doesn't stay stiff.

To spread the meringue easily over the filling, dip the spatula in hot water.

For the best walnut flavor, buy fresh California walnut halves and chop them, rather than buying prechopped.

- **Preheat oven to 350°F (180°C)**
- **13- by 9-inch (3 L) cake pan, greased**

BASE

1/2 cup	butter, softened	125 mL
1 cup	granulated sugar	250 mL
1	egg	1
2	egg yolks	2
1 1/2 cups	all-purpose flour	375 mL
1 tsp	baking powder	5 mL
1/4 tsp	salt	1 mL

FILLING

1 cup	chopped walnuts	250 mL
1 cup	milk chocolate chips	250 mL
1 cup	miniature marshmallows	250 mL

TOPPING

2	egg whites	2
1 cup	packed brown sugar	250 mL

1. *Base:* In a bowl, using an electric mixer on high speed, beat butter, sugar, egg and egg yolks until light and creamy. Combine flour, baking powder and salt. Stir into creamed mixture until well blended. Spread evenly in prepared pan.

2. *Filling:* Sprinkle walnuts, chocolate chips and marshmallows evenly over batter.

3. *Topping:* In a small bowl, using an electric mixer with clean beaters on high speed, beat egg whites until stiff. Gently fold in brown sugar. Spread evenly over filling.

4. Bake in preheated oven until golden brown, 25 to 30 minutes. Let cool completely in pan on rack. Cut into bars.

Variations

For a stronger hit of chocolate, use semisweet instead of milk chocolate chips.

Replace walnuts with pecans.

Good 'n' Gooey Chocolate Cashew Squares

Try serving these squares warm with a scoop of vanilla ice cream on the side.

**MAKES 24 SQUARES
(see Cutting Guide, page 10)**

- **Preparation: 20 minutes**
- **Baking: 37 minutes**
- **Freezing: excellent**

TIPS

If you prefer, mix the crust in a food processor or cut the butter in using a pastry blender, 2 knives or your fingers. In both cases, use cold butter, cubed, rather than softened butter. Whichever method you use, the mixture should resemble coarse crumbs.

When baking bars in dark nonstick pans, reduce the baking time of the crust and topping by about 5 minutes.

- **Preheat oven to 350°F (180°C)**
- **13- by 9-inch (3 L) cake pan, greased**

CRUST

1 ½ cups	all-purpose flour	375 mL
⅓ cup	packed brown sugar	75 mL
½ cup	butter, softened	125 mL

TOPPING

3	eggs	3
¾ cup	granulated sugar	175 mL
¾ cup	corn syrup	175 mL
3 tbsp	butter, melted	45 mL
1 ½ cups	coarsely chopped cashews	375 mL
1 ½ cups	semisweet chocolate chips	375 mL

1. *Crust:* In a bowl, combine flour, brown sugar and butter. Using an electric mixer on low speed, beat until crumbly. Press evenly into prepared pan. Bake in preheated oven until golden around the edges, 10 to 12 minutes.

2. *Topping:* In a bowl, whisk eggs, sugar, syrup and melted butter until smooth. Stir in cashews and chocolate chips. Spread evenly over base.

3. Return to oven and bake until set and golden, about 25 minutes. Let cool completely in pan on rack. Cut into squares.

Variations

Use white or milk chocolate chips instead of semisweet.
Replace the cashews with walnuts.

1-2-3 Chocolate Bars

Here's a delicious treat that's quick and easy to make. If you have the ingredients on hand, it's perfect for unexpected company.

MAKES 20 TO 54 BARS
(see Cutting Guide,
page 10)

- **Preparation: 15 minutes**
- **Baking: 25 minutes**
- **Freezing: excellent**

TIPS

Brands of sweetened condensed milk vary in consistency. Some, usually the cheaper brands, are very thin. I recommend that you try several, choose your favorite and stick to it. Condensed milk should be pourable but not too thin. The recipes in this book were tested using whole or regular condensed milk. Lower-fat versions are available and, in most cases, make a satisfactory substitute.

These bars are very rich and chocolaty. One pan goes a long way.

- **Preheat oven to 350°F (180°C)**
- **13- by 9-inch (3 L) cake pan, greased**

CRUST

1 ⅓ cups	graham wafer crumbs	325 mL
¼ cup	unsweetened cocoa powder, sifted	60 mL
¼ cup	granulated sugar	60 mL
½ cup	butter, melted	125 mL

TOPPING

1	can (10 oz/300 mL) sweetened condensed milk	1
1	egg	1
¼ cup	all-purpose flour	60 mL
¼ cup	unsweetened cocoa powder, sifted	60 mL
½ tsp	baking powder	2 mL
½ tsp	vanilla	2 mL
1 cup	chopped pecans	250 mL
2 cups	semisweet chocolate chips, divided	500 mL

1. *Crust:* In a bowl, combine graham wafer crumbs, cocoa powder and granulated sugar. Stir well. Add melted butter and mix well. Press evenly into prepared pan. Set aside.

2. *Topping:* In a bowl, whisk sweetened condensed milk, egg, flour, cocoa powder, baking powder and vanilla until smoothly blended. Stir in pecans and 1½ cups (375 mL) of the chocolate chips. Spread evenly over base. Sprinkle remaining ½ cup (125 mL) chocolate chips evenly on top. Press in lightly.

3. Bake in preheated oven until set, 20 to 25 minutes. Let cool completely in pan on rack. Cut into bars.

Variation
Vary the type of nut or chip to suit your taste.

Chocolate Sandwich Squares

This sandwich cookie is very easy to make. The filling bakes right in so no last-minute filling is required.

**MAKES 24 SQUARES
(see Cutting Guide, page 10)**

- **Preparation: 20 minutes**
- **Baking: 35 minutes**
- **Freezing: excellent**

TIPS

For easy pouring, melt the butter in a measuring cup or a bowl with a spout.

When measuring brown sugar, pack it firmly into a dry measuring cup. It should hold its shape when turned out.

- **Preheat oven to 350°F (180°C)**
- **13- by 9-inch (3 L) cake pan, greased**

FILLING

1¾ cups	semisweet chocolate chips	425 mL
1	can (10 oz/300 mL) sweetened condensed milk	1
2 tbsp	butter	30 mL

BASE

2¼ cups	packed brown sugar	550 mL
2	eggs	2
1 cup	butter, melted	250 mL
1 tsp	vanilla	5 mL
2 cups	all-purpose flour	500 mL
1 cup	chopped unblanched almonds	250 mL

1. *Filling:* In a saucepan over low heat, combine chocolate chips, sweetened condensed milk and butter. Heat, stirring constantly, until chocolate is melted and mixture is smooth. Remove from heat and set aside.

2. *Base:* In a bowl, whisk brown sugar, eggs, melted butter and vanilla until smooth. Stir in flour, mixing just until blended. Stir in almonds. Mix well. Spread half in prepared pan. Spread filling evenly over base. Dot spoonfuls of remaining batter on top. Spread lightly with knife to cover filling.

3. Bake in preheated oven until set, 30 to 35 minutes. Let cool completely in pan on rack. Cut into squares.

Variation

For a blond bar, replace the chocolate chips with butterscotch or peanut butter chips, and the almonds with peanuts.

Chocolate Peanut Chews

The combination of peanut butter and chocolate has been a favorite for a long time and will likely always be.

MAKES 24 TO 60 BARS OR SQUARES
(see Cutting Guide, page 10)

- **Preparation: 15 minutes**
- **Baking: 15 minutes**
- **Freezing: excellent**

TIPS

When measuring sticky ingredients (such as syrup or honey) that are to be combined with melted butter, measure the melted butter first. (You can also spray the measuring cup with cooking spray.) Then the syrup will slip out of the measuring cup easily.

In this recipe and most others, except for shortbread, hard margarine may be used in place of butter. However, hard margarine likely contains hydrogenated or partially hydrogenated oils, which are unhealthy trans fats. Although soft margarine has a more positive nutritional profile, its consistency differs from butter's so it cannot be used in its place.

- **Preheat oven to 375°F (190°C)**
- **15- by 10- by 1-inch (2 L) jelly roll pan, greased**

BASE

2 cups	quick-cooking rolled oats	500 mL
1 cup	graham wafer crumbs	250 mL
¾ cup	packed brown sugar	175 mL
¼ tsp	baking soda	1 mL
1 cup	chopped peanuts	250 mL
½ cup	butter, melted	125 mL
½ cup	corn syrup	125 mL

TOPPING

1 cup	semisweet chocolate chips	250 mL
⅓ cup	creamy peanut butter	75 mL
½ cup	finely chopped peanuts	125 mL

1. *Base:* In a bowl, combine oats, graham wafer crumbs, brown sugar, baking soda and chopped peanuts. In a large measure or small bowl, combine melted butter and corn syrup. Stir into oat mixture, mixing well. Press evenly into prepared pan. Bake in preheated oven until edges are lightly browned, 12 to 15 minutes.

2. *Topping:* In a small saucepan over low heat, melt chocolate chips and peanut butter, stirring constantly, until smooth. Spread evenly over warm base. Sprinkle with finely chopped peanuts. Let cool completely in pan on rack. Cut into bars or squares.

Variation

If you're watching calories, omit the topping. On the plus side, the plain bars pack well for storage.

Chocolate Caramel Cashew Slices

These look great and taste even better. They have lots of caramel, with a nice hit of chocolate and an appealing crunch of cashews.

MAKES 48 SLICES (see Cutting Guide, page 10)

- Preparation: 20 minutes
- Baking: 14 minutes
- Freezing: excellent

(see **Cutting Guide, page 10**)

TIPS

To retain freshness, store nuts in the freezer. Bring them to room temperature before using in baking.

If you prefer, melt the caramels in the microwave. Combine with the cream and microwave on High until caramels are softened, about 2 minutes. Stir well to blend.

- Preheat oven to 350°F (180°C)
- 15- by 10- by 1-inch (2 L) jelly roll pan, greased

1 cup	butter, softened	250 mL
1/2 cup	packed brown sugar	125 mL
2 cups	all-purpose flour	500 mL
2 cups	semisweet chocolate chips	500 mL
1 lb	soft caramels, unwrapped (about 60)	500 g
1/3 cup	whipping (35%) cream	75 mL
1 cup	coarsely chopped cashews, divided	250 mL

1. In a large bowl, using an electric mixer on medium speed, beat butter and brown sugar until light and creamy, about 3 minutes. Add flour and mix on low speed until crumbly. Press evenly into prepared pan.

2. Bake in preheated oven until golden around edges, 10 to 12 minutes. Sprinkle with chocolate chips. Return to oven to melt chocolate, about 2 minutes. Spread chocolate over base. Let cool in pan on rack or until chocolate is set, about 30 minutes.

3. In a saucepan, combine caramels and whipping cream. Heat over low heat, stirring constantly, until caramels are melted and mixture is smooth. Stir in 3/4 cup (175 mL) of the cashews. Spread carefully over chocolate layer. Sprinkle with remaining cashews. Let cool completely in pan on rack. Cut into thin bars.

Variation

Use walnuts, almonds or pecans in place of cashews.

Chocolate Hazelnut Bars

These yummy bars taste like a big chocolate chip oatmeal cookie. They're easy to make and a good choice if you're in a hurry.

MAKES 36 TO 66 BARS (see Cutting Guide, page 10)

- **Preparation: 15 minutes**
- **Baking: 15 minutes**
- **Freezing: excellent**

TIPS

For a softer cookie, prepare these bars the day before you intend to serve them.

When a recipe calls for all-purpose flour, you can substitute whole wheat flour; the texture will be a little drier, and the product will have a nice nutty flavor. I often use half of each kind of flour, for the best qualities of both.

Hazelnuts are also called filberts. If you prefer, remove the outer brown skin before using them in baking. Toast the nuts on a rimmed baking sheet at 350°F (180°C) for about 5 minutes. Transfer the warm nuts to a towel and rub together. The skins should come off in the towel.

- **Preheat oven to 375°F (190°C)**
- **17- by 11- by 1-inch (3 L) jelly roll pan, greased**

1 cup	butter, softened	250 mL
1 cup	packed brown sugar	250 mL
1/2 cup	granulated sugar	125 mL
2	eggs	2
1 tsp	vanilla	5 mL
1 3/4 cups	all-purpose flour	425 mL
1 cup	quick-cooking rolled oats	250 mL
1 tsp	baking soda	5 mL
1/4 tsp	salt	1 mL
2 cups	semisweet chocolate chips	500 mL
1 1/2 cups	coarsely chopped hazelnuts	375 mL

1. In a bowl, using an electric mixer on medium speed, beat butter and brown and granulated sugars until light and creamy, about 3 minutes. Add eggs, one at a time, beating well after each addition. Beat in vanilla. Stir in flour, oats, baking soda and salt, mixing well. Stir in chocolate chips and hazelnuts. Spread dough evenly in prepared pan.

2. Bake in preheated oven until golden, about 15 minutes. Let cool completely in pan on rack. Cut into bars.

Variation

Macadamia nuts make a wonderful substitution for the hazelnuts in this bar.

Chewy Cranberry, Coconut and Chocolate Chip Bars

This bar is particularly nice for holiday entertaining. One pan goes a long way, and the bars keep well.

MAKES 36 TO 66 BARS (see Cutting Guide, page 10)

- **Preparation: 15 minutes**
- **Baking: 15 minutes**
- **Freezing: excellent**

TIPS

I have specified sweetened coconut because it seems to be more readily available than the unsweetened variety. But sweetened and unsweetened coconut can be used interchangeably in any recipe to suit your preference.

It's best to purchase coconut in packages rather than in bulk as it will retain its freshness longer. Coconut purchased in bulk tends to dry out quickly.

Be sure to use the larger jelly roll pan, as recommended, when making this recipe. If you use the smaller 15- by 10-inch (2 L) one, it will overflow.

- **Preheat oven to 375°F (190°C)**
- **17- by 11- by 1-inch (3 L) jelly roll pan, greased**

1 cup	butter, softened	250 mL
¾ cup	granulated sugar	175 mL
¾ cup	packed brown sugar	175 mL
2	eggs	2
2 cups	all-purpose flour	500 mL
1 tsp	baking soda	5 mL
2 cups	milk chocolate chips, divided	500 mL
1 cup	sweetened flaked coconut (see Tips, left)	250 mL
1 cup	dried cranberries	250 mL

1. In a large bowl, using an electric mixer on medium speed, beat butter and granulated and brown sugars until light and creamy, about 3 minutes. Add eggs, one at a time, beating well after each addition. Add flour and baking soda and beat on low speed, mixing well. Stir in 1⅓ cups (325 mL) of the chocolate chips, coconut and cranberries, blending thoroughly. Spread evenly in prepared pan. Sprinkle remaining chocolate chips over top.

2. Bake in preheated oven until set and golden, about 15 minutes. Let cool completely in pan on rack. Cut into bars.

Variations

Substitute dried cherries for the cranberries. Because they're larger than cranberries, use 1 tbsp (15 mL) or so more, and chop them a little.

White chocolate chips in place of the milk chocolate also look nice in this bar, and they create a different but equally great taste.

Chocolate Coconut Squares

Even though these squares are rich, they're so good it's hard to stop at just one. Cut them small to control your consumption.

MAKES 24 SQUARES
(see Cutting Guide, page 10)

- **Preparation: 25 minutes**
- **Baking: 40 minutes**
- **Chilling: 30 minutes**
- **Freezing: excellent**

TIPS

The filling is quite thick. If you drop it by small spoonfuls over the entire surface of the bars, you can easily spread it to cover.

To toast almonds, place them on a baking sheet in a 350°F (180°C) oven and stir often until golden, 5 to 10 minutes.

There are a number of ways to melt chocolate chips. You can place them in a double boiler over hot, not boiling, water or in a small saucepan over low heat. In both cases, stir frequently until smooth. Melt them in a microwave oven on Medium power until softened (about 1 minute for 1/4 cup/60 mL), then stir until smooth.

- **Preheat oven to 350°F (180°C)**
- **13- by 9-inch (3 L) cake pan, greased**

BASE

4	squares (1 oz/28 g each) unsweetened chocolate, chopped	4
1 cup	butter	250 mL
2 cups	granulated sugar	500 mL
3	eggs	3
1 1/4 cups	all-purpose flour	300 mL

FILLING

3 cups	unsweetened flaked coconut	750 mL
1	can (10 oz/300 mL) sweetened condensed milk	1
3/4 tsp	almond extract	3 mL

TOPPING

1 1/2 cups	semisweet chocolate chips, melted (see Tips, left)	375 mL
2/3 cup	sliced almonds, toasted (see Tips, left)	150 mL

1. *Base:* In a saucepan over low heat, melt chocolate and butter, stirring constantly, until smooth. Remove from heat. Stir in sugar until blended. Whisk in eggs, one at a time, mixing lightly after each addition. Stir in flour, mixing well. Spread half of the batter in prepared pan. Set remainder aside.

2. *Filling:* In a bowl, combine coconut, sweetened condensed milk and almond extract, mixing well. Drop by small spoonfuls over base and spread evenly. Cover with reserved batter and spread evenly.

3. Bake in preheated oven until set, 35 to 40 minutes. Let cool completely in pan on rack.

4. *Topping:* Spread melted chocolate chips evenly over baked bar. Sprinkle almonds on top. Chill until chocolate is set, about 30 minutes. Cut into squares.

Variations

For the holiday season, substitute mint extract for the almond and sprinkle crushed candy canes on top.

If nut allergies are a concern, replace the almond extract with vanilla and omit the nuts on top.

Praline Bars

These bars are a real favorite. The crisp toffee crust and chocolate toffee nut top remind me of a chocolate toffee bar.

MAKES 20 TO 54 BARS (see Cutting Guide, page 10)

- **Preparation: 20 minutes**
- **Baking: 20 minutes**
- **Freezing: excellent**

TIPS

My favorite brand of toffee bits is Skor, and I like to buy them in bulk. Others, such as Heath bits, are also available in bulk, but I don't recommend being over-inventoried on this product. If toffee bits become stale, they take longer to soften.

If the chocolate chips aren't melted enough to swirl after standing for 3 minutes, return the pan to the oven for 1 minute.

Be sure to use fresh, pure chocolate chips. When chocolate chips get older or are made from imitation chocolate, they don't melt as easily, making spreading difficult. Store chocolate in a cool, dry place, not in the freezer or refrigerator.

- **Preheat oven to 350°F (180°C)**
- **13- by 9-inch (3 L) cake pan, greased**

CRUST

½ cup	butter	125 mL
½ cup	packed brown sugar	125 mL
1	egg	1
1 cup	all-purpose flour	250 mL
¼ tsp	baking powder	1 mL
¼ cup	toffee bits (see Tips, left)	60 mL
¼ cup	chopped pecans	60 mL

TOPPING

1 cup	semisweet chocolate chips	250 mL
1 cup	white chocolate chips	250 mL
¼ cup	toffee bits	60 mL
¼ cup	chopped pecans	60 mL

1. *Crust:* In a large saucepan over low heat, melt butter. Remove from heat. Stir in brown sugar. Whisk in egg, mixing well. Stir in flour and baking powder, mixing well. Stir in toffee bits and pecans. Spread evenly in prepared pan. Bake in preheated oven until edges are lightly browned, 15 to 20 minutes.

2. *Topping:* Sprinkle semisweet and white chocolate chips evenly over hot crust. Let stand for 3 minutes to melt chocolate. Swirl lightly with the tip of a knife to create a marbled effect. Sprinkle toffee bits and pecans evenly over top. Let cool completely in pan on rack. Cut into bars.

Variation

Replace pecans with almonds or hazelnuts.

Chocolate Caramel Pecan Bars

I love how these bars combine crisp and chewy textures in one bar. They resemble the popular Turtles or Slow Pokes chocolates.

MAKES 20 TO 54 BARS (see Cutting Guide, page 10)

- **Preparation: 20 minutes**
- **Baking: 20 minutes**
- **Freezing: excellent**

TIPS

If you prefer, use a large wooden spoon to mix the crust.

If the chocolate chips aren't melted enough to swirl after standing for 3 minutes, return the pan to the oven for 1 minute.

Store nuts in the freezer to retain freshness. Let them come to room temperature before using them in baking.

Store brown sugar in a sealed heavy plastic bag. It stays moist and can easily be measured by placing a measuring cup in the bag and packing it into the cup through the bag — no messy hands.

If you're using a dark pan, reduce the time slightly to avoid overbaking.

- **Preheat oven to 350°F (180°C)**
- **13- by 9-inch (3 L) cake pan, greased**

CRUST

2 cups	all-purpose flour	500 mL
¾ cup	packed brown sugar	175 mL
½ cup	butter, softened	125 mL
1½ cups	pecan halves	375 mL

CARAMEL FILLING

1 cup	butter	250 mL
¾ cup	packed brown sugar	175 mL

CHOCOLATE GLAZE

1⅓ cups	semisweet chocolate chips	325 mL

1. *Crust:* In a large bowl, combine flour, brown sugar and butter. Using an electric mixer on medium speed, beat until crumbly. Press firmly into prepared pan. Sprinkle pecans evenly in a single layer over crust.

2. *Caramel Filling:* In a saucepan over medium heat, combine butter and brown sugar. Cook, stirring constantly, until mixture begins to boil, forming bubbles over the entire surface, about 1½ minutes. Pour evenly over pecans on crust.

3. Bake in preheated oven until caramel is bubbly, about 20 minutes. Remove from oven.

4. *Chocolate Glaze:* Immediately sprinkle chocolate chips evenly over bar. Let stand for 3 minutes to melt chocolate. Swirl lightly with the tip of a knife to create a marbled effect, leaving a few chips whole. Let cool completely in pan on rack. Cut into bars.

Variation

Replace pecans with walnut halves. Cut them in half if large.

Coconut Chocolate Caramel Squares

Packed into a colorful box or tin, these make a wonderful hostess gift.

MAKES 16 TO 36 SQUARES
(see Cutting Guide, page 10)

- **Preparation: 25 minutes**
- **Cooking: 10 minutes**
- **Baking: 24 minutes**
- **Chilling: 4 hours**
- **Freezing: excellent**

TIPS

Be aware that sweetened condensed milk burns very quickly. So don't leave it unattended on the stove.

These bars can be made up to 3 days ahead of serving. Store them in an airtight container in the refrigerator but let stand for about 30 minutes at room temperature before serving.

- **Preheat oven to 350°F (180°C)**
- **8-inch (2 L) square cake pan, lined with parchment paper**

BASE

¾ cup	all-purpose flour	175 mL
⅔ cup	flaked coconut	150 mL
½ cup	packed brown sugar	125 mL
1 tsp	baking powder	5 mL
⅓ cup	butter, melted	75 mL

CARAMEL FILLING

1	can (10 oz/300 mL) sweetened condensed milk	1
2 tbsp	butter	30 mL
1 tbsp	corn syrup	15 mL

CHOCOLATE TOPPING

4	squares (1 oz/28 g each) bittersweet chocolate, chopped	4
3 tbsp	butter	45 mL

1. *Base:* In a bowl, combine flour, coconut, brown sugar and baking powder. Stir in melted butter, mixing well. Press evenly into prepared pan. Bake in preheated oven until golden around the edges, 10 to 12 minutes.

2. *Caramel Filling:* In a small heavy saucepan, combine sweetened condensed milk, butter and corn syrup. Cook over medium heat, stirring constantly, until mixture thickens slightly, about 10 minutes. Spread evenly over base. Return to oven and bake until lightly browned around the edges, 10 to 12 minutes. Let cool completely in pan on rack.

3. *Chocolate Topping:* In a small saucepan over low heat, melt chocolate and butter, stirring constantly, until smooth. Spread quickly over filling. Let cool at room temperature for 1 hour. Transfer to refrigerator and chill thoroughly, about 3 hours. Cut into squares.

Variation

Replace coconut with ground almonds and add ½ tsp (2 mL) almond extract to the filling.

Chocolate Almond Toffee Bars

◆

A great treat to enjoy with a cold glass of milk or a steaming cup of coffee.

**MAKES 20 TO 54 BARS
(see Cutting Guide, page 10)**

- **Preparation: 15 minutes**
- **Baking: 25 minutes**
- **Freezing: excellent**

TIP

Ovens are often inaccurate, so a good oven thermometer is a wise investment. You can check your temperature and adjust the control accordingly. Whenever a range is given, check your bars at the earliest baking time.

- **Preheat oven to 325°F (160°C)**
- **13- by 9-inch (3 L) cake pan, ungreased**

½ cup	butter	125 mL
1 cup	quick-cooking rolled oats	250 mL
1 cup	graham wafer crumbs	250 mL
1¼ cups	semisweet chocolate chips	300 mL
1 cup	toffee bits (see Tips, page 56)	250 mL
1 cup	chopped unblanched almonds	250 mL
1	can (10 oz/300 mL) sweetened condensed milk	1

1. Place butter in pan and place in preheated oven until butter melts. Remove from oven. Tilt the pan to cover the bottom evenly with melted butter. Sprinkle oats and graham wafer crumbs evenly over top, pressing with a spatula, if necessary, to ensure oats and crumbs are thoroughly moistened.

2. Sprinkle chocolate chips, toffee bits and almonds evenly over base. Drizzle sweetened condensed milk evenly over top. Bake until golden around the edges, 20 to 25 minutes. Let cool completely in pan on rack. Cut into bars.

Variation

For a fruity version, replace half of the chocolate chips with dried cranberries or chopped dried apricots.

White Chocolate Pecan Cranberry Squares

Fresh cranberries add a festive touch to these deliciously decadent squares.

MAKES 24 SQUARES (see Cutting Guide, page 10)

- Preparation: 25 minutes
- Baking: 55 minutes
- Freezing: excellent

TIPS

If you prefer, mix the crust in a food processor. Use cubed cold butter rather than softened. You can also mix the crust in a bowl, cutting cold butter in using a pastry blender, 2 knives or your fingers. Whichever method you use, the mixture should resemble coarse crumbs.

Try a new look for bar cookies: cut them into triangles or diamonds instead of the traditional squares and rectangles. See the Cutting Guide, page 10.

For a fancier presentation, drizzle the cooled bars with melted white chocolate.

- Preheat oven to 350°F (180°C)
- 13- by 9-inch (3 L) cake pan, greased

CRUST

2 cups	all-purpose flour	500 mL
1/2 cup	granulated sugar	125 mL
3/4 cup	butter, softened	175 mL
1/4 cup	ground pecans	60 mL

TOPPING

4	eggs	4
1 cup	granulated sugar	250 mL
1 cup	corn syrup	250 mL
3 tbsp	butter, melted	45 mL
1 cup	coarsely chopped pecans	250 mL
3/4 cup	coarsely chopped cranberries	175 mL
3/4 cup	white chocolate chips	175 mL

1. *Crust:* In a large bowl, combine flour, sugar and butter. Using an electric mixer on low speed, beat until mixture resembles coarse crumbs. Stir in ground pecans. Press evenly into prepared pan. Bake in preheated oven until golden around the edges, 12 to 15 minutes.

2. *Topping:* In a bowl, whisk eggs, sugar, corn syrup and melted butter until blended. Stir in pecans, cranberries and white chocolate chips. Pour evenly over warm crust.

3. Return to oven and bake until set and golden, 35 to 40 minutes. Let cool completely in pan on rack. Cut into squares.

Variation

Replace pecans with walnuts, slivered almonds or cashews.

White Chocolate Cream Bars

These look a bit like Nanaimo bars but taste quite different — they aren't nearly as sweet.

MAKES 18 TO 48 BARS (see Cutting Guide, page 10)

- **Preparation: 20 minutes**
- **Baking: 35 minutes**
- **Chilling: 2 hours**
- **Freezing: excellent**

TIPS

If serving these at a special occasion, garnish with some shaved white or milk chocolate.

If you prefer, use the microwave to make the topping. Combine the ingredients in a microwave-safe dish and microwave on Medium for about 1 minute, until chocolate is softened. Stir until smooth.

- **Preheat oven to 350°F (180°C)**
- **8-inch (2 L) square cake pan, greased**

BASE

1 ½ cups	chocolate wafer crumbs	375 mL
⅓ cup	butter, melted	75 mL

FILLING

1 cup	white chocolate chips	250 mL
¾ cup	whipping (35%) cream	175 mL
3	eggs	3
⅓ cup	granulated sugar	75 mL

TOPPING

4	squares (1 oz/28 g each) semisweet chocolate, chopped	4
2 tbsp	butter	30 mL

1. *Base:* In a bowl, combine chocolate wafer crumbs and melted butter. Mix well. Press evenly into prepared pan. Bake in preheated oven until set, about 10 minutes.

2. *Filling:* In a saucepan over low heat, combine white chocolate chips and whipping cream. Heat, stirring constantly, until chocolate is melted and mixture is smooth. Remove from heat and let cool for 10 minutes.

3. In a bowl, whisk eggs and sugar until frothy. Add melted chocolate mixture, stirring until smoothly blended. Pour over base. Bake in preheated oven until set and golden, 20 to 25 minutes. Let cool for 20 minutes in pan on rack.

4. *Topping:* In a saucepan over low heat, melt chocolate and butter, stirring constantly, until smooth. Spread evenly over base. Refrigerate until cold, about 2 hours. Cut into bars.

Variations

Replace white chocolate chips with milk chocolate chips.

For a different three-layer treat, use white chocolate in the topping.

Heavenly White Chocolate Macadamia Bars

One bite of these sensational bars and you'll think you're in heaven.

MAKES 20 TO 54 BARS (see Cutting Guide, page 10)

- **Preparation: 20 minutes**
- **Baking: 37 minutes**
- **Freezing: excellent**

TIPS

In this bar, I like the look of coarsely chopped chocolate instead of chips. The irregularity of shreds and chunks gives a more interesting appearance. But you can use 1¼ cups (300 mL) chips if you prefer.

Buy good-quality white chocolate that's flavorful and creamy. Look for cocoa butter, not vegetable shortening, as the main ingredient. Ghirardelli is a reliable brand of white chocolate.

- **Preheat oven to 350°F (180°C)**
- **13- by 9-inch (3 L) cake pan, greased**

CRUST

½ cup	butter, softened	125 mL
½ cup	granulated sugar	125 mL
1½ cups	all-purpose flour	375 mL

TOPPING

1 cup	packed brown sugar	250 mL
¼ cup	granulated sugar	60 mL
½ tsp	baking powder	2 mL
3	eggs	3
1 tsp	vanilla	5 mL
2 tbsp	butter, melted	30 mL
¼ cup	all-purpose flour	60 mL
2 cups	coarsely chopped macadamia nuts	500 mL
8	squares (1 oz/28 g each) white chocolate, coarsely chopped	8

1. *Crust:* In a bowl, using a wooden spoon, beat butter and sugar until light and creamy, about 2 minutes. Add flour and beat until mixture resembles coarse crumbs. Press evenly into prepared pan. Bake in preheated oven until golden around the edges, 10 to 12 minutes.

2. *Topping:* In a bowl, whisk brown and granulated sugars, baking powder, eggs, vanilla and melted butter. Whisk until smooth. Whisk in flour, mixing well. Stir in nuts and chocolate. Spread evenly over crust.

3. Return to oven and bake until top is set and golden, 20 to 25 minutes. Let cool completely in pan on rack. Cut into bars.

Variations

Macadamia nuts are expensive. If the cost seems outrageous, substitute blanched almonds for half of them. You can also use a mixture of macadamia nuts, almonds and Brazil nuts, keeping the total amount at 2 cups (500 mL).

Chocolate Raspberry Crumble Bars

The combo of chocolate and raspberry is a perennial hit.

MAKES 18 TO 48 BARS (see Cutting Guide, page 10)

- **Preparation: 20 minutes**
- **Baking: 35 minutes**
- **Freezing: excellent**

TIPS

If you prefer, use a large wooden spoon to mix the crust.

Use a good-quality, thick jam with great flavor. The taste of the bar is only as good as the ingredients that go in it.

To soften jam for easy spreading, stir it well.

- **Preheat oven to 375°F (190°C)**
- **8-inch (2 L) or 9-inch (2.5 L) square cake pan, greased**

TOPPING

²⁄₃ cup	all-purpose flour	150 mL
½ cup	chopped pecans	125 mL
⅓ cup	packed brown sugar	75 mL
¼ cup	cold butter, cubed	60 mL

CRUST

1 ¼ cups	all-purpose flour	300 mL
½ cup	packed brown sugar	125 mL
½ cup	butter, softened	125 mL
⅓ cup	raspberry jam	75 mL
1 cup	milk chocolate chips	250 mL

1. *Topping:* In a food processor fitted with a metal blade, combine flour, pecans, brown sugar and butter. Pulse until crumbly. Set aside.

2. *Crust:* In a bowl, combine flour, brown sugar and butter. Using an electric mixer on low speed, beat until crumbly. Press firmly into prepared pan. Bake in preheated oven until edges are lightly browned, 12 to 15 minutes. Spread with jam and sprinkle chocolate chips evenly over top. Sprinkle with topping.

3. Return to oven and bake until lightly browned, 15 to 20 minutes. Let cool completely in pan on rack. Cut into bars.

Variation

Vary the jam to suit your taste. Apricot and strawberry also work well in this recipe.

Creamy Caramel Chocolate Bars

These yummy bars are like caramel-filled chocolate on a cookie crust, with the addition of nuts.

MAKES 18 TO 48 BARS
(see Cutting Guide, page 10)

- **Preparation: 20 minutes**
- **Cooking: 14 minutes**
- **Baking: 25 minutes**
- **Chilling: 90 minutes**
- **Freezing: excellent**

TIPS

Cooling the baked crust before you add the filling prevents it from becoming soggy.

Keep a close eye on sweetened condensed milk when cooking. The minute you leave it unattended it will burn.

These squares are very rich. For a pretty presentation, cut them small and serve in small paper cups like the ones boxed chocolates come in.

- **Preheat oven to 350°F (180°C)**
- **9-inch (2.5 L) square cake pan, greased**

CRUST

1 1/4 cups	all-purpose flour	300 mL
1/4 cup	granulated sugar	60 mL
1/2 cup	cold butter, cubed	125 mL

FILLING

1	can (10 oz/300 mL) sweetened condensed milk	1
1/2 cup	granulated sugar	125 mL
1/2 cup	butter	125 mL
2 tbsp	corn syrup	30 mL
1 tsp	vanilla	5 mL
1 cup	coarsely chopped pecans	250 mL

TOPPING

4	squares (1 oz/28 g each) semisweet chocolate, chopped	4
2 tbsp	butter	30 mL

1. *Crust:* In a bowl, combine flour and sugar. Using a pastry blender, 2 knives or your fingers, cut in butter until mixture resembles coarse crumbs. Press evenly into prepared pan. Bake in preheated oven until golden, 20 to 25 minutes. Let cool in pan on rack for 15 minutes.

2. *Filling:* In a heavy saucepan over medium heat, combine sweetened condensed milk, sugar, butter and corn syrup. Cook, stirring constantly, until sugar is dissolved and mixture comes to a boil, about 5 minutes. Reduce heat to medium-low and simmer, stirring constantly, until mixture thickens and turns a light caramel color, 6 to 9 minutes. Remove from heat. Stir in vanilla and pecans. Spread evenly over cooled crust. Chill until set, about 1 hour.

3. *Topping:* In a saucepan over low heat, melt chocolate and butter, stirring constantly, until smooth. Spread over filling. Chill for about 30 minutes to set chocolate. Cut into bars.

Variations

Decorate each bar with a pecan half.

Replace pecans with walnuts.

Caramel Apple Bars

Fruit Bars and Squares

Fruit bars and squares are extremely varied. They can be plain or fancy or something in between. They may include fresh fruits such as apples and oranges, dried fruits such as apricots and figs, candied fruits and even canned fruits. Some are so much like cake they make great desserts — top with a dollop of whipped cream or a scoop of ice cream to finish them off. Others are perfect finger food, the final embellishment to a cookie tray, passed at festivities during the holiday season. There is so much variety in this chapter, I'm sure you'll find recipes that will become favorites for every occasion.

Caramel Apple Bars

These bars bring back fond memories of the caramel apples I enjoyed as a kid at fall fairs, exhibitions and Halloween.

MAKES 20 TO 54 BARS (see Cutting Guide, page 10)

- **Preparation: 25 minutes**
- **Baking: 30 minutes**
- **Freezing: not recommended**

TIPS

Use a firm, crisp apple like Granny Smith or Spartan to avoid a soggy crust.

For a special treat, serve these bars with hot or cold mulled cider.

If you're using a glass baking dish, remember to decrease the oven temperature by 25°F (10°C).

- **Preheat oven to 350°F (180°C)**
- **13- by 9-inch (3 L) cake pan, greased**

2/3 cup	butter, softened	150 mL
3/4 cup	packed brown sugar	175 mL
1 tsp	vanilla	5 mL
1 3/4 cups	quick-cooking rolled oats	425 mL
1 1/2 cups	all-purpose flour	375 mL
1 1/4 tsp	ground cinnamon	6 mL
2 cups	grated, peeled apple (4 large)	500 mL
1/2 cup	caramel sundae sauce	125 mL
3/4 cup	chopped peanuts	175 mL

1. In a bowl, combine butter, brown sugar and vanilla. Using an electric mixer on medium speed, beat until blended. Add oats, flour and cinnamon. Beat on low speed until crumbly. Set aside 1 1/2 cups (375 mL) for topping. Press remainder into prepared pan. Scatter apples evenly over crust. Sprinkle reserved topping over apples. Drizzle caramel sauce over crumbs. Sprinkle peanuts on top.

2. Bake in preheated oven until top is set and golden, 25 to 30 minutes. Let cool completely in pan on rack. Cut into bars.

Variations

Use half pears and half apples.

Replace peanuts with cashews.

Cherry Lime Squares

Here's a square for all seasons. I love these flavors during the holiday season, but the refreshing combination of fruit is great in the summer as well.

MAKES 24 SQUARES (see Cutting Guide, page 10)

- **Preparation: 25 minutes**
- **Baking: 40 minutes**
- **Chilling: 2 hours**
- **Freezing: excellent**

TIPS

Always use freshly squeezed lime juice for the best flavor.

To get the most juice out of limes, warm them for about 10 seconds on High in the microwave. Grate the zest off first.

This crust is a little crumbly to cut, but I think it contributes to the appeal of these bars.

- **Preheat oven to 350°F (180°C)**
- **13- by 9-inch (3 L) cake pan, greased**

CRUST

2 cups	all-purpose flour	500 mL
1/2 cup	confectioners' (icing) sugar	125 mL
1 tbsp	grated lime zest	15 mL
1/4 tsp	salt	1 mL
1 cup	cold butter, cubed	250 mL

TOPPING

4	eggs	4
2 cups	granulated sugar	500 mL
1 tbsp	grated lime zest	15 mL
1/3 cup	freshly squeezed lime juice	75 mL
1/4 cup	all-purpose flour	60 mL
1 tsp	baking powder	5 mL
1 cup	chopped dried cherries	250 mL
	Confectioners' (icing) sugar	

1. *Crust:* In a bowl, combine flour, confectioners' sugar, lime zest and salt. Using a pastry blender, 2 knives or your fingers, cut in butter until mixture resembles coarse crumbs. Press evenly into prepared pan. Bake in preheated oven until edges are lightly browned, 12 to 15 minutes.

2. *Topping:* In a bowl, whisk eggs and sugar until blended. Whisk in lime zest and juice, mixing well. Combine flour and baking powder. Whisk into egg mixture until smooth. Stir in cherries. Pour over crust.

3. Return to oven and bake just until set, 20 to 25 minutes. Let cool completely in pan on rack. Chill for 2 hours for easy cutting. Sprinkle with confectioners' sugar. Cut into squares.

Variations

Substitute an equal quantity of lemon juice and zest for the lime.

Add 1/3 cup (75 mL) ground almonds to the crust, along with the flour.

Festive Fruit Triangles

This is an attractive candied fruit and almond Florentine cookie on a shortbread crust with a drizzle of chocolate to top it off. Tasty and elegant.

MAKES 48 TO 120 TRIANGLES
(see Cutting Guide, page 10)

- **Preparation: 25 minutes**
- **Cooking: 3 minutes**
- **Baking: 20 minutes**
- **Freezing: excellent**

TIPS

If you prefer, buy deluxe mixed candied (glacé) fruit for use in this recipe (the mixture includes cherries and pineapple). Use 1 2/3 cups (400 mL) in place of the cherries and pineapple.

If you don't care for triangles, make these cookies any shape you like. Strips, bars and squares also work well.

- **Preheat oven to 375°F (190°C)**
- **15- by 10- by 1-inch (2 L) jelly roll pan, greased**

CRUST

1 1/2 cups	all-purpose flour	375 mL
1/2 cup	confectioners' (icing) sugar, sifted	125 mL
1/2 cup	cold butter, cubed	125 mL
2 tbsp	whipping (35%) cream	30 mL
1 tsp	vanilla	5 mL

TOPPING

3/4 cup	butter	175 mL
1/2 cup	granulated sugar	125 mL
1/4 cup	whipping (35%) cream	60 mL
2/3 cup	chopped red candied (glacé) cherries	150 mL
1/3 cup	chopped green candied (glacé) cherries	75 mL
2/3 cup	chopped candied (glacé) pineapple	150 mL
1 cup	sliced blanched almonds	250 mL
2	squares (1 oz/28 g each) semisweet chocolate, melted	2

1. *Crust:* In a bowl, combine flour and confectioners' sugar. Using a pastry blender, 2 knives or your fingers, cut in butter until mixture resembles coarse crumbs. Stir in whipping cream and vanilla, mixing until dough clings together. Press dough evenly into prepared pan. Chill while preparing topping.

2. *Topping:* In a saucepan over medium heat, combine butter, sugar and whipping cream. Bring to a boil, stirring often. Boil, stirring constantly, until thickened, 1 to 2 minutes. Remove from heat. Stir in red and green cherries, pineapple and almonds. Spread evenly over chilled crust.

3. Bake in preheated oven until top is golden, 15 to 20 minutes. Let cool completely in pan on rack.

4. Drizzle melted chocolate over top. Let cool until chocolate sets, about 1 hour. Cut into squares, then cut into triangles.

Variations

If you prefer, you can use all red or all green cherries.

Omit the chocolate drizzle and dip the triangles in melted chocolate. Use about 8 (1 oz/28 g each) squares.

Fruit 'n' Nut Squares

Sweet and yummy, these squares are a bit like fruitcake on a crust. Since they are quite rich, cut them into small bites.

MAKES 24 SQUARES (see Cutting Guide, page 10)

- **Preparation: 25 minutes**
- **Baking: 42 minutes**
- **Freezing: excellent**

TIPS

Theses squares freeze well, so they're a great make-ahead treat for the festive season.

It pays to buy fresh glacé fruit when you're ready to bake rather than using leftovers. When stored, the fruit dries out and forms sugar crystals, which will affect your baked goods.

In my opinion, the tastiest walnuts are from California. Always taste nuts before using to make sure they're not rancid. This is especially true of walnuts, as their healthful oils spoil very quickly.

- **Preheat oven to 350°F (180°C)**
- **13- by 9-inch (3 L) cake pan, greased**

CRUST

1 1/4 cups	all-purpose flour	300 mL
1/2 cup	granulated sugar	125 mL
1/2 cup	cold butter, cubed	125 mL
1	egg yolk, beaten	1

TOPPING

1	can (10 oz/300 mL) sweetened condensed milk	1
2 tbsp	all-purpose flour	30 mL
1/4 tsp	ground nutmeg	1 mL
2 tbsp	brandy	30 mL
3/4 cup	sweetened flaked coconut	175 mL
1/2 cup	chopped walnuts	125 mL
1/2 cup	slivered almonds	125 mL
2/3 cup	chopped candied (glacé) cherries	150 mL
1/3 cup	chopped candied (glacé) pineapple	75 mL

1. *Crust:* In a food processor fitted with a metal blade, combine flour, sugar and butter. Process until mixture resembles coarse crumbs. With machine running, add egg yolk, mixing just until moist crumbs form. Press evenly into prepared pan. Bake in preheated oven until golden around edges, 10 to 12 minutes.

2. *Topping:* In a bowl, stir together sweetened condensed milk, flour, nutmeg and brandy until well blended. Stir in coconut, walnuts, almonds, cherries and pineapple, mixing well. Spread evenly over warm crust.

3. Return to oven and bake until set and golden, 25 to 30 minutes. Let cool completely in pan on rack. Cut into squares.

Variations

Replace candied pineapple with candied mixed peel.

Replace brandy with an equal quantity of orange or almond liqueur, or apple juice.

Cranberry Apricot Oat Bars

Apricots and cranberries are a dynamite combination. This flavor combination always seems to be a hit, no matter what you make.

MAKES 20 TO 54 BARS (see Cutting Guide, page 10)

- **Preparation: 20 minutes**
- **Baking: 37 minutes**
- **Freezing: excellent**

TIPS

The filling will spread more easily if, after dropping it over the crust, you let it sit for a minute to warm, then spread gently with a small spatula.

Use regular jam rather than a light variety, which will be quite a bit thinner in consistency.

- **Preheat oven to 350°F (180°C)**
- **13- by 9-inch (3 L) cake pan, greased**

CRUST

2 cups	quick-cooking rolled oats	500 mL
1 ½ cups	all-purpose flour	375 mL
1 ½ cups	packed brown sugar	375 mL
1 tsp	baking powder	5 mL
½ tsp	baking soda	2 mL
1 tsp	ground cinnamon	5 mL
1 cup	cold butter, cubed	250 mL

FILLING

2 cups	apricot jam	500 mL
1 ½ cups	dried cranberries	375 mL
1 tbsp	grated orange zest	15 mL

TOPPING

⅔ cup	slivered almonds	150 mL

1. *Crust:* In a bowl, combine oats, flour, brown sugar, baking powder, baking soda and cinnamon. Using a pastry blender, 2 knives or your fingers, cut in butter until mixture resembles coarse crumbs. Set aside 1 cup (250 mL) for topping. Press remainder evenly into prepared pan. Bake in preheated oven until golden around edges, 10 to 12 minutes.

2. *Filling:* In a bowl, combine apricot jam, dried cranberries and orange zest, mixing well. Drop small spoonfuls over hot crust. Spread gently, leaving a ¾-inch (2 cm) border of crust.

3. *Topping:* Stir almonds into reserved crumble mixture. Sprinkle evenly over filling.

4. Return to oven and bake until golden, 20 to 25 minutes. Let cool completely in pan on rack. Cut into bars.

Variations

Replace apricot jam with an equal quantity of strawberry jam.

Substitute an equal quantity of cherry jam for the apricot and chopped dried cherries for the cranberries.

Replace almonds with chopped pecans.

Marmalade Bars

These tasty bars couldn't be easier. Keep a jar of marmalade on hand to prepare them at a moment's notice.

MAKES 18 TO 48 BARS (see Cutting Guide, page 10)

- **Preparation: 20 minutes**
- **Baking: 35 minutes**
- **Freezing: excellent**

TIPS

When making bars, use jams that are fairly stiff in consistency. Lighter, lower-sugar versions are too moist and too loose to set firmly.

A drizzle of confectioners' (icing) sugar mixed with a little orange juice to make a pouring consistency looks nice on these bars. Add after they've cooled.

If you're a ginger lover, add 3 tbsp (45 mL) finely chopped crystallized ginger to the marmalade.

- **Preheat oven to 350°F (180°C)**
- **9-inch (2.5 L) square cake pan, greased**

BASE

2 cups	all-purpose flour	500 mL
¾ cup	packed brown sugar	175 mL
¾ cup	butter, softened	175 mL
2 tsp	grated orange zest	10 mL
¼ tsp	ground ginger	1 mL
Pinch	salt	Pinch
1	egg, beaten	1

TOPPING

1 cup	orange marmalade	250 mL
3 tbsp	all-purpose flour	45 mL

1. *Base:* In a bowl, combine flour, brown sugar, butter, orange zest, ginger and salt. Using an electric mixer on medium speed, beat until crumbly, about 2 minutes. Add egg and mix to form a soft dough. Set aside one-third of the dough for topping. Press remainder evenly into prepared pan.

2. *Topping:* Spread marmalade evenly over crust. Stir flour into reserved dough and work with fingers until crumbly. Sprinkle over marmalade.

3. Bake in preheated oven until golden, 30 to 35 minutes. Let cool completely in pan on rack. Cut into bars.

Variations

Try making these bars with other kinds of jam. Red ones like sour cherry, strawberry and plum, look and taste great.

Replace ginger with nutmeg.

Cranberry Coconut Oat Bars

I like these bars because they aren't too sweet. They're also easy to make and freeze well.

MAKES 18 TO 48 BARS (see Cutting Guide, page 10)

- **Preparation: 25 minutes**
- **Baking: 40 minutes**
- **Freezing: excellent**

TIPS

Be sure to use regular quick-cooking oats, not the instant variety that just requires the addition of boiling water. Large-flake rolled oats also work well in this recipe.

For added flavor, toast oats before using. To toast oats, spread in a thin layer on a large rimmed baking sheet. Bake in a 350°F (180°C) oven for about 10 minutes, stirring often, until lightly browned. Let cool completely before using.

- **Preheat oven to 350°F (180°C)**
- **9-inch (2.5 L) square cake pan, greased**

CRUST

1/2 cup	butter, melted	125 mL
1/3 cup	granulated sugar	75 mL
1 cup	all-purpose flour	250 mL
1/2 cup	quick-cooking rolled oats (see Tips, left)	125 mL

TOPPING

2	eggs	2
1 cup	packed brown sugar	250 mL
1/3 cup	all-purpose flour	75 mL
1/2 tsp	baking powder	2 mL
3/4 tsp	cinnamon	3 mL
1 1/3 cups	dried cranberries	325 mL
1 cup	unsweetened flaked coconut	250 mL

1. *Crust:* In a bowl, combine melted butter, sugar, flour and oats, mixing well. Press evenly into prepared pan. Bake in preheated oven until lightly browned, about 15 minutes. Let cool in pan on rack.

2. *Topping:* In a large bowl, whisk eggs and brown sugar until blended. Whisk in flour, baking powder and cinnamon until blended. Stir in dried cranberries and coconut. Spread evenly over cooled base.

3. Return to oven and bake until set and golden, 20 to 25 minutes. Let cool completely in pan on rack. Cut into bars.

Variations

Replace 1/3 cup (75 mL) of the dried cranberries with chopped dried apricots.

Replace cinnamon with 1 tsp (5 mL) grated orange zest.

Blueberry Cheesecake Bars

These bars are just like cheesecake — but smaller in size.

MAKES 20 TO 54 BARS (see Cutting Guide, page 10)

- **Preparation: 30 minutes**
- **Baking: 45 minutes**
- **Freezing: not recommended**

TIPS

Be sure to have eggs and cream cheese at room temperature for smooth blending.

If you've forgotten to remove eggs from the refrigerator to allow them to come to room temperature, place them in a bowl of warm water for a few minutes.

To soften cream cheese in a microwave, place an unwrapped 8 oz (250 g) block in a microwaveable bowl. Microwave on High for 15 seconds. Add 15 seconds for each additional block of cream cheese.

- **Preheat oven to 350°F (180°C)**
- **13- by 9-inch (3 L) cake pan, greased**

CRUST

2 cups	all-purpose flour	500 mL
1/2 cup	granulated sugar	125 mL
2/3 cup	cold butter, cubed	150 mL

FILLING

2	package (8 oz/250 g each) cream cheese, softened	2
3/4 cup	granulated sugar	175 mL
2	eggs	2
1 tbsp	grated lemon zest	15 mL
1 tbsp	freshly squeezed lemon juice	15 mL
1 cup	blueberry jam	250 mL
1 cup	fresh blueberries	250 mL

1. *Crust:* In a bowl, combine flour and sugar. Using a pastry blender, 2 knives or your fingers, cut in butter until mixture resembles coarse crumbs. Press evenly into prepared pan. Bake in preheated oven until edges are lightly browned, 12 to 15 minutes. Let cool in pan on rack.

2. *Filling:* In a bowl, using an electric mixer on medium speed, beat cream cheese and sugar until smooth. Add eggs and lemon zest and juice, beating until smooth.

3. Spread jam evenly over crust. Sprinkle blueberries on top. Drop cream cheese mixture by spoonfuls over berries, then spread evenly. Return to oven and bake just until set, 25 to 30 minutes. Let cool completely in pan on rack. Cut into bars.

Variation

Try replacing blueberry jam and fresh blueberries with strawberry or raspberry jam and sliced fresh strawberries or fresh raspberries.

Frosted Banana Bars

These yummy bars taste like a mini version of banana cake. How can you go wrong?

MAKES 36 TO 48 BARS (see Cutting Guide, page 10)

- **Preparation: 25 minutes**
- **Baking: 25 minutes**
- **Freezing: excellent**

TIP

The riper the banana the better the flavor in baked goods. I like to buy extra bananas so I always have some that are at the baking stage. I prefer to use them fresh rather than mashing and freezing them. Frozen bananas always seem too wet, which means you need to adjust the recipe.

- **Preheat oven to 375°F (190°C)**
- **15- by 10- by 1-inch (2 L) jelly roll pan, greased**

BATTER

½ cup	butter, softened	125 mL
1 ½ cups	granulated sugar	375 mL
1 cup	sour cream	250 mL
2	eggs	2
1 ½ cups	mashed ripe banana (3 large)	375 mL
1 ½ tsp	vanilla	7 mL
2 cups	all-purpose flour	500 mL
1 tsp	baking soda	5 mL
½ tsp	salt	2 mL
½ cup	chopped walnuts	125 mL

FROSTING

¼ cup	butter, softened	60 mL
2 cups	confectioners' (icing) sugar, sifted	500 mL
¼ cup	milk	60 mL
1 tsp	vanilla	5 mL

1. *Batter:* In a large bowl, using an electric mixer on low speed, beat butter, sugar, sour cream and eggs for 1 minute. Beat in mashed bananas and vanilla. Combine flour, baking soda and salt. On low speed, beat into creamed mixture, mixing until smooth. Stir in walnuts. Spread evenly in prepared pan.

2. Bake in preheated oven until a toothpick inserted in the center comes out clean, 20 to 25 minutes. Let cool completely in pan on rack.

3. *Frosting:* In a saucepan, over medium heat, heat butter until it melts and turns a delicate brown color, about 10 minutes. Remove from heat. Stir in confectioners' sugar, milk and vanilla. Beat until smooth and spreadable. Spread quickly over cooled bars. Let cool until set. Cut into bars.

Variation

Replace walnuts with pecans or omit the nuts if allergies are a concern.

Apple Streusel Squares

With a tender melt-in-your-mouth crust, a tart apple filling and walnut streusel topping, these delicious squares taste like old-fashioned apple pie in a new shape.

MAKES 24 TO 60 SQUARES
(see Cutting Guide, page 10)

- **Preparation: 40 minutes**
- **Cooking: 16 minutes**
- **Baking: 55 minutes**
- **Freezing: not recommended**

TIPS

There seems to be a lot of steps in this recipe, but each is easy and the large yield is well worth the extra time.

If you prefer, mix the crust in a food processor.

You'll need about 3 lbs (1.5 kg) or 8 large apples to make these squares.

Use Golden Delicious apples or Matsu apples for a great flavor and texture.

Because ovens are often not accurate in their temperature, a good oven thermometer is a worthwhile investment. Set your timer for the minimum recommended time. You can always bake a little longer, but you can't fix an overbaked product.

- **Preheat oven to 375°F (190°C)**
- **15- by 10- by 1-inch (2 L) jelly roll pan, greased**

STREUSEL TOPPING

1 cup	all-purpose flour	250 mL
1 cup	chopped walnuts	250 mL
½ cup	packed brown sugar	125 mL
½ cup	butter, softened	125 mL
1 tsp	cinnamon	5 mL

CRUST

3 cups	all-purpose flour	750 mL
⅓ cup	granulated sugar	75 mL
1 cup	cold butter, cubed	250 mL

FILLING

3 tbsp	butter	45 mL
7 cups	sliced (½ inch/1 cm), cored, peeled apples	1.75 L
1 cup	dried cranberries	250 mL
½ cup	packed brown sugar	125 mL
1 tsp	ground cinnamon	5 mL
2 tbsp	cornstarch	30 mL
3 tbsp	freshly squeezed lemon juice	45 mL

1. *Streusel Topping:* In a bowl, combine flour, walnuts, brown sugar, butter and cinnamon. Mix with a wooden spoon, then knead until the dough comes together. Shape into a ball. Cover and chill until ready to use.

2. *Crust:* In a bowl, combine flour and sugar. Using a pastry blender, 2 knives or your fingers, cut in butter until mixture resembles coarse crumbs. Press evenly into prepared pan. Bake in preheated oven until lightly browned all over, about 20 minutes. (Don't worry if crust cracks a little).

3. *Filling:* In a large skillet, melt butter over medium heat. Add apples, cranberries, brown sugar and cinnamon. Cook, stirring occasionally, until apples are tender-crisp, about 15 minutes. In a small bowl, combine cornstarch and lemon juice, mixing until smooth. Stir into apples and cook, stirring, until slightly thickened, about 1 minute. Spoon evenly over warm crust. Crumble chilled streusel mixture evenly over fruit.

4. Return to oven and bake until golden, 30 to 35 minutes. Let cool completely in pan on rack. Cut into squares.

Crunchy Raisin Pecan Bars with Broiled Topping

These bars are easy as well as delicious. A crunchy coconut nut topping is baked right on, so you don't need to add a frosting later.

MAKES 20 TO 54 BARS
(see Cutting Guide, page 10)

- **Preparation: 25 minutes**
- **Baking: 37 minutes**
- **Freezing: excellent**

TIPS

To ease cleanup, rather than combining the dry ingredients in a bowl (Step 1), place a large piece of waxed paper on the counter. Spread the flour on the paper and sprinkle with the baking powder, baking soda, salt and cinnamon. Using the paper as a funnel, transfer the dry ingredients to the butter mixture.

The topping can burn quickly. Watch it carefully so it just gets to the bubbly, golden brown stage.

I recommend the use of unsweetened coconut in this recipe because it won't burn as quickly under the broiler. Leave the door slightly ajar and watch closely when broiling.

- **Preheat oven to 350°F (180°C)**
- **13- by 9-inch (3 L) cake pan, greased**

BAR

1 1/2 cups	all-purpose flour	375 mL
1 tsp	baking powder	5 mL
1 tsp	baking soda	5 mL
1/2 tsp	salt	2 mL
1 tsp	ground cinnamon	5 mL
1 cup	quick-cooking rolled oats	250 mL
1 1/4 cups	boiling water	300 mL
1/2 cup	butter, softened	125 mL
1 1/2 cups	packed brown sugar	375 mL
2	eggs	2
1 1/4 cups	raisins	300 mL

TOPPING

1/4 cup	butter	60 mL
3/4 cup	packed brown sugar	175 mL
1/4 cup	half-and-half (10%) cream	60 mL
1 1/4 cups	chopped pecans	300 mL
1 cup	unsweetened flaked coconut	250 mL

1. *Bar:* Combine flour, baking powder, baking soda, salt and cinnamon. Place oats in a bowl. Add boiling water and mix to moisten oats. Let stand for 5 to 10 minutes.

2. In a bowl, using an electric mixer on medium speed, beat butter, brown sugar and eggs until light. Stir in flour mixture and oats, mixing well. Stir in raisins. Spread evenly in prepared pan.

3. Bake in preheated oven until a toothpick inserted in center comes out clean, 30 to 35 minutes. Do not remove from pan.

4. *Topping:* Preheat broiler. In a saucepan over low heat, melt butter. Stir in brown sugar, cream, pecans and coconut, mixing well. Remove from heat. Spread evenly over hot bar. Broil 6 inches (15 cm) below element, until topping is bubbly and golden brown, 1 to 2 minutes. Let cool completely in pan on rack. Cut into bars.

Almond Cranberry Lemon Bars

◆

Lemon juice enhances the tart flavor of cranberries in these wonderful almond bars.

MAKES 20 TO 54 BARS (see Cutting Guide, page 10)

- **Preparation: 25 minutes**
- **Baking: 65 minutes**
- **Freezing: excellent**

TIPS

If you prefer, you can mix the crust in a food processor. Use cubed cold butter, not softened. You can also mix the crust in a bowl, cutting in the cold butter using a pastry blender, 2 knives or your fingers. Whichever method you use, the mixture should resemble coarse crumbs.

When freezing bars and squares, chill the whole bar well before cutting. Cut as desired then wrap tightly in plastic wrap, individually or 6 per package. Freeze for up to 3 months.

To get the maximum amount of juice from lemons, warm them in the microwave on High for 30 seconds or place in a bowl of boiling water for a minute.

- **Preheat oven to 350°F (180°C)**
- **13- by 9-inch (3 L) cake pan, greased**

CRUST

2 cups	all-purpose flour	500 mL
1/3 cup	confectioners' (icing) sugar, sifted	75 mL
1 cup	butter, softened	250 mL

TOPPING

1 1/4 cups	dried cranberries	300 mL
7	eggs	7
2 1/4 cups	granulated sugar	550 mL
4 tsp	grated lemon zest	20 mL
3/4 cup	freshly squeezed lemon juice	175 mL
1/4 cup	butter, melted	60 mL
1/2 cup	all-purpose flour	125 mL
2 tsp	baking powder	10 mL
1 1/4 cups	ground or finely chopped almonds	300 mL
	Confectioners' (icing) sugar for dusting	

1. *Crust:* In a bowl, combine flour, confectioners' sugar and butter. Using an electric mixer on low speed, beat until crumbly. Press evenly into prepared pan. Bake in preheated oven until edges are lightly browned, 12 to 15 minutes.

2. *Topping:* Reduce oven temperature to 325°F (160°C). Sprinkle dried cranberries evenly over crust. In a bowl, using an electric mixer on high speed, beat eggs and sugar until light and slightly thickened, about 5 minutes. Stir in lemon zest and juice, melted butter, flour, baking powder and ground almonds, mixing well. Pour over cranberries.

3. Return to oven and bake until set and golden, about 50 minutes. Let cool completely in pan on rack. Cut into bars. Dust with confectioners' sugar before serving.

Variations

Replace almonds with hazelnuts.
Replace dried cranberries with dried blueberries or cherries.

Lemony Lemon Squares

If, like me, you enjoy lots of lemon flavor, you'll love these squares. They really make you pucker up.

MAKES 16 TO 36 SQUARES (see Cutting Guide, page 10)

- **Preparation: 20 minutes**
- **Baking: 45 minutes**
- **Freezing: excellent**

TIPS

For less pucker-up lemon flavor, decrease the lemon juice to $1/3$ cup (75 mL) and the flour to 2 tbsp (30 mL).

Just before serving, dust these squares lightly with confectioners' (icing) sugar, if desired. Don't do it too far ahead, as it will soak into the topping on standing.

Don't worry if these squares crack on top during cooling. The fabulous flavor outweighs the cracked appearance.

- **Preheat oven to 350°F (180°C)**
- **8-inch (2 L) square cake pan, greased**

CRUST

1 cup	all-purpose flour	250 mL
$1/4$ cup	granulated sugar	60 mL
$1/2$ cup	cold butter, cubed	125 mL

TOPPING

3	eggs	3
1 cup	granulated sugar	250 mL
3 tbsp	all-purpose flour	45 mL
2 tsp	grated lemon zest	10 mL
$1/2$ cup	freshly squeezed lemon juice	125 mL

1. *Crust:* In a bowl, combine flour and sugar. Using a pastry blender, 2 knives or your fingers, cut in butter until mixture resembles coarse crumbs. Press evenly into prepared pan. Bake in preheated oven until lightly browned around the edges, 12 to 15 minutes.

2. *Topping:* In a bowl, whisk eggs, sugar, flour, lemon zest and juice just until smooth. Don't overbeat. Pour over crust.

3. Return to oven and bake just until set, 25 to 30 minutes. Let cool completely in pan on rack. Cut into squares.

Variation

You can transform these into a citrus square by substituting an equal quantity of lime juice and zest for half of the lemon juice and zest.

Apricot Orange Almond Bars

The combination of a crisp crust with a tangy apricot-almond topping is delightful. Nothing fancy, just plain good.

MAKES 20 TO 54 BARS
(see Cutting Guide, page 10)

- **Preparation: 25 minutes**
- **Cooking: 10 minutes**
- **Baking: 45 minutes**
- **Freezing: excellent**

TIPS

For convenience, chop the apricots in a food processor fitted with a steel blade. Process just until finely chopped but not mushy.

Bars with an acid such as lemon juice in the filling should not be stored in the baking pan because the acid cuts into the pan.

Line the pan with parchment paper for easy removal.

- **Preheat oven to 350°F (180°C)**
- **13- by 9-inch (3 L) cake pan, greased**

CRUST

2 cups	all-purpose flour	500 mL
1/2 cup	granulated sugar	125 mL
3/4 cup	butter, softened	175 mL

FILLING

2 cups	dried apricots, finely chopped	500 mL
1/2 cup	water	125 mL
1/4 cup	orange liqueur	60 mL
2 tsp	freshly squeezed lemon juice	10 mL
2	eggs	2
1/3 cup	granulated sugar	75 mL
1 cup	chopped toasted almonds	250 mL

GLAZE

1/2 cup	confectioners' (icing) sugar, sifted	125 mL
2 tbsp	orange liqueur	30 mL

1. *Crust:* In a bowl, combine flour, sugar and butter. Using an electric mixer on low speed, beat until crumbly. Press evenly into prepared pan. Bake in preheated oven until golden around the edges, 12 to 15 minutes. Let cool in pan on rack.

2. *Filling:* In a saucepan over medium heat, bring apricots, water, orange liqueur and lemon juice to a boil. Reduce heat and simmer, stirring occasionally, until apricots are tender and liquid is evaporated, about 10 minutes. Remove from heat. Let cool. Stir in eggs and sugar until blended. Spread evenly over crust. Sprinkle with almonds.

3. Return to oven and bake until top is set and golden, 25 to 30 minutes. Let cool completely in pan on rack.

4. *Glaze:* In a bowl, combine confectioners' sugar and orange liqueur, stirring until smooth. Drizzle over filling. Let stand until set. Cut into bars.

Variations

Hazelnuts work well in place of almonds.

Replace orange liqueur with almond liqueur.

Pear and Mincemeat Oatmeal Bars

Prepared mincemeat gives you a head start on these fabulous bars. Take them along with some eggnog or sparkling cider as a hostess gift for a holiday party.

MAKES 20 TO 54 BARS
(see Cutting Guide, page 10)

- **Preparation: 20 minutes**
- **Baking: 30 minutes**
- **Freezing: excellent**

TIPS

For baking, pears should be ripe but firm.

Try cutting these bars in large squares and serve them slightly warm with a scoop of French vanilla or eggnog ice cream.

Prepared mincemeats vary considerably among brands. Experiment and pick your favorite before using it in baking.

- **Preheat oven to 375°F (190°C)**
- **13- by 9-inch (3 L) cake pan, greased**

BASE

3/4 cup	butter, softened	175 mL
3/4 cup	packed brown sugar	175 mL
1 1/2 cups	all-purpose flour	375 mL
1 1/4 cups	quick-cooking rolled oats	300 mL
3/4 cup	chopped walnuts	175 mL
1 tsp	cinnamon	5 mL
1/2 tsp	baking soda	2 mL
1/2 tsp	salt	2 mL

FILLING

2	large Anjou or Bartlett pears, peeled, cored and chopped	2
1 cup	prepared mincemeat	250 mL
1 tsp	grated lemon zest	5 mL
1 tbsp	freshly squeezed lemon juice	15 mL

1. *Base:* In a bowl, using an electric mixer on medium speed, beat butter and brown sugar until blended. Stir in flour, oats, walnuts, cinnamon, baking soda and salt, mixing until crumbly. Set aside 1 1/2 cups (375 mL) for topping. Press remainder evenly into prepared pan. Set aside.

2. *Filling:* In a bowl, combine pears, mincemeat and lemon zest and juice, mixing well. Spread evenly over crust. Sprinkle reserved topping evenly over mincemeat mixture.

3. Bake in preheated oven until top is golden brown, 25 to 30 minutes. Let cool completely in pan on rack. Cut into bars.

Variation

Replace lemon juice with an equal quantity of rum or brandy.

Replace pears with apples.

Pineapple Squares

These squares have been in my family for as long as I can remember. They were one of my grandmother's specialties, probably because they're easy to make and use only a few ingredients, all shelf stable.

MAKES 16 TO 36 SQUARES
(see Cutting Guide, page 10)

- **Preparation: 25 minutes**
- **Baking: 37 minutes**
- **Freezing: excellent**

TIPS

Use a good-quality crushed pineapple that has coarse chunks and a high fruit-to-juice ratio.

I have specified sweetened coconut because it seems to be more readily available than the unsweetened variety. But sweetened and unsweetened coconut can be used interchangeably in any recipe to suit your preference.

Bars and squares always taste better when enjoyed with a hot cup of tea or coffee. To personalize a cookie gift, pack them with a mug or teacup containing a package of gourmet coffee or herbal tea bags.

- **Preheat oven to 350°F (180°C)**
- **8-inch (2 L) square cake pan, greased**

CRUST

1/2 cup	butter, softened	125 mL
1/4 cup	granulated sugar	60 mL
1 1/3 cups	all-purpose flour	325 mL
1/4 tsp	baking powder	1 mL

FILLING

1	can (19 oz/540 mL) crushed pineapple, well drained	1

TOPPING

1/4 cup	butter, melted	60 mL
1/2 cup	granulated sugar	125 mL
1	egg	1
1 tsp	vanilla	5 mL
1 1/4 cups	sweetened flaked coconut	300 mL

1. *Crust:* In a bowl, using an electric mixer on medium speed, beat butter and sugar until blended. Stir in flour and baking powder, mixing until crumbly. Press evenly into prepared pan. Bake in preheated oven until golden around edges, 10 to 12 minutes. Let cool for 30 minutes.

2. *Filling:* Spread pineapple evenly over cooled crust.

3. *Topping:* In a bowl, whisk melted butter, sugar, egg and vanilla until well blended. Stir in coconut. Spread evenly over pineapple.

4. Return to oven and bake until set, 20 to 25 minutes. Let cool completely in pan on rack. Cut into squares.

Variations

Add 1/4 cup (60 mL) ground almonds to the crust and replace the vanilla with 1/2 tsp (2 mL) almond extract.

Use shredded coconut for a slightly different texture in the topping.

Apricot Coconut Chews

You don't have to like coconut to love these squares.

MAKES 18 TO 48 BARS OR 16 TO 36 SQUARES
(see Cutting Guide, page 10)

- **Preparation: 25 minutes**
- **Baking: 50 minutes**
- **Freezing: excellent**

TIPS

I have specified sweetened coconut because it seems to be more readily available than the unsweetened variety. But sweetened and unsweetened coconut can be used interchangeably in any recipe to suit your preference.

If your apricots seem very dry, plump them in boiling water for 5 minutes. Pat dry with paper towel before using.

- **Preheat oven to 350°F (180°C)**
- **9-inch (2.5 L) square cake pan, greased**

CRUST

1 cup	all-purpose flour	250 mL
1 cup	graham wafer crumbs	250 mL
1 cup	packed brown sugar	250 mL
1/2 cup	sweetened flaked coconut	125 mL
1/2 cup	butter, melted	125 mL

TOPPING

2	eggs	2
1 cup	packed brown sugar	250 mL
1 tbsp	freshly squeezed lemon juice	15 mL
1/3 cup	all-purpose flour	75 mL
1/2 tsp	baking powder	2 mL
1 cup	chopped dried apricots	250 mL

1. *Crust:* In a bowl, combine flour, graham wafer crumbs, brown sugar and coconut. Stir in melted butter, mixing well. Set aside 1 cup (250 mL) of the mixture for topping. Press remainder evenly into prepared pan. Bake in preheated oven until golden around edges, about 15 minutes.

2. *Topping:* In a bowl, whisk eggs until frothy. Add brown sugar and lemon juice, whisking until smooth. Whisk in flour and baking powder until smooth. Stir in apricots. Spread evenly over base. Sprinkle reserved crust mixture over top.

3. Return to oven and bake until top is set, 30 to 35 minutes. Let cool completely in pan on rack. Cut into bars or squares.

Variations

Replace coconut in crust with an equal quantity of ground almonds.

Replace graham wafer crumbs with vanilla wafer crumbs.

Cranberry Orange Apricot Bars

Here's a tasty bar that isn't too sweet. It's particularly enjoyable during the holiday season when there are plenty of other sweet treats available.

MAKES 18 TO 48 BARS (see Cutting Guide, page 10)

- **Preparation: 25 minutes**
- **Baking: 42 minutes**
- **Standing: 20 minutes**
- **Freezing: excellent**

TIP

Spices don't last forever. Their flavor comes from volatile oils that lose their punch over time. Buy in small amounts that will be used fairly quickly. To ensure optimum flavor, keep spices in airtight containers in a cool, dry place. Put the date of purchase on the container.

- **Preheat oven to 350°F (180°C)**
- **9-inch (2.5 L) square cake pan, greased**

CRUST

1 cup	all-purpose flour	250 mL
1/3 cup	packed brown sugar	75 mL
1/3 cup	cold butter, cubed	75 mL

FILLING

1/2 cup	golden raisins	125 mL
1/2 cup	dried cranberries	125 mL
1/2 cup	chopped dried apricots	125 mL
1/3 cup	freshly squeezed orange juice	75 mL
2	eggs	2
1 cup	packed brown sugar	250 mL
1/3 cup	all-purpose flour	75 mL
1/2 tsp	ground cinnamon	2 mL
1/3 cup	chopped pecans	75 mL

1. *Crust:* In a bowl, combine flour and brown sugar. Using a pastry blender, 2 knives or your fingers, cut in butter until mixture resembles coarse crumbs. Press evenly into prepared pan. Bake in preheated oven until golden around the edges, 10 to 12 minutes.

2. *Filling:* In a saucepan, combine raisins, cranberries, apricots and orange juice. Bring to a boil over medium heat. Remove from heat and let stand for 20 minutes. Liquid should be absorbed. If necessary, drain off any excess.

3. In a bowl, whisk eggs and brown sugar until blended. Add flour and cinnamon, whisking until smooth. Stir in pecans and fruit mixture. Spread evenly over crust.

4. Return to oven and bake until top is set and golden, 25 to 30 minutes. Let cool completely in pan on rack. Cut into bars.

Variations

Replace raisins with chopped dates or dried figs.
Replace orange juice with apple juice, brandy or water.

Cranberry Rhubarb Meringue Squares

These squares taste like old-fashioned cranberry rhubarb pie. They're pleasantly tart and best enjoyed the same day they're baked.

MAKES 16 TO 36 SQUARES
(see Cutting Guide, page 10)

- **Preparation: 30 minutes**
- **Baking: 70 minutes**
- **Freezing: not recommended**

TIPS

Fresh rhubarb is always better than frozen. If using frozen rhubarb, thaw it first and pat dry so the filling won't seep through the crust and make it soggy.

When beating egg whites, to get the maximum volume, have them at room temperature and be sure your bowl and beaters are free of any trace of grease.

When browning, watch meringue closely. It can burn very quickly.

- **Preheat oven to 350°F (180°C)**
- **8-inch (2 L) square cake pan, greased**

CRUST

1 cup	all-purpose flour	250 mL
2 tbsp	granulated sugar	30 mL
½ cup	cold butter, cubed	125 mL

FILLING

2 cups	chopped rhubarb	500 mL
⅔ cup	granulated sugar	150 mL
½ cup	dried cranberries	125 mL
3 tbsp	all-purpose flour	45 mL
3	eggs yolks, beaten	3
2 tsp	grated orange zest	10 mL
½ cup	freshly squeezed orange juice	125 mL
¼ tsp	almond extract	1 mL

TOPPING

3	egg whites, at room temperature	3
¼ cup	confectioners' (icing) sugar	60 mL
1 tsp	vanilla	5 mL
¼ cup	sweetened flaked coconut	60 mL

1. *Crust:* In a bowl, combine flour and sugar. Using a pastry blender, 2 knives or your fingers, cut in butter until mixture resembles coarse crumbs. Press evenly into prepared pan. Bake in preheated oven until golden around the edges, 10 to 12 minutes.

2. *Filling:* In a bowl, combine rhubarb, sugar, cranberries and flour. Stir in egg yolks, orange zest and juice and almond extract, mixing well. Pour over crust. Bake until rhubarb is tender, 40 to 45 minutes.

3. *Topping:* In a clean bowl, using an electric mixer on high speed, beat egg whites until frothy. Gradually add confectioners' sugar and vanilla, beating until stiff peaks form. Spread evenly over hot filling. Sprinkle with coconut. Return to oven and bake until topping is golden, 10 to 13 minutes. Let cool completely in pan on rack. Cut into squares.

Cranberry Orange Squares

A hazelnut crust, tart cranberry filling and sweet crumble topping make these squares irresistible. They're best enjoyed the same day they're baked.

MAKES 16 TO 36 SQUARES
(see Cutting Guide, page 10)

- **Preparation: 30 minutes**
- **Cooking: 5 minutes**
- **Baking: 45 minutes**
- **Freezing: not recommended**

TIP

This makes a wonderful dessert served warm with vanilla ice cream or orange sherbet.

- **Preheat oven to 350°F (180°C)**
- **8-inch (2 L) square cake pan, greased**

CRUST

3/4 cup	all-purpose flour	175 mL
1/2 cup	chopped hazelnuts	125 mL
1/3 cup	packed brown sugar	75 mL
1/4 cup	cold butter, cubed	60 mL
1/4 tsp	baking soda	1 mL
1/4 tsp	salt	1 mL
1	egg yolk, beaten	1

FILLING

2 cups	cranberries, thawed if frozen	500 mL
1/3 cup	dried cranberries	75 mL
1/2 cup	frozen orange juice concentrate, thawed	125 mL
1/3 cup	granulated sugar	75 mL
2 tbsp	cornstarch	30 mL

TOPPING

1/3 cup	all-purpose flour	75 mL
1/3 cup	packed brown sugar	75 mL
3/4 tsp	cinnamon	3 mL
1/4 cup	cold butter, cubed	60 mL
1/2 cup	chopped hazelnuts	125 mL

1. *Crust:* In a food processor fitted with a metal blade, combine flour, hazelnuts and sugar. Process until nuts are ground. Add butter, baking soda, salt and egg yolk; process until moist crumbs form. Press evenly into prepared pan. Bake in preheated oven until golden around the edges, 20 to 25 minutes.

2. *Filling:* In a saucepan, combine cranberries, dried cranberries, orange juice concentrate, sugar and cornstarch. Cook over medium heat, stirring often, until thickened, about 5 minutes. Remove from heat. Set aside.

3. *Topping:* In a bowl, combine flour, brown sugar and cinnamon. Using a pastry blender, 2 knives or your fingers, cut in butter until mixture resembles coarse crumbs. Stir in hazelnuts. Spread filling over base. Sprinkle topping evenly over filling.

4. Meanwhile, increase oven temperature to 375°F (190°C). Bake until top is golden and filling is bubbly, 15 to 20 minutes. Let cool completely in pan on rack. Cut into squares.

Triple Treat Fruit Bars

I've been making this bar for years. When my neighbor heard I was doing a book on bars and squares, his first comment was "Don't forget my favorite bar." So here it is.

MAKES 18 TO 48 BARS (see Cutting Guide, page 10)

- **Preparation: 20 minutes**
- **Baking: 45 minutes**
- **Chilling: 1 hour**
- **Freezing: excellent**

TIPS

These bars look festive with a pink frosting. Replace the lemon juice with maraschino cherry juice and replace the lemon zest with ¼ tsp (1 mL) almond extract.

Maraschino cherries are packed in liquid, so it's important to dry them well on paper towels before adding to the other ingredients. I like to dry them whole, then again after I've chopped them. That way you ensure you don't end up with pink filling.

- **Preheat oven to 350°F (180°C)**
- **9-inch (2.5 L) square cake pan, greased**

CRUST

1 cup	all-purpose flour	250 mL
¼ cup	granulated sugar	60 mL
½ cup	cold butter, cubed	125 mL

FILLING

2	eggs	2
1 cup	granulated sugar	250 mL
1 tsp	vanilla	5 mL
½ cup	chopped walnuts	125 mL
½ cup	raisins	125 mL
½ cup	sweetened flaked coconut	125 mL
½ cup	chopped, well-drained maraschino cherries	125 mL
2 tbsp	all-purpose flour	30 mL
1 tsp	baking powder	5 mL

LEMON FROSTING

¼ cup	butter, softened	60 mL
2 cups	confectioners' (icing) sugar, sifted	500 mL
2 tbsp	milk	30 mL
1½ tsp	grated lemon zest	7 mL
1 tbsp	freshly squeezed lemon juice	15 mL

1. *Crust:* In a bowl, combine flour and sugar. Using a pastry blender, 2 knives or your fingers, cut in butter until mixture resembles coarse crumbs. Press firmly into prepared pan. Bake in preheated oven until golden all over, 12 to 15 minutes.

2. *Filling:* In a bowl, whisk eggs, sugar and vanilla until blended. Stir in walnuts, raisins, coconut, maraschino cherries, flour and baking powder, mixing well. Spread evenly over crust.

3. Return to oven and bake until top is set and golden, 25 to 30 minutes. Let cool completely in pan on rack.

4. *Lemon Frosting:* In a bowl, using an electric mixer on medium speed, beat butter and half of the confectioners' sugar until light and creamy. Add milk and lemon zest and juice. Gradually add remaining confectioners' sugar, beating until smooth. Spread evenly over cooled filling. Refrigerate until frosting is firm, about 1 hour. Cut into bars.

Happy Holiday Fruit Squares

An attractive mixture of candied and dried fruits with crunchy cashews nestles on top of a buttery shortbread base.

MAKES 24 SQUARES (see Cutting Guide, page 10)

- **Preparation: 25 minutes**
- **Baking: 45 minutes**
- **Freezing: excellent**

TIPS

If you prefer, use a microwave to soak the raisins in brandy. Cover and heat on High for 1 minute.

Use the kind of cashews you usually buy. Both salted and unsalted work fine.

Sometimes when candied (glacé) cherries settle in the container, there's a lot of syrup at the bottom of the pot. Wipe the cherries to eliminate this or you'll end up with a red topping.

- **Preheat oven to 350°F (180°C)**
- **13- by 9-inch (3 L) cake pan, greased**

CRUST

1 ½ cups	all-purpose flour	375 mL
½ cup	confectioners' (icing) sugar, sifted	125 mL
⅔ cup	cold butter, cubed	150 mL

TOPPING

½ cup	golden raisins	125 mL
2 tbsp	brandy	30 mL
2	eggs	2
⅓ cup	packed brown sugar	75 mL
2 tbsp	all-purpose flour	30 mL
¾ cup	corn syrup	175 mL
1 tsp	vanilla	5 mL
1 cup	coarsely chopped red candied (glacé) cherries	250 mL
1 cup	coarsely chopped cashews	250 mL
¾ cup	coarsely chopped candied (glacé) pineapple	175 mL

1. *Crust:* In a food processor, combine flour, confectioners' sugar and butter. Pulse to form coarse crumbs. Press evenly into prepared pan. Bake in preheated oven until lightly browned all over, 12 to 15 minutes.

2. *Topping:* In a small saucepan over medium heat, combine raisins and brandy. Bring just to a boil, then set aside. Let cool to lukewarm, about 20 minutes.

3. In a large bowl, whisk eggs, brown sugar, flour, corn syrup and vanilla until blended. Stir in soaked raisins, cherries, cashews and pineapple, mixing well. Spread evenly over crust.

4. Return to oven and bake until set, 25 to 30 minutes. Let cool completely in pan on rack. Cut into squares.

Variations

Replace light raisins with sultanas or dried cranberries.
Replace brandy with rum, orange liqueur or apple juice.
Use a mixture of red and green candied (glacé) cherries.

Raspberry Almond Holiday Bars

Here's a delicious and colorful bar to jazz up your holiday cookie tray. Swirls of pink and green batter on a shortbread crust, topped with snowy white almond-flavored frosting, fit right into the festive season.

MAKES 18 TO 48 BARS (see Cutting Guide, page 10)

- **Preparation: 25 minutes**
- **Baking: 47 minutes**
- **Freezing: excellent**

TIPS

Although the filling has a tender but dense, cake-like texture, it doesn't contain any leavening agents such as baking soda or baking powder. Beating the eggs into the batter provides the lift.

Add a sprinkling of toasted sliced almonds after the bar has been frosted.

If you want to make a big batch of these bars, double the recipe. Bake in a 13- by 9-inch (3 L) pan for 35 to 40 minutes.

- **Preheat oven to 350°F (180°C)**
- **8-inch (2 L) square cake pan, greased**

CRUST

1 cup	all-purpose flour	250 mL
3 tbsp	granulated sugar	45 mL
1/3 cup	cold butter, cubed	75 mL

FILLING

1/2 cup	raspberry jam	125 mL
1/2 cup	butter, softened	125 mL
2/3 cup	granulated sugar	150 mL
2	eggs	2
2/3 cup	all-purpose flour	150 mL
1/4 tsp	salt	1 mL
	Red and green food coloring	

FROSTING

2 tbsp	butter, softened	30 mL
2 cups	confectioners' (icing) sugar, sifted	500 mL
2 tbsp	half-and-half (10%) cream	30 mL
1 tsp	almond extract	5 mL

1. *Crust:* In a bowl, combine flour and sugar. Using a pastry blender, 2 knives or your fingers, cut in butter until mixture resembles coarse crumbs. Press evenly into prepared pan. Bake in preheated oven until light golden around edges, 10 to 12 minutes.

2. *Filling:* Spread jam evenly over crust. In a bowl, using an electric mixer on medium speed, beat butter and sugar until blended, about 3 minutes. Add eggs, one at a time, beating lightly after each addition. Stir in flour and salt, mixing well. Divide batter evenly between 2 bowls. Add red food coloring to one of the bowls a few drops at a time, stirring, to make pastel pink. Using green food coloring, repeat with the other bowl to make pastel green. Drop small spoonfuls of each batter alternately over jam. Tap pan gently on counter to even out batter.

3. Return to oven and bake until top is set and golden, 30 to 35 minutes. Let cool completely in pan on rack.

4. *Frosting:* In a bowl, using an electric mixer on medium speed, beat butter, confectioners' sugar, cream and almond extract until smooth and creamy. Spread over filling. Cut into bars.

Raspberry Coconut Squares

These squares are similar to Raspberry Coconut Walnut Bars (see recipe, page 150) but different enough that I wanted to include them. I love them both and can't decide which I like better.

MAKES 16 TO 36 SQUARES
(see Cutting Guide, page 10)

- **Preparation: 25 minutes**
- **Baking: 42 minutes**
- **Freezing: excellent**

TIPS

Chill the bars for easy cutting but serve at room temperature for the nicest flavor.

Try these bars slightly warm with a scoop of French vanilla ice cream or raspberry sherbet.

When cutting bars containing flaked or shredded coconut, use a straight blade like a chef's knife and cut straight down. A serrated knife drags the coconut down rather than cutting it.

- **Preheat oven to 425°F (220°C)**
- **9-inch (2.5 L) square cake pan, greased**

CRUST

1 ¼ cups	all-purpose flour	300 mL
¼ cup	granulated sugar	60 mL
½ cup	cold butter, cubed	125 mL
3 tbsp	cold water	45 mL

TOPPING

⅓ cup	raspberry jam	75 mL
2	eggs	2
½ cup	packed brown sugar	125 mL
2 cups	sweetened flaked coconut	500 mL

1. *Crust:* In a bowl, combine flour and sugar. Using a pastry blender, 2 knives or your fingers, cut in butter until mixture resembles coarse crumbs. Add water and, using a fork, mix until moistened. Press firmly into prepared pan. Bake in preheated oven until golden around edges, 10 to 12 minutes. Reduce oven temperature to 350°F (180°C).

2. *Topping:* Spread jam evenly over crust, leaving a ½-inch (1 cm) border of crust. In a small bowl, using an electric mixer on high speed, beat eggs until frothy. Gradually add sugar, beating until mixture is thick, about 5 minutes. Stir in coconut, mixing well until moistened. Drop by spoonfuls over jam and, using a spatula or the back of a spoon, carefully spread evenly.

3. Return to oven and bake until topping is light golden, 25 to 30 minutes. Let cool completely in pan on rack. Chill (see Tips, left). Cut into squares.

Variations

Replace ½ cup (125 mL) of the coconut with finely chopped almonds.

Use strawberry, peach or pineapple jam.

Coconut Lemon Bars

◆

The tart lemon flavor mingles beautifully with the crunchy almonds in this easy-to-make bar.

MAKES 20 TO 54 BARS (see Cutting Guide, page 10)

- **Preparation: 20 minutes**
- **Baking: 50 minutes**
- **Freezing: excellent**

TIPS

If you prefer, mix the crust using an electric mixer on medium speed. It will take about 3 minutes.

Using a toothbrush makes cleaning a zester or grater easier.

When a microwave isn't handy and you have hard butter, here's how to soften it quickly: set it in a dish and leave a heated saucepan upside down over the dish for a few minutes.

- **Preheat oven to 325°F (160°C)**
- **13- by 9-inch (3 L) cake pan, greased**

CRUST

³⁄₄ cup	butter, softened	175 mL
¹⁄₂ cup	granulated sugar	125 mL
1 ¹⁄₂ cups	all-purpose flour	375 mL
¹⁄₃ cup	flaked coconut	75 mL

TOPPING

4	eggs	4
1 ¹⁄₂ cups	granulated sugar	375 mL
¹⁄₄ cup	all-purpose flour	60 mL
1 ¹⁄₂ tbsp	grated lemon zest	22 mL
¹⁄₃ cup	freshly squeezed lemon juice	75 mL
1 ¹⁄₃ cups	sliced almonds	325 mL
	Confectioners' (icing) sugar, optional	

1. *Crust:* In a bowl, using a wooden spoon, beat butter and sugar until smooth and creamy. Stir in flour and coconut, mixing until thoroughly blended. Press evenly into prepared pan. Bake in preheated oven until golden, 20 to 25 minutes.

2. *Topping:* In a bowl, whisk eggs and sugar until blended. Whisk in flour and lemon zest, mixing until smooth. Whisk in lemon juice. Pour evenly over crust. Sprinkle almonds evenly over top.

3. Return to oven and bake until topping is set and almonds are golden, 20 to 25 minutes. Let cool completely in pan on rack. Before serving, dust lightly with confectioners' sugar, if desired. Cut into bars.

Variation

Replace half of the lemon zest and juice with lime zest and juice for a citrus bar.

Raspberry Crisscross Squares

This variation on the classic Austrian linzertorte is delicious, but very easy to make, unlike the original.

**MAKES 16 TO 36 SQUARES
(see Cutting Guide, page 10)**

- **Preparation: 25 minutes**
- **Baking: 30 minutes**
- **Freezing: excellent**

TIPS

Look for a jam that has a bright red color. It will darken a little during baking, so the brighter it is to start, the nicer it will be after baking.

Omit the glaze if time is a factor or if you would rather not have a leftover egg white. The glaze makes the lattice a nice golden color.

When adding liquid such as water, milk or egg to pastry crumbs, toss the mixture lightly with a fork to keep it crumbly. When you use a spoon, it tends to mash the crumbs, making the dough tough.

- **Preheat oven to 375°F (190°C)**
- **9-inch (2.5 L) square cake pan, greased**

DOUGH

1 1/4 cups	all-purpose flour	300 mL
1/2 cup	packed brown sugar	125 mL
1/3 cup	ground almonds	75 mL
1/4 cup	granulated sugar	60 mL
2 tsp	grated lemon zest	10 mL
1/2 tsp	baking powder	2 mL
1/4 tsp	salt	1 mL
3/4 tsp	ground cinnamon	3 mL
1/2 cup	cold butter, cubed	125 mL
1	egg, beaten	1
1 tsp	almond extract	5 mL

TOPPING

1 cup	raspberry jam	250 mL
2 tbsp	all-purpose flour	30 mL
1 tbsp	water (approx.)	15 mL

GLAZE, OPTIONAL

1	egg yolk	1
1 tsp	milk	5 mL

1. *Dough:* In a bowl, combine flour, brown sugar, ground almonds, granulated sugar, lemon zest, baking powder, salt and cinnamon. Using a pastry blender, 2 knives or your fingers, cut in butter until mixture resembles coarse crumbs. Add egg and almond extract. Mix with a fork until moistened. Set 1/2 cup (125 mL) of the mixture aside for topping. Press remainder evenly into prepared pan.

2. *Topping:* Spread jam evenly over base. Add flour to reserved dough and stir with a fork to blend. Stir in water until dough holds together, adding a little more, if necessary. Divide into 10 portions and roll each into a pencil-like strip. Crisscross strips diagonally over jam to form a lattice.

3. *Glaze (if using):* Mix together egg yolk and milk. Brush over lattice.

4. Bake in preheated oven until golden, 25 to 30 minutes. Let cool completely in pan on rack. Cut into squares.

Lemon-Frosted Cherry Bars

◆

The tart flavors of lemon and sour cherry combine in a bar that's not too sweet. It makes a refreshing treat at the end of a busy day.

MAKES 18 TO 48 BARS (see Cutting Guide, page 10)

- **Preparation: 30 minutes**
- **Baking: 47 minutes**
- **Chilling: 1 hour**
- **Freezing: excellent**

TIPS

If there are large pieces of fruit in the jam, chop them to get an even distribution of pieces over the crust.

When you only need a little lemon juice, poke holes in a whole lemon with a fork or the tip of a knife and squeeze out the juice required. The lemon can then be refrigerated and will keep longer than a cut lemon.

- **Preheat oven to 350°F (180°C)**
- **9-inch (2.5 L) square cake pan, greased**

CRUST

1 cup	all-purpose flour	250 mL
¼ cup	granulated sugar	60 mL
⅓ cup	cold butter, cubed	75 mL

FILLING

½ cup	sour cherry jam	125 mL
½ cup	butter, softened	125 mL
⅔ cup	granulated sugar	150 mL
2	eggs	2
⅔ cup	all-purpose flour	150 mL
2 tsp	grated lemon zest	10 mL

LEMON FROSTING

2 tbsp	butter, softened	30 mL
1½ cups	confectioners' (icing) sugar, sifted	375 mL
2 tsp	grated lemon zest	10 mL
1 to 2 tbsp	freshly squeezed lemon juice	15 to 30 mL

1. *Crust:* In a bowl, combine flour and sugar. Using a pastry blender, 2 knives or your fingers, cut in butter until mixture resembles coarse crumbs. Press evenly into prepared pan. Bake in preheated oven until golden around edges, 10 to 12 minutes. Let cool in pan on rack for 15 minutes.

2. *Filling:* Spread jam evenly over crust. In a bowl, using an electric mixer on medium speed, beat butter, sugar and eggs for 3 minutes. On low speed, beat in flour and lemon zest, mixing well. Drop filling by spoonfuls over jam and, using a spatula or the back of a spoon, spread evenly.

3. Return to oven and bake until top is set and golden, 30 to 35 minutes. Let cool completely in pan on rack.

4. *Lemon Frosting:* In a bowl, using an electric mixer on medium speed, beat butter, confectioners' sugar and lemon zest and juice until light and creamy. Spread evenly over cooled bars. Chill until frosting is firm, about 1 hour. Cut into bars.

Variation
Replace cherry jam with blackcurrant or strawberry.

Party Pink Coconut Squares

This creamy, soft frosting is a perfect match for a moist coconut filling and graham wafer crust.

MAKES 16 TO 36 SQUARES
(see Cutting Guide, page 10)

- **Preparation: 30 minutes**
- **Baking: 37 minutes**
- **Chilling: 1 hour**
- **Freezing: excellent**

TIPS

I have specified sweetened coconut because it seems to be more readily available than the unsweetened variety. But sweetened and unsweetened coconut can be used interchangeably in any recipe to suit your preference.

The smooth, rich, creamy texture of the frosting is thanks to the long beating. It may seem to have a lot of liquid for a frosting, but believe me, it's wonderful.

I like the pastel pink frosting, but if you prefer, leave it plain or color it other pastel colors.

This bar cuts very nicely. It looks pretty cut into small squares and put into tiny pastel paper cups.

- **Preheat oven to 350°F (180°C)**
- **9-inch (2.5 L) square cake pan, greased**

CRUST

1 ½ cups	graham wafer crumbs	375 mL
¼ cup	packed brown sugar	60 mL
1 tbsp	all-purpose flour	15 mL
½ cup	butter, melted	125 mL

FILLING

1	can (10 oz/300 mL) sweetened condensed milk	1
2 cups	sweetened flaked coconut	500 mL

FROSTING

½ cup	butter, softened	125 mL
2 cups	confectioners' (icing) sugar, sifted	500 mL
1 tbsp	half-and-half (10%) cream	15 mL
1 tbsp	boiling water	15 mL
2	drops red food coloring	2

1. *Crust:* In a bowl, combine graham wafer crumbs, brown sugar, flour and melted butter, mixing well until all ingredients are moistened. Press evenly into prepared pan. Bake in preheated oven until firm, 10 to 12 minutes.

2. *Filling:* In a bowl, combine sweetened condensed milk and coconut, mixing until coconut is thoroughly moistened. Spread evenly over crust, being careful not to break the delicate crust.

3. Return to oven and bake until filling is set and top is light golden, 20 to 25 minutes. Let cool completely in pan on rack.

4. *Frosting:* In a small bowl, using an electric mixer on low speed, beat butter and confectioners' (icing) sugar for 2 minutes. Add cream. Beat on medium speed until smooth, about 2 minutes. Add boiling water and beat for 2 minutes. Add food coloring and beat until very smooth and creamy, about 2 minutes. Spread evenly over filling. Chill until frosting is firm, about 1 hour. Cut into squares.

Variation

Add ½ tsp (2 mL) almond extract to the filling.

Overloaded Nut Squares

Nut Bars and Squares

If you enjoy eating nuts — and now that nutritionists tell us including moderate amounts of nuts in our diets is a healthy strategy, you can do this guilt-free — there are lots of recipes to choose from in this chapter. Almost every kind of nut is featured, but since nuts are usually interchangeable, you can adapt most recipes to include your favorites or the kind you have on hand.

I've included recipes to meet the needs of every occasion. Many of the bars contain two layers, which include a cookie-like crust pressed into the pan and a topping that includes an abundance of nuts, often mixed with other ingredients such as fruit and chocolate. There are also single-layer bars, where nuts are combined with mixtures of other yummy ingredients scattered through a cookie dough. These bars have only one step in the method and are particularly quick and easy.

Overloaded Nut Squares

The topping soaks into the crust of these squares, making the base more cake-like, which is a refreshing change from the crisp shortbread base usually found in bars. The softer texture goes well with the overload of crunchy, chunky mixed nuts on top.

MAKES 24 SQUARES
(see Cutting Guide, page 10)

- **Preparation: 20 minutes**
- **Baking: 50 minutes**
- **Freezing: excellent**

TIPS

If you don't have buttermilk, here's a handy substitute: Place 1 tbsp (15 mL) lemon juice or white vinegar in a measuring cup and add milk to make 1 cup (250 mL). Let stand for 5 minutes, then stir. Add to recipe.

If the filling is sticky, make cutting easier by running a knife around the edge of the pan as soon as you remove it from the oven. Let bars cool completely before cutting. Bars with a soft filling or frosting are usually easier to cut neatly if they're first chilled until firm.

- Preheat oven to 350°F (180°C)
- 13- by 9-inch (3 L) cake pan, greased

CRUST

1¾ cups	all-purpose flour	425 mL
⅓ cup	packed brown sugar	75 mL
¾ cup	butter, softened	175 mL

TOPPING

1⅔ cups	granulated sugar	400 mL
¼ cup	all-purpose flour	60 mL
3	eggs	3
1 cup	buttermilk (see Tips, left)	250 mL
¼ cup	butter, melted and cooled	60 mL
1 tsp	vanilla	5 mL
2 cups	coarsely chopped deluxe salted mixed nuts (no peanuts)	500 mL

1. *Crust:* In a bowl, combine flour, brown sugar and butter. Using an electric mixer on low speed, beat until crumbly. Press evenly into prepared pan. Bake in preheated oven until golden around edges, 12 to 15 minutes.
2. *Topping:* In a bowl, combine sugar and flour. Whisk in eggs, buttermilk, melted butter and vanilla, whisking just until smooth. Stir in nuts. Pour over crust.
3. Return to oven and bake until topping is set and golden, 30 to 35 minutes. Let cool completely in pan on rack. Cut into squares.

Variation

I like the flavor of salted nuts in these bars, but if you're trying to cut down on salt, make your own mixture of nuts using unsalted pecans, almonds, hazelnuts, cashews and Brazil nuts.

Crunchy Caramel Almond Squares

These squares are one of the simplest recipes in the book. They're also one of my favorites. With a recipe like this, there's no excuse for not making homemade treats.

MAKES 24 TO 60 SQUARES (see Cutting Guide, page 10)

- **Preparation: 5 minutes**
- **Baking: 10 minutes**
- **Freezing: excellent**

TIPS

Be careful not to boil the sugar mixture or it will become sugary and too thick.

Instead of cutting this bar into neat squares, break it into irregular pieces after it has cooled. Lift the bar off the pan in large pieces, then break into smaller ones.

I like the look of unblanched almonds, which are available presliced in some bulk stores, although you'll get the same flavor using the blanched variety.

- Preheat oven to 375°F (190°C)
- 15- by 10- by 1-inch (2 L) jelly roll pan, greased

28	graham wafers	28
1 cup	butter	250 mL
1 cup	packed brown sugar	250 mL
1 1/2 cups	sliced almonds	375 mL

1. In prepared pan, arrange graham crackers in single layer. Set aside.

2. In a saucepan, melt butter over medium heat. Whisk in brown sugar until combined. Bring just to a boil, reduce heat to low and simmer for 2 minutes. (Do not boil.) Remove from heat. Stir in almonds. Quickly pour over crackers and spread evenly to cover.

3. Bake in preheated oven until golden and bubbly, about 10 minutes. Let cool in pan on rack for 10 minutes. Cut into squares. Let cool completely.

Variations

Substitute an equal quantity of sliced hazelnuts for the almonds.

Spread or drizzle melted chocolate over the squares.

Try making these squares into ice cream sandwiches by placing a scoop of ice cream on one square, then topping with another.

Chocolate Raspberry Almond Bars

The combination of raspberry and almond is always delicious. Add a shortbread crust and creamy butter frosting and the results are nothing short of sensational.

MAKES 20 TO 54 BARS (see Cutting Guide, page 10)

- **Preparation: 30 minutes**
- **Baking: 37 minutes**
- **Chilling: 1 hour**
- **Freezing: excellent**

TIPS

Be sure to buy almond paste, not marzipan, which contains a much higher proportion of sugar. Squeeze the almond paste to make sure it's soft and fresh. It tends to harden in storage, which makes it difficult to blend smoothly.

If you prefer, make the crust in a food processor. Just substitute cold butter, cubed, for the softened.

- **Preheat oven to 350°F (180°C)**
- **13- by 9-inch (3 L) cake pan, greased**

CRUST

½ cup	butter, softened	125 mL
½ cup	packed brown sugar	125 mL
1 tsp	vanilla	5 mL
1½ cups	all-purpose flour	375 mL
¼ tsp	salt	1 mL
¾ cup	raspberry jam	175 mL

FILLING

8 oz	almond paste (see Tips, left)	250 g
½ cup	granulated sugar	125 mL
1 tsp	vanilla	5 mL
3	eggs	3

BUTTERY CHOCOLATE FROSTING

2 tbsp	butter, softened	30 mL
1½ cups	confectioners' (icing) sugar, sifted	375 mL
1 tsp	vanilla	5 mL
2 to 3 tbsp	milk	30 to 45 mL
1	square (1 oz/28 g) semisweet chocolate, melted	1

1. *Crust:* In a bowl, using a wooden spoon, beat butter, brown sugar and vanilla until smooth and creamy, about 2 minutes. Stir in flour and salt, mixing until crumbly. Press evenly into prepared pan. Bake in preheated oven until golden around edges, 10 to 12 minutes. Let cool slightly. Spread jam evenly over warm crust, leaving a ½-inch (1 cm) border of crust.
2. *Filling:* In a food processor fitted with a metal blade, process almond paste, sugar and vanilla until smoothly blended. Add eggs, one at a time, pulsing a few times after each addition. Process until smooth. Spread evenly over jam.
3. Return to oven and bake until set and golden, 20 to 25 minutes. Let cool completely in pan on rack.
4. *Frosting:* In a bowl, using an electric mixer on medium speed, beat butter, confectioners' sugar and vanilla just until combined. Gradually beat in milk, adding just enough to reach a spreadable consistency. Beat in chocolate. Spread over filling. Chill for 1 hour to firm up frosting. Cut into bars.

Maraschino Cherry and Almond Bars

◆

Here's a colorful holiday bar to brighten up a cookie tray. I love the almond flavor with the cherries.

MAKES 18 TO 48 BARS (see Cutting Guide, page 10)

- **Preparation: 30 minutes**
- **Baking: 37 minutes**
- **Freezing: excellent**

TIPS

Red maraschino cherries are flavored with almond. If you'd like a stronger almond flavor in the topping, add ½ tsp (2 mL) almond extract.

Green maraschino cherries are often flavored with mint, but they work in this recipe.

- **Preheat oven to 350°F (180°C)**
- **9-inch (2.5 L) square cake pan, greased**

CRUST

1 cup	all-purpose flour	250 mL
¼ cup	confectioners' (icing) sugar	60 mL
½ cup	cold butter, cubed	125 mL

TOPPING

2	eggs	2
½ cup	granulated sugar	125 mL
¼ cup	all-purpose flour	60 mL
½ tsp	baking powder	2 mL
1 cup	sliced almonds	250 mL
1 cup	drained red maraschino cherries, chopped	250 mL

GLAZE, OPTIONAL

½ cup	confectioners' (icing) sugar, sifted	125 mL
¼ tsp	almond extract	1 mL
2 tsp	reserved maraschino cherry juice	10 mL
1 to 2 tsp	milk	5 to 10 mL

1. *Crust:* In a bowl, combine flour and confectioners' sugar. Using a pastry blender, 2 knives or your fingers, cut in butter until mixture resembles coarse crumbs. Press evenly into prepared pan. Bake in preheated oven until golden around the edges, 10 to 12 minutes.

2. *Topping:* In a bowl, whisk eggs and sugar until blended. Whisk in flour and baking powder, mixing well. Stir in almonds and cherries. Spread evenly over crust.

3. Return to oven and bake until topping is set and golden, 20 to 25 minutes. Let cool completely in pan on rack.

4. *Glaze (if using):* In a small bowl, combine confectioners' sugar, almond extract and cherry juice. Gradually whisk in enough milk to make a smooth, pourable consistency. Drizzle over top of cooled bars. Let glaze set. Cut into bars.

Butterscotch Peanut Squares

A crisp crust and chewy caramel top with lots of peanuts in the middle make these bars the perfect partner for a cold glass of milk.

MAKES 24 TO 60 SQUARES
(see Cutting Guide, page 10)

- **Preparation: 15 minutes**
- **Baking: 27 minutes**
- **Freezing: excellent**

TIPS

Like all nuts, peanuts become rancid quickly because they're high in fat. Keep them in your freezer in airtight containers to retain freshness. Taste nuts before using to make sure they're fresh.

If you prefer, you can mix the crust in a bowl. Combine the flour and brown sugar, then cut in butter using a pastry blender, 2 knives or your fingers. Whichever method you use, the mixture should resemble coarse crumbs.

- **Preheat oven to 350°F (180°C)**
- **15- by 10- by 1-inch (2 L) jelly roll pan, greased**

CRUST

1 1/2 cups	all-purpose flour	375 mL
3/4 cup	packed brown sugar	175 mL
1/2 cup	cold butter, cubed	125 mL

TOPPING

3 1/2 cups	salted peanuts	875 mL
1/2 cup	corn syrup	125 mL
2 tbsp	butter	30 mL
1 tbsp	water	15 mL
1 cup	butterscotch chips	250 mL

1. *Crust:* In a food processor fitted with a metal blade, combine flour, brown sugar and butter. Process until mixture resembles coarse crumbs. Press evenly into prepared pan. Bake in preheated oven until golden around edges, 10 to 12 minutes.

2. *Topping:* Sprinkle peanuts over crust. In a saucepan over low heat, combine corn syrup, butter, water and butterscotch chips. Cook, stirring often, until chips are melted and mixture is smooth. Pour evenly over peanuts.

3. Return to oven and bake until set, 12 to 15 minutes. Let cool completely in pan on rack. Cut into squares.

Variations

Replace butterscotch chips with peanut butter chips or semisweet chocolate chips.

Use dry-roasted peanuts for an extra-crunchy filling.

Apricot Almond Bars

The almond paste gives these bars a strong but appealing almond flavor. I find it works particularly well with a tart apricot jam.

MAKES 20 TO 54 BARS (see Cutting Guide, page 10)

- **Preparation: 25 minutes**
- **Baking: 40 minutes**
- **Freezing: excellent**

TIPS

Almond paste is a mixture of ground almonds and sugar. Marzipan is too, but it has a much higher sugar content. It's sold in tubes, cans or pieces, by weight, in the baking section of supermarkets.

Use cold butter when cutting it into a dry mixture with a pastry blender or in a food processor. Let it soften if you're using a mixer or beating with a spoon.

- **Preheat oven to 350°F (180°C)**
- **13- by 9-inch (3 L) cake pan, greased**

CRUST

1 1/2 cups	all-purpose flour	375 mL
1/4 cup	granulated sugar	60 mL
1/2 cup	butter, softened	125 mL

TOPPING

7 1/2 oz	almond paste, crumbled	225 g
1/2 cup	all-purpose flour	125 mL
1/4 cup	granulated sugar	60 mL
1/4 cup	butter, softened	60 mL
1 cup	apricot jam	250 mL
1/2 cup	sliced almonds	125 mL

1. *Crust:* In a bowl, combine flour, sugar and butter. Using an electric mixer on low speed, beat until crumbly. Press evenly into prepared pan. Bake in preheated oven until golden all over, 12 to 15 minutes.

2. *Topping:* In a bowl, combine almond paste, flour and sugar. Using a pastry blender, 2 knives or your fingers, cut in butter until mixture resembles coarse crumbs. Set aside.

3. Spread jam over crust, leaving a 1/2-inch (1 cm) border of crust. Sprinkle almond paste mixture evenly over top. Sprinkle sliced almonds evenly over topping.

4. Return to oven and bake until top is set and golden, 20 to 25 minutes. Let cool completely in pan on rack. Cut into bars.

Variations

Use other soft spreads, such as raspberry or peach jam or marmalade.

Dust with confectioners' (icing) sugar or drizzle with a mixture of 2/3 cup (150 mL) confectioners' (icing) sugar and 1 to 2 tbsp (15 to 30 mL) milk.

Peanut Chocolate Candy Bars

Kids young and old love these bars. A generous layer of caramel peanuts smothers a tender, melt-in-your-mouth crust.

MAKES 36 TO 48 BARS
(see Cutting Guide, page 10)

- **Preparation: 20 minutes**
- **Baking: 27 minutes**
- **Freezing: excellent**

TIPS

It's always best to use the pan size recommended in a recipe because it's the one in which the recipe was tested. However, if you don't have a jelly roll pan, you can use two 9-inch (2.5 L) square pans. In any recipe, check for doneness 5 minutes before the minimum time suggested.

When serving bars like these, which may stick to the plate, first dust the plate lightly with confectioners' (icing) sugar.

- **Preheat oven to 350°F (180°C)**
- **15- by 10- by 1-inch (2 L) jelly roll pan, greased**

CRUST

2 cups	all-purpose flour	500 mL
½ cup	packed brown sugar	125 mL
¾ cup	butter, softened	175 mL

TOPPING

2 cups	peanuts	500 mL
1 ¼ cups	milk chocolate chips	300 mL
3 tbsp	all-purpose flour	45 mL
1 ½ cups	caramel sundae sauce	375 mL

1. *Crust:* In a bowl, combine flour, brown sugar and butter. Using an electric mixer on low speed, beat until crumbly. Press evenly into prepared pan. Bake in preheated oven until golden around the edges, 10 to 12 minutes.

2. *Topping:* Sprinkle peanuts and chocolate chips evenly over crust. In a small bowl, stir flour into sundae sauce, mixing until smooth. Pour evenly over peanuts and chocolate chips.

3. Return to oven and bake until caramel is bubbly, 12 to 15 minutes. Let cool completely in pan on rack. Cut into bars.

Variations

Substitute semisweet chocolate chips for the milk chocolate chips.

Use butterscotch sundae sauce if you prefer a milder caramel flavor.

Raspberry Hazelnut Bars

These bars, which feature a light and tender nut top on a layer of jam and a shortbread crust, are a favorite in Austria. They're pretty delicious on this side of the ocean, too.

MAKES 20 TO 54 BARS (see Cutting Guide, page 10)

- **Preparation: 20 minutes**
- **Baking: 47 minutes**
- **Freezing: excellent**

TIPS

Hazelnuts are also called filberts.

It's not a mistake — there's no flour in the topping. The ground hazelnuts take its place.

When folding stiff egg whites into a stiff batter, add one-quarter of the egg whites first and stir them into the batter to soften it. Then gently fold in the remaining egg whites. This helps keep the mixture light, tender and airy.

- **Preheat oven to 325°F (160°C)**
- **13- by 9-inch (3 L) cake pan, greased**

CRUST

1 1/4 cups	all-purpose flour	300 mL
3 tbsp	granulated sugar	45 mL
1 cup	cold butter, cubed	250 mL

TOPPING

1/2 cup	raspberry jam	125 mL
3 tbsp	butter, softened	45 mL
1 1/4 cups	granulated sugar	300 mL
6	eggs, separated	6
1 2/3 cups	coarsely ground hazelnuts	400 mL

1. *Crust:* In a bowl, combine flour and sugar. Using a pastry blender, 2 knives or your fingers, cut in butter until mixture resembles coarse crumbs. Press evenly into prepared pan. Bake in preheated oven until golden around edges, 10 to 12 minutes. Let cool on rack for 30 minutes.

2. *Topping:* Spread jam evenly over cooled crust, leaving a 1/2-inch (1 cm) border. In a bowl, using an electric mixer on medium speed, beat butter and sugar until blended. In a small bowl, using an electric mixer on high speed, beat egg yolks until light and creamy, about 5 minutes. Stir into butter mixture along with ground hazelnuts, mixing well. In a clean bowl, using an electric mixer with clean beaters on high speed, beat egg whites until stiff, shiny peaks form. Gently fold into nut mixture. Spread carefully over jam.

3. Return to oven and bake until topping is set and golden, 30 to 35 minutes. Let cool completely in pan on rack. Cut into bars.

Variations

Use raspberry, strawberry or pineapple jam.
Substitute unblanched ground almonds for the hazelnuts.

Mom's Dream Cake

For as long as I can remember, my mother, who was fond of nuts of any kind, loved making — and eating — these delicious bars.

MAKES 16 TO 48 BARS OR SQUARES (see Cutting Guide, page 10)

- **Preparation: 20 minutes**
- **Baking: 42 minutes**
- **Freezing: excellent**

TIPS

Shortbread crusts like this can be prepared quickly in a food processor. They can also be mixed with an electric mixer on low speed or with a wooden spoon when using softened butter. Whichever method you choose, the butter should be evenly distributed throughout the mixture, so it resembles coarse crumbs.

I have specified sweetened coconut because it seems to be more readily available than the unsweetened variety. But sweetened and unsweetened coconut can be used interchangeably in any recipe to suit your preference.

- **Preheat oven to 350°F (180°C)**
- **9-inch (2.5 L) square cake pan, greased**

CRUST

1 cup + 2 tbsp	all-purpose flour	280 mL
3 tbsp	granulated sugar	45 mL
1/4 tsp	salt	1 mL
1/2 cup	cold butter, cubed	125 mL

TOPPING

2	eggs	2
1 1/4 cups	packed brown sugar	300 mL
1 tsp	vanilla	5 mL
2 tbsp	all-purpose flour	30 mL
1 tsp	baking powder	5 mL
1 cup	chopped walnuts	250 mL
1/2 cup	sweetened flaked coconut	125 mL

1. *Crust:* In a bowl, combine flour, sugar and salt. Using a pastry blender, 2 knives or your fingers, cut in butter until mixture resembles coarse crumbs. Press evenly into prepared pan. Bake in preheated oven until golden around edges, 10 to 12 minutes.

2. *Topping:* In a bowl, whisk eggs, brown sugar and vanilla until smooth. Whisk in flour and baking powder, mixing well. Stir in walnuts and coconut. Spread evenly over crust.

3. Return to oven and bake until topping is set and golden, 25 to 30 minutes. Let cool completely in pan on rack. Cut into bars or squares.

Variations

Replace walnuts with pecans or almonds.

Add 1/3 cup (75 mL) chopped red candied (glacé) cherries to topping.

Maple Nut Bars

These delicious bars start with a shortbread crust and add a slightly gooey maple topping loaded with your favorite nuts. What could be better?

MAKES 20 TO 54 BARS (see Cutting Guide, page 10)

- **Preparation: 25 minutes**
- **Baking: 40 minutes**
- **Freezing: excellent**

TIPS

If you prefer, mix the crust in a food processor. Use cold butter rather than softened. You can also mix the crust in a bowl, cutting in cold cubed butter using a pastry blender, 2 knives or your fingers.

Use pure maple syrup for baking. Pancake syrup doesn't have enough maple flavor and can react differently in baking.

Buy California walnuts for baking. If you have the time, buy walnut halves and chop them rather than using pieces. They're fresher and of a higher quality.

In all your baking, you can replace all-purpose flour with unbleached all-purpose flour, if you prefer. They are interchangeable.

- **Preheat oven to 350°F (180°C)**
- **13- by 9-inch (3 L) cake pan, greased**

CRUST

1 cup	butter, softened	250 mL
1/2 cup	packed brown sugar	125 mL
2 cups	all-purpose flour	500 mL

TOPPING

3	eggs	3
1 cup	packed brown sugar	250 mL
1/4 cup	pure maple syrup	60 mL
2 tbsp	butter, melted	30 mL
1/4 cup	all-purpose flour	60 mL
1/2 tsp	baking powder	2 mL
1 cup	coarsely chopped pecans	250 mL
3/4 cup	sliced hazelnuts	175 mL
2/3 cup	coarsely chopped walnuts	150 mL

1. *Crust:* In a bowl, using an electric mixer on medium speed, beat butter and brown sugar until smooth and creamy. On low speed, beat in flour until thoroughly blended and crumbly. Press evenly into prepared pan. Bake in preheated oven until golden around edges, 12 to 15 minutes.

2. *Topping:* In a bowl, whisk eggs, brown sugar, maple syrup and melted butter until smoothly blended. Whisk in flour and baking powder. Mix well. Stir in pecans, hazelnuts and walnuts. Spread evenly over warm crust.

3. Return to oven and bake until topping is set, 20 to 25 minutes. Let cool completely in pan on rack. Cut into bars.

Variation

Use the same quantities of your favorite combination of nuts. To make the texture more interesting, use a combination of sliced and chopped nuts.

Caramel Peanut Squares

Dieters, beware. These are definitely not on your list.

MAKES 24 SQUARES (see Cutting Guide, page 10)

- **Preparation: 15 minutes**
- **Baking: 35 minutes**
- **Freezing: excellent**

TIPS

Look for good-quality caramel sauce that's thick and has a rich caramel flavor. If it's thin, add an additional 1 tbsp (15 mL) flour.

I like to use salted peanuts in this recipe because the salt complements the caramel flavor. But if you're trying to decrease your salt intake, unsalted peanuts work well, too.

- **Preheat oven to 350°F (180°C)**
- **13- by 9-inch (3 L) cake pan, greased**

1 2/3 cups	all-purpose flour, divided	400 mL
2/3 cup	quick-cooking rolled oats	150 mL
1/2 cup	packed brown sugar	125 mL
3/4 tsp	baking soda	3 mL
1/2 cup	butter, melted	125 mL
1 1/2 cups	caramel sundae sauce	375 mL
1 2/3 cups	peanut butter chips	400 mL
1 cup	coarsely chopped peanuts	250 mL

1. In a bowl, combine 1 1/3 cups (325 mL) of the flour, oats, brown sugar and baking soda. Stir well. Stir in melted butter, mixing well. Press evenly into prepared pan. Bake in preheated oven until edges are lightly browned, about 10 minutes.

2. In another bowl, combine caramel sauce and remaining 1/3 cup (75 mL) of the flour, mixing until smooth. Sprinkle peanut butter chips and chopped peanuts over warm crust. Drizzle caramel mixture evenly over top.

3. Return to oven and bake until bubbly and browned, 20 to 25 minutes. Let cool completely in pan on rack. Cut into squares.

Chocolate-Glazed Almond Squares

These squares combine two favorites — cookies and candy. It's no wonder they don't last long.

MAKES 16 TO 36 SQUARES
(see Cutting Guide, page 10)

- **Preparation: 25 minutes**
- **Baking: 27 minutes**
- **Freezing: excellent**

TIPS

Corn syrup comes in white and golden colors. The white is used mainly for candy making while the golden is used for baking.

To cut bars neatly, use a sharp knife in a gentle sawing motion to avoid squashing the filling.

- **Preheat oven to 350°F (180°C)**
- **8-inch (2 L) square cake pan, greased**

CRUST

1/4 cup	butter, softened	60 mL
2/3 cup	confectioners' (icing) sugar, sifted	150 mL
1/2 cup	ground almonds	125 mL
1/4 cup	all-purpose flour	60 mL

TOPPING

1/3 cup	butter	75 mL
1/2 cup	packed brown sugar	125 mL
1/2 cup	corn syrup (see Tips, left)	125 mL
1 tbsp	water	15 mL
1 tbsp	freshly squeezed lemon juice	15 mL
3/4 cup	sliced almonds	175 mL
1/4 tsp	almond extract	1 mL

GLAZE, OPTIONAL

1	square (1 oz/28 g) semisweet chocolate, chopped	1
1 tbsp	butter	15 mL

1. *Crust:* In a bowl, using an electric mixer on medium speed, beat butter and confectioners' sugar until creamy. On low speed, beat in ground almonds and flour, mixing until crumbly. Press evenly into prepared pan. Bake in preheated oven until golden around the edges, 10 to 12 minutes.

2. *Topping:* In a saucepan, melt butter over medium heat. Add brown sugar, corn syrup, water and lemon juice, whisking until smooth. Bring to a boil over medium-high heat and boil for 3 minutes, stirring constantly, until thickened. Remove from heat. Stir in almonds and almond extract. Spread evenly over crust.

3. Return to oven and bake until topping is set and golden, about 15 minutes. Let cool completely in pan on rack.

4. *Glaze (if using):* In a saucepan over low heat, melt chocolate and butter, stirring until smooth. Drizzle over topping. Let cool until chocolate is set, about 30 minutes. Cut into squares.

Apple Pecan Bars

These bars remind me of an apple nut cake in bite-size form. It's nice to be able to pop them in your mouth without having to use a plate and fork.

MAKES 18 TO 48 BARS (see Cutting Guide, page 10)

- **Preparation: 20 minutes**
- **Baking: 35 minutes**
- **Freezing: excellent**

TIPS

Choose apples that are best for baking. Apples that are too wet, like McIntosh, will make your bars too gooey. Firmer apples, such as Granny Smith, Northern Spy and Spartan, work well for baking.

Using the largest holes on a box grater, grate the apple fairly coarsely for use in this recipe. Since the apple will turn brown quickly when exposed to air, grate it just before using.

- **Preheat oven to 350°F (180°C)**
- **9-inch (2.5 L) square cake pan, greased**

6 tbsp	butter	90 mL
1 cup	packed brown sugar	250 mL
2	eggs	2
1 cup	all-purpose flour	250 mL
1 tsp	baking powder	5 mL
3/4 tsp	ground cinnamon	3 mL
1/4 tsp	salt	1 mL
1/4 tsp	ground nutmeg	1 mL
3/4 cup	chopped pecans	175 mL
1	medium apple, peeled and coarsely grated (see Tips, left)	1

1. In a large saucepan, melt butter over medium heat. Stir in brown sugar. Bring mixture to a boil, stirring often. Remove from heat and let cool to room temperature. Add eggs, one at a time, whisking until smooth.

2. Combine flour, baking powder, cinnamon, salt and nutmeg. Add to saucepan, mixing until smooth. Stir in pecans and grated apple, mixing well. Spread evenly in prepared pan.

3. Bake in preheated oven until a toothpick inserted in center comes out clean, 25 to 35 minutes. Let cool completely in pan on rack. Cut into bars.

Variations

Replace the apple with a pear.

Dried cranberries are a nice touch in autumn. Add 1/2 cup (125 mL) to the batter.

Applesauce Praline Bars

Not only does applesauce give these bars a great flavor, but it also helps to keep them moist. In fact, they actually taste better the second day. The crunchy praline topping is the crowning touch.

MAKES 20 TO 54 BARS (see Cutting Guide, page 10)

- **Preparation: 25 minutes**
- **Baking: 35 minutes**
- **Freezing: excellent**

TIPS

Peel and chop apples just before using, to prevent them from turning brown.

Golden Delicious apples work particularly well in these bars.

This recipe works well with chunky applesauce, so homemade is ideal. Use unsweetened applesauce since there's already sugar in the batter. If your applesauce is sweetened, decrease the amount of sugar in the batter to 1/3 cup (75 mL).

- **Preheat oven to 350°F (180°C)**
- **13- by 9-inch (3 L) cake pan, greased**

BATTER

1/4 cup	butter, softened	60 mL
1/2 cup	packed brown sugar	125 mL
1	egg	1
1 tsp	vanilla	5 mL
1 cup	unsweetened applesauce (see Tips, left)	250 mL
1 1/2 cups	all-purpose flour	375 mL
1 tsp	cinnamon	5 mL
1/2 tsp	baking powder	2 mL
1/2 tsp	baking soda	2 mL
1/4 tsp	ground cloves	1 mL
1/4 tsp	salt	1 mL
1 1/2 cups	chopped, peeled apples (2 large apples)	375 mL
2/3 cup	chopped pecans	150 mL

TOPPING

2/3 cup	packed brown sugar	150 mL
3 tbsp	butter, softened	45 mL
1 tbsp	all-purpose flour	15 mL
1 tsp	cinnamon	5 mL
1 cup	chopped pecans	250 mL

1. *Batter:* In a bowl, using an electric mixer on medium speed, beat butter and brown sugar until light and fluffy. Add egg and vanilla, beating well. Stir in applesauce just until blended. (The mixture will look curdled.)

2. Combine flour, cinnamon, baking powder, baking soda, cloves and salt. Add to batter, mixing on low speed just until blended. Stir in apples and pecans. Spread batter evenly in prepared pan.

3. *Topping:* In a bowl, combine brown sugar, butter, flour and cinnamon. Blend with a fork until crumbly. Stir in pecans. Crumble the mixture evenly over batter.

4. Bake in preheated oven until set and golden, 30 to 35 minutes. Let cool completely in pan on rack. Cut into bars.

Toffee Almond Triangles

◆

The crisp, candy-like oatmeal crust is a perfect match for the thin caramel almond top.

MAKES 48 TRIANGLES (see Cutting Guide, page 10)

- **Preparation: 20 minutes**
- **Cooking: 2 minutes**
- **Baking: 32 minutes**
- **Freezing: excellent**

TIP

When deciding on bars and squares to include on an assorted cookie tray or in a gift box, look for a variety of textures, colors and shapes. That way, you're sure to have something that will please everyone.

- **Preheat oven to 350°F (180°C)**
- **13- by 9-inch (3 L) cake pan, greased**

CRUST

1 cup	all-purpose flour	250 mL
1 cup	quick-cooking rolled oats	250 mL
1 cup	packed brown sugar	250 mL
1 tsp	baking soda	5 mL
1/2 cup	cold butter, cubed	125 mL

TOPPING

1/2 cup	corn syrup	125 mL
1/3 cup	packed brown sugar	75 mL
1/4 cup	butter	60 mL
1/4 cup	whipping (35%) cream	60 mL
1 2/3 cups	sliced almonds	400 mL
1 tsp	vanilla	5 mL

1. *Crust:* In a food processor fitted with a metal blade, combine flour, oats, brown sugar, baking soda and butter. Process until crumbly. Press evenly into prepared pan. Bake in preheated oven until golden around the edges, 10 to 12 minutes.

2. *Topping:* In a heavy saucepan over medium-high heat, combine corn syrup, brown sugar, butter and whipping cream. Cook, stirring, until mixture boils. Remove from heat. Stir in almonds and vanilla. Pour over crust, using a spatula or the back of a spoon to spread evenly.

3. Return to oven and bake until topping is bubbly, 15 to 20 minutes. Let cool completely in pan on rack. Cut into squares, then triangles.

Variations

You can also make the crust using half all-purpose and half whole wheat flour.

For a less rich, more intense caramel flavor, replace the whipping cream with evaporated milk.

Bite-Size Pecan Pie

I love pecan pie, but because it's so rich, I always feel guilty eating an entire piece. Enjoying it in smaller bites in these squares makes me feel less self-indulgent.

MAKES 16 TO 36 SQUARES
(see Cutting Guide, page 10)

- **Preparation: 20 minutes**
- **Baking: 47 minutes**
- **Freezing: excellent**

TIPS

Bars like these, with a slightly soft topping, will be easier to cut if they're cold.

Use a sharp serrated knife in a sawing motion to cut neat pieces.

If you like the filling a little gooey, underbake slightly. Bake a little longer for a firmer texture.

- **Preheat oven to 350°F (180°C)**
- **9-inch (2.5 L) square cake pan, greased**

CRUST

1⅓ cups	all-purpose flour	325 mL
3 tbsp	granulated sugar	45 mL
½ cup	cold butter, cubed	125 mL

TOPPING

2	eggs	2
½ cup	granulated sugar	125 mL
½ cup	corn syrup	125 mL
2 tbsp	butter, melted	30 mL
1¾ cups	coarsely chopped pecans	425 mL

1. *Crust:* In a bowl, combine flour and sugar. Using a pastry blender, 2 knives or your fingers, cut in butter until mixture resembles coarse crumbs. Press evenly into prepared pan. Bake in preheated oven until golden around the edges, 10 to 12 minutes.

2. *Topping:* In a bowl, whisk eggs, sugar, corn syrup and melted butter until smoothly blended. Stir in pecans. Pour evenly over crust.

3. Return to oven and bake until set and golden, 25 to 35 minutes. Let cool completely in pan on rack. Cut into squares.

Variations

Replace pecans with walnuts and half of the corn syrup with pure maple syrup.

Decrease pecans to 1¼ cups (300 mL) and add ½ cup (125 mL) dried cranberries or raisins.

Chewy Toffee Almond Squares

◆

These bars have a delicate candy-like base and a crunchy layer of sliced almonds covered by a thin, chewy caramel coating. It's a mouthwatering combination.

MAKES 24 SQUARES (see Cutting Guide, page 10)

- **Preparation: 20 minutes**
- **Cooking: 12 minutes**
- **Baking: 30 minutes**
- **Freezing: excellent**

TIPS

Toffee bits are available in bags. They're broken pieces of the toffee part of Heath or Skor bars (no chocolate).

I have specified sweetened coconut because it seems to be more readily available than the unsweetened variety. But sweetened and unsweetened coconut can be used interchangeably in any recipe to suit your preference.

If your coconut seems dry, sprinkle it with a little milk and let it stand until softened.

- **Preheat oven to 350°F (180°C)**
- **13- by 9-inch (3 L) cake pan, greased**

CRUST

1 cup	butter, softened	250 mL
½ cup	granulated sugar	125 mL
2 cups	all-purpose flour	500 mL

TOPPING

1⅓ cups	toffee bits (see Tips, left)	325 mL
¾ cup	corn syrup	175 mL
1 cup	sliced almonds, divided	250 mL
¾ cup	sweetened flaked coconut, divided (see Tips, left)	175 mL

1. *Crust:* In a bowl, using an electric mixer on medium speed, beat butter and sugar until smooth, about 2 minutes. On low speed, gradually add flour, beating until well blended and crumbly. Press evenly into prepared pan. Bake in preheated oven until edges are lightly browned, 12 to 15 minutes.

2. *Topping:* In a saucepan over medium heat, combine toffee bits and corn syrup. Cook, stirring constantly, until toffee is melted, about 12 minutes. Stir in ½ cup (125 mL) of the almonds and ½ cup (125 mL) of the coconut. Spread evenly over crust, leaving ½-inch (1 cm) border of crust. Sprinkle remaining almonds and coconut over top.

3. Return to oven and bake until bubbly and golden, about 15 minutes. Let cool completely in pan on rack. Cut into squares.

Variations

Cut these squares into triangles for an interesting alternative shape.

Use unblanched sliced almonds for an attractive top. The taste is the same as the blanched variety, but I like the contrasting colors.

Apricot Pecan Bars

A tender shortbread crust, a layer of apricot jam and crunchy but chewy pecan meringue make one great bar.

MAKES 18 TO 48 BARS (see Cutting Guide, page 10)

- **Preparation: 25 minutes**
- **Baking: 37 minutes**
- **Freezing: excellent**

TIPS

When making meringue, be sure your bowl and beaters are clean and free of any trace of grease. Otherwise, your egg whites won't stiffen.

When beating egg whites, have them at room temperature to ensure the best volume.

To fancy these up, drizzle melted chocolate over top.

- **Preheat oven to 350°F (180°C)**
- **9-inch (2.5 L) square cake pan, greased**

CRUST

½ cup	butter, softened	125 mL
½ cup	confectioners' (icing) sugar, sifted	125 mL
2	egg yolks	2
1¼ cups	all-purpose flour	300 mL

TOPPING

¾ cup	apricot jam	175 mL
2	egg whites	2
Pinch	cream of tartar	Pinch
½ cup	granulated sugar	125 mL
1¼ cups	ground toasted pecans	300 mL

1. *Crust:* In a bowl, using an electric mixer on medium speed, beat butter, confectioners' sugar and egg yolks until smooth. Gradually add flour, mixing on low speed until well blended. Press firmly into prepared pan. Bake in preheated oven until golden around edges, 10 to 12 minutes. Let cool for 15 minutes.

2. *Topping:* Spread jam evenly over crust. In a bowl, using an electric mixer on high speed, beat egg whites and cream of tartar until soft peaks form. Gradually add sugar, beating until stiff peaks form. Fold in pecans. Drop by spoonfuls on top of jam and spread carefully to edges.

3. Return to oven and bake until lightly browned, 20 to 25 minutes. Let cool completely in pan on rack. Cut into bars.

Variation

Other kinds of jam, such as marmalade and peach, also work well in this recipe.

Caramel Cappuccino Bars

The combination of coffee flavor and crunchy toffee bits makes these bars an outstanding coffee time treat.

MAKES 20 TO 54 BARS (see Cutting Guide, page 10)

- **Preparation: 25 minutes**
- **Baking: 45 minutes**
- **Freezing: excellent**

TIPS

My favorite brand of toffee bits is Skor bits and I like to buy them in bulk. Others, such as Heath bits, are also available in bulk.

If you don't have instant espresso coffee powder, use double the amount of regular instant coffee granules. Use the back of a spoon to grind them to a fine powder before combining with water.

I prefer to leave the coffee powder dry in the crust, but you can dissolve it in 2 tsp (10 mL) hot water if you prefer.

To make a wonderful Valentine gift, cut these bars into heart shapes using a cookie cutter.

- **Preheat oven to 325°F (160°C)**
- **13- by 9-inch (3 L) cake pan, greased**

CRUST

½ cup	butter, softened	125 mL
¾ cup	packed brown sugar	175 mL
2 tsp	instant espresso coffee powder (see Tips, left)	10 mL
1 ¼ cups	all-purpose flour	300 mL
⅓ cup	ground almonds	75 mL
⅔ cup	toffee bits (see Tips, left)	150 mL

TOPPING

1 tbsp	instant espresso coffee powder	15 mL
2 tsp	hot water	10 mL
1 cup	granulated sugar	250 mL
⅔ cup	sweetened condensed milk	150 mL
3	eggs	3
2 tbsp	all-purpose flour	30 mL
½ tsp	baking powder	2 mL
⅓ cup	toffee bits	75 mL
¼ cup	finely chopped almonds	60 mL

1. *Crust:* In a bowl, using an electric mixer on medium speed, beat butter, brown sugar and coffee powder until light and creamy. Add flour and ground almonds and mix on low speed until thoroughly blended. Press evenly into prepared pan. Sprinkle toffee bits evenly over crust. Press in lightly. Bake in preheated oven until lightly browned all over, 12 to 15 minutes.

2. *Topping:* In a bowl, dissolve espresso powder in hot water. Whisk in sugar, sweetened condensed milk and eggs until smooth. Whisk in flour and baking powder, mixing well. Pour evenly over crust.

3. Return to oven and bake until topping is golden, 25 to 30 minutes. Remove from oven and immediately sprinkle toffee bits and almonds evenly over top. Let cool completely in pan on rack. Cut into bars.

Variation

If you prefer a milder coffee flavor, use half the suggested amount of espresso coffee powder.

Chewy Cherry Date and Nut Bars

The combination of dates and nuts has been popular for years. They fit into the "comfort food" category, and so do these bars.

MAKES 20 TO 54 BARS
(see Cutting Guide, page 10)

- **Preparation: 30 minutes**
- **Baking: 40 minutes**
- **Chilling: 1 hour**
- **Freezing: excellent**

TIPS

For a bar that's less sweet, omit the frosting and dust lightly with confectioners' (icing) sugar.

The easiest way to cut dates is to use kitchen shears sprayed with cooking spray. Be sure your dates are soft. They'll be easier to cut and taste better in your baking.

Confectioners' (icing) sugar is often lumpy. Measure it, then sift it in a sifter or sieve before adding to your other ingredients.

For dusting confectioners' (icing) sugar over a bar, use a small sieve with a very fine mesh.

- **Preheat oven to 350°F (180°C)**
- **13- by 9-inch (3 L) cake pan, greased**

CRUST

¾ cup	butter, softened	175 mL
½ cup	granulated sugar	125 mL
2 cups	all-purpose flour	500 mL

FILLING

2	eggs	2
1½ cups	packed brown sugar	375 mL
1 tsp	vanilla	5 mL
2 tbsp	all-purpose flour	30 mL
½ tsp	baking powder	2 mL
1¼ cups	chopped walnuts, toasted	300 mL
1 cup	candied (glacé) cherries, quartered	250 mL
½ cup	chopped dates	125 mL

FROSTING

½ cup	butter, softened	125 mL
2 cups	confectioners' (icing) sugar, sifted	500 mL
2 tbsp	milk	30 mL
1 tbsp	freshly squeezed lemon juice	15 mL

1. *Crust:* In a bowl, using an electric mixer on medium speed, beat butter and sugar until creamy. Beat in flour, mixing until crumbly. Press evenly into prepared pan. Bake in preheated oven until golden all over, 12 to 15 minutes. Let cool in pan on rack.

2. *Filling:* In a bowl, whisk eggs, brown sugar and vanilla until blended. Whisk in flour and baking powder, mixing until smooth. Stir in walnuts, cherries and dates. Spread evenly over cooled crust.

3. Return to oven and bake until top is set and golden, 20 to 25 minutes. Let cool completely in pan on rack.

4. *Frosting:* In a bowl, using an electric mixer on medium speed, beat butter, half of the confectioners' sugar, milk and lemon juice until light and creamy. Gradually add remaining confectioners' sugar, beating until smooth. Spread evenly over cooled filling. Refrigerate until frosting is firm, about 1 hour. Cut into bars.

Double Almond Strawberry Jam Squares

These bars are an example of how the simplest things often taste the best.

MAKES 16 TO 36 SQUARES
(see Cutting Guide, page 10)

- Preparation: 25 minutes
- Baking: 45 minutes
- Freezing: excellent

TIPS

For the best flavor, grind nuts just before using.

If you prefer, use unbleached flour in all your baking. Unbleached and regular all-purpose flours are interchangeable.

- **Preheat oven to 350°F (180°C)**
- **9-inch (2.5 L) square cake pan, greased**

CRUST

1 cup	all-purpose flour	250 mL
¼ cup	confectioners' (icing) sugar, sifted	60 mL
½ cup	cold butter, cubed	125 mL
¼ cup	ground almonds	60 mL

TOPPING

¾ cup	firmly packed ground almonds	175 mL
⅓ cup	granulated sugar	75 mL
2 tbsp	butter, softened	30 mL
1	egg	1
½ tsp	almond extract	2 mL
1 tbsp	all-purpose flour	15 mL
¾ cup	strawberry jam	175 mL
¾ cup	sliced almonds	175 mL

1. *Crust:* In a bowl, combine flour and confectioners' sugar. Using a pastry blender, 2 knives or your fingers, cut in butter until mixture resembles coarse crumbs. Press evenly into bottom of prepared pan. Bake in preheated oven until golden all over, 12 to 15 minutes. Let cool for 15 minutes.

2. *Topping:* In a bowl, combine ground almonds, sugar, butter, egg and almond extract. Using a wooden spoon, mix until smooth. Stir in flour. Spread jam evenly over base. Drop topping by spoonfuls over jam and, using a spatula or the back of a spoon, spread evenly. Sprinkle sliced almonds evenly over top.

3. Return to oven and bake until set and golden, 25 to 30 minutes. Let cool completely in pan on rack. Cut into squares.

> **Variation**
> Replace strawberry jam with apricot or blueberry.

Frosted Carrot Nut Bars

Here's a great way to enjoy carrot cake in a bite-size form.

MAKES 18 TO 48 BARS (see Cutting Guide, page 10)

- **Preparation: 25 minutes**
- **Baking: 30 minutes**
- **Freezing: excellent**

TIPS

To ease cleanup, rather than combining the dry ingredients in a bowl, place a large piece of waxed paper on the counter. Spread the flour on the paper. Sprinkle with the baking soda, cinnamon, nutmeg and cloves. Using the paper as a funnel, transfer the dry ingredients to the chocolate mixture.

Minimizing the number of times you open the oven door and the amount of time you keep it open helps maintain the oven temperature, which is important to successful baking.

- **Preheat oven to 350°F (180°C)**
- **9-inch (2.5 L) square cake pan, greased**

BAR

¼ cup	butter, softened	60 mL
⅔ cup	packed brown sugar	150 mL
1	egg	1
1 tsp	vanilla	5 mL
1 cup	all-purpose flour	250 mL
1 tsp	baking soda	5 mL
¾ tsp	ground cinnamon	3 mL
¼ tsp	ground nutmeg	1 mL
¼ tsp	ground cloves	1 mL
1 cup	shredded carrots	250 mL
½ cup	chopped walnuts	125 mL

FROSTING

1½ cups	confectioners' (icing) sugar, sifted	375 mL
¼ cup	butter, softened	60 mL
1 tsp	grated lemon zest	5 mL
1 to 2 tbsp	milk	15 to 30 mL
¼ cup	finely chopped walnuts	60 mL

1. *Bar:* In a bowl, using an electric mixer on medium speed, beat butter, brown sugar, egg and vanilla until light and creamy, about 3 minutes. Combine flour, baking soda, cinnamon, nutmeg and cloves. Stir into butter mixture, mixing well. Stir in carrots and walnuts. Spread evenly in prepared pan.

2. Bake in preheated oven until a toothpick inserted in center comes out clean, 25 to 30 minutes. Let cool completely in pan on rack.

3. *Frosting:* In a bowl, using an electric mixer on medium speed, beat confectioners' sugar, butter and lemon zest, adding just enough milk to make a smooth, spreadable consistency. Spread evenly over cooled bar. Sprinkle walnuts evenly over top. Cut into bars.

Variation

Replace walnuts with dried cranberries.

Raspberry Coconut Walnut Bars

These are a bit chewy and a little gooey, but a big success. They look messy when cut, but that's why they're so delicious.

MAKES 18 TO 48 BARS (see Cutting Guide, page 10)

- **Preparation: 25 minutes**
- **Baking: 37 minutes**
- **Freezing: excellent**

(see Cutting Guide, page 10)

TIPS

The jam will ooze during baking. Line the pan completely with parchment paper (overhanging the sides), so the bars will be easy to remove.

Combine crust ingredients in a food processor for convenience.

Store nuts in the freezer to retain their freshness. Label the package with the date so you'll be sure to rotate the containers and use in order.

- **Preheat oven to 425°F (220°C)**
- **9-inch (2.5 L) square cake pan, lined with parchment paper**

CRUST

1 ⅓ cups	all-purpose flour	325 mL
⅓ cup	packed brown sugar	75 mL
½ tsp	baking powder	2 mL
½ cup	cold butter, cubed	125 mL
1	egg, beaten	1

TOPPING

⅓ cup	raspberry jam	75 mL
2	eggs	2
1 cup	packed brown sugar	250 mL
¾ cup	chopped walnuts	175 mL
¾ cup	sweetened flaked coconut	175 mL
2 tbsp	all-purpose flour	30 mL
2 tsp	freshly squeezed lemon juice	10 mL
1 tsp	baking powder	5 mL

1. *Crust:* In a bowl, combine flour, brown sugar and baking powder. Using a pastry blender, 2 knives or your fingers, cut in butter until mixture resembles coarse crumbs. Add egg and, using a fork, mix thoroughly until moistened. Press mixture evenly into prepared pan. Bake in preheated oven until golden around the edges, 10 to 12 minutes. Reduce oven temperature to 350°F (180°C).

2. *Topping:* Spread jam evenly over crust, leaving a ½-inch (1 cm) border of crust. In a bowl, whisk eggs and brown sugar until blended. Stir in walnuts, coconut, flour, lemon juice and baking powder, mixing well. Spread evenly over jam.

3. Return to oven and bake until topping is set and golden, 20 to 25 minutes. Let cool completely in pan on rack. Cut into bars.

Variations

Strawberry and apricot jam work well in these bars.

Replace flaked coconut with shredded coconut for a different texture.

Cranberry Raspberry Almond Bars

With their bright red filling, these bars are a great choice for holiday baking. The large pan makes a lot of bars, but they keep and freeze well, allowing you to get a head start on the festive season.

MAKES 36 TO 48 BARS
(see Cutting Guide, page 10)

- **Preparation: 25 minutes**
- **Baking: 37 minutes**
- **Freezing: excellent**

TIPS

If you're using frozen cranberries, pat them dry with paper towel to eliminate excess moisture.

Buy good-quality jam. The flavor of this bar is highly dependent on the jam.

You can use regular jam in place of seedless, but the flavor will not be as robust.

When jam is baked, the sugar caramelizes, causing it to stick to the pan. This makes cleanup difficult. Leaving a small border of crust around the jam helps alleviate this problem.

- **Preheat oven to 350°F (180°C)**
- **15- by 10- by 1-inch (2 L) jelly roll pan, greased**

CRUST

2 cups	quick-cooking rolled oats	500 mL
1 1/4 cups	all-purpose flour	300 mL
1/3 cup	ground almonds	75 mL
1 1/3 cups	packed brown sugar	325 mL
1 tsp	baking powder	5 mL
1/2 tsp	baking soda	2 mL
1 cup	cold butter, cubed	250 mL

FILLING

1 1/2 cups	seedless raspberry jam (see Tips, left)	375 mL
1 cup	fresh or frozen (thawed) cranberries	250 mL
1 tbsp	grated lemon zest	15 mL

TOPPING

1 1/4 cups	sliced almonds	300 mL

1. *Crust:* In a bowl, combine oats, flour, ground almonds, brown sugar, baking powder and baking soda. Using a pastry blender, 2 knives or your fingers, cut in butter until mixture resembles coarse crumbs. Set 1 1/4 cups (300 mL) aside for topping. Press remainder evenly into prepared pan. Bake in preheated oven until golden around edges, 10 to 12 minutes.

2. *Filling:* In a bowl, combine jam, cranberries and lemon zest. Drop spoonfuls over crust. Spread evenly, leaving a 1/2-inch (1 cm) border of crust.

3. *Topping:* Stir almonds into reserved crumb mixture. Sprinkle over filling. Return to oven and bake until golden, 20 to 25 minutes. Let cool completely in pan on rack. Cut into bars.

Variation

Other flavors of jam, such as strawberry, cherry or blueberry, also work well in this recipe.

Lemon Almond Bars

Here's a traditional favorite, but with a touch of almonds. It's an exquisite combination.

MAKES 20 TO 54 BARS (see Cutting Guide, page 10)

- **Preparation: 15 minutes**
- **Baking: 45 minutes**
- **Freezing: excellent**

TIPS

Lemons often contain a lot of seeds, so be sure to strain the juice before using.

A medium lemon yields 2 to 3 tbsp (30 to 45 mL) juice and 1 tbsp (15 mL) zest.

- **Preheat oven to 350°F (180°C)**
- **13- by 9-inch (3 L) cake pan, greased**

ALMOND CRUST

1¾ cups	all-purpose flour	425 mL
⅔ cup	ground almonds	150 mL
⅓ cup	granulated sugar	75 mL
1 cup	cold butter, cubed	250 mL

TOPPING

4	eggs	4
2 cups	granulated sugar	500 mL
2 tsp	grated lemon zest	10 mL
⅓ cup	freshly squeezed lemon juice	75 mL
¼ cup	all-purpose flour	60 mL
1 tsp	baking powder	5 mL
	Confectioners' (icing) sugar, optional	

1. *Almond Crust:* In a bowl, combine flour, almonds and sugar. Using a pastry blender, 2 knives or your fingers, cut in butter until mixture resembles coarse crumbs. Press evenly into prepared pan. Bake in preheated oven until golden around edges, 12 to 15 minutes. Let cool in pan on rack for 10 minutes.

2. *Topping:* In a bowl, whisk eggs, sugar, lemon zest and juice until blended. Combine flour and baking powder. Whisk into egg mixture, whisking until smooth. Pour over crust.

3. Return to oven and bake just until set and light golden, 25 to 30 minutes. Let cool completely in pan on rack. Cut into bars. Sprinkle with confectioners' sugar before serving, if desired.

Variation

Replace ground almonds with ground hazelnuts.

Apricot Walnut Squares

I love the way the tangy apricots set off the sweet brown sugar topping. The addition of walnuts is, for me, the pièce de résistance, but if you're not a fan, replace them with almonds (see Variations).

MAKES 16 TO 36 SQUARES
(see **Cutting Guide, page 10**)

- **Preparation: 25 minutes**
- **Baking: 47 minutes**
- **Freezing: excellent**

TIP

To chop apricots easily, use kitchen shears. Lightly spray the blades with vegetable oil spray.

- **Preheat oven to 350°F (180°C)**
- **9-inch (2.5 L) cake pan, greased**

1 cup	dried apricots	250 mL
	Boiling water	
CRUST		
1 cup	all-purpose flour	250 mL
1/4 cup	granulated sugar	60 mL
1/2 cup	cold butter, cubed	125 mL
TOPPING		
2	eggs	2
1 cup	packed brown sugar	250 mL
1 tsp	baking powder	5 mL
1/4 tsp	salt	1 mL
1 1/4 tsp	vanilla	6 mL
1 cup	chopped walnuts	250 mL

1. In a small bowl, combine apricots with boiling water to cover. Let stand until apricots are softened, about 15 minutes. Drain well and chop. Set aside.

2. *Crust:* In a food processor fitted with a metal blade, combine flour, sugar and butter. Process until mixture resembles coarse crumbs. Press evenly into prepared pan. Bake in preheated oven until golden around edges, 10 to 12 minutes.

3. *Topping:* In a bowl, whisk eggs, brown sugar, baking powder, salt and vanilla until blended. Stir in walnuts and reserved apricots. Spread evenly over warm crust.

4. Return to oven and bake until set and golden, 30 to 35 minutes. Let cool completely in pan on rack. Cut into squares.

Variations

Replace one-third of the apricots with 1/3 cup (75 mL) dried cranberries.

Replace walnuts with almonds and vanilla with 1/2 tsp (2 mL) almond extract.

Caramel Honey Pecan Bars

There's nothing I'd want to change in these bars, which are a favorite in my family. The honey gives them a special flavor. Making a large pan is a good idea because they go quickly.

**MAKES 40 TO 48 BARS
(see Cutting Guide, page 10)**

- **Preparation: 15 minutes**
- **Cooking: 7 minutes**
- **Baking: 30 minutes**
- **Freezing: excellent**

TIPS

It takes a little extra time, but if you place the pecans right side up before adding the syrup, your squares will be more visually appealing.

Look for large, light-colored pecans, and taste them before using, to ensure they have a fresh, nutty taste. It doesn't make sense to spoil the bar by using nuts that aren't up to par.

- **Preheat oven to 350°F (180°C)**
- **15- by 10- by 1-inch (2 L) jelly roll pan, greased**

CRUST

½ cup	pecan halves	125 mL
2½ cups	all-purpose flour	625 mL
1 cup	cold butter, cubed	250 mL
⅓ cup	granulated sugar	75 mL
1	egg, beaten	1

FILLING

3½ cups	pecan halves	875 mL
¾ cup	butter	175 mL
½ cup	liquid honey	125 mL
¾ cup	packed brown sugar	175 mL
½ tsp	cinnamon	2 mL
¼ cup	whipping (35%) cream	60 mL

1. *Crust*: In a food processor, process pecans until fine. Add flour, butter, sugar and egg. Process until mixture resembles coarse crumbs. Press evenly into prepared pan. Bake in preheated oven until edges are lightly browned, 12 to 15 minutes.

2. *Filling*: Sprinkle pecans evenly over hot crust. Set aside. In a large heavy saucepan over medium-high heat, melt butter and honey. Add brown sugar and cinnamon and boil, stirring constantly, until mixture is a rich caramel color, 5 to 7 minutes. Remove from heat. Stir in whipping cream, mixing well. Pour evenly over pecans.

3. Return to oven and bake until top is bubbly, about 15 minutes. Let cool completely in pan on rack. Cut into bars.

Chunky Chocolate Shortbread and
Lemon Poppy Seed Shortbread

Shortbread

This section was the most surprising to my tasters, who couldn't believe there are so many versions of shortbread. Shortbread has three basic ingredients — butter, flour and sugar. It's amazing how slight variations in the way they're combined can produce such a wide range of tastes and textures.

Shortbread is actually very easy to make. You can mix it by hand for about 5 minutes, or with a wooden spoon or using an electric mixer on medium speed for about 3 minutes. You can also use a food processor or pastry blender, in which case the butter should be cold and cut into 1-inch (2.5 cm) cubes. Most recipes require a bit of kneading to smooth out the dough after mixing.

To get even edges, plain shortbread bars should be cut when they come out of the oven and are still warm, then cut again when they're cool. They tend to break unevenly if they aren't cut until cold. Another unusual element to making shortbread is that the pan is always ungreased — there's so much butter in the dough, it almost greases the pan, preventing sticking. Use a sharp knife to cut shortbread. Store it in a cool, dry place or in the refrigerator for up to 1 month. You can freeze shortbread for up to 3 months, but the texture will change slightly.

You probably have a favorite shortbread recipe — the one you have traditionally enjoyed. But it's fun to try others and compare. I know I changed my "favorite" several times while preparing this chapter. Maybe you will, too.

Chunky Chocolate Shortbread

This crisp shortbread cookie has lots of crunch from the nuts and a great chocolate flavor from the chopped chocolate.

MAKES 20 TO 54 BARS OR 24 SQUARES
(see Cutting Guide, page 10)

- **Preparation: 20 minutes**
- **Baking: 35 minutes**
- **Freezing: excellent**

- **Preheat oven to 350°F (180°C)**
- **13- by 9-inch (3 L) cake pan, ungreased**

1 cup	butter, softened	250 mL
½ cup	superfine granulated sugar (see Tips, page 170)	125 mL
1¾ cups	all-purpose flour	425 mL
¼ cup	cornstarch	60 mL
4	squares (1 oz/28 g each) bittersweet chocolate, coarsely chopped	4
⅔ cup	coarsely chopped pecans, toasted	150 mL

1. In a bowl, beat butter and sugar until light and creamy. Combine flour and cornstarch. Stir into butter mixture, mixing well. Stir in chocolate and pecans. Press evenly into pan.
2. Bake in preheated oven until lightly browned around edges, 30 to 35 minutes. Let cool completely in pan on rack. Cut into bars or squares.

Lemon Poppy Seed Shortbread

The poppy seeds give an interesting crunch and attractive look to these rich, buttery bars.

MAKES 18 TO 48 BARS
(see Cutting Guide, page 10)

- **Preparation: 20 minutes**
- **Baking: 35 minutes**
- **Freezing: excellent**

- **Preheat oven to 300°F (150°C)**
- **9-inch (2.5 L) square cake pan, ungreased**

1 cup	butter, softened	250 mL
1 cup	confectioners' (icing) sugar, sifted	250 mL
2 cups	all-purpose flour	500 mL
2 tbsp	poppy seeds	30 mL
2 tbsp	grated lemon zest	30 mL
1 tbsp	freshly squeezed lemon juice	15 mL
2 tbsp	granulated sugar	30 mL

1. In a bowl, beat butter and confectioners' sugar until light and creamy. Stir in flour, poppy seeds and lemon zest and juice, mixing well. Knead to form a smooth dough. Press evenly into pan. Sprinkle with granulated sugar.
2. Bake in preheated oven until lightly browned around the edges, 30 to 35 minutes. Cut into bars while warm. Let cool completely in pan on rack. Recut.

Hazelnut Shortbread Bars

Hazelnuts have a unique flavor that really shines in a shortbread dough.

MAKES 18 TO 48 BARS (see Cutting Guide, page 10)

- **Preparation: 15 minutes**
- **Baking: 35 minutes**
- **Freezing: excellent**

TIP

There's no substitute for butter when making shortbread.

- **Preheat oven to 300°F (150°C)**
- **9-inch (2.5 L) square cake pan, ungreased**

1 cup	butter, softened	250 mL
½ cup	superfine granulated sugar (see Tips, page 170)	125 mL
1½ cups	all-purpose flour	375 mL
¾ cup	cornstarch	175 mL
½ cup	finely chopped hazelnuts	125 mL

1. In a bowl, using an electric mixer on medium speed, beat butter and sugar until light and creamy, about 3 minutes. Stir in flour, cornstarch and hazelnuts, mixing well. Using your hands, knead to form a smooth dough. Press evenly into pan. Prick surface all over with a fork.
2. Bake in preheated oven until lightly browned, 30 to 35 minutes. Cut into bars just as the pan comes out of the oven, then let cool completely in pan on rack. Recut.

Chocolate Shortbread Bars

Because there are so many chocolate lovers in the world, I've always believed you should have a chocolate version of every cookie to satisfy them all. These bars are thin, crisp and chocolaty.

MAKES 20 TO 54 BARS (see Cutting Guide, page 10)

- **Preparation: 20 minutes**
- **Baking: 40 minutes**
- **Freezing: excellent**

- **Preheat oven to 300°F (150°C)**
- **13- by 9-inch (3.5 L) cake pan, ungreased**

1 cup	butter, softened	250 mL
½ cup	granulated sugar	125 mL
2 cups	all-purpose flour	500 mL
2	squares (1 oz/28 g each) semisweet chocolate, melted and cooled	2

1. In a bowl, using an electric mixer on medium speed, beat butter and sugar until light and creamy, about 3 minutes. Stir in flour, mixing well. Stir in melted chocolate, mixing well. Using your hands, knead to form a smooth dough. Press evenly into pan.
2. Bake in preheated oven until firm and dry, 35 to 40 minutes. Cut into bars just as the pan comes out of the oven, then let cool completely in pan on rack. Recut.

Cornmeal Shortbread

This Italian favorite gets an extra-crunchy texture from cornmeal and almonds. The cornmeal also provides a wonderful yellow color. This is a particularly nice cookie to serve with fresh or stewed fruit.

MAKES 18 TO 48 BARS OR 16 TO 36 SQUARES
(see Cutting Guide, page 10)

- **Preparation: 20 minutes**
- **Baking: 30 minutes**
- **Freezing: excellent**

- **Preheat oven to 350°F (180°C)**
- **9-inch (2.5 L) square cake pan, ungreased**

3/4 cup	whole unblanched almonds	175 mL
1/2 cup	yellow cornmeal	125 mL
1 3/4 cups	all-purpose flour	425 mL
3/4 cup	granulated sugar	175 mL
1 cup	cold butter, cubed	250 mL

1. In a food processor, pulse almonds until coarsely chopped. Add cornmeal, flour, sugar and butter. Pulse until mixture resembles coarse crumbs. Press three-quarters of the dough evenly into pan. Using your fingers, scatter remainder on top.

2. Bake in preheated oven until light golden, 25 to 30 minutes. Cut into bars or squares just as the pan comes out of the oven, then let cool completely in pan on rack. Recut.

Rice Flour Shortbread

This thick, melt-in-your-mouth shortbread is similar to the Scottish shortbread usually baked in rounds or shortbread moulds and cut in wedges.

MAKES 18 TO 48 BARS OR 16 TO 36 SQUARES
(see Cutting Guide, page 10)

- **Preparation: 15 minutes**
- **Baking: 35 minutes**
- **Freezing: excellent**

- **Preheat oven to 300°F (150°C)**
- **8-inch (2 L) square cake pan, ungreased**

1 1/2 cups	all-purpose flour	375 mL
1/3 cup	superfine granulated sugar	75 mL
1/3 cup	rice flour	75 mL
1/4 tsp	salt	1 mL
3/4 cup	cold butter, cubed	175 mL

1. In a bowl, combine all-purpose flour, sugar, rice flour and salt. Using a pastry blender, 2 knives or your fingers, work in butter until mixture resembles coarse crumbs. Knead dough on a lightly floured surface until very smooth, about 5 minutes. Press evenly into pan. Prick surface all over with a fork.

2. Bake in preheated oven until lightly browned around edges, 30 to 35 minutes. Cut into bars or squares just as the pan comes out of the oven, then let cool completely in pan on rack. Recut.

Oatmeal Shortbread

The large-flake oats give this shortbread a wonderful nutty flavor and an appealingly rustic appearance. These cookies taste terrific with a glass of cold milk or a mug of hot chocolate.

MAKES 20 TO 54 BARS OR 24 SQUARES
(see Cutting Guide, page 10)

- **Preparation: 15 minutes**
- **Baking: 30 minutes**
- **Freezing: excellent**

- **Preheat oven to 350°F (180°C)**
- **13- by 9-inch (3 L) cake pan, ungreased**

1 cup	butter, softened	250 mL
2/3 cup	packed brown sugar	150 mL
1 1/2 cups	all-purpose flour	375 mL
1 tsp	ground cinnamon	5 mL
1 1/4 cups	old-fashioned (large-flake) rolled oats	300 mL

1. In a bowl, using an electric mixer on medium speed, beat butter and brown sugar until light and creamy, about 3 minutes. Stir in flour, cinnamon and oats, mixing well. Using your hands, knead to form a smooth dough. Press evenly into pan. Prick surface all over with a fork.

2. Bake in preheated oven until light golden, 25 to 30 minutes. Cut into bars or squares just as the pan comes out of the oven, then let cool completely in pan on rack. Recut.

Brown Sugar Shortbread

When I was growing up, one of our neighbors made shortbread with brown sugar. I remember especially enjoying its nice butterscotch flavor and wonderful melt-in-your-mouth texture.

MAKES 18 TO 48 BARS OR 16 TO 36 SQUARES
(see Cutting Guide, page 10)

- **Preparation: 20 minutes**
- **Baking: 55 minutes**
- **Freezing: excellent**

- **Preheat oven to 300°F (150°C)**
- **9-inch (2.5 L) square cake pan, ungreased**

2 1/4 cups	all-purpose flour	550 mL
3/4 cup	packed dark brown sugar, divided	175 mL
1 cup	cold butter, cubed, divided	250 mL

1. In a bowl, combine flour and 2/3 cup (150 mL) of the sugar. Using a pastry blender, 2 knives or your fingers, cut in 3/4 cup (175 mL) of the butter until mixture resembles coarse crumbs. Melt remaining butter. Work into flour mixture. Using your hands, knead dough on floured surface until smooth, about 2 minutes. Press evenly into pan. Prick surface all over with a fork. Sprinkle remaining brown sugar evenly over top.

2. Bake in preheated oven until light golden, 45 to 55 minutes. Cut into bars or squares just as the pan comes out of the oven, then let cool completely in pan on rack. Recut.

Cherry Pecan Shortbread Squares

◆

Here's a recipe based on a soft shortbread dough. It's enhanced with favorite holiday ingredients — candied cherries and pecans.

MAKES 24 SQUARES (see Cutting Guide, page 10)

- **Preparation: 20 minutes**
- **Baking: 30 minutes**
- **Freezing: excellent**

TIP

When shortbread contains a significant quantity of chunky ingredients, such as the pecans and cherries in this recipe, precutting isn't necessary.

- **Preheat oven to 325°F (160°C)**
- **13- by 9-inch (3 L) cake pan, ungreased**

1 cup	butter, softened	250 mL
2/3 cup	granulated sugar	150 mL
2	egg yolks	2
2 cups	all-purpose flour	500 mL
1 tbsp	grated lemon zest	15 mL
3/4 cup	chopped pecans	175 mL
2/3 cup	chopped red candied (glacé) cherries	150 mL

1. In a bowl, using an electric mixer on medium speed, beat butter, sugar and egg yolks until smooth and creamy. Stir in flour and lemon zest, mixing well. Stir in pecans and cherries, mixing well. Using your hands, knead to form a smooth dough. Press evenly into pan.

2. Bake in preheated oven until lightly browned, 25 to 30 minutes. Let cool completely in pan on rack. Cut into squares.

Variations

Add 4 oz (125 g) chopped bittersweet chocolate to dough.

Replace lemon zest with 1 tsp (5 mL) vanilla.

Cherry Almond Shortbread Bars

The fabulous flavor of almond paste is combined with a crisp crust and the addition of glacé cherries for decoration. All are included in one-step baking, so no last-minute decorating is required.

**MAKES 48 BARS
(see Cutting Guide, page 10)**

- **Preparation: 20 minutes**
- **Baking: 37 minutes**
- **Freezing: excellent**

TIPS

If you prefer, mix the topping in an electric mixer on medium speed for 3 minutes.

If using a mixer, ensure the almond paste is soft and cut into small cubes for easy blending.

If your almond paste seems hard, soften it in a microwave oven on High power for about 30 seconds.

- **Preheat oven to 350°F (180°C)**
- **13- by 9-inch (3 L) cake pan, ungreased**

CRUST

½ cup	butter, softened	125 mL
½ cup	granulated sugar	125 mL
1¼ cups	all-purpose flour	300 mL

TOPPING

7 oz	almond paste	210 g
¼ cup	granulated sugar	60 mL
¼ cup	butter, softened	60 mL
2	eggs	2
¼ tsp	almond extract	1 mL
48	red candied (glacé) cherries	48
2	squares (1 oz/28 g each) semisweet chocolate, melted, optional	2

1. *Crust:* In a bowl, using an electric mixer on medium speed, beat butter and sugar until light and creamy, about 3 minutes. Stir in flour, mixing until thoroughly combined and crumbly. Press evenly into pan. Bake until golden around the edges, 10 to 12 minutes.

2. *Topping:* In a food processor, combine almond paste, sugar, butter, eggs and almond extract. Process until blended and smooth. Spread evenly over crust. Arrange cherries on top in 6 rows of 8, evenly spaced.

3. Bake in preheated oven until set and lightly browned around the edges, 20 to 25 minutes. Cut into bars just as the pan comes out of the oven, then let cool completely in pan on rack. If desired, drizzle with melted chocolate. Let stand until chocolate is set. Recut into bars with a cherry in the center of each.

Variations

Use a mixture of red and green cherries.

Omit chocolate drizzle and sprinkle lightly with confectioners' (icing) sugar.

I like to make these squares with cherries during the holiday season, but if you prefer, you can substitute an equal number of whole blanched almonds, which may be more appropriate at other times of the year.

Almond Spice Shortbread

A hint of spice in the dough and a crunchy almond topping give these bars a wonderful flavor and a texture that's quite different from plain shortbread.

MAKES 20 TO 54 BARS OR 24 SQUARES
(see Cutting Guide, page 10)

- **Preparation: 20 minutes**
- **Baking: 35 minutes**
- **Freezing: excellent**

TIPS

When creaming butter and sugar, it's important to have the butter at the right temperature. It should be a spreadable consistency. If it's too hard, it won't mix to a creamy light texture, and if it's too soft, the dough will be too soft.

Due to the addition of an egg yolk, this dough is a little softer than regular shortbread dough. That's the advantage of bars — the pan holds the shape. Softer dough in cookies will spread out and flatten, resulting in crisp, potentially overbaked cookies.

- **Preheat oven to 300°F (150°C)**
- **13- by 9-inch (3 L) cake pan, ungreased**

1 cup	butter, softened	250 mL
¾ cup	granulated sugar	175 mL
1	egg, separated	1
½ tsp	almond extract	2 mL
2 cups	all-purpose flour	500 mL
1 tsp	cinnamon	5 mL
¼ tsp	ground nutmeg	1 mL
¾ cup	sliced almonds	175 mL

1. In a bowl, using an electric mixer on medium speed, beat butter, sugar, egg yolk and almond extract until smooth and creamy. Stir in flour, cinnamon and nutmeg, mixing well. Using your hands, knead to form a smooth dough. Press evenly into pan.

2. In a bowl, whisk egg white lightly (you don't want it to be frothy). Brush lightly over dough. Sprinkle almonds evenly over top.

3. Bake in preheated oven until light golden all over, 30 to 35 minutes. Cut into bars or squares just as the pan comes out of the oven, then let cool completely in pan on rack. Recut.

Variations

Omit almond extract. Replace almonds with hazelnuts.

Unblanched sliced almonds look nice on these bars. They're available in some bulk food stores.

Ginger Shortbread

Filled with bits of sweet yet tangy crystallized ginger, these buttery bars are a hit with ginger fans. They're perfect with a cup of tea.

MAKES 20 TO 54 BARS OR 24 SQUARES
(see Cutting Guide, page 10)

- **Preparation: 20 minutes**
- **Baking: 25 minutes**
- **Freezing: excellent**

- **Preheat oven to 350°F (180°C)**
- **13- by 9-inch (3 L) cake pan, ungreased**

2¼ cups	all-purpose flour	550 mL
½ cup	packed brown sugar	125 mL
1 tsp	ground ginger	5 mL
½ tsp	baking powder	2 mL
¼ tsp	salt	1 mL
1 cup	butter, softened	250 mL
⅔ cup	finely chopped crystallized ginger	150 mL

1. In a large bowl, combine flour, brown sugar, ground ginger, baking powder and salt. Add butter and, using an electric mixer on low speed, beat until mixture resembles coarse crumbs, about 3 minutes. Stir in crystallized ginger, mixing well. Using your hands, knead to form a smooth dough. Press evenly into pan.

2. Bake in preheated oven until lightly browned, 20 to 25 minutes. Let cool completely in pan on rack (see Tips, page 170). Cut into bars or squares.

Chocolate Ginger Shortbread

Chocolate and ginger are one of my favorite flavor combinations. They're especially delicious in a buttery shortbread dough.

MAKES 18 TO 48 BARS OR 16 TO 36 SQUARES
(see Cutting Guide, page 10)

- **Preparation: 20 minutes**
- **Baking: 45 minutes**
- **Freezing: excellent**

- **Preheat oven to 300°F (150°C)**
- **9-inch (2.5 L) square cake pan, ungreased**

1 cup	butter, softened	250 mL
½ cup	superfine granulated sugar (see Tips, page 170)	125 mL
2 cups	all-purpose flour	500 mL
½ cup	finely chopped crystallized ginger	125 mL
½ cup	chopped milk chocolate (3 oz/84 g)	125 mL

1. In a bowl, using an electric mixer on medium speed, beat butter and sugar until light and creamy. Stir in flour, ginger and chocolate, mixing well. Using your hands, knead to form a smooth dough. Press evenly into pan.

2. Bake in preheated oven until light golden all over, 40 to 45 minutes. Let cool completely in pan on rack (see Tips, page 170). Cut into bars or squares.

Citrus Shortbread Bars

You can leave these bars plain or finish them by dipping the cooled bars in melted chocolate or drizzling melted chocolate on top. Plain or fancy — the choice is yours.

MAKES 36 TO 48 BARS (see Cutting Guide, page 10)

- Preparation: 20 minutes
- Baking: 45 minutes
- Freezing: excellent

- **Preheat oven to 300°F (150°C)**
- **15- by 10- by 1-inch (2 L) jelly roll pan, ungreased**

1 lb	butter, softened	500 g
1 cup	superfine granulated sugar (see Tips, page 170)	250 mL
1 1/2 tbsp	grated lemon zest	22 mL
1 1/2 tbsp	grated orange zest	22 mL
1/2 tsp	salt	2 mL
3 cups	all-purpose flour	750 mL
1 1/2 cups	cornstarch	375 mL

1. In a bowl, using an electric mixer on medium speed, beat butter, sugar, lemon and orange zests and salt until light and creamy. Combine flour and cornstarch. Stir one-third into butter mixture, mixing well. Repeat twice. Using your hands, knead to form a smooth dough. Press evenly into pan. Prick surface all over with a fork.

2. Bake in preheated oven until lightly browned around edges, 40 to 45 minutes. Cut into bars while warm. Let cool completely in pan on rack. Recut.

Mocha Java Shortbread Sticks

The crushed coffee beans add unique crunch and flavor to this shortbread. They're particularly good with a steamy mug of café au lait or cappuccino.

MAKES 48 BARS (see Cutting Guide, page 10)

- Preparation: 20 minutes
- Baking: 40 minutes
- Freezing: excellent

- **Preheat oven to 325°F (160°C)**
- **9-inch (2.5 L) square cake pan, ungreased**

1 cup	butter, softened	250 mL
1/2 cup	granulated sugar	125 mL
2 cups	all-purpose flour	500 mL
2 tbsp	cornstarch	30 mL
3 tbsp	coffee beans, crushed	45 mL

1. In a bowl, using an electric mixer on medium speed, beat butter and sugar until light and creamy, about 3 minutes. Stir in flour, cornstarch and crushed coffee beans, mixing well. Using your hands, knead to form a smooth dough. Press evenly into pan.

2. Bake in preheated oven until lightly browned around edges, 35 to 40 minutes. Cut into thin bars while warm. Let cool completely in pan on rack. Recut.

Chocolate-Dipped Peanut Butter Chocolate Shortbread Sticks

The great thing about making shortbread bars is that one large pan makes a large quantity with a minimum amount of work. They taste every bit as good as those you roll out and cut individually.

MAKES 48 BARS
(see Cutting Guide, page 10)

- **Preparation: 20 minutes**
- **Baking: 15 minutes**
- **Freezing: excellent**

TIPS

Coating or moulding chocolate, sold in wafer shapes in bulk stores and cake supply stores, is ideal for dipping. It hardens quickly and, unlike real chocolate, doesn't melt after it's on the product. It tastes great, too.

For an attractive presentation, cut these bars into triangles, dip the base in chocolate and sprinkle finely chopped peanuts on top.

- **Preheat oven to 375°F (190°C)**
- **15- by 10- by 1-inch (2 L) jelly roll pan, ungreased**

SHORTBREAD

³⁄₄ cup	butter, softened	175 mL
¹⁄₃ cup	creamy peanut butter	75 mL
¹⁄₃ cup	granulated sugar	75 mL
¹⁄₃ cup	packed brown sugar	75 mL
2 cups	all-purpose flour	500 mL
³⁄₄ cup	miniature semisweet chocolate chips	175 mL

CHOCOLATE DIP

1¹⁄₃ cups	semisweet chocolate chips	325 mL
2 tbsp	vegetable oil	30 mL

1. *Shortbread:* In a bowl, using an electric mixer on medium speed, beat butter, peanut butter and granulated and brown sugars until smooth and creamy, about 3 minutes. Stir in flour, mixing well. Using your hands, knead to form a smooth dough. Stir in chocolate chips. Press evenly into pan.

2. Bake in preheated oven until lightly browned around edges, 12 to 15 minutes. Cut into thin bars while warm. Let cool completely in pan on rack. Recut.

3. *Chocolate Dip:* In a small saucepan, combine chocolate chips and oil. Heat over low heat, stirring constantly, until chocolate is melted and mixture is smooth. Dip one or both ends of each bar into chocolate. Place on wire rack over waxed paper. Let stand until chocolate is set, about 1 hour.

Variations

Add ¹⁄₃ cup (75 mL) finely chopped peanuts to the dough.

Make half the quantity of chocolate dip and drizzle it over top of the bars.

White Chocolate Cranberry Shortbread Squares

Tart dried cranberries offset the sweet creamy white chocolate in this delicious and easy-to-make shortbread.

**MAKES 24 SQUARES
(see Cutting Guide, page 10)**

- **Preparation: 20 minutes**
- **Baking: 30 minutes**
- **Freezing: excellent**

(see Cutting Guide, page 10)

TIPS

If you don't have superfine sugar, whirl regular granulated sugar in a blender or food processor until fine.

When shortbread contains a significant quantity of chunky ingredients, precutting isn't necessary.

Unsalted and salted butter are interchangeable in baking. The only difference is the taste. The sweet, delicate flavor of unsalted butter really comes through when butter is the main ingredient.

- **Preheat oven to 350°F (180°C)**
- **13- by 9-inch (3 L) cake pan, ungreased**

SHORTBREAD

1 cup	butter, softened	250 mL
1/2 cup	superfine granulated sugar (see Tips, left)	125 mL
1 1/2 tsp	vanilla	7 mL
2 1/3 cups	all-purpose flour	575 mL
1 cup	chopped dried cranberries	250 mL
3/4 cup	white chocolate chips	175 mL

DRIZZLE

1/2 cup	white chocolate chips	125 mL
2 tsp	vegetable oil	10 mL

1. *Shortbread:* In a bowl, using an electric mixer on medium speed, beat butter, sugar and vanilla until light and creamy. Stir in flour, mixing well. Using your hands, knead to form a smooth dough. Knead in cranberries and white chocolate chips. Press evenly into pan.

2. Bake in preheated oven until lightly browned around the edges, 25 to 30 minutes. Let cool completely in pan on rack (see Tips, left).

3. *Drizzle:* In a small saucepan, heat chocolate and oil over low heat, stirring constantly, until chocolate is melted and mixture is smooth. Drizzle over shortbread. Let stand until chocolate is set. Cut into squares.

Variations

Replace white chocolate with semisweet chocolate chips.

Replace dried cranberries with dried cherries.

Try cherry-flavored cranberries for another great taste.

Cranberry Lemon Shortbread

◆

There's nothing better than the combination of cranberries and lemon. The delicate flavor of buttery shortbread really shows off the taste.

MAKES 20 TO 54 BARS OR 24 SQUARES
(see Cutting Guide, page 10)

- **Preparation: 25 minutes**
- **Baking: 35 minutes**
- **Freezing: excellent**

TIPS

Depending on your food processor, you may not be able to mix the cranberries thoroughly into the dough. If so, remove the dough from the food processor and knead gently with hands to distribute cranberries evenly. Most of the cranberries should be chopped, with a few still in large pieces.

Use a small offset spatula to easily spread frosting or glazes on bars. It gets into the corners nicely.

- **Preheat oven to 300°F (150°C)**
- **13- by 9-inch (3 L) cake pan, ungreased**

SHORTBREAD

¾ cup	cold butter, cubed	175 mL
½ cup	confectioners' (icing) sugar, sifted	125 mL
¼ cup	granulated sugar	60 mL
2 tbsp	grated lemon zest	30 mL
1 tbsp	freshly squeezed lemon juice	15 mL
2 cups	all-purpose flour	500 mL
⅔ cup	dried cranberries	150 mL

GLAZE

1 cup	confectioners' (icing) sugar, sifted	250 mL
1 tsp	grated lemon zest	5 mL
1 tbsp	freshly squeezed lemon juice (approx.)	15 mL

1. *Shortbread:* In a food processor, combine butter, confectioners' sugar, granulated sugar, lemon zest and lemon juice. Process until blended. Add flour. Pulse until mixture resembles coarse crumbs. Add cranberries. Pulse until evenly mixed. Press evenly into pan.

2. Bake in preheated oven until lightly browned around the edges, 30 to 35 minutes. Let cool completely in pan on rack.

3. *Glaze:* In a bowl, whisk confectioners' sugar and lemon zest and juice until smooth. Add a little more lemon juice, if necessary, to make a spreadable consistency. Spread over shortbread. Let stand until glaze sets, about 30 minutes. Cut into bars or squares.

Variations

Omit glaze if desired.

Replace cranberries with dried cherries.

Replace lemon zest and juice with orange.

Nutty Shortbread Bars

These bars, which are not too sweet, have a nice nutty flavor and a very "short" texture.

MAKES 18 TO 48 BARS
(see Cutting Guide, page 10)

- **Preparation: 20 minutes**
- **Baking: 45 minutes**
- **Freezing: excellent**

- **Preheat oven to 300°F (150°C)**
- **9-inch (2.5 L) square cake pan, ungreased**

1 cup	butter, softened	250 mL
1/3 cup	granulated sugar	75 mL
2 tbsp	cornstarch	30 mL
1 tsp	vanilla	5 mL
2 cups	all-purpose flour	500 mL
1/3 cup	finely chopped walnuts	75 mL
1/3 cup	finely chopped pecans	75 mL

1. In a bowl, using an electric mixer on medium speed, beat butter, sugar, cornstarch and vanilla until light and creamy. Stir in flour, walnuts and pecans, mixing well. Using your hands, knead to form a smooth dough. Press evenly into pan.
2. Bake in preheated oven until light golden around edges, 40 to 45 minutes. Cut into bars just as the pan comes out of the oven, then let cool completely in pan on rack. Recut.

Coconut Shortbread Bars

Funny thing — this shortbread was a favorite of friends who claim to hate coconut. The coconut flavor isn't strong, but the texture is crisp, light and tender.

MAKES 20 TO 54 BARS
(see Cutting Guide, page 10)

- **Preparation: 20 minutes**
- **Baking: 40 minutes**
- **Freezing: excellent**

- **Preheat oven to 300°F (150°C)**
- **13- by 9-inch (3 L) cake pan, ungreased**

1 cup	butter, softened	250 mL
1/2 cup	granulated sugar	125 mL
1 tsp	vanilla	5 mL
2 cups	all-purpose flour	500 mL
1/2 cup	rice flour	125 mL
1 cup	sweetened flaked coconut	250 mL

1. In a bowl, using an electric mixer on medium speed, beat butter, sugar and vanilla until smooth and creamy, about 3 minutes. Stir in all-purpose and rice flours and coconut, mixing well. Using your hands, knead to form a smooth dough. Press evenly into pan.
2. Bake in preheated oven until light golden, 35 to 40 minutes. Let cool completely in pan on rack. Cut into bars.

Chocolate Nougat Shortbread

The bars are strong competitors to that all-time favorite, chocolate chip cookies.

MAKES 18 TO 48 BARS (see Cutting Guide, page 10)

- **Preparation: 20 minutes**
- **Baking: 40 minutes**
- **Freezing: excellent**

TIP

You'll need about 6 oz (170 g) chocolate to make ¾ cup (175 mL) coarsely chopped.

- **Preheat oven to 325°F (160°C)**
- **9-inch (2.5 L) square cake pan, ungreased**

1 cup	butter, softened	250 mL
½ cup	superfine granulated sugar (see Tips, page 170)	125 mL
1⅔ cups	all-purpose flour	400 mL
¼ cup	cornstarch	60 mL
¾ cup	coarsely chopped milk chocolate honey almond nougat chocolate bars (such as Toblerone)	175 mL

1. In a bowl, using an electric mixer on medium speed, beat butter and sugar until light and creamy, about 3 minutes. Stir in flour and cornstarch, mixing well. Using your hands, knead to form a smooth dough. Work in chopped chocolate bars with your hands. Press evenly into pan.
2. Bake in preheated oven until lightly browned around the edges, 35 to 40 minutes. Let cool completely in pan on rack. Cut into bars.

Almond Shortbread Squares

Tender but crisp, the crunchy almonds give these squares an unusual texture for shortbread.

MAKES 24 SQUARES (see Cutting Guide, page 10)

- **Preparation: 20 minutes**
- **Baking: 35 minutes**
- **Freezing: excellent**

- **Preheat oven to 325°F (160°C)**
- **13- by 9-inch (3 L) cake pan, ungreased**

¾ cup	sliced almonds, toasted	175 mL
2 cups	all-purpose flour	500 mL
1 cup	cold butter, cubed	250 mL
½ cup	granulated sugar	125 mL
½ cup	cornstarch	125 mL
2 tbsp	grated orange zest	30 mL
¾ tsp	almond extract	3 mL

1. In a food processor, pulse almonds until coarsely chopped. Add flour, butter, sugar, cornstarch, orange zest and almond extract and pulse until crumbly. Press evenly into pan.
2. Bake in preheated oven until lightly browned around edges, 30 to 35 minutes. Cut into squares just as the pan comes out of the oven, then let cool completely in pan on rack. Recut.

Triple-Layer Chocolate Peanut Butter Bars

No-Bake Bars and Squares

In this chapter, I've tried to expand the horizon of no-bake bars beyond the all-time favorite, Rice Krispies Squares. No-bake bars are perfect for hot summer days when it's too hot to turn the oven on. They're also great to make when there's already something in the oven. No-bake bars usually consist of a warm mixture made on top of the stove, mixed with yummy, crunchy ingredients like cereal, nuts, dried fruit and marshmallows. The entire concoction is simply pressed into a pan and left to set for about 30 minutes. All you do is cut to eat.

In most cases, no-bake bars are quick and easy to prepare, with relatively few ingredients, which are readily available. Because they aren't baked and cooking time is short, you get to enjoy them much faster than most bars, which also means they're great to make with kids. And they don't use many dishes, which reduces washing-up time.

No-bake bars are generally cut into larger pieces than baked bars. They are firm and not as delicate or crumbly as baked bars. They usually keep for several weeks without freezing — if they're well hidden.

Triple-Layer Chocolate Peanut Butter Bars

If you're someone who gets cravings for chocolate and peanut butter, these chewy bars fit the bill. Keep a pan in the refrigerator at all times. Just like peanut butter cookies, they're great with a glass of milk.

MAKES 20 TO 54 BARS
(see Cutting Guide, page 10)

- **Preparation: 30 minutes**
- **Cooking: 10 minutes**
- **Chilling: 3 hours**
- **Freezing: excellent**

TIP

Always sift confectioners' (icing) sugar before using to get rid of any lumps that have formed during storage.

- **13- by 9-inch (3 L) cake pan, lined with greased aluminum foil or waxed paper**

BASE

³⁄₄ cup	butter	175 mL
¹⁄₃ cup	granulated sugar	75 mL
¹⁄₃ cup	unsweetened cocoa powder, sifted	75 mL
2	eggs, beaten	2
2¹⁄₂ cups	graham wafer crumbs	625 mL
³⁄₄ cup	sweetened fine or medium coconut	175 mL
³⁄₄ cup	finely chopped peanuts	175 mL

FILLING

1 cup	creamy peanut butter	250 mL
¹⁄₃ cup	butter	75 mL
3 cups	confectioners' (icing) sugar, sifted	750 mL
¹⁄₃ cup	half-and-half (10%) cream	75 mL

TOPPING

8	squares (1 oz/28 g each) semisweet chocolate, chopped	8
3 tbsp	butter	45 mL
¹⁄₂ cup	finely chopped peanuts	125 mL

1. *Base:* In a large heavy saucepan, melt butter over low heat. Add sugar, cocoa and eggs and cook, stirring constantly, until mixture starts to thicken, about 5 minutes. Remove from heat. Stir in graham wafer crumbs, coconut and peanuts, mixing well. Press evenly into prepared pan. Refrigerate until cold, about 30 minutes.

2. *Filling:* Meanwhile, in a clean saucepan over low heat, melt peanut butter and butter, stirring until smooth. Remove from heat. Add confectioners' sugar alternately with cream, beating until smooth and creamy. Spread evenly over base. Refrigerate until firm, about 2 hours.

3. *Topping:* In a small saucepan over low heat, melt chocolate and butter over, stirring until smooth. Pour over filling and quickly spread to cover evenly. Sprinkle peanuts evenly over top. Refrigerate until chocolate is set, about 30 minutes. Cut into bars. Store bars in refrigerator for up to 3 weeks.

Chocolate Ginger Bars

Two different looks from one bar. You can leave them plain or dust with confectioners' sugar. Both taste great.

MAKES 18 TO 48 BARS
(see Cutting Guide, page 10)

- **Preparation: 15 minutes**
- **Cooking: 5 minutes**
- **Chilling: 2 hours**
- **Freezing: not recommended**

- **8-inch (2 L) square cake pan, lined with greased aluminum foil or waxed paper**

1/3 cup	butter	75 mL
8	squares (1 oz/28 g each) semisweet chocolate, chopped	8
3 tbsp	corn syrup	45 mL
8 oz	ginger cookies, crushed	250 g
1/4 cup	chopped crystallized ginger	60 mL
	Confectioners' (icing) sugar, optional	

1. In a heavy saucepan over low heat, combine butter, chocolate and corn syrup. Heat, stirring constantly, until chocolate is melted and mixture is smooth. Remove from heat. Set aside.

2. In a food processor, chop cookies to make coarse crumbs. Measure 2 cups (500 mL). Stir into chocolate mixture along with ginger, mixing well. Spread evenly in prepared pan. Refrigerate until firm, about 2 hours. Cut into bars. Dust with confectioners' sugar, if desired.

Mix 'n' Match Chocolate Bars

I love this combination of sweet chocolate and crunchy, salty pretzels and peanuts.

MAKES 20 TO 54 BARS
(see Cutting Guide, page 10)

- **Preparation: 15 minutes**
- **Cooking: 5 minutes**
- **Chilling: 30 minutes**
- **Freezing: not recommended**

- **13- by 9-inch (3 L) cake pan, lined with greased aluminum foil or waxed paper**

3 cups	semisweet chocolate chips	750 mL
2 tbsp	butter	30 mL
4 cups	miniature marshmallows	1 L
1 1/4 cups	candy-coated chocolate pieces (Smarties or M&M's)	300 mL
1 cup	chopped pretzel sticks (1/2-inch/1 cm pieces)	250 mL
1/2 cup	chopped peanuts	125 mL

1. In a saucepan over low heat, melt chocolate chips and butter, stirring constantly, until smooth. Remove from heat. Let cool until just slightly warm.

2. In a large bowl, combine marshmallows, candies, pretzels and peanuts. Stir in chocolate mixture, mixing well. Press evenly into prepared pan. Chill until firm, about 30 minutes. Cut into bars.

Peanut Butter Honey Date Crisps

◆

Besides making wonderful sandwiches, peanut butter is a favorite ingredient for bakers. It gives bars and other treats a rich, nutty flavor.

MAKES 20 TO 54 BARS OR 24 SQUARES
(see Cutting Guide, page 10)

- **Preparation: 10 minutes**
- **Cooking: 5 minutes**
- **Chilling: 1 hour**
- **Freezing: excellent**

- **13- by 9-inch (3 L) cake pan, greased**

½ cup	liquid honey	125 mL
½ cup	creamy peanut butter	125 mL
⅓ cup	packed brown sugar	75 mL
3 cups	crisp rice cereal	750 mL
1 cup	finely chopped dates	250 mL
½ cup	chopped peanuts	125 mL
3 tbsp	sesame seeds, toasted	45 mL

1. In a heavy saucepan over low heat, combine honey, peanut butter and brown sugar. Heat, stirring, until smooth.

2. In a large bowl, combine cereal, dates and peanuts. Stir in honey mixture, mixing well. Press firmly into prepared pan. Sprinkle with sesame seeds. Chill until set, about 1 hour. Cut into bars or squares.

Chocolate Caramel Crisps

◆

These bars save you time because the flavor combination of chocolate and caramel is already in the chocolate bar. You don't need to mix it up.

MAKES 20 TO 54 BARS OR 24 SQUARES
(see Cutting Guide, page 10)

- **Preparation: 10 minutes**
- **Cooking: 5 minutes**
- **Chilling: 1 hour**
- **Freezing: excellent**

- **13- by 9-inch (3 L) cake pan, greased**

1 cup	corn syrup	125 mL
⅓ cup	butter	75 mL
3 cups	crisp rice cereal	750 mL
1 cup	corn flakes cereal, slightly crushed	250 mL
1 cup	chocolate-coated caramel bars, chopped	250 mL
½ cup	chopped cashews	125 mL

1. In a large saucepan over medium heat, combine corn syrup and butter. Heat, stirring, until butter is melted and mixture is smooth. Continue cooking, stirring often, until mixture begins to thicken, about 4 minutes. Remove from heat.

2. Stir in rice and corn flakes cereals, caramel bars and cashews, mixing well. Press firmly into prepared pan. Chill until firm, about 1 hour. Cut into bars or squares.

Chocolate Peanut Butter Bars

These are chewy like a chocolate peanut butter candy bar that's loaded with nuts. Just like peanuts, these bars can quickly become addictive.

MAKES 20 TO 54 BARS
(see Cutting Guide, page 10)

- **Preparation: 10 minutes**
- **Cooking: 4 minutes**
- **Chilling: 1 hour**
- **Freezing: excellent**

- **13- by 9-inch (3 L) cake pan, greased**

1²⁄₃ cups	milk chocolate chips	400 mL
1 cup	corn syrup	250 mL
²⁄₃ cup	creamy peanut butter	150 mL
2 cups	quick-cooking rolled oats, toasted (see Tip, page 91)	500 mL
2 cups	peanuts	500 mL

1. In a large heavy saucepan over medium heat, combine chocolate chips, corn syrup and peanut butter. Heat, stirring, until mixture comes to a boil. Boil, stirring constantly, until mixture thickens slightly, about 2 minutes. Remove from heat. Stir in toasted oats and peanuts, mixing well. Press firmly into prepared pan. Chill until firm, about 1 hour. Cut into bars.

Date and Almond Crisps

Most no-bake bars fit equally well in the kids' section. Make them together for some family fun. These are a nice backpack or school lunch bar that they can share with friends.

MAKES 18 TO 48 BARS OR 16 TO 36 SQUARES
(see Cutting Guide, page 10)

- **Preparation: 15 minutes**
- **Cooking: 10 minutes**
- **Chilling: 1 hour**
- **Freezing: excellent**

- **9-inch (2.5 L) square cake pan, greased**

³⁄₄ cup	butter	175 mL
²⁄₃ cup	packed brown sugar	150 mL
1¹⁄₂ cups	chopped dates	375 mL
1	square (1 oz/28 g) semisweet chocolate, chopped	1
2³⁄₄ cups	crisp rice cereal	675 mL
³⁄₄ cup	chopped almonds	175 mL

1. In a large heavy saucepan over medium heat, combine butter, brown sugar, dates and chocolate. Cook, stirring often, until thickened, about 10 minutes. Remove from heat. Stir in cereal and almonds, mixing well. Press firmly into prepared pan. Chill until firm, about 1 hour. Cut into bars or squares.

Variations

Replace almonds with walnuts or pecans.

Replace ¹⁄₂ cup (125 mL) dates with dried apricots.

Cool Cranberry Pistachio Squares

◆

The red and green layers on a dark chocolate base make a colorful and tasty square. These look particularly festive on Christmas cookie trays. Cut them into triangles for a different look.

MAKES 16 TO 36 SQUARES
(see Cutting Guide, page 10)

- **Preparation: 15 minutes**
- **Cooking: 5 minutes**
- **Chilling: 2 hours**
- **Freezing: excellent**

TIP

White chocolate must be a good quality or it will be difficult to melt. It never pays to scrimp when it comes to ingredients for baking. One ingredient that's not up to par can ruin your finished product.

• 9-inch (2.5 L) square cake pan, lined with aluminum foil

1/3 cup	butter	75 mL
7	squares (1 oz/28 g each) semisweet chocolate, chopped	7
3 tbsp	corn syrup	45 mL
2 cups	chocolate wafer crumbs	500 mL
1 1/3 cups	white chocolate chips	325 mL
2/3 cup	chopped dried cranberries	150 mL
1/4 cup	chopped pistachios	60 mL

1. In a saucepan over low heat, combine butter, chocolate and corn syrup. Heat, stirring constantly, until chocolate is melted and mixture is smooth. Remove from heat. Stir in chocolate wafer crumbs, mixing well. Spread evenly in prepared pan.

2. In a saucepan over low heat, melt white chocolate chips, stirring constantly, until smooth. Stir in cranberries. Spread evenly over base. Sprinkle pistachios over top. Refrigerate until chocolate is firm, about 2 hours. Cut into squares.

Variations

For an all-chocolate treat, use semisweet chocolate chips instead of the white.

Replace dried cranberries with finely chopped candied pineapple.

Chocolate Trail Mix Bars

Each bite tastes like a combination of a chocolate bar mixed with trail mix. How can you go wrong with these two favorites?

MAKES 18 TO 48 BARS (see Cutting Guide, page 10)

- **Preparation: 15 minutes**
- **Cooking: 3 minutes**
- **Chilling: 1 hour**
- **Freezing: not recommended**

- **9-inch (2.5 L) square cake pan, lined with greased aluminum foil or waxed paper**

2 1/2 cups	quick-cooking rolled oats	625 mL
1 cup	sweetened flaked coconut	250 mL
1 cup	sliced almonds, toasted	250 mL
1/2 cup	dried cranberries	125 mL
1/2 cup	chopped dried pineapple or mango	125 mL
1/2 cup	butter	125 mL
1/2 cup	milk	125 mL
1 1/3 cups	granulated sugar	325 mL
1/3 cup	unsweetened cocoa powder, sifted	75 mL
3/4 tsp	vanilla	3 mL

1. In a large bowl, combine oats, coconut, almonds, dried cranberries and dried pineapple. Set aside.

2. In a heavy saucepan, combine butter, milk and sugar. Bring to a boil over medium heat, stirring until smooth. Remove from heat. Stir in cocoa and vanilla, mixing well. Stir into dry ingredients, mixing well. Press evenly into prepared pan. Refrigerate until firm, about 1 hour. Cut into bars.

Crispy Nougat Bars

You don't have to spend all day in the kitchen to make fantastic bars. Just don't tell anyone how easy these are.

MAKES 18 TO 48 BARS (see Cutting Guide, page 10)

- **Preparation: 5 minutes**
- **Cooking: 5 minutes**
- **Freezing: excellent**

- **8-inch (2 L) square cake pan, greased**

3	chocolate caramel nougat bars, such as Snickers or Mars (2 oz/56 g each), chopped	3
1/4 cup	butter	60 mL
3 cups	crisp rice cereal	750 mL

1. In a large saucepan over low heat, melt chocolate bars and butter, stirring constantly, until smooth. Add cereal and mix until thoroughly coated. Press firmly into prepared pan. Let set for 30 minutes. Cut into bars.

Variation
Add 1/2 cup (125 mL) chopped peanuts or almonds.

Chocolate Nut Candy Crunch

These crunchy treats make a welcome hostess gift any time of the year.

**MAKES ABOUT
2 DOZEN PIECES OR
1 1/2 LB (750 G) CANDY**

- **Preparation: 15 minutes**
- **Cooking: 6 minutes**
- **Chilling: 2 hours**
- **Freezing: not recommended**

TIP

Try using salted cashews and almonds in this recipe for a pleasantly different taste.

- **9-inch (2.5 L) square cake pan, lined with greased aluminum foil**

2 cups	semisweet chocolate chips	500 mL
3/4 cup	coarsely chopped cashews	175 mL
3/4 cup	slivered almonds	175 mL
1/2 cup	granulated sugar	125 mL
1/2 cup	butter	125 mL
2 tbsp	corn syrup	30 mL

1. Sprinkle chocolate chips evenly over bottom of prepared pan. In a large skillet over low heat, combine cashews, almonds, sugar, butter and corn syrup. Cook, stirring, until butter is melted. Increase heat to medium and cook, stirring constantly, until mixture comes together and turns light golden, about 5 minutes. Pour over chocolate chips. Spread evenly in pan.

2. Let stand for 1 hour then chill until chocolate is firm, about 1 hour. Remove from pan. Peel off foil. Break into pieces. Store in a cool, dry place.

Caramel Chews

This tasty combination of crisp cereals, chewy coconut, tart dried cranberries and crunchy cashews is held together with creamy caramel.

**MAKES 18 TO 48 BARS
OR 16 TO 36 SQUARES
(see Cutting Guide,
page 10)**

- **Preparation: 5 minutes**
- **Cooking: 10 minutes**
- **Chilling: 1 hour**
- **Freezing: excellent**

- **9-inch (2.5 L) square cake pan, greased**

11 oz	soft caramels, unwrapped (43)	330 g
3 tbsp	half-and-half (10%) cream	45 mL
2 cups	crisp rice cereal	500 mL
1 cup	corn flakes cereal, slightly crushed	250 mL
3/4 cup	sweetened flaked coconut	175 mL
1/2 cup	chopped cashews	125 mL
1/2 cup	dried cranberries	125 mL

1. In a heavy saucepan over low heat, combine caramels and cream. Heat, stirring constantly, until caramels are melted and mixture is smooth.

2. In a large bowl, combine rice and corn flakes cereals, coconut, cashews and dried cranberries. Stir in caramel mixture, mixing well. Press firmly into prepared pan. Chill until firm, about 1 hour. Cut into bars or squares.

Inside-Out Nanaimo Bars

Reverse the dark and light colors of this popular no-bake bar for a different look and taste.

**MAKES 18 TO 48 BARS
(see Cutting Guide, page 10)**

- **Preparation: 30 minutes**
- **Cooking: 5 minutes**
- **Chilling: 3 hours**
- **Freezing: excellent**

TIPS

White chocolate can burn quickly, so be sure to use a heavy saucepan over low heat and stir constantly. If the element seems to be too hot, take the pan off the heat and continue to stir until the mixture is smooth.

Custard powder is usually sold in cans or envelopes. Bird's, Horne's and Dr. Oetker are popular brands. If you can't find it, substitute an equal quantity of vanilla pudding powder (the kind that you have to cook, not instant).

- **8-inch (2 L) square cake pan, lined with greased aluminum foil or waxed paper**

BASE

1/4 cup	butter	60 mL
2	squares (1 oz/28 g each) white chocolate, chopped	2
1	egg, beaten	1
2 cups	vanilla wafer crumbs	500 mL
1/2 cup	sweetened flaked coconut	125 mL
1/3 cup	finely chopped walnuts	75 mL

FILLING

1/3 cup	butter	75 mL
1/2 cup	unsweetened cocoa powder, sifted	125 mL
1 1/2 cups	confectioners' (icing) sugar, sifted	375 mL
2 tbsp	custard powder, sifted (see Tips, left)	30 mL
1/4 cup	half-and-half (10%) cream	60 mL

TOPPING

4	squares (1 oz/28 g each) white chocolate, chopped	4
1 tbsp	vegetable oil	15 mL

1. *Base:* In a heavy saucepan over low heat, melt butter and white chocolate, stirring until smooth. Stir in beaten egg. Heat, stirring, for 1 minute. Remove from heat. Stir in vanilla wafer crumbs, coconut and walnuts, mixing well. Press evenly into prepared pan. Chill until cold, about 30 minutes.

2. *Filling:* Meanwhile, in saucepan, melt butter over low heat. Add cocoa, stirring until smooth. In a bowl, combine confectioners' sugar and custard powder. Add cocoa mixture and cream. Using an electric mixer on medium speed, beat until smooth and creamy. Spread over chilled base. Refrigerate until firm, about 2 hours.

3. *Topping:* In a small saucepan over low heat, combine white chocolate and oil. Heat, stirring constantly, until smooth. Pour over filling, quickly spreading to cover evenly. Refrigerate until chocolate is set, about 30 minutes. Cut into bars. Store bars in refrigerator for up to 3 weeks.

Cappuccino Nanaimo Bars

Nanaimo bars, which originated in Nanaimo, British Columbia, have become a favorite around the world. Not only do they taste delicious, but they keep extremely well in the refrigerator or freezer.

**MAKES 18 TO 48 BARS
(see Cutting Guide, page 10)**

- **Preparation: 30 minutes**
- **Cooking: 5 minutes**
- **Chilling: 3 hours**
- **Freezing: excellent**

TIPS

I have specified sweetened coconut because it seems to be more readily available than the unsweetened variety. But sweetened and unsweetened coconut can be used interchangeably in any recipe to suit your preference.

Replace espresso powder with double the amount of instant coffee granules. Look for finely ground coffee granules so they will dissolve easily, or crush them with the back of a spoon to make them finer.

Lining the pan with foil or waxed paper makes it easier to remove the bars.

- **8-inch (2 L) square cake pan, lined with greased aluminum foil or waxed paper (see Tips, left)**

BASE

⅔ cup	butter	150 mL
⅓ cup	unsweetened cocoa powder, sifted	75 mL
¼ cup	granulated sugar	60 mL
1 tbsp	instant espresso powder	15 mL
1	egg, beaten	1
1½ cups	graham wafer crumbs	375 mL
¾ cup	sweetened flaked coconut	175 mL
¾ cup	finely chopped almonds	175 mL

FILLING

2 cups	confectioners' (icing) sugar	500 mL
¼ cup	butter, softened	60 mL
1 tbsp	instant espresso powder	15 mL
2 tbsp	hot water	30 mL

TOPPING

2 tbsp	butter	30 mL
1 tbsp	instant espresso powder	15 mL
4	squares (1 oz/28 g each) semisweet chocolate, chopped	4

1. *Base:* In a saucepan over low heat, combine butter, cocoa, sugar, espresso powder and egg. Cook, stirring constantly, until mixture starts to thicken, about 5 minutes. Remove from heat. Mix in graham wafer crumbs, coconut and almonds. Press evenly into prepared pan. Refrigerate until cold, about 30 minutes.

2. *Filling:* Meanwhile, in a bowl, using an electric mixer on low speed, beat half of the confectioners' sugar and the butter until blended. Mix espresso powder and hot water until dissolved. On medium speed, beat espresso powder into butter mixture along with remaining confectioners' sugar until smooth and creamy. Spread evenly over base. Refrigerate until firm, about 2 hours. Lift out of pan and transfer to a cutting board.

3. *Topping:* In a saucepan over low heat, combine butter, espresso powder and chocolate. Heat, stirring constantly, until smooth. Pour over filling and quickly spread to cover evenly. Refrigerate until chocolate is set, about 30 minutes. Cut into bars. Store bars in refrigerator for up to 3 weeks.

Crispy Cereal Bars

Good for You, Too

I've tried to make these recipes healthy and delicious, using ingredients that are readily available. You won't need to shop in specialty stores to make these bars. Although they aren't designed for special diets, some are nut-free, lactose-free or egg-free. They use ingredients that nutritionists say are good for us: nuts and seeds; dried fruits; and whole grain cereals, such as oats, bran and wheat germ. I've tried to cut down on sugar and fat and increase dietary fiber, keeping the calories as low as possible without sacrificing flavor. I've used unbleached flour because some people avoid flour that has been chemically bleached. If you enjoy the nutty taste and slightly drier texture, you can substitute whole wheat flour, which contains more fiber, for all or half of the all-purpose flour called for.

Enjoy the recipes in this chapter as guilt-free snacks and treats. The key to healthy eating is moderation, so when eating these bars and squares, as well as others in the book, bear in mind that the richer it is, the smaller you cut it. Often a small taste of something delicious is far more satisfying than a big piece of mediocrity.

Crispy Cereal Bars

These no-bake bars are a great way for kids to enjoy their breakfast cereal. Add a glass of milk and they'll be happy campers.

MAKES 20 TO 54 BARS (see Cutting Guide, page 10)

- **Preparation: 15 minutes**
- **Baking: 10 minutes**
- **Freezing: excellent**

TIP

Lightly butter an offset spatula or the back of a spoon to press the cereal mixture into the pan. It keeps it from sticking to the gooey mixture. You can also use your fingers — butter them, too, to ease sticking.

- **Preheat oven to 350°F (180°C)**
- **13- by 9-inch (3 L) cake pan, ungreased**

1 cup	quick-cooking rolled oats	250 mL
1/4 cup	butter	60 mL
8 oz	marshmallows (about 40 regular size)	250 g
1 tsp	vanilla	5 mL
5 cups	crisp rice cereal	1.25 L
3/4 cup	raisins	175 mL
1/3 cup	sunflower seeds	75 mL
1/3 cup	chopped dried apricots	75 mL
1/4 cup	chopped unblanched almonds	60 mL

1. Sprinkle oats evenly in pan. Bake in preheated oven, stirring occasionally, until lightly toasted, about 10 minutes. Transfer to a bowl and let cool for 15 minutes. Spray pan lightly with cooking spray. Set aside.

2. In a large saucepan, combine butter and marshmallows. Cook over low heat, stirring often, until melted and smooth. Remove from heat. Stir in vanilla. Stir in oats, cereal, raisins, sunflower seeds, apricots and almonds, mixing well. Using an offset spatula or the back of a spoon, press mixture evenly into prepared pan. Let cool completely, about 1 hour. Cut into bars.

Variations

If you prefer a nut-free bar, omit the almonds.

Replace raisins with dried cranberries.

Replace almonds with another type of nut.

Replace sunflower seeds with pumpkin seeds.

Replace apricots with dried apples.

Three-Simple-Steps Squares

Here's a healthy version of an old classic. I think I prefer it to the original layered bar. If you're watching calories, cut these squares in half (into triangles).

**MAKES 24 SQUARES
(see Cutting Guide, page 10)**

- **Preparation: 20 minutes**
- **Baking: 25 minutes**
- **Freezing: excellent**

TIPS

Store wheat germ in the freezer to keep it fresh.

Sweetened and unsweetened coconut are interchangeable in recipes. I have specified unsweetened in this recipe with a view to reducing sugar consumption.

- **Preheat oven to 350°F (180°C)**
- **13- by 9-inch (3 L) cake pan, ungreased**

½ cup	butter	125 mL
1 cup	graham wafer crumbs	250 mL
⅓ cup	wheat germ (see Tips, left)	75 mL
1	can (10 oz/300 mL) light sweetened condensed milk	1
1 cup	chopped dried apricots	250 mL
¾ cup	dried cranberries	175 mL
¾ cup	unsweetened flaked coconut	175 mL
½ cup	chopped unblanched almonds	125 mL
⅓ cup	pumpkin seeds	75 mL

1. Place butter in cake pan and melt in preheated oven. Remove from oven and tilt pan to cover bottom evenly with melted butter. Combine graham wafer crumbs and wheat germ. Sprinkle evenly over butter, pressing with an offset spatula or the back of a spoon to moisten.

2. Drizzle sweetened condensed milk evenly over crumbs. Sprinkle apricots, cranberries, coconut, almonds and pumpkin seeds over top. Press in lightly.

3. Bake in preheated oven until lightly browned around edges, 20 to 25 minutes. Let cool completely in pan on rack. Cut into squares.

Variations

Replace dried cranberries with raisins, chopped dried cherries or chopped dried figs.

Replace pumpkin seeds with sunflower seeds.

Replace almonds with pecans or walnuts.

Tropical Fruit and Nut Bars

A lighter version of an old-time favorite.

MAKES 18 TO 48 BARS (see Cutting Guide, page 10)

- **Preparation: 20 minutes**
- **Baking: 45 minutes**
- **Freezing: excellent**

TIP

Older baking recipes tend to be high in fat, sugar and salt, ingredients we are trying to cut back on. Experiment with your favorite recipes by decreasing these ingredients by about 25% and see how they turn out. You may prefer the lighter version.

- **Preheat oven to 350°F (180°C)**
- **8-inch (2 L) square cake pan, greased**

³⁄₄ cup	dried apricots, chopped	175 mL
¹⁄₄ cup	dried cherries	60 mL
¹⁄₄ cup	dried mango, chopped	60 mL
CRUST		
1 cup	unbleached all-purpose flour	250 mL
¹⁄₄ cup	packed brown sugar	60 mL
¹⁄₄ cup	cold butter, cubed	60 mL
TOPPING		
2	eggs	2
¹⁄₂ cup	packed brown sugar	125 mL
1 tsp	freshly squeezed lemon juice	5 mL
¹⁄₂ cup	pine nuts	125 mL

1. In a saucepan, combine apricots and cherries with water to cover. Bring to a boil, then remove from heat. Stir in mango and let stand while preparing crust.

2. *Crust:* In a bowl, combine flour and brown sugar. Using a pastry blender, 2 knives or your fingers, cut in butter until mixture resembles coarse crumbs. Press firmly into prepared pan. Bake in preheated oven until lightly browned around the edges, 12 to 15 minutes.

3. *Topping:* In a bowl, whisk eggs, brown sugar and lemon juice until smooth. Stir in pine nuts and apricot mixture, mixing well. Spread evenly over crust.

4. Return to oven and bake until topping is set and golden, 25 to 30 minutes. Let cool completely in pan on rack. Cut into bars.

Variations

Replace dried cherries with dried cranberries or more dried apricots.

Replace pine nuts with chopped almonds or pecans.

Chewy Honey Apple Fig Bars

In these moist, chewy bars, I've used applesauce to replace the fat. It also adds great flavor.

MAKES 20 TO 54 BARS (see Cutting Guide, page 10)

- **Preparation: 25 minutes**
- **Baking: 25 minutes**
- **Freezing: excellent**

TIP

Because honey replaces sugar in these bars, they have a dense, moist, chewy texture and a delightful honey flavor. Often you see both honey and sugar in a recipe because using honey only would result in too much liquid, which interferes with proper baking.

- **Preheat oven to 350°F (180°C)**
- **13- by 9-inch (3 L) cake pan, greased**

1 cup	unbleached all-purpose flour	250 mL
¾ cup	whole wheat flour	175 mL
1 tsp	baking soda	5 mL
1 tsp	cinnamon	5 mL
½ tsp	ground ginger	2 mL
¼ tsp	ground nutmeg	1 mL
1	egg	1
1 cup	liquid honey	250 mL
½ cup	unsweetened applesauce	125 mL
2 tsp	grated lemon zest	10 mL
¾ cup	finely chopped dried figs	175 mL
¾ cup	finely chopped dried apricots	175 mL
½ cup	chopped pecans	125 mL

1. In a bowl, combine all-purpose and whole wheat flours, baking soda, cinnamon, ginger and nutmeg. In a separate bowl, whisk egg, honey, applesauce and lemon zest until smooth. Stir into dry ingredients, mixing well. Stir in figs, apricots and pecans. Spread evenly in prepared pan.

2. Bake in preheated oven until top is set and lightly browned, 20 to 25 minutes. Let cool completely in pan on rack. Cut into bars.

Variations

Replace apricots with figs for an all-fig bar.

Replace pecans with walnuts.

Apricot Seed Bars

Packed full of dried fruits and seeds, these bars make a great addition to a backpack, if you're hiking or biking.

MAKES 20 TO 54 BARS, see Cutting Guide, page 10

- **Preparation: 20 minutes**
- **Baking: 30 minutes**
- **Freezing: excellent**

TIPS

To prevent sticking, use cooking spray to get a light, even coating of grease on baking pans.

To ease cleanup, rather than combining the dry ingredients in a bowl (in Step 1), place a large piece of waxed paper on the counter. Spread the flour on the paper and sprinkle the baking soda, salt and cinnamon over it. Using the paper as a funnel, transfer the dry ingredients to the egg mixture.

- **Preheat oven to 350°F (180°C)**
- **13- by 9-inch (3 L) cake pan, greased**

³⁄₄ cup	butter, softened	175 mL
³⁄₄ cup	packed brown sugar	175 mL
1	egg	1
1 cup	unbleached all-purpose flour	250 mL
¹⁄₂ tsp	baking soda	2 mL
¹⁄₄ tsp	salt	1 mL
³⁄₄ tsp	ground cinnamon	3 mL
1 cup	quick-cooking rolled oats	250 mL
³⁄₄ cup	finely chopped dried apricots	175 mL
³⁄₄ cup	dried cranberries	175 mL
¹⁄₄ cup	sesame seeds	60 mL
¹⁄₄ cup	flax seeds	60 mL
¹⁄₄ cup	sunflower seeds	60 mL

1. In a bowl, using an electric mixer on medium speed, beat butter, brown sugar and egg until smooth and creamy. Combine flour, baking soda, salt and cinnamon. Stir into creamed mixture, mixing well. Stir in rolled oats, apricots, cranberries, sesame seeds, flax seeds and sunflower seeds. Spread evenly in prepared pan.

2. Bake in preheated oven until top is set and golden, 25 to 30 minutes. Let cool completely in pan on rack. Cut into bars.

Variations

Replace cranberries with chopped dried figs or raisins.

Add ¹⁄₃ cup (75 mL) chopped almonds along with the seeds.

Lighten-Up Cookie Bars

This is a lighter version of one of my favorite bar cookies, and it's still very delicious.

MAKES 20 TO 54 BARS (see Cutting Guide, page 10)

- **Preparation: 25 minutes**
- **Baking: 25 minutes**
- **Freezing: excellent**

TIPS

Miniature chocolate chips are great to use when you're trying to cut down on calories. There are a lot more chips per bar than with regular chips, so you can reduce the quantity and still get a good chocolate impact in every bite.

If you like the nutty flavor of whole wheat, you can reverse the proportions of the unbleached all-purpose and whole wheat flour. You'll increase your fiber intake.

- **Preheat oven to 375°F (190°C)**
- **13- by 9-inch (3 L) cake pan, greased**

½ cup	butter, softened	125 mL
¾ cup	granulated sugar	175 mL
¾ cup	packed brown sugar	175 mL
½ cup	unsweetened applesauce	125 mL
1	egg	1
1 tsp	vanilla	5 mL
1½ cups	unbleached all-purpose flour	375 mL
1 cup	whole wheat flour	250 mL
1 tsp	baking soda	5 mL
½ tsp	salt	2 mL
¾ cup	miniature chocolate chips	175 mL
¾ cup	chopped dried apricots	175 mL
¾ cup	dried cranberries	175 mL
½ cup	sunflower seeds	125 mL

1. In a bowl, using an electric mixer on medium speed, beat butter, granulated and brown sugars, applesauce, egg and vanilla until creamy, about 3 minutes. Combine all-purpose and whole wheat flours, baking soda and salt. Stir into creamed mixture, mixing well. Stir in chocolate chips, apricots, cranberries and sunflower seeds. Spread evenly in prepared pan.

2. Bake in preheated oven until light golden, about 25 minutes. Let cool completely in pan on rack. Cut into bars.

Variations

Replace apricots with chopped dates or raisins.

Replace dried cranberries with chopped dried pineapple or mango.

Replace sunflower seeds with chopped almonds.

Raisin Applesauce Squares

This moist square has a soft, cake-like texture. It gets its wonderful flavor from applesauce and dates.

MAKES 16 TO 36 SQUARES
(see Cutting Guide, page 10)

- **Preparation: 20 minutes**
- **Baking: 30 minutes**
- **Freezing: excellent**

TIP

To ease cleanup, rather than combining the dry ingredients in a bowl (Step 2), place a large piece of waxed paper on the counter. Spread the flours on the paper. Sprinkle with the baking powder, baking soda, cinnamon and cloves. Using the paper as a funnel, transfer the dry ingredients to the butter mixture.

- **Preheat oven to 350°F (180°C)**
- **8-inch (2 L) square cake pan, greased**

¼ cup	butter, softened	60 mL
½ cup	packed brown sugar	125 mL
1	egg	1
1 tbsp	grated orange zest	15 mL
1 tsp	vanilla	5 mL
1 cup	unbleached all-purpose flour	250 mL
½ cup	whole wheat flour	125 mL
½ tsp	baking powder	2 mL
½ tsp	baking soda	2 mL
1 tsp	ground cinnamon	5 mL
¼ tsp	ground cloves	1 mL
1 cup	unsweetened applesauce	250 mL
¾ cup	raisins	175 mL

1. In a large bowl, using an electric mixer on low speed, beat butter, brown sugar, egg, orange zest and vanilla until blended, about 3 minutes.
2. Combine all-purpose and whole wheat flours, baking powder, baking soda, cinnamon and cloves. Stir into creamed mixture alternately with applesauce, making 3 additions and mixing lightly after each addition. Stir in raisins. Spread evenly in prepared pan.
3. Bake in preheated oven until a toothpick inserted in center comes out clean, 25 to 30 minutes. Let cool completely in pan on rack. Cut into squares.

Variations

Replace orange zest with lemon zest.

Replace raisins with dried cranberries or cherries.

Oatmeal Crisps

Enjoy your morning oats baked in a bar rather than warm in a cereal bowl. Accompany with a glass of cold milk for more nutrients.

MAKES ABOUT 24 PIECES

- **Preparation: 15 minutes**
- **Cooking: 1 minute**
- **Baking: 15 minutes**
- **Freezing: excellent**

TIPS

Store these crisps in an airtight container with waxed paper between the layers to prevent them from becoming soft. They also freeze well for up to 3 months.

Use cooking spray to grease pans. It doesn't burn like butter.

- **Preheat oven to 350°F (180°C)**
- **13- by 9-inch (3 L) cake pan, lined with aluminum foil and greased**

⅔ cup	butter	150 mL
⅔ cup	packed brown sugar	150 mL
2⅔ cups	old-fashioned (large-flake) rolled oats	650 mL
1 tsp	ground cinnamon	5 mL
Pinch	salt	Pinch

1. In a large saucepan, melt butter over medium heat. Add brown sugar. Cook, stirring constantly, until sugar is melted and mixture is smooth, about 1 minute. Stir in oats, cinnamon and salt, mixing until oats are thoroughly moistened. Press evenly into prepared pan.

2. Bake in preheated oven until top is golden, about 15 minutes. Let cool completely in pan on rack. Break into irregular pieces.

Variations

Decrease oats to 2⅓ cups (575 mL) and add ⅓ cup (75 mL) toasted wheat germ.

Add ¼ cup (60 mL) sesame or flax seeds.

Pick-Me-Up Bars

This dense, slightly chewy bar is a great boost if you're experiencing an afternoon slump and is an ideal after-school snack.

MAKES 18 TO 48 BARS (see Cutting Guide, page 10)

- **Preparation: 20 minutes**
- **Baking: 20 minutes**
- **Freezing: excellent**

(see Cutting Guide, page 10)

TIPS

When baking, you can usually use 1 whole egg in place of 2 egg whites or vice versa. However, in desserts like custards, where the yolk is needed for thickening, this rule doesn't apply.

Small seeds, like sesame, flax and sunflower, can easily be added to your favorite cookie and bar recipes in small amounts.

- **Preheat oven to 350°F (180°C)**
- **8-inch (2 L) square cake pan, greased**

1 cup	graham wafer crumbs	250 mL
2/3 cup	packed brown sugar	150 mL
1/2 cup	whole wheat flour	125 mL
1/2 cup	butterscotch chips	125 mL
1/3 cup	quick-cooking rolled oats	75 mL
1/3 cup	sunflower seeds	75 mL
1 tsp	baking powder	5 mL
2	egg whites (see Tips, left)	2
1 tbsp	vegetable oil	15 mL
1 1/2 tsp	vanilla	7 mL

1. In a bowl, combine graham wafer crumbs, brown sugar, flour, butterscotch chips, oats, sunflower seeds and baking powder.
2. In a separate bowl, whisk egg whites, oil and vanilla until blended. Stir into dry ingredients, mixing well. Press evenly into prepared pan.
3. Bake in preheated oven until top is golden, about 20 minutes. Let cool completely in pan on rack. Cut into bars.

Variations

Replace whole wheat flour with all-purpose, but be aware that you'll lose some of the health benefits, such as added fiber.

Replace sunflower seeds with a mixture of sesame and flax seeds.

Coconut Almond Raspberry Bars

A little like store-bought soft jam-filled granola bars but with a whole lot more flavor.

MAKES 18 TO 48 BARS
(see Cutting Guide, page 10)

- **Preparation: 20 minutes**
- **Baking: 30 minutes**
- **Freezing: excellent**

TIPS

I suggest lining the pan with parchment or greased aluminum foil because the jam will stick and caramelize on the pan making it difficult to cut.

Although sweetened and unsweetened coconut are interchangeable in baking, I recommend the use of unsweetened in this recipe to cut down on sugar.

- **Preheat oven to 350°F (180°C)**
- **9-inch (2.5 L) square cake pan, greased and lined with parchment or greased aluminum foil**

1³⁄₄ cups	quick-cooking rolled oats	425 mL
1 cup	unbleached all-purpose flour	250 mL
1 cup	packed brown sugar	250 mL
¼ cup	unsweetened flaked coconut	60 mL
1 tsp	baking powder	5 mL
¼ tsp	salt	1 mL
¾ cup	butter, melted	175 mL
¾ cup	raspberry jam	175 mL
1 tsp	grated lemon zest	5 mL
²⁄₃ cup	sliced almonds	150 mL

1. In a large bowl, combine oats, flour, brown sugar, coconut, baking powder and salt. Stir in melted butter, mixing well. Press two-thirds of the mixture evenly into prepared pan. Set remainder aside.

2. In a bowl, combine jam and lemon zest. Spread evenly over crust, leaving a ¹⁄₂-inch (1 cm) border of crust. Stir almonds into reserved crust mixture and sprinkle over jam. Pat down lightly.

3. Bake in preheated oven until top is golden, 25 to 30 minutes. Let cool completely in pan on rack. Cut into bars.

Variations

Replace raspberry jam with strawberry, apricot, peach or cherry.

Replace almonds with sliced hazelnuts.

Replace some of the all-purpose flour with whole wheat flour for a little more fiber.

Fruit and Seed Granola Bars

You won't be tempted to buy granola bars again after making these tasty nibblers. Keep a supply on hand for lunch-box treats.

MAKES 36 TO 48 BARS
(see Cutting Guide, page 10)

- **Preparation: 20 minutes**
- **Baking: 25 minutes**
- **Freezing: excellent**

TIPS

If you prefer a chewy texture, underbake these bars. Bake longer for crisp bars.

Vary the dried fruit and seeds to suit your taste. A mixture looks nice, but you can use just one fruit and one kind of seed.

- **Preheat oven to 350°F (180°C)**
- **15- by 10- by 1-inch (2 L) jelly roll pan, greased**

1 cup	butter, softened	250 mL
1 cup	packed brown sugar	250 mL
1/2 cup	corn syrup	125 mL
3 cups	quick-cooking rolled oats	750 mL
1 cup	whole wheat flour	250 mL
1/2 tsp	baking soda	2 mL
1 tsp	ground cinnamon	5 mL
1 cup	crisp rice cereal	250 mL
3/4 cup	raisins	175 mL
3/4 cup	chopped dried apricots	175 mL
1/4 cup	sunflower seeds	60 mL
1/4 cup	pumpkin seeds	60 mL
1/4 cup	flax seeds	60 mL

1. In a small saucepan over medium heat, heat butter and brown sugar, stirring until butter is melted and mixture is smooth. Stir in corn syrup.

2. In a large bowl, combine rolled oats, whole wheat flour, baking soda, cinnamon, cereal, raisins, apricots, and sunflower, pumpkin and flax seeds. Pour sugar mixture over top. Mix until ingredients are moistened. Press evenly into prepared pan.

3. Bake in preheated oven until top is light golden, 20 to 25 minutes. Let cool completely in pan on rack. Cut into bars.

Variations

Add 1/2 cup (125 mL) chopped almonds, pecans or peanuts to the dry ingredients.

Replace whole wheat flour with unbleached all-purpose, or use half of each kind.

Fabulous Fig Bars

These bars are a childhood favorite. I'm not sure whether I love making these for the taste of the moist fig filling in the buttery crust or just for the memories.

MAKES 18 TO 48 BARS,
(see Cutting Guide, page 10)

- **Preparation: 35 minutes**
- **Cooking: 25 minutes**
- **Cooling: 30 minutes**
- **Baking: 35 minutes**
- **Freezing: excellent**

TIPS

I like to use a combination of Calimyrna (golden) and Mission (black) figs in this recipe.

If your dough seems soft after mixing, chill for 30 to 60 minutes. It will roll out much more easily.

Don't worry if the dough tears when you transfer it to the pan. You can patch any tears by pressing it together with your fingertips. The bottom crust can extend a bit up the side before filling. The top crust is trimmed to fit over it.

This recipe can be doubled and baked in a 13- by 9-inch (3 L) pan.

- **Preheat oven to 350°F (180°C)**
- **8-inch (2 L) square cake pan, greased**

FILLING

8 oz	dried figs, chopped	250 g
1 cup	water	250 mL
1 tbsp	freshly squeezed lemon juice	15 mL

CRUST

¾ cup	unbleached all-purpose flour	175 mL
½ cup	whole wheat flour	125 mL
¾ tsp	baking powder	3 mL
¾ tsp	ground cinnamon	3 mL
Pinch	salt	Pinch
¼ cup	butter, softened	60 mL
½ cup	granulated sugar	125 mL
1	egg	1

1. *Filling:* In a saucepan, combine figs, water and lemon juice. Bring to a boil over medium heat, reduce heat to low and simmer, uncovered, until water is absorbed and figs are tender, about 25 minutes. Let cool to lukewarm. Transfer to a food processor and purée. Set aside until cool, about 30 minutes.

2. *Crust:* Combine all-purpose and whole wheat flours, baking powder, cinnamon and salt. In a large bowl, using an electric mixer on medium speed, beat butter, sugar and egg until light and creamy, about 3 minutes. On low speed, gradually add dry ingredients, mixing just until dough comes together. Using floured hands, knead dough to form a smooth ball. Divide in half.

3. Between 2 sheets of waxed paper, roll out one half of the dough to an 8-inch (20 cm) square. Remove top sheet of waxed paper and transfer dough upside down into prepared pan. Remove second sheet of waxed paper. Spread cooled fig filling evenly over dough. Repeat rolling with other half of dough. Trim edges to make an even square. Place over filling.

4. Bake in preheated oven until crust is golden, 30 to 35 minutes. Let cool completely in pan on rack. Cut into bars.

Apple Fruit Bars

This moist, cake-like bar is as good for dessert as it is for snack time.

MAKES 20 TO 54 BARS (see Cutting Guide, page 10)

- **Preparation: 20 minutes**
- **Baking: 30 minutes**
- **Freezing: excellent**

(see Cutting Guide, page 10)

TIPS

If you're concerned about fat and cholesterol, replace 1 egg with 2 egg whites. When your recipe calls for 2 eggs, use 1 whole egg and 2 egg whites.

Add ¼ cup (60 mL) flax seeds to increase the fiber content.

- **Preheat oven to 350°F (180°C)**
- **13- by 9-inch (3 L) cake pan, greased**

2	eggs	2
¾ cup	packed brown sugar	175 mL
½ cup	vegetable oil	125 mL
½ cup	unbleached all-purpose flour	125 mL
½ cup	whole wheat flour	125 mL
1 tsp	baking soda	5 mL
¾ tsp	ground cinnamon	3 mL
¼ tsp	ground nutmeg	1 mL
2 cups	chopped peeled apples (2 to 3 apples)	500 mL
⅔ cup	dried cranberries	150 mL
½ cup	chopped dates	125 mL

1. In a bowl, whisk eggs, brown sugar and oil. Combine all-purpose and whole wheat flours, baking soda, cinnamon and nutmeg. Stir into egg mixture, mixing until blended. Stir in apples, cranberries and dates, mixing well. Spread evenly in prepared pan.

2. Bake in preheated oven until set and golden, 25 to 30 minutes. Let cool completely in pan on rack. Cut into bars.

Variations

Replace dried cranberries with raisins.

Replace dates with chopped dried apricots.

High-Energy Granola Bars

This granola bar is nice and chewy but not too sweet, with lots of healthy, tasty ingredients. It's also easy to make. Take a few to work for an afternoon energy boost.

MAKES 20 TO 54 BARS (see Cutting Guide, page 10)

- **Preparation: 20 minutes**
- **Baking: 20 minutes**
- **Freezing: excellent**

TIPS

Underbaking granola bars gives them a chewy texture, whereas baking for a little longer makes a crisp bar. Use whichever technique your family prefers.

After cutting, wrap these into individual bars so they're ready to pack in lunch boxes or knapsacks when needed.

- **Preheat oven to 350°F (180°C)**
- **13- by 9-inch (3 L) cake pan, greased**

½ cup	butter, melted	125 mL
¾ cup	corn syrup	175 mL
2 cups	quick-cooking rolled oats	500 mL
¾ cup	natural bran	175 mL
½ cup	chopped unblanched almonds	125 mL
½ cup	sunflower seeds	125 mL
⅓ cup	chopped dried apricots	75 mL
⅓ cup	chopped dates	75 mL
⅓ cup	chopped dried cranberries	75 mL
¼ cup	wheat germ	60 mL
¼ cup	pumpkin seeds	60 mL
¼ cup	flax seeds	60 mL
¼ cup	sesame seeds	60 mL

1. In a bowl, combine melted butter and corn syrup. Stir in rolled oats, bran, almonds, sunflower seeds, apricots, dates, cranberries, wheat germ, pumpkin seeds, flax seeds and sesame seeds, mixing well until all ingredients are moistened. Press evenly into prepared pan.

2. Bake in preheated oven until top is golden, 15 to 20 minutes. Let cool completely in pan. Cut into bars.

Variations

There's no end to the variety of dried fruit combinations you can use. Dried cherries, raisins, mango and papaya all work well in this recipe. Just keep the total amount to 1 cup (250 mL).

Replace almonds with your favorite nut.

Mixed Fruit Bran Bars

Enjoy your breakfast bran flakes in an easy-to-eat-on-the-run fruit and fiber bar.

MAKES 20 TO 54 BARS
(see Cutting Guide, page 10)

- **Preparation: 20 minutes**
- **Baking: 25 minutes**
- **Freezing: excellent**

TIPS

When choosing a healthy snack, look for those containing dried fruits, such as apricots and dates, which are high in iron and fiber. And they taste great!

For added fiber, substitute whole wheat flour for all or half of the all-purpose.

- **Preheat oven to 375°F (190°C)**
- **13- by 9-inch (3 L) cake pan, greased**

2 cups	bran flake cereal	500 mL
1 cup	unbleached all-purpose flour	250 mL
2/3 cup	packed brown sugar	150 mL
2 tsp	baking soda	10 mL
1/4 tsp	salt	1 mL
1 cup	buttermilk	250 mL
2 tbsp	vegetable oil	30 mL
2	eggs	2
1 tbsp	grated lemon zest	15 mL
3/4 cup	chopped dried apricots	175 mL
1/2 cup	chopped dried apples	125 mL
1/2 cup	chopped dates	125 mL
1/2 cup	dried cranberries	125 mL
1/3 cup	chopped pecans	75 mL

1. In a food processor fitted with a metal blade, combine cereal, flour, brown sugar, baking soda and salt. Pulse until coarsely chopped, about 1 minute. Add buttermilk, vegetable oil, eggs and lemon zest and process until cereal is crushed and mixture is blended. Stir in apricots, apples, dates, cranberries and pecans. Spread evenly in prepared pan.

2. Bake in preheated oven until set and golden, 20 to 25 minutes. Let cool completely in pan on rack. Cut into bars.

Variations

Replace lemon zest with orange or tangerine zest.

Replace dried cranberries with chopped dried cherries or raisins.

Honey Granola Breakfast Bars

Keep some of these on hand for the days when the need for a little extra sleep takes priority over a sit-down breakfast. They also make a great pick-me-up any time of the day.

MAKES 20 TO 54 BARS (see Cutting Guide, page 10)

- **Preparation: 20 minutes**
- **Baking: 30 minutes**
- **Freezing: excellent**

TIPS

Ground flax seeds are available in the health food section of grocery stores or specialty health food stores. Keep a containerful handy in the freezer so you can add a little to baking.

Always use liquid honey unless specified otherwise.

When making these bars, measure the oil in your measuring cup first, then measure the honey. That way, the honey will slip easily out of the cup without sticking.

- **Preheat oven to 350°F (180°C)**
- **13- by 9-inch (3 L) cake pan, greased**

2 cups	old-fashioned (large-flake) rolled oats	500 mL
1 cup	whole wheat flour	250 mL
¾ cup	packed brown sugar	175 mL
¼ cup	wheat germ	60 mL
¼ cup	ground flax seeds	60 mL
1 tsp	ground cinnamon	5 mL
½ tsp	salt	2 mL
1	egg	1
½ cup	vegetable oil	125 mL
½ cup	liquid honey	125 mL
1 tsp	vanilla	5 mL
¾ cup	raisins	175 mL
½ cup	chopped dried apricots	125 mL

1. In a bowl, combine rolled oats, whole wheat flour, brown sugar, wheat germ, flax seeds, cinnamon and salt. In a small bowl, whisk egg, oil, honey and vanilla until blended. Pour over oat mixture, mixing until dry ingredients are moistened. Stir in raisins and apricots. Press evenly into prepared pan.

2. Bake in preheated oven until light golden, 20 to 30 minutes. Let cool completely in pan on rack. Cut into bars.

Variations

Replace raisins with dried cranberries.
Replace apricots with more raisins or dried apple.

Rocky Road Chocolate Bars

Not Just for Kids

Kid-friendly ingredients — such as cereal, graham wafers, marshmallows, chocolate chips, peanut butter and caramels — dominate this section, making the recipes favorites for the young as well as the young at heart. These bars are also relatively easy to make, which means that kids can help out in the kitchen because their attention span isn't taxed. Not only does baking provide an opportunity to share quality family time together, but it also helps kids develop practical skills like counting. They'll also learn how to measure, mix and chop, preparing them for the days when they'll be responsible for food preparation themselves. I've tried to keep an eye on cleanup so they won't be daunted by it.

These foolproof recipes guarantee that kids will end up with treats they can be proud to share with their family and friends. Let them choose the recipes and make their own lunch-box treats and after-school snacks. It's fun for everyone.

Rocky Road Chocolate Bars

Kids know the ingredients in rocky roads long before they learn to make them, so it won't be hard to get them in the kitchen for these.

MAKES 18 TO 48 BARS (see Cutting Guide, page 10)

- **Preparation: 20 minutes**
- **Cooking: 5 minutes**
- **Chilling: 1 hour**
- **Freezing: excellent**

TIPS

Let kids count the marshmallows as they put them in the measuring cup. If you have two helpers, they can each count enough to fill ³⁄₄ cup (175 mL) and see if they get the same number.

Use a fine strainer to sift the confectioners' (icing) sugar. Measure it first in a dry measure, then sift it, pushing it through the sieve with the back of a spoon.

- **8-inch (2 L) square cake pan, greased**

CRUMB MIXTURE

1 ¹⁄₂ cups	graham wafer crumbs	375 mL
1 ¹⁄₂ cups	miniature marshmallows	375 mL
¹⁄₂ cup	chopped pecans	125 mL
¹⁄₂ cup	confectioners' (icing) sugar, sifted	125 mL
2 tbsp	milk	30 mL

CHOCOLATE MIXTURE

2 cups	semisweet chocolate chips	500 mL
¹⁄₂ cup	milk	125 mL
3 tbsp	butter	45 mL
¹⁄₄ cup	confectioners' (icing) sugar, sifted	60 mL

1. *Crumb Mixture:* In a bowl, combine graham wafer crumbs, marshmallows, pecans, confectioners' sugar and milk. Mix well until all ingredients are moistened. Set aside.

2. *Chocolate Mixture:* In a saucepan, combine chocolate chips, milk and butter. Heat over low heat, stirring constantly, until chocolate is melted and mixture is smooth. Remove from heat. Pour half (about ³⁄₄ cup/175 mL) over reserved crumb mixture. Mix well. Spread evenly in prepared pan.

3. Stir confectioners' sugar into remaining chocolate mixture in saucepan, mixing well. Spread evenly over base in pan. Chill until chocolate is set, about 1 hour. Cut into bars.

Variations

Replace pecans with walnuts, almonds or peanuts.

Sprinkle finely chopped nuts over the chocolate topping.

Use colored marshmallows for fun.

Peter Pumpkin Bars

Make these a Halloween tradition. Kids can take them to school for their Halloween party or just enjoy them as a special treat. They're as soft as cheesecake, which is nice for small children.

MAKES 18 TO 48 BARS
(see Cutting Guide, page 10)

- **Preparation: 25 minutes**
- **Baking: 25 minutes**
- **Freezing: excellent**

TIPS

If you prefer, use unbleached all-purpose flour in all your baking. It's the same as regular all-purpose flour but has not been chemically bleached.

Be sure to buy pumpkin purée, not pumpkin pie filling, which contains spices and sugar.

This batter doesn't require a mixer, which makes it fun and easy for children to help. They enjoy beating things with a wooden spoon.

It's fun for kids to decorate the frosting with their favorite Halloween candies, such as licorice bats, brooms and witches, candy corn, candy pumpkins and orange and black M&M's or Smarties.

- **Preheat oven to 350°F (180°C)**
- **9-inch (2.5 L) square cake pan, greased**

BARS

1 cup	all-purpose flour	250 mL
¾ cup	granulated sugar	175 mL
1 tsp	baking powder	5 mL
1 tsp	ground cinnamon	5 mL
¼ tsp	salt	1 mL
¼ tsp	ground nutmeg	1 mL
2	eggs	2
1 cup	pumpkin purée (not pie filling)	250 mL
½ cup	vegetable oil	125 mL

FROSTING

4 oz	cream cheese, softened	125 g
¼ cup	butter, softened	60 mL
2 cups	confectioners' (icing) sugar, sifted, divided	500 mL
1 tsp	vanilla	5 mL
2 to 3 tsp	milk	10 to 15 mL

1. *Bars:* In a bowl, combine flour, sugar, baking powder, cinnamon, salt and nutmeg. In a separate bowl, whisk together eggs, pumpkin and oil until blended. Stir into dry mixture, mixing until smooth. Spread evenly in prepared pan.

2. Bake in preheated oven until a toothpick inserted in center comes out clean, 20 to 25 minutes. Let cool completely in pan on rack.

3. *Frosting:* In a bowl, using an electric mixer on medium speed, beat cream cheese and butter until creamy, about 3 minutes. Add 1 cup (250 mL) of the confectioners' sugar and vanilla, beating until smooth. Add remaining confectioners' sugar and enough milk to make a soft, spreadable consistency. Spread over cooled bar. Cut into bars.

Variations

Omit the frosting. Dust with confectioners' (icing) sugar or leave plain.

Add ½ cup (125 mL) raisins to the batter.

Chocolate Toffee Cookie Brittle

Kids love to help when they get to enjoy their efforts. The hardest part of the job is waiting for their masterpieces to cool.

**MAKES ABOUT
4 DOZEN PIECES**

- **Preparation: 20 minutes**
- **Baking: 25 minutes**
- **Freezing: excellent**

TIP
The mixture will be crumbly when pressed in the pan, but as it bakes it all comes together.

- **Preheat oven to 325°F (160°C)**
- **15- by 10- by 1-inch (2 L) jelly roll pan, greased**

1 cup	butter, softened	250 mL
1 cup	granulated sugar	250 mL
1 tsp	vanilla	5 mL
2 cups	all-purpose flour	500 mL
1/4 tsp	salt	1 mL
1 cup	semisweet chocolate chips	250 mL
4	crunchy chocolate-covered toffee bars (1.4 oz/39 g each), coarsely chopped, (see Tips, page 145)	4
1/2 cup	finely chopped almonds	125 mL

1. In a large bowl, using an electric mixer on medium speed, beat butter, sugar and vanilla until light and creamy, about 3 minutes. Stir in flour, salt, chocolate chips, chocolate bars and almonds, mixing well. Press firmly into prepared pan.

2. Bake in preheated oven until top is golden, 20 to 25 minutes. Let cool completely in pan on rack. Break into pieces.

Corn Flake Peanut Squares

Here's an excellent cereal square that kids can easily learn to make for their own lunch box and afternoon snack.

**MAKES 16 TO
36 SQUARES
(see Cutting Guide,
page 10)**

- **Preparation: 15 minutes**
- **Cooking: 5 minutes**
- **Cooling: 30 minutes**
- **Freezing: excellent**

- **9-inch (2.5 L) square cake pan, greased**

3/4 cup	packed brown sugar	175 mL
3/4 cup	creamy peanut butter	175 mL
3/4 cup	corn syrup	175 mL
6 cups	corn flakes cereal, slightly crushed	1.5 L
1 cup	coarsely chopped peanuts	250 mL

1. In a saucepan, heat brown sugar, peanut butter and corn syrup over medium heat, stirring until smooth. In a large bowl, combine cereal and peanuts. Pour syrup mixture over top and, using a large wooden spoon, stir until cereal and nuts are evenly coated. Press evenly into prepared pan. Let cool until set, about 30 minutes. Cut into squares.

Chocolate Candy Cookie Bars

Here's a perfect recipe for children with a short attention span. It's in the oven in a flash so there's no time for them to get bored.

MAKES 20 TO 54 BARS
(see Cutting Guide, page 10)

- **Preparation: 15 minutes**
- **Baking: 25 minutes**
- **Freezing: excellent**

- **Preheat oven to 350°F (180°C)**
- **13- by 9-inch (3 L) cake pan, ungreased**

1/2 cup	butter, melted	125 mL
1 1/3 cups	graham wafer crumbs	325 mL
1	can (10 oz/300 mL) sweetened condensed milk	1
2 cups	semisweet chocolate chips	500 mL
3/4 cup	mini candy-coated chocolate pieces (such as M&M's)	175 mL

1. Pour butter into cake pan and tilt to coat the bottom evenly. Sprinkle graham wafer crumbs evenly over top, moistening all the crumbs. Pour condensed milk evenly over crumbs. Sprinkle chocolate chips, then candies, evenly over top.

2. Bake in preheated oven until golden around the edges, 20 to 25 minutes. Let cool completely in pan on rack. Cut into bars.

S'more Cookie Bars

No kids' section would be complete if it didn't contain some version of the classic s'mores. It goes without saying that this will be on their list of most requested recipes.

MAKES 20 TO 54 BARS
(see Cutting Guide, page 10)

- **Preparation: 15 minutes**
- **Baking: 25 minutes**
- **Freezing: excellent**

- **Preheat oven to 350°F (180°C)**
- **13- by 9-inch (3 L) cake pan, ungreased**

1/2 cup	butter, melted	125 mL
1 1/4 cups	graham wafer crumbs	300 mL
1/2 cup	quick-cooking rolled oats	125 mL
1	can (10 oz/300 mL) sweetened condensed milk	1
1 1/4 cups	miniature marshmallows	300 mL
1 cup	milk chocolate chips	250 mL
1 cup	peanut butter chips	250 mL

1. Pour butter into cake pan and tilt to coat the bottom evenly. Sprinkle graham wafer crumbs and oats evenly over top. Press down lightly with the back of a spoon to moisten crumb mixture. Pour sweetened condensed milk evenly over crumbs. Sprinkle marshmallows, then chips, evenly over top.

2. Bake in preheated oven until golden around the edges, about 25 minutes. Let cool completely in pan on rack. Cut into bars.

Blueberry Cookie Bars

These bars are easy enough for kids to make themselves and so attractive they'll be proud to show them off.

MAKES 18 TO 48 BARS (see Cutting Guide, page 10)

- **Preparation: 20 minutes**
- **Baking: 40 minutes**
- **Freezing: excellent**

TIP

If your jam seems a little sweet, try adding 2 to 3 tsp (10 to 15 mL) lemon juice to it.

- **Preheat oven to 350°F (180°C)**
- **8-inch (2 L) square cake pan, greased**

½ cup	butter, softened	125 mL
½ cup	granulated sugar	125 mL
1	egg	1
1½ cups	all-purpose flour	375 mL
¾ cup	blueberry jam	175 mL
⅓ cup	sliced almonds	75 mL

1. In a bowl, using an electric mixer on medium speed, beat butter, sugar and egg until light and creamy, about 3 minutes. On low speed, gradually beat in flour, until mixture is crumbly. Set aside 1 cup (250 mL) of the mixture for topping. Press remainder evenly into prepared pan. Spread jam evenly over top, leaving a ½-inch (1 cm) border of crust around edges. Stir almonds into reserved mixture and sprinkle evenly over jam.

2. Bake in preheated oven until golden, 35 to 40 minutes. Let cool completely in pan on rack. Cut into bars.

Variations

Try jams such as cherry, apricot and strawberry.

Replace almonds with pecans or omit them for a nut-free bar.

Chocolate Chip Cookie Bars

No kids' section is complete without the ultimate favorite cookie. In this case, it's the same taste in an easy-to-make bar shape.

MAKES 20 TO 54 BARS (see Cutting Guide, page 10)

- **Preparation: 15 minutes**
- **Baking: 20 minutes**
- **Freezing: excellent**

TIPS

When pressing this dough into the pan, lightly flour your fingers to prevent it from sticking.

This dough also makes wonderful cookies, which can be fun for kids to shape. Drop dough by rounded spoonfuls onto a greased baking sheet and bake for 8 to 10 minutes or until light golden but still soft. They'll firm up on cooling.

You don't need an electric mixer for many cookie doughs. A big wooden spoon works well and gives a more homemade look. It's also more kid friendly.

- Preheat oven to 375°F (190°C)
- 13- by 9-inch (3 L) cake pan, greased

1 cup	butter, softened	250 mL
¾ cup	granulated sugar	175 mL
¾ cup	packed brown sugar	175 mL
1	egg	1
1 tsp	vanilla	5 mL
2¼ cups	all-purpose flour	550 mL
1 tsp	baking soda	5 mL
¼ tsp	salt	1 mL
2 cups	semisweet chocolate chips	500 mL
1 cup	coarsely chopped pecans	250 mL

1. In a bowl, using a wooden spoon, beat butter, granulated and brown sugars, egg and vanilla until smooth, about 5 minutes. Combine flour, baking soda and salt. Stir into creamed mixture, mixing well. Stir in chocolate chips and pecans. Using floured fingers, press dough evenly into prepared pan.

2. Bake in preheated oven until golden, about 20 minutes. Let cool completely in pan on rack. Cut into bars.

Variations

For a birthday party loot bag treat, replace the chocolate chips with candy-coated chocolate pieces like Smarties or M&M's.

Replace pecans with walnuts or cashews.

Oatmeal Raisin Cookie Bars

Second to chocolate chip cookies in the list of favorites is oatmeal raisin. These take half the time to shape, which means they're ready for eating sooner.

MAKES 20 TO 54 BARS
(see Cutting Guide, page 10)

- **Preparation: 20 minutes**
- **Baking: 25 minutes**
- **Freezing: excellent**

TIPS

I like to use some shortening in these bars because it produces a cookie with better texture. Since traditional shortening is loaded with unhealthy trans fats, I recommend purchasing a brand that's trans fat–free. Check the label.

Use old-fashioned (large-flake) rolled oats for a more "oaty" flavor.

To prevent sticking, use floured fingers or the heel of your hand to press the dough into the pan. Don't worry about gooey hands. Kids enjoy this.

These are like a big, thick, chewy cookie. Bake them a little longer to make them crisper.

- **Preheat oven to 375°F (190°C)**
- **13- by 9-inch (3 L) cake pan, greased**

½ cup	butter, softened	125 mL
½ cup	shortening (see Tips, left)	125 mL
⅔ cup	granulated sugar	150 mL
⅔ cup	packed brown sugar	150 mL
2	eggs	2
1 cup	all-purpose flour	250 mL
1 tsp	baking soda	5 mL
1 tsp	ground cinnamon	5 mL
½ tsp	baking powder	2 mL
¼ tsp	salt	1 mL
3 cups	quick-cooking rolled oats	750 mL
1⅓ cups	raisins	325 mL

1. In a bowl, using a wooden spoon, beat butter, shortening, granulated and brown sugars and eggs until smooth and creamy, about 5 minutes. Combine flour, baking soda, cinnamon, baking powder and salt. Stir into creamed mixture, mixing well. Stir in oats and raisins until thoroughly blended. Using floured fingers, press dough evenly into prepared pan.

2. Bake in preheated oven until light golden, 20 to 25 minutes. Let cool completely in pan on rack. Cut into bars.

Variation

Replace raisins with dried cranberries, chocolate chips or chopped walnuts.

Chocolate-Topped Peanut Butter Oat Bars

It's hard to find a kid who doesn't like the combination of peanut butter and chocolate in any form — bars, cookies, candy, ice cream and cake.

MAKES 20 TO 54 BARS (see Cutting Guide, page 10)

- **Preparation: 15 minutes**
- **Baking: 15 minutes**
- **Chilling: 30 minutes**
- **Freezing: excellent**

TIP

Use a small offset spatula or the back of a soup spoon to spread soft ingredients like peanut butter and melted chocolate.

- **Preheat oven to 350°F (180°C)**
- **13- by 9-inch (3 L) cake pan, greased**

BASE

½ cup	butter, softened	125 mL
1 cup	packed brown sugar	250 mL
½ cup	corn syrup	125 mL
¼ tsp	salt	1 mL
4 cups	quick-cooking rolled oats	1 L
¾ cup	crunchy peanut butter	175 mL

TOPPING

6	squares (1 oz/28 g each) semisweet chocolate, chopped	6
¼ cup	butter	60 mL
½ cup	peanut butter chips	125 mL

1. *Base:* In a bowl, using a wooden spoon, beat butter and brown sugar until light and creamy, about 5 minutes. Stir in corn syrup, salt and oats, mixing well. Spread evenly in prepared pan. Bake in preheated oven until top is set and golden, about 15 minutes. Let cool in pan on rack for 15 minutes. Drop peanut butter by spoonfuls over base and spread evenly.

2. *Topping:* In a saucepan over low heat, melt chocolate, butter and peanut butter chips, stirring constantly, until smooth. Drop by spoonfuls over peanut butter and spread evenly. Chill until chocolate is set, about 30 minutes. Cut into bars.

Variations

If you prefer an all-chocolate topping, replace peanut butter chips with 2 additional (1 oz/28 g each) squares of chocolate.

Use creamy peanut butter instead of crunchy, reducing the amount to ½ cup (125 mL).

Sprinkle ⅓ cup (75 mL) finely chopped peanuts evenly over chocolate topping.

Use old-fashioned (large-flake) rolled oats for a more oaty taste and appearance.

Thumbprint Jam Cookie Squares

Thumbprint cookies have been around as long as I can remember. My grandmother and mother always made them at Christmas. It was my job to put the thumbprint in the dough.

MAKES 54 SQUARES (see Cutting Guide page 10)

- **Preparation: 20 minutes**
- **Baking: 20 minutes**
- **Chilling: 15 minutes**
- **Freezing: excellent**

TIPS

If the jam seems skimpy after baking (it will settle when warm), top up with a little more as soon as the squares come out of the oven.

Stir jam to soften before spooning into thumbprint.

- **Preheat oven to 400°F (200°C)**
- **15- by 10- by 1-inch (2 L) jelly roll pan, greased**

3 cups	all-purpose flour	750 mL
1 ¼ cups	confectioners' (icing) sugar, sifted	300 mL
1 ¼ cups	butter, softened	300 mL
1 ½ tsp	vanilla	7 mL
1	egg, beaten	1
1 cup	raspberry jam	250 mL
2	squares (1 oz/28 g each) bittersweet chocolate, melted	2

1. In a bowl, combine flour, confectioners' sugar, butter, vanilla and egg. Using a large wooden spoon, beat until dough comes together, about 5 minutes. Transfer to a lightly floured surface and, using your hands, knead until smooth. Press evenly into prepared pan. Using the tip of a knife, mark dough into 54 squares. With your thumb or the handle of a wooden spoon, press an indentation in the center of each square. Place a scant teaspoon (5 mL) of jam in each thumbprint.

2. Bake in preheated oven until lightly browned around edges, 15 to 20 minutes. Let cool completely in pan on rack.

3. Drizzle melted chocolate randomly over squares. Chill until chocolate is set, about 15 minutes. Cut into squares.

Variations

Vary the jam to suit your taste or to have a variety of colors. Blackberry and apricot are nice.

Omit chocolate drizzle. Leave the squares plain or dust them with confectioners' (icing) sugar before serving.

Sprinkle ¾ cup (175 mL) finely chopped walnuts over dough before making thumbprints.

Chocolate Caramel Peanut Bars

The best part of having little helpers with this recipe is that they can unwrap the caramels. Count the unwrapped caramels to be sure the total matches the wrapped number. Some usually get lost in the unwrapping process.

MAKES 20 TO 54 BARS
(see Cutting Guide, page 10)

- **Preparation: 25 minutes**
- **Cooking: 10 minutes**
- **Baking: 35 minutes**
- **Freezing: excellent**

TIPS

Caramels are easier to unwrap if you chill them first.

If you prefer, use a wooden spoon to mix the base. It will take about 5 minutes.

Always assemble your ingredients before starting to bake. That way you'll be sure you have everything and will not leave anything out.

Don't keep opened baking soda longer than 6 months. Invest in a new box and retire the old one to the refrigerator as a deodorizer.

- **Preheat oven to 350°F (180°C)**
- **13- by 9-inch (3 L) cake pan, greased**

BASE

2 cups	all-purpose flour	500 mL
2 cups	quick-cooking rolled oats	500 mL
1 1/3 cups	packed brown sugar	325 mL
1 tsp	baking soda	5 mL
1/4 tsp	salt	1 mL
1 cup	butter, softened	250 mL
1	egg, beaten	1

TOPPING

1 lb	soft caramels, unwrapped (about 60)	500 g
1/3 cup	evaporated milk	75 mL
1 1/4 cups	semisweet chocolate chips	300 mL
1 cup	chopped dry-roasted peanuts	250 mL

1. *Base:* In a large bowl, combine flour, oats, brown sugar, baking soda and salt. Add butter and egg. On low speed, beat until mixture is crumbly, about 2 minutes. Press half of the mixture evenly into prepared pan. Bake in preheated oven until set, about 10 minutes.

2. *Topping:* In a heavy saucepan over low heat, combine caramels and evaporated milk. Heat, stirring, until caramels are melted and mixture is smooth. Remove from heat and set aside. Sprinkle chocolate chips and peanuts evenly over base. Drizzle melted caramel mixture evenly over top. Sprinkle remaining oat mixture over caramel.

3. Return to oven and bake until top is golden brown, 20 to 25 minutes. Let cool in pan on rack for 30 minutes. Loosen edges from sides of pan with a sharp knife. Let cool completely in pan on rack. Cut into bars.

Variations

Replace peanuts with pecans or cashews.

Replace chocolate chips with peanut butter chips.

Frosted Honey Zucchini Bars

Here's a great way to get kids to enjoy vegetables — in a cake-like base with frosting.

MAKES 20 TO 54 BARS
(see Cutting Guide, page 10)

- **Preparation: 25 minutes**
- **Baking: 30 minutes**
- **Freezing: excellent**

TIPS

I like to leave the zucchini unpeeled because I think the specks of green add interesting detail, but by all means peel it if you prefer.

To dress up these bars, sprinkle the frosting with finely chopped nuts.

Serve larger squares as a dessert.

If you omit the frosting, these bars taste like a moist and delicious breakfast muffin.

Not only does the honey add flavor, it also keeps the bars moist.

These bars are easier to cut if chilled.

- **Preheat oven to 350°F (180°C)**
- **13- by 9-inch (3 L) cake pan, greased**

BASE

1 cup	all-purpose flour	250 mL
1 tsp	baking powder	5 mL
1 tsp	baking soda	5 mL
1 tsp	ground cinnamon	5 mL
1/4 tsp	salt	1 mL
1/4 tsp	ground nutmeg	1 mL
2	eggs	2
1/3 cup	vegetable oil	75 mL
1/3 cup	liquid honey	75 mL
2 tbsp	milk	30 mL
1 cup	shredded zucchini	250 mL
1/2 cup	well-drained crushed pineapple	125 mL
1/2 cup	raisins	125 mL
1/3 cup	chopped pecans	75 mL

FROSTING

4 oz	cream cheese, softened	125 g
2 tbsp	butter, softened	30 mL
1 1/2 cups	confectioners' (icing) sugar, sifted	375 mL
1 tsp	freshly squeezed lemon juice	5 mL

1. *Base:* In a bowl, combine flour, baking powder, baking soda, cinnamon, salt and nutmeg. In a separate bowl, whisk eggs, oil, honey and milk until smooth. Stir into dry ingredients, mixing well. Stir in zucchini, pineapple, raisins and pecans, mixing until all ingredients are thoroughly combined. Spread batter evenly in prepared pan.

2. Bake in preheated oven until a toothpick inserted in center comes out clean, 25 to 30 minutes. Let cool completely in pan on rack.

3. *Frosting:* In a small bowl, using an electric mixer on low speed, beat cream cheese and butter until smooth. Gradually beat in confectioners' sugar and lemon juice, beating until smooth. Spread evenly over cooled base. Cut into bars. Store in refrigerator for up to 1 week.

Seeds and Coconut Cereal Squares

A combination of coconut and seeds adds fiber and flavor to these addictive squares. They make a wonderful snack to pack for long car rides. Luckily, the recipe makes a large pan.

MAKES 24 TO 60 SQUARES
(see Cutting Guide, page 10)

- **Preparation: 10 minutes**
- **Cooking: 2 minutes**
- **Baking: 10 minutes**
- **Freezing: excellent**

TIPS

Sweetened and unsweetened coconut are interchangeable in baking. I have specified unsweetened here with a view to limiting kids' sugar consumption.

Teach kids how to measure brown sugar properly. Unlike granulated sugar, which is simply scooped into a dry measuring cup then leveled off, brown sugar is packed into the cup. To test if they did it right, turn the filled cup upside down on a piece of waxed paper. When you remove the cup the sugar should hold its shape.

- **Preheat oven to 375°F (190°C)**
- **15- by 10- by 1-inch (2 L) jelly roll pan, greased**

³⁄₄ cup	butter	175 mL
1 ¹⁄₄ cups	packed brown sugar	300 mL
1 tsp	vanilla	5 mL
2 ¹⁄₄ cups	quick-cooking rolled oats	550 mL
¹⁄₄ cup	sesame seeds	60 mL
¹⁄₄ cup	flax seeds	60 mL
¹⁄₄ cup	sunflower seeds	60 mL
¹⁄₄ cup	unsweetened flaked coconut	60 mL
³⁄₄ tsp	baking powder	3 mL
¹⁄₄ tsp	salt	1 mL

1. In a large saucepan, melt butter over medium heat. Stir in brown sugar and vanilla. Cook, stirring often, until mixture is bubbly, about 2 minutes. Remove from heat. Stir in rolled oats, sesame seeds, flax seeds, sunflower seeds, coconut, baking powder and salt, mixing well until all ingredients are moistened. Press evenly into prepared pan.

2. Bake in preheated oven until light golden, about 10 minutes. Let cool completely in pan on rack. Cut into squares.

Variation

Use other kinds of seeds. Pumpkin seeds add an interesting appearance, texture and flavor.

Double Granola Bars

Two layers of granola bars in one means double the flavor and nutrition in every bite. Kids can help pick some of their favorite ingredients to put in the top layer.

MAKES 18 TO 48 BARS
(see Cutting Guide, page 10)

- **Preparation: 30 minutes**
- **Baking: 32 minutes**
- **Freezing: excellent**

TIPS

Sweetened and unsweetened coconut are interchangeable in recipes. I have specified the use of unsweetened in this chapter with a view to limiting kids' sugar consumption.

Granola bars keep very well if they're well wrapped and stored in a cool, dry place — for up to 2 weeks.

These bars aren't too sweet and are easy to eat, which makes them very versatile. They're a good choice for lunches, breakfast on the run, snacks and coffee time.

- **Preheat oven to 325°F (160°C)**
- **8-inch (2 L) square cake pan, greased**

CRUST

½ cup	whole wheat flour	125 mL
⅓ cup	quick-cooking rolled oats	75 mL
¼ cup	ground almonds	60 mL
3 tbsp	packed brown sugar	45 mL
¼ tsp	baking powder	1 mL
3 tbsp	butter, melted	45 mL

TOPPING

¼ cup	butter, melted	60 mL
2 tbsp	packed brown sugar	30 mL
2 tbsp	liquid honey	30 mL
½ cup	quick-cooking rolled oats	125 mL
½ cup	finely chopped almonds	125 mL
½ cup	unsweetened flaked coconut (see Tips, left)	125 mL
⅓ cup	pumpkin seeds	75 mL
¼ cup	chopped dried mango	60 mL
2 tbsp	sesame seeds	30 mL

1. *Crust:* In a bowl, combine flour, oats, ground almonds, brown sugar and baking powder. Stir in melted butter, mixing well. Press evenly into prepared pan. Bake in preheated oven until set and golden around the edges, 10 to 12 minutes.

2. *Topping:* In a bowl, whisk melted butter, brown sugar and honey. Stir in oats, almonds, coconut, pumpkin seeds, dried mango and sesame seeds, mixing well. Spread evenly over crust. Press down gently using the heel of your hand, an offset spatula or the back of a spoon.

3. Return to oven and bake until set and golden, 15 to 20 minutes. Let cool completely in pan on rack. Cut into bars.

Variations

Replace whole wheat flour with all-purpose flour.

Decrease flour to ⅓ cup (75 mL) and add 3 tbsp (45 mL) wheat germ or 2 tbsp (30 mL) ground flax seeds.

Replace pumpkin seeds with sunflower seeds.

Raisin Pecan Tart Squares

A combination of butter tarts and pecan tarts baked into one delicious square, these are great on their own or served with ice cream for a scrumptious dessert.

MAKES 16 TO 36 SQUARES
(see Cutting Guide, page 10)

- **Preparation: 20 minutes**
- **Baking: 40 minutes**
- **Freezing: excellent**

(see Cutting Guide, page 10)

TIPS

The center of the square should be slightly soft when you take it from the oven. It firms up on cooling.

These bars are nice but not too firm, like a butter tart that's almost drippy.

Use real vanilla in baking. No matter how much you use, you'll never get the authentic flavor using artificial vanilla. It may seem expensive, but it is well worth the cost.

- **Preheat oven to 350°F (180°C)**
- **9-inch (2.5 L) square cake pan, greased**

CRUST

1 cup	all-purpose flour	250 mL
1/4 cup	granulated sugar	60 mL
1/2 cup	cold butter, cubed	125 mL

TOPPING

2	eggs	2
1 cup	packed brown sugar	250 mL
2 tbsp	all-purpose flour	30 mL
1/2 tsp	baking powder	2 mL
1/4 tsp	salt	1 mL
1 tsp	vanilla	5 mL
3/4 cup	raisins	175 mL
3/4 cup	coarsely chopped pecans	175 mL

1. *Crust:* In a bowl, combine flour and sugar. Using a pastry blender, 2 knives or your fingers, cut in butter until mixture resembles coarse crumbs. Press evenly into prepared pan. Bake in preheated oven until golden around the edges, 10 to 12 minutes.

2. *Topping:* In a bowl, whisk eggs and brown sugar until blended. Whisk in flour, baking powder, salt and vanilla until smooth. Stir in raisins and pecans. Spread evenly over crust.

3. Return to oven and bake just until top is set and golden, 23 to 28 minutes. Let cool completely in pan on rack. Cut into squares.

Variations

Use all raisins or all pecans.

Replace raisins with dried cranberries.

Replace pecans with walnuts.

Strawberry Cheesecake Squares

Cake Mix Bars and Squares

The convenience of a cake mix makes it especially quick and easy to bake bars and squares. Not only does it eliminate the need to measure many ingredients, but it also reduces the room for error and saves on washing up. You can use a cake mix to form the base of layered bars or to provide the batter to hold crunchy, chunky ingredients in single-layer bars. And, like other bars, those made with cake mix can be dressed up with a frosting (ready to serve for speed and convenience) or a dusting of confectioners' (icing) sugar.

I'm sure after you try a few bars made with cake mix, you'll agree they're quick, easy and delicious — a perfect choice for spur-of-the-moment baking. With a chocolate and a white mix on hand, there's no excuse for not baking.

Strawberry Cheesecake Squares

Cut these into large squares for a dessert or into bite-size morsels for a cookie tray.

MAKES 24 SQUARES
(see Cutting Guide, page 10)

- **Preparation: 25 minutes**
- **Baking: 45 minutes**
- **Chilling: 3 hours**
- **Freezing: excellent**

TIP

Cooking spray is an easy way to grease baking pans. Don't overdo it though — a fine spray will do the trick.

- **Preheat oven to 350°F (180°C)**
- **13- by 9-inch (3 L) cake pan, greased**

CRUST

1	package (18.25 oz/515 g) white cake mix	1
¾ cup	finely chopped almonds	175 mL
¾ cup	cold butter, cubed	175 mL

FILLING

2	package (8 oz/250 g each) cream cheese, softened	2
⅔ cup	granulated sugar	150 mL
2	eggs	2
½ tsp	almond extract	2 mL
1 cup	strawberry jam	250 mL
¾ cup	sliced almonds	175 mL

1. *Crust:* In a bowl, combine cake mix and chopped almonds. Using a pastry blender, 2 knives or your fingers, cut in butter until mixture resembles coarse crumbs. Set aside 1 cup (250 mL) for topping. Press remainder evenly into prepared pan. Bake in preheated oven until light golden, about 15 minutes.

2. *Filling:* In a large bowl, using an electric mixer on medium speed, beat cream cheese, sugar, eggs and almond extract until smooth and creamy, about 3 minutes. Spread evenly over hot crust.

3. Return to oven and bake until set, about 15 minutes. Let cool in pan on rack for 10 minutes. Stir jam until smooth and spread evenly over filling. Stir sliced almonds into reserved crust mixture. Sprinkle evenly over jam. Bake until top is golden, about 15 minutes. Let cool completely in pan on rack. Chill until set, about 3 hours, or overnight before cutting into squares. Refrigerate leftover cheesecake squares for up to 3 days.

Variations

Replace strawberry jam with raspberry, apricot or cherry.
Replace almond extract with vanilla.

Cherry Cheesecake Bars

Enjoy bite-size cheesecakes for dessert or a snack. Vary the flavor to suit your own family's favorites.

MAKES 20 TO 54 BARS
(see Cutting Guide, page 10)

- **Preparation: 20 minutes**
- **Baking: 50 minutes**
- **Freezing: excellent**

TIP

For easy drizzling, melt butter in a glass measuring cup with a spout.

- **Preheat oven to 350°F (180°C)**
- **13- by 9-inch (3 L) cake pan, greased**

CRUST

1	package (18.25 oz/515 g) white cake mix, divided	1
½ cup	corn flakes cereal crumbs	125 mL
1	egg, beaten	1
½ cup	butter, melted	125 mL

FILLING

2	package (8 oz/250 g each) cream cheese, softened	2
⅓ cup	granulated sugar	75 mL
2	eggs	2
1 tsp	grated lemon zest	5 mL
1 tbsp	freshly squeezed lemon juice	15 mL
1	can (19 oz/540 mL) cherry pie filling	1

TOPPING

½ cup	chopped pecans	125 mL
½ tsp	ground cinnamon	2 mL
¼ cup	butter, melted	60 mL

1. *Crust:* Set aside ½ cup (125 mL) cake mix for topping. In a large bowl, combine remaining cake mix, corn flakes crumbs, egg and melted butter, mixing until well blended. Press evenly into bottom and slightly up sides of prepared pan. Chill while preparing filling.

2. *Filling:* In a large bowl, using an electric mixer on medium speed, beat cream cheese and sugar until blended, about 3 minutes. Add eggs, one at a time, beating thoroughly after each addition. Beat in lemon zest and juice. Spread evenly over crust. Dollop spoonfuls of cherry pie filling over cheese mixture.

3. *Topping:* In a bowl, combine reserved cake mix, pecans and cinnamon. Sprinkle over filling. Drizzle with melted butter.

4. Bake in preheated oven until topping is just set, 40 to 50 minutes. Let cool completely in pan on rack. Refrigerate until serving. Cut into bars. Refrigerate leftover bars for up to 3 days.

Chocolate Pecan Bars

One pan goes a long way, so this recipe is a good choice for gift giving.

MAKES 36 TO 66 BARS (see Cutting Guide, page 10)

- **Preparation: 20 minutes**
- **Baking: 47 minutes**
- **Cooking: 5 minutes**
- **Freezing: excellent**

TIPS

If you don't do much baking, shop at bulk stores for specialty items and smaller quantities. Remember to store nuts in the freezer.

Purchase good-quality shiny metal pans for baking. They bake evenly and don't rust. Dark metal pans can cause overbrowning of edges before the center of the pan is cooked. If using glass dishes, decrease the oven temperature by 25°F (10°C).

These bars will store better if you omit the chocolate drizzle.

- **Preheat oven to 350°F (180°C)**
- **17- by 11- by 1-inch (3 L) jelly roll pan, greased**

CRUST

1	package (18.25 oz/515 g) white cake mix	1
2/3 cup	butter, melted	150 mL

TOPPING

5	squares (1 oz/28 g each) semisweet chocolate, chopped	5
1 cup	corn syrup	250 mL
1 cup	granulated sugar	250 mL
3	eggs	3
1 tsp	vanilla	5 mL
2 1/2 cups	chopped pecans	625 mL

DRIZZLE, OPTIONAL

2	squares (1 oz/28 g each) semisweet chocolate, melted	2

1. *Crust:* In a large bowl, combine cake mix and melted butter, mixing until well blended. Press evenly into prepared pan. Bake in preheated oven until light golden, 10 to 12 minutes.

2. *Topping:* In a saucepan over low heat, combine chocolate and corn syrup. Heat, stirring constantly, until smooth. Remove from heat. Whisk in sugar, eggs and vanilla until blended. Stir in pecans. Spread evenly over warm crust.

3. Return to oven and bake until filling is set around edges and slightly soft in the center, 30 to 35 minutes. Let cool completely in pan on rack.

4. *Drizzle (if using):* Drizzle melted chocolate randomly over bars. Chill until chocolate is set, about 30 minutes. Cut into bars.

Candy Bar Bars

The name says it all. These are just like a candy bar.

MAKES 20 TO 54 BARS (see Cutting Guide, page 10)

- **Preparation: 25 minutes**
- **Baking: 20 minutes**
- **Cooking: 5 minutes**
- **Cooling: 2 hours**
- **Freezing: excellent**

(see Cutting Guide, page 10)

TIP

There are several brands of soft caramels. Choose ones that are easy to unwrap, unless you have kids to do that job for you.

- **Preheat oven to 350°F (180°C)**
- **13- by 9-inch (3 L) cake pan, greased**

CRUST

1	package (18.25 oz/515 g) white cake mix	1
¾ cup	butter, melted	175 mL

FILLING

14 oz	soft caramels, unwrapped (about 60)	425 g
⅓ cup	evaporated milk	75 mL
⅓ cup	butter	75 mL
1⅔ cups	confectioners' (icing) sugar, sifted	400 mL
1 cup	chopped pecans	250 mL

GLAZE

1 cup	semisweet chocolate chips	250 mL

1. *Crust:* In a large bowl, combine cake mix and melted butter, mixing until well blended. Press evenly into prepared pan. Bake in preheated oven until light golden, 15 to 20 minutes.

2. *Filling:* In a saucepan over low heat, combine caramels and evaporated milk. Heat, stirring constantly, until caramels are melted and mixture is smooth. Stir in butter until melted. Remove from heat. Stir in confectioners' sugar and pecans, mixing well. Spread evenly over crust. Let cool until set, about 1 hour.

3. *Glaze:* In a small saucepan over low heat, melt chocolate chips, stirring constantly, until smooth. Drop by spoonfuls over filling and spread evenly. Chill until chocolate is set, about 1 hour. Cut into bars.

Variation

Peanuts, or a combination of peanuts and pecans, also work well in this bar.

Chewy Coconut Nut Bars

These bars are quick to make and a treat to eat.

MAKES 20 TO 54 BARS (see Cutting Guide, page 10)

- **Preparation: 20 minutes**
- **Baking: 45 minutes**
- **Freezing: excellent**

TIPS

I prefer flaked or shredded coconut. Desiccated coconut is very fine and results in drier baked products.

If you like the topping to be a little less sweet, add 1 tbsp (15 mL) lemon juice.

Pecans or walnuts work well in this recipe.

- **Preheat oven to 350°F (180°C)**
- **13- by 9-inch (3 L) cake pan, greased**

CRUST

1	package (18.25 oz/515 g) white cake mix	1
½ cup	butter, melted	125 mL

TOPPING

4	eggs	4
1¾ cups	packed brown sugar	425 mL
¼ cup	all-purpose flour	60 mL
2 tsp	baking powder	10 mL
1 tsp	vanilla	5 mL
1½ cups	chopped nuts (see Tips, left)	375 mL
1 cup	sweetened flaked coconut	250 mL

1. *Crust:* In a large bowl, combine cake mix and melted butter, mixing until well blended. Press evenly into prepared pan. Bake in preheated oven until light golden, about 15 minutes.
2. *Topping:* In a bowl, whisk eggs and brown sugar until blended. Whisk in flour, baking powder and vanilla, mixing well. Stir in nuts and coconut. Spread evenly over warm crust.
3. Return to oven and bake until set and golden, 25 to 30 minutes. Let cool completely in pan on rack. Cut into bars.

Toffee Chocolate Bars

Layers of crunchy toffee bits, creamy caramel and chocolate cover a crisp, cookie-like base, making every bite a sensation.

MAKES 20 TO 54 BARS (see Cutting Guide, page 10)

- **Preparation: 20 minutes**
- **Cooking: 10 minutes**
- **Baking: 30 minutes**
- **Cooling: 1 hour**
- **Freezing: excellent**

TIPS

The toffee bits get softer if you freeze these bars. We love them both ways — frozen and soft or unfrozen and crunchy. Take your pick.

Toffee bits are available in bags. They are broken pieces of the toffee part of Heath or Skor bars (no chocolate).

Don't leave the filling unattended on the stove, even for a minute. It burns very quickly.

- **Preheat oven to 350°F (180°C)**
- **13- by 9-inch (3 L) cake pan, greased**

CRUST

1	package (18.25 oz/515 g) white cake mix	1
2 tbsp	packed brown sugar	30 mL
½ cup	butter, melted	125 mL

FILLING

1	can (10 oz/300 mL) sweetened condensed milk	1
2 tbsp	butter	30 mL

TOPPING

1⅔ cups	semisweet chocolate chips	400 mL
1 cup	toffee bits (see Tips, left)	250 mL

1. *Crust:* In a bowl, combine cake mix, brown sugar and melted butter, mixing until well blended. Press evenly into prepared pan. Bake in preheated oven until light golden, about 15 minutes. Let cool in pan on rack while preparing filling.

2. *Filling:* In a heavy saucepan over low heat, combine sweetened condensed milk and butter. Heat, stirring constantly, until thickened, 5 to 10 minutes. Spread evenly over crust.

3. Return to oven and bake until top is golden, 10 to 15 minutes. Let cool in pan on rack for 1 hour.

4. *Topping:* In a heavy saucepan over low heat, melt chocolate chips, stirring until smooth. (You can also do this in a microwave on Medium for 2 minutes.) Drop by spoonfuls over filling and spread evenly. Sprinkle toffee bits on top, pressing lightly into chocolate. Let cool completely. If necessary, chill briefly to set chocolate. Cut into bars.

Variation

Use milk chocolate chips in place of semisweet.

Cranberry Pecan Bars

You'll love this combination of sweet pecan pie with tart cranberries in an easy-to-eat, bite-size bar.

MAKES 20 TO 54 BARS (see Cutting Guide, page 10)

- **Preparation: 20 minutes**
- **Baking: 50 minutes**
- **Freezing: excellent**

TIP
The crust will puff slightly during baking but settles down again on cooling.

- **Preheat oven to 350°F (180°C)**
- **13- by 9-inch (3 L) cake pan, greased**

CRUST

1	package (18.25 oz/515 g) white cake mix	1
½ cup	butter, melted	125 mL

TOPPING

4	eggs	4
1 cup	granulated sugar	250 mL
1 cup	corn syrup	250 mL
3 tbsp	butter, melted	45 mL
1½ cups	coarsely chopped pecans	375 mL
¾ cup	dried cranberries	175 mL

1. *Crust:* In a large bowl, combine cake mix and melted butter. Mix until well blended. Press evenly into prepared pan. Bake in preheated oven until light golden, about 15 minutes. Let cool in pan on rack for 5 minutes before adding topping.

2. *Topping:* In a bowl, whisk eggs, sugar, syrup and melted butter until blended. Stir in pecans and dried cranberries. Pour evenly over crust.

3. Return to oven and bake until set and golden, 30 to 35 minutes. Let cool completely in pan on rack. Cut into bars.

Variation
Replace dried cranberries with chocolate chips.

Raspberry Meringue Bars

A chewy meringue topping with lots of nuts and coconut covers a layer of jam on a shortbread-like base.

MAKES 20 TO 54 BARS (see Cutting Guide, page 10)

- **Preparation: 20 minutes**
- **Baking: 40 minutes**
- **Freezing: excellent**

TIPS

I have specified sweetened coconut because it seems to be more readily available than the unsweetened variety. But sweetened and unsweetened coconut can be used interchangeably in any recipe to suit your preference.

Before beating egg whites, wipe the bowl with the cut surface of a lemon to make sure it's free of grease.

Cut these bars with a hot, damp knife.

- **Preheat oven to 350°F (180°C)**
- **13- by 9-inch (3 L) cake pan, greased**

CRUST

1	package (18.25 oz/515 g) white cake mix	1
1/2 cup	butter, melted	125 mL
2	egg yolks	2

TOPPING

1 cup	raspberry jam	250 mL
1/2 cup	sweetened flaked coconut	125 mL
2	egg whites (see Tips, left)	2
1/2 cup	granulated sugar	125 mL
1 cup	chopped walnuts	250 mL

1. *Crust:* In a large bowl, using an electric mixer on low speed, beat cake mix, melted butter and egg yolks until well blended, about 1 minute. Press evenly into prepared pan. Bake in preheated oven until very light golden, 12 to 15 minutes.

2. *Topping:* Spread jam evenly over warm crust. Sprinkle coconut evenly over top. In a small bowl, using an electric mixer with clean beaters on high speed, beat egg whites until frothy. Gradually beat in sugar, beating until stiff peaks form. Fold in walnuts. Drop by spoonfuls over coconut and spread evenly.

3. Return to oven and bake until topping is light golden, 20 to 25 minutes. Let cool completely in pan on rack. Cut into bars.

Variation

Try other flavors of jam and nuts, such as apricot jam with hazelnuts.

Pecan Toffee Bars

This easy-to-make treat is quite sweet and will be very popular.

MAKES 20 TO 54 BARS (see Cutting Guide, page 10)

- **Preparation: 15 minutes**
- **Baking: 50 minutes**
- **Freezing: excellent**

TIPS

Toffee bits are available in bags. They're broken pieces of the toffee part of Heath or Skor bars (no chocolate).

Cut cooled bars and pack them in a single layer to freeze. If the bars are precut, you can thaw just the number you want to serve.

A drizzle of melted chocolate makes these bars special. If they have been frozen, add the drizzle just before serving.

- **Preheat oven to 350°F (180°C)**
- **13- by 9-inch (3 L) cake pan, greased**

CRUST

1	package (18.25 oz/515 g) white cake mix	1
1/2 cup	butter, melted	125 mL
1	egg, beaten	1

TOPPING

1	can (10 oz/300 mL) sweetened condensed milk	1
1	egg	1
1 1/4 cups	chopped pecans	300 mL
1 1/3 cups	toffee bits (see Tips, left)	325 mL

1. *Crust:* In a large bowl, using an electric mixer on low speed, beat cake mix, melted butter and egg until well blended, about 1 minute. Press evenly into prepared pan. Bake in preheated oven until light golden, 15 to 20 minutes.
2. *Topping:* In a bowl, whisk sweetened condensed milk and egg until smooth. Stir in pecans and toffee bits. Pour evenly over crust.
3. Return to oven and bake until topping is set, 25 to 30 minutes. Let cool completely in pan on rack. Cut into bars.

Variation

Replace toffee bits with chopped crunchy chocolate-covered toffee bars, such as Skor or Heath.

Chewy Peanut Candy Bars

These bars are a big hit with kids, young and old.

MAKES 40 TO 48 BARS (see Cutting Guide, page 10)

- **Preparation: 15 minutes**
- **Baking: 17 minutes**
- **Freezing: excellent**

> **TIP**
>
> To retain the fresh taste in baked goods, buy peanut butter just as you need it.

- **Preheat oven to 350°F (180°C)**
- **15- by 10- by 1-inch (2 L) jelly roll pan, greased**

CRUST

1	package (18.25 oz/515 g) white cake mix	1
½ cup	butter, softened	125 mL
1	egg, beaten	1

TOPPING

3½ cups	miniature marshmallows	875 mL
¾ cup	packed brown sugar	175 mL
¾ cup	corn syrup	175 mL
¾ cup	creamy peanut butter	175 mL
2 cups	crisp rice cereal	500 mL
1¾ cups	salted peanuts	425 mL
1¼ cups	miniature candy-coated chocolate pieces (such as M&M's)	300 mL

1. *Crust:* In a large bowl, using an electric mixer on low speed, beat cake mix, butter and egg until well blended and crumbly, about 1 minute. Press evenly into prepared pan. Bake in preheated oven until light golden, 10 to 15 minutes.

2. *Topping:* Sprinkle marshmallows evenly over hot crust. Return to oven and bake just until marshmallows begin to puff, 1 to 2 minutes. Let cool in pan on rack for 30 minutes.

3. In a large saucepan over low heat, combine brown sugar, syrup and peanut butter. Heat, stirring constantly, until smooth. Let cool for 5 minutes. Stir in cereal and peanuts. Mix well, then stir in candy. Spread evenly over marshmallows. Let cool completely before cutting into bars.

> **Variation**
>
> Colored marshmallows are a fun choice.

Caramel-Filled Brownies

There are many varieties of bars inspired by chocolate caramel candies, but this is one of our favorites — decided on after many taste comparisons!

MAKES 20 TO 54 BARS OR 24 SQUARES
(see Cutting Guide, page 10)

- **Preparation: 20 minutes**
- **Cooking: 5 minutes**
- **Baking: 35 minutes**
- **Freezing: excellent**

TIPS

The brownies may seem soft when you take them out of the oven, but they will firm up on cooling.

Chill caramels for easier unwrapping. It's still a frustrating job but easily forgotten when you taste these squares.

- **Preheat oven to 350°F (180°C)**
- **13- by 9-inch (3 L) cake pan, greased**

FILLING

1 lb	soft caramels, unwrapped (about 60)	500 g
½ cup	evaporated milk	125 mL

BASE & TOPPING

1	package (18.25 oz/515 g) devil's food cake mix	1
1 cup	chopped pecans	250 mL
½ cup	cold butter, cubed	125 mL
½ cup	evaporated milk	125 mL
1 cup	semisweet chocolate chips	250 mL

1. *Filling:* In a saucepan over low heat, combine caramels and evaporated milk. Heat, stirring constantly, until caramels are melted and mixture is smooth. Set aside. Keep warm while preparing batter.

2. *Base & Topping:* In a bowl, combine cake mix and pecans. Using a pastry blender, 2 knives or your fingers, cut in butter until mixture resembles coarse crumbs. Add evaporated milk and, using a wooden spoon, mix until well blended. (The batter will be thick.) Set half aside. Spread remaining batter in prepared pan. Bake in preheated oven until set, 12 to 15 minutes.

3. Sprinkle chocolate chips evenly over base. Drizzle caramel sauce evenly over chips. Spread carefully to cover base. Drop remaining batter by spoonfuls over caramel.

4. Return to oven and bake just until set, 15 to 20 minutes. Let cool completely in pan on rack. Cut into bars or squares.

Variation

Try using chocolate caramels. It doesn't look as attractive, but real chocoholics won't care.

Butterscotch Nut Bars

This versatile bar is also great cut into larger squares and served warm with ice cream for dessert.

MAKES 20 TO 54 BARS (see Cutting Guide, page 10)

- **Preparation: 20 minutes**
- **Baking: 50 minutes**
- **Freezing: excellent**

TIP

Store nuts in the freezer to keep them fresh.

- **Preheat oven to 350°F (180°C)**
- **13- by 9-inch (3 L) cake pan, greased**

CRUST

1	package (18.25 oz/515 g) white cake mix	1
2/3 cup	butter, melted	150 mL

TOPPING

4	eggs	4
1 cup	granulated sugar	250 mL
1 cup	corn syrup	250 mL
1/4 cup	butter, melted	60 mL
1 2/3 cups	butterscotch chips	400 mL
1 1/2 cups	coarsely chopped pecans	375 mL

1. *Crust:* In a large bowl, combine cake mix and melted butter, mixing until well blended. Press evenly into prepared pan. Bake in preheated oven until light golden, about 15 minutes. Let cool on rack for 5 minutes before adding topping.

2. *Topping:* In a bowl, whisk eggs, sugar, syrup and melted butter until well blended. Stir in butterscotch chips and nuts. Pour evenly over crust.

3. Return to oven and bake until set and golden, 30 to 35 minutes. Let cool completely in pan on rack. Cut into bars.

Variation

Semisweet chocolate chips and walnuts are another good combination.

Cranberry White Chocolate Chip Bars

Creamy white chocolate, crunchy nuts and tart cranberries combine in this colorful, festive bar.

MAKES 20 TO 54 BARS (see Cutting Guide, page 10)

- **Preparation: 20 minutes**
- **Baking: 30 minutes**
- **Freezing: excellent**

TIPS

If you prefer, use a wooden spoon to mix the batter. If beating by hand, beat for about 3 minutes.

When baking, check for doneness at the minimum time recommended to avoid being disappointed with an overdone item. You can always bake it longer.

It's a good idea to keep a reliable oven thermometer in your oven to check on the temperature.

- **Preheat oven to 350°F (180°C)**
- **13- by 9-inch (3 L) cake pan, greased**

1	package (18.25 oz/515 g) white cake mix	1
1/4 cup	packed brown sugar	60 mL
2	eggs	2
1/4 cup	butter, softened	60 mL
1/4 cup	water	60 mL
1 cup	dried cranberries	250 mL
1 cup	white chocolate chips	250 mL
1 cup	chopped almonds	250 mL

LEMON GLAZE, OPTIONAL

2 cups	confectioners' (icing) sugar, sifted	500 mL
1 tbsp	butter, softened	15 mL
2 tsp	grated lemon zest	10 mL
2 to 4 tbsp	freshly squeezed lemon juice	30 to 60 mL

1. In a large bowl, using an electric mixer on low speed, beat cake mix, brown sugar, eggs, butter and water until smooth, about 1 minute. Stir in cranberries, chocolate chips and almonds. Spread batter evenly in prepared pan.

2. Bake in preheated oven until set and golden, 25 to 30 minutes. Let cool completely in pan on rack.

3. *Lemon Glaze (if using):* In a bowl, combine confectioners' sugar, butter, lemon zest and lemon juice. Using a wooden spoon, mix until blended, adding just enough juice to make a smooth, spreadable consistency. Cut into bars.

Variations

If you prefer, top this bar with Lemon Frosting (page 108).

Replace the almonds with pecans or walnuts and the cranberries with chopped dried apricots.

Chewy Cherry Bars

These bars make a colorful addition to a holiday cookie tray. You'll never go wrong with extras in the freezer.

MAKES 20 TO 54 BARS
(see Cutting Guide,
page 10)

- **Preparation: 25 minutes**
- **Baking: 45 minutes**
- **Chilling: 1 hour**
- **Freezing: excellent**

- **Preheat oven to 350°F (180°C)**
- **13- by 9-inch (3 L) cake pan, greased**

CRUST

1	package (18.25 oz/515 g) white cake mix	1
¾ cup	butter, softened	175 mL

FILLING

2	eggs	2
1 cup	packed brown sugar	250 mL
½ tsp	almond extract	2 mL
2 tbsp	all-purpose flour	30 mL
1 tsp	baking powder	5 mL
1 cup	sweetened flaked coconut	250 mL
1 cup	chopped drained maraschino cherries	250 mL
½ cup	chopped pecans or walnuts	125 mL

ALMOND FROSTING

¼ cup	butter, softened	60 mL
½ tsp	almond extract	2 mL
2 cups	confectioners' (icing) sugar, sifted	500 mL
3 to 4 tbsp	half-and-half (10%) cream	45 to 60 mL

1. *Crust:* In a large bowl, using an electric mixer on low speed, beat cake mix and butter until well blended. Press evenly into prepared pan. Bake in preheated oven until light golden, 12 to 15 minutes.

2. *Filling:* In a bowl, whisk eggs, brown sugar and almond extract until well blended. Whisk in flour and baking powder, mixing well. Stir in coconut, cherries and nuts. Spread evenly over warm crust.

3. Return to oven and bake until set and golden, 25 to 30 minutes. Let cool completely in pan on rack.

4. *Almond Frosting:* In a small bowl, using an electric mixer on medium speed, beat butter and almond extract until smooth. Gradually beat in confectioners' sugar and cream until smooth and creamy, adding more cream as necessary. Spread over cooled bars. Chill until frosting is firm, about 1 hour. Cut into bars.

Chocolate Caramel Pecan Crumble Bars

◆

Easy to make and easy to eat! These bars are an excellent choice to keep on hand in the freezer.

MAKES 20 TO 54 BARS (see Cutting Guide, page 10)

- **Preparation: 20 minutes**
- **Cooking: 5 minutes**
- **Baking: 40 minutes**
- **Freezing: excellent**

TIPS

Chill caramels to make unwrapping a little easier. Slit wrapper with a small sharp knife to start.

Break up any large lumps in crust mixture with your fingers.

- **Preheat oven to 350°F (180°C)**
- **13- by 9-inch (3 L) cake pan, greased**

CRUST

1	package (18.25 oz/515 g) devil's food cake mix	1
1 cup	chopped pecans	250 mL
¾ cup	quick-cooking rolled oats	175 mL
¾ cup	butter, melted	175 mL

TOPPING

1	can (10 oz/300 mL) sweetened condensed milk	1
8 oz	caramels, unwrapped (about 30)	250 g
¼ cup	butter	60 mL

1. *Crust:* In a large bowl, combine cake mix, pecans, oats and melted butter, mixing until well blended. Set aside 1⅓ cups (325 mL) for topping. Press remainder evenly into prepared pan. Bake in preheated oven until set, about 15 minutes.

2. *Topping:* In a heavy saucepan over low heat, combine sweetened condensed milk, caramels and butter. Heat, stirring constantly, until caramels are melted and mixture is smooth. Pour evenly over warm crust. Sprinkle reserved crust mixture evenly over top.

3. Return to oven and bake until topping is golden and bubbly, 20 to 25 minutes. Let cool completely in pan on rack. Cut into bars.

Variation

Use your favorite nut in place of the pecans. Walnuts, hazelnuts, cashews and almonds all work well.

Chocolate Raspberry Almond Oat Bars

♦

The best of both worlds — healthy oats and decadent chocolate chips.

**MAKES 20 TO 54 BARS
(see Cutting Guide, page 10)**

- **Preparation: 20 minutes**
- **Baking: 40 minutes**
- **Freezing: excellent**

TIPS

Stir jam to soften for easy spreading.

Leaving a $1/2$-inch (1 cm) border when spreading jam over crust prevents the jam from sticking to the sides of pan.

Regular raspberry jam works fine, although the seedless variety has a more intense flavor.

- **Preheat oven to 375°F (190°C)**
- **13- by 9-inch (3 L) cake pan, greased**

1	package (18.25 oz/515 g) white cake mix	1
2 $1/2$ cups	quick-cooking rolled oats	625 mL
1 cup	butter, melted	250 mL
1 cup	seedless raspberry jam	250 mL
1 $1/3$ cups	semisweet chocolate chips	325 mL
$3/4$ cup	chopped almonds or pecans	175 mL
	Confectioners' (icing) sugar, optional	

1. In a large bowl, combine cake mix, oats and melted butter. Mix until well blended. Press half (3 cups/750 mL) evenly into prepared pan. Set remainder aside. Spread jam evenly over unbaked crust, leaving a $1/2$-inch (1 cm) border of crust. Sprinkle chocolate chips over jam. Stir almonds into remaining crumble mixture. Sprinkle evenly over chocolate chips.

2. Bake in preheated oven until golden, 35 to 40 minutes. Let cool completely in pan on rack. Cut into bars. Dust with confectioners' sugar before serving, if desired.

Variations

Replace raspberry jam with apricot. It's not as pretty, but it tastes good. Seedless strawberry jam is also great.

Lots of Lemon Squares

These squares have a hazelnut cookie base with a tart lemony topping. They make a refreshing complement to decadent chocolate delights.

MAKES 24 SQUARES (see Cutting Guide, page 10)

- **Preparation: 20 minutes**
- **Baking: 40 minutes**
- **Freezing: excellent**

TIP
Toast hazelnuts for the best flavor. There's no need to remove the skins. They add a wonderful nutty color and flavor.

- **Preheat oven to 350°F (180°C)**
- **13- by 9-inch (3 L) cake pan, greased**

CRUST

1	package (18.25 oz/515 g) lemon cake mix	1
½ cup	finely chopped hazelnuts	125 mL
½ cup	butter, melted	125 mL

TOPPING

4	eggs	4
2 cups	granulated sugar	500 mL
1 tsp	grated lemon zest	5 mL
⅓ cup	freshly squeezed lemon juice	75 mL
¼ cup	all-purpose flour	60 mL
1 tsp	baking powder	5 mL
	Confectioners' (icing) sugar, optional	

1. *Crust:* In a large bowl, combine cake mix, hazelnuts and melted butter. Mix until well blended. Press evenly into prepared pan. Bake in preheated oven until light golden, about 15 minutes.

2. *Topping:* In a bowl, whisk eggs, sugar and lemon zest and juice until blended. Whisk in flour and baking powder, mixing well. Pour evenly over hot crust.

3. Return to oven and bake until set and light golden, 20 to 25 minutes. Let cool completely in pan on rack. Dust with confectioners' sugar before serving, if desired. Cut into squares.

Variation
Replace hazelnuts with unblanched almonds.

Part 2
Cookies

Cranberry Almond Oatmeal Cookies
and Seeds and Coconut Oatmeal Crisps

Drop Cookies

Drop cookies are the most common type of cookie, likely because they are the easiest to make. After you've prepared the dough, simply scoop out a spoonful and, using another spoon or a spatula, push the mound onto a cookie sheet. Or use a small ice cream scoop with a wire release, which ensures evenly sized and nicely rounded cookies. Keep the mounds of dough uniform in size to ensure even baking, and space them about 2 inches (5 cm) apart to allow for spreading.

Drop cookies are versatile. I've suggested plenty of variations to encourage you to have fun experimenting with your favorites.

Cranberry Almond Oatmeal Cookies

◆

The dried fruit makes this old-fashioned oatmeal cookie chewy, and the nuts provide pleasing crunch.

MAKES ABOUT 4 DOZEN COOKIES

- **Preparation: 25 minutes**
- **Baking: 14 minutes**
- **Freezing: excellent**

TIPS

I prefer combining the dry ingredients on a piece of waxed paper instead of dirtying a bowl. Then I use the paper as a funnel when adding them to the butter mixture.

I prefer to use parchment paper rather than just greasing the cookie sheet because it makes cleanup easy. It also solves the problem of cookies sticking to the pan.

Although recipes usually call for an electric mixer to blend ingredients, you can almost always use a wooden spoon when making cookies. It just takes more physical effort. With either method, it usually takes about 3 minutes to get a butter-and-sugar mixture light and creamy.

- **Preheat oven to 350°F (180°C)**
- **Cookie sheet, greased or lined with parchment paper**

1 ½ cups	all-purpose flour	375 mL
½ tsp	baking soda	2 mL
½ tsp	baking powder	2 mL
¼ tsp	salt	1 mL
½ tsp	ground cinnamon	2 mL
1 cup	butter, softened	250 mL
1 cup	packed brown sugar	250 mL
½ cup	granulated sugar	125 mL
2	eggs	2
½ tsp	almond extract	2 mL
2 cups	quick-cooking rolled oats	500 mL
1 ½ cups	dried cranberries	375 mL
1 cup	slivered almonds	250 mL

1. On a sheet of waxed paper or in a bowl, combine flour, baking soda, baking powder, salt and cinnamon. Set aside.

2. In a large bowl, using an electric mixer on medium speed, beat butter and brown and granulated sugars until blended. Add eggs and almond extract, beating until light and creamy, about 3 minutes. On low speed, gradually add flour mixture, beating until blended. With a wooden spoon, stir in oats, cranberries and almonds.

3. Drop dough by tablespoonfuls (15 mL) about 2 inches (5 cm) apart on prepared cookie sheet. Bake in preheated oven for 10 to 14 minutes or until golden. Cool for 5 minutes on sheet, then transfer to a rack and cool completely.

Variations

Replace cranberries with chopped dried cherries or apricots.
Replace almonds with pecans.

Seeds and Coconut Oatmeal Crisps

With three kinds of seeds, these cookies have lots of crunch and flavor.

MAKES ABOUT 2½ DOZEN COOKIES

- **Preparation: 25 minutes**
- **Standing: 2 hours**
- **Baking: 14 minutes**
- **Freezing: excellent**

TIPS

Don't be surprised — there is no flour in this recipe.

I like to use toasted wheat germ that is sold in bottles. It has a nice nutty flavor and crunchier texture than wheat germ that isn't toasted.

If you prefer chewy cookies, bake these for 10 minutes or until golden around the edges. For crisp cookies, bake for 14 minutes or until golden overall.

- **Preheat oven to 350°F (180°C)**
- **Cookie sheet, greased or lined with parchment paper**

2	eggs	2
1 cup	packed brown sugar	250 mL
½ cup	vegetable oil	125 mL
1 tsp	vanilla	5 mL
2 cups	quick-cooking rolled oats	500 mL
1 cup	sweetened flaked coconut	250 mL
½ cup	chopped pecans	125 mL
¼ cup	wheat germ	60 mL
¼ cup	sesame seeds	60 mL
¼ cup	sunflower seeds	60 mL
3 tbsp	flax seeds	45 mL

1. In a large bowl, using a wooden spoon, beat eggs, brown sugar, oil and vanilla until blended. Stir in oats, coconut, pecans, wheat germ, and sesame, sunflower and flax seeds. Cover bowl with plastic wrap and let stand at room temperature for 2 hours.

2. Drop dough by tablespoonfuls (15 mL) about 2 inches (5 cm) apart on prepared cookie sheet. Using an offset spatula or the back of a spoon, press until thin and flat. Bake in preheated oven for 10 to 14 minutes (see Tips, left). Cool for 10 minutes on sheet, then transfer to a rack and cool completely.

Variation

Vary the kinds of seeds you use. Try pumpkin seeds in place of the sunflower seeds or black sesame seeds in place of the white ones.

Cranberry Cashew Cookies

When you combine cashews with white chocolate and cranberries, a mouthwatering cookie is guaranteed.

MAKES ABOUT 4½ DOZEN COOKIES

- **Preparation: 25 minutes**
- **Baking: 12 minutes**
- **Freezing: excellent**

TIPS

I prefer combining the dry ingredients on a piece of waxed paper instead of dirtying a bowl. Then I use the paper as a funnel when adding them to the butter mixture.

Store nuts in the freezer to retain their freshness.

Although recipes usually call for an electric mixer to blend ingredients, you can almost always use a wooden spoon when making cookies. It just takes more physical effort. With either method, it usually takes about 3 minutes to get a butter-and-sugar mixture light and creamy.

- **Preheat oven to 375°F (190°C)**
- **Cookie sheet, ungreased**

2¼ cups	all-purpose flour	550 mL
1 tsp	baking soda	5 mL
¼ tsp	salt	1 mL
1 cup	butter, softened	250 mL
¾ cup	granulated sugar	175 mL
¾ cup	packed brown sugar	175 mL
2	eggs	2
1 tsp	vanilla	5 mL
1¾ cups	white chocolate chips	425 mL
1 cup	dried cranberries	250 mL
1 cup	coarsely chopped cashews	250 mL

1. On a sheet of waxed paper or in a bowl, combine flour, baking soda and salt. Set aside.

2. In a large bowl, using an electric mixer on medium speed, beat butter, granulated and brown sugars, eggs and vanilla until light and creamy, about 3 minutes. On low speed, gradually add flour mixture, beating until blended. With a wooden spoon, stir in chocolate chips, cranberries and cashews.

3. Drop dough by tablespoonfuls (15 mL) about 2 inches (5 cm) apart on cookie sheet. Bake in preheated oven for 8 to 12 minutes or until golden. Cool for 5 minutes on sheet, then transfer to a rack and cool completely.

Variation

Substitute an equal quantity of chopped dried cherries or apricots for the cranberries.

White Chocolate Nut Crisps

Lots of crunchy nuts and creamy white chocolate make these cookies irresistible.

MAKES ABOUT 4 DOZEN COOKIES

- **Preparation: 25 minutes**
- **Baking: 18 minutes**
- **Freezing: excellent**

TIPS

I prefer combining the dry ingredients on a piece of waxed paper instead of dirtying a bowl. Then I use the paper as a funnel when adding them to the butter mixture.

Parchment paper makes cleanup easy. It also solves the problem of cookies sticking to the pan. Washable silicone sheets also work well.

For chewy cookies, bake about 14 minutes or until golden around the edges. For crisp cookies, bake about 18 minutes or until top of cookie is also light golden.

- **Preheat oven to 300°F (150°C)**
- **Cookie sheet, greased or lined with parchment paper**

2 cups	all-purpose flour	500 mL
1 tsp	baking soda	5 mL
1/4 tsp	salt	1 mL
3/4 cup	butter, softened	175 mL
1 cup	packed brown sugar	250 mL
3/4 cup	granulated sugar	175 mL
2	eggs	2
1 tsp	vanilla	5 mL
10	squares (1 oz/28 g each) white chocolate, cut in chunks	10
1 cup	coarsely chopped macadamia nuts	250 mL
1/2 cup	coarsely chopped pecans	125 mL

1. On a sheet of waxed paper or in a bowl, combine flour, baking soda and salt. Set aside.

2. In a large bowl, using an electric mixer on medium speed, beat butter and brown and granulated sugars until blended. Add eggs, one at a time, beating well after each addition. Add vanilla. On low speed, gradually add flour mixture, beating until blended. With a wooden spoon, stir in chocolate, macadamia nuts and pecans.

3. Drop dough by heaping tablespoonfuls (20 mL) about 2 inches (5 cm) apart on prepared cookie sheet. Bake in preheated oven for 14 to 18 minutes (see Tips, left). Cool for 5 minutes on sheet, then transfer to a rack and cool completely.

Variation

Replace macadamia nuts with slivered almonds.

Frosted Carrot Cake Cookies

◆

These cookies taste like bite-size morsels of carrot cake. Better still, you don't need a plate and fork to eat them.

MAKES ABOUT 4 DOZEN COOKIES

- **Preparation: 35 minutes**
- **Baking: 14 minutes**
- **Freezing: excellent**

TIPS

When making these cookies, I prefer to combine the flour, baking soda, salt, cinnamon, nutmeg and cloves on a piece of waxed paper instead of dirtying a bowl. Then I use the paper as a funnel when adding it to the egg mixture.

Be sure to peel the carrots. If peel is left on, sometimes it will show up as green flecks in baked cookies.

Parchment paper makes cleanup easy. It also solves the problem of cookies sticking to the pan. Washable silicone sheets also work well.

- **Preheat oven to 350°F (180°C)**
- **Cookie sheet, greased or lined with parchment paper**

COOKIE

2½ cups	all-purpose flour	625 mL
½ tsp	baking soda	2 mL
¼ tsp	salt	1 mL
1 tsp	ground cinnamon	5 mL
¼ tsp	ground nutmeg	1 mL
¼ tsp	ground cloves	1 mL
1 cup	butter, softened	250 mL
¾ cup	granulated sugar	175 mL
¾ cup	packed brown sugar	175 mL
2	eggs	2
2 cups	shredded peeled carrots	500 mL
1 cup	chopped pecans	250 mL

FROSTING

4 oz	cream cheese, softened	125 g
¼ cup	butter, softened	60 mL
2 cups	confectioners' (icing) sugar, sifted	500 mL
	Chopped pecans, optional	

1. *Cookie:* Combine flour, baking soda, salt, cinnamon, nutmeg and cloves. Set aside.

2. In a bowl, using an electric mixer on medium speed, beat butter and granulated and brown sugars until blended. Beat in eggs until light and creamy. On low speed, gradually beat in flour mixture. Stir in carrots and pecans.

3. Drop dough by tablespoonfuls (15 mL) about 2 inches (5 cm) apart on prepared cookie sheet. Bake in preheated oven for 10 to 14 minutes or until golden. Cool for 5 minutes on sheet, then transfer to a rack and cool completely.

4. *Frosting:* In a bowl, using an electric mixer on medium speed, beat cream cheese and butter until smooth. On low speed, gradually add confectioners' sugar, beating until blended. Spread over tops of cookies and sprinkle with nuts, if using.

Variation

Substitute walnuts, raisins or dried cranberries for the pecans.

Chocolate Caramel Oat Cookies

These taste like a mound of soft chocolate caramels in cookie form.

**MAKES ABOUT
4 DOZEN COOKIES**

- **Preparation: 25 minutes**
- **Baking: 12 minutes**
- **Freezing: excellent**

TIPS

Be sure to use parchment paper when baking with caramels as, once melted, they stick to the pan, making cleanup difficult.

You can use four 1.8-oz (52 g) chocolate-covered caramel bars in place of the rolls.

I use Rolo rolls. You can also buy bags of chocolate-covered caramels. Chill chocolate caramel candy for easier cutting.

A reliable oven thermometer is a good investment. It will tell you whether your oven heat is aligned with the setting. If not, you can adjust it accordingly.

- **Preheat oven to 375°F (190°C)**
- **Cookie sheet, lined with parchment paper**

2 cups	all-purpose flour	500 mL
1 cup	quick-cooking rolled oats	250 mL
1 tsp	baking soda	5 mL
1/4 tsp	salt	1 mL
1 cup	butter, softened	250 mL
3/4 cup	packed brown sugar	175 mL
1/2 cup	granulated sugar	125 mL
1	egg	1
1 tsp	vanilla	5 mL
4	rolls (1.8 oz/52 g each) chocolate-covered caramels, quartered	4
3/4 cup	coarsely chopped cashews	175 mL

1. On a sheet of waxed paper or in a bowl, combine flour, oats, baking soda and salt. Set aside.

2. In a large bowl, using an electric mixer on medium speed, beat butter, brown and granulated sugars, egg and vanilla until smooth and creamy, about 3 minutes. On low speed, gradually add flour mixture, beating until blended. With a wooden spoon, stir in chocolate caramels and cashews.

3. Drop dough by tablespoonfuls (15 mL) about 2 inches (5 cm) apart on prepared cookie sheet. Bake in preheated oven for 8 to 12 minutes or until golden around edges. Cool for 5 minutes on sheet, then transfer to a rack and cool completely.

Variation

Replace cashews with pecans.

Chocolate Apricot Pecan Cookies

If you're a fan of apricots, you'll love these cookies.

MAKES ABOUT 5 DOZEN COOKIES

- **Preparation: 25 minutes**
- **Baking: 12 minutes**
- **Freezing: excellent**

TIP

If you like your cookies chewy, bake for the minimum time, about 8 minutes. Bake longer if you like crisp cookies.

- **Preheat oven to 375°F (190°C)**
- **Cookie sheet, ungreased**

2 1/4 cups	all-purpose flour	550 mL
1 tsp	baking soda	5 mL
1/4 tsp	salt	1 mL
1 cup	butter, softened	250 mL
3/4 cup	granulated sugar	175 mL
3/4 cup	packed brown sugar	175 mL
2	eggs	2
1 tsp	vanilla	5 mL
2 cups	milk chocolate chips	500 mL
1 cup	chopped dried apricots	250 mL
1 cup	chopped pecans	250 mL

1. On a sheet of waxed paper or in a bowl, combine flour, baking soda and salt. Set aside.

2. In a large bowl, using an electric mixer on medium speed, beat butter and granulated and brown sugars until blended. Add eggs and vanilla, beating until light and creamy, about 3 minutes. On low speed, gradually add flour mixture, beating until blended. With a wooden spoon, stir in chocolate chips, apricots and pecans.

3. Drop dough by tablespoonfuls (15 mL) about 2 inches (5 cm) apart on cookie sheet. Bake in preheated oven for 8 to 12 minutes or until golden around edges. Cool for 5 minutes on sheet, then transfer to a rack and cool completely.

Variations

Replace apricots with dried cranberries.

Use white chocolate chips or a combination of white and milk chocolate chips.

Crunchy Cereal Cookies

Breakfast couldn't taste better. These cookies are delicious any time of the day.

MAKES ABOUT 4 DOZEN COOKIES

- **Preparation: 25 minutes**
- **Baking: 13 minutes**
- **Freezing: excellent**

TIPS

I like to use toasted wheat germ, which is sold in bottles. It has a nice nutty flavor and pleasing texture.

Store wheat germ in the freezer to keep it fresh.

Although recipes usually call for an electric mixer to blend ingredients, you can almost always use a wooden spoon when making cookies. It just takes more physical effort. With either method, it usually takes about 3 minutes to get a butter-and-sugar mixture light and creamy.

- **Preheat oven to 350°F (180°C)**
- **Cookie sheet, ungreased**

1 1/2 cups	all-purpose flour	375 mL
1/2 tsp	baking soda	2 mL
1/2 tsp	cream of tartar	2 mL
1/4 tsp	salt	1 mL
1/2 cup	butter, softened	125 mL
1 cup	packed brown sugar	250 mL
1/2 cup	vegetable oil	125 mL
1	egg	1
1 tsp	vanilla	5 mL
1 cup	crisp rice cereal	250 mL
1/2 cup	quick-cooking rolled oats	125 mL
1/2 cup	sliced almonds	125 mL
1/3 cup	unsweetened flaked coconut	75 mL
1/3 cup	sunflower seeds	75 mL
1/4 cup	wheat germ	60 mL

1. On a sheet of waxed paper or in a bowl, combine flour, baking soda, cream of tartar and salt. Set aside.

2. In a large bowl, using an electric mixer on medium speed, beat butter, brown sugar, oil, egg and vanilla until smooth and creamy, about 3 minutes. On low speed, gradually add flour mixture, beating until blended. With a wooden spoon, stir in rice cereal, oats, almonds, coconut, sunflower seeds and wheat germ.

3. Drop dough by tablespoonfuls (15 mL) about 2 inches (5 cm) apart on cookie sheet. Bake in preheated oven for 9 to 13 minutes or until light golden. Cool for 5 minutes on sheet, then transfer to a rack and cool completely.

Variations

Other crisp cereals, such as crushed corn flakes, work well in place of the rice cereal.

Replace almonds with pecans or walnuts.

Ragged Robins

I'm not sure where the name originated, but the basic recipe for these cookies qualifies as "heritage." Obviously, they endured because they taste so good.

MAKES ABOUT 2½ DOZEN COOKIES

- **Preparation: 20 minutes**
- **Baking: 23 minutes**
- **Freezing: excellent**

TIPS

Measure the cereal, then crush it slightly.

These cookies will hold together when baked, although they may not seem like they will in the dough state.

- **Preheat oven to 325°F (160°C)**
- **Cookie sheet, greased or lined with parchment paper**

1¾ cups	corn flakes cereal, slightly crushed	425 mL
1½ cups	chopped dates	375 mL
1 cup	chopped walnuts	250 mL
½ cup	chopped red candied (glacé) cherries	125 mL
3	egg whites	3
Pinch	salt	Pinch
½ tsp	vanilla	2 mL
½ cup	granulated sugar	125 mL

1. In a large bowl, combine cereal, dates, walnuts and cherries. Set aside.
2. In a small bowl, using an electric mixer on high speed, beat egg whites, salt and vanilla until stiff. With a wooden spoon, stir in sugar. Add to cereal mixture, mixing until well coated.
3. Drop dough by tablespoonfuls (15 mL) about 2 inches (5 cm) apart on prepared cookie sheet. Bake in preheated oven for 18 to 23 minutes or until set and light golden. Cool for 5 minutes on sheet, then transfer to a rack and cool completely.

Variations

Replace cherries with flaked coconut.

Replace corn flakes cereal with crisp rice cereal.

Raspberry Coconut Pinwheels

Here's an easy way to make an attractive swirl on top of a cookie.

**MAKES ABOUT
5 DOZEN COOKIES**

- **Preparation: 30 minutes**
- **Baking: 14 minutes**
- **Freezing: excellent**

TIPS

Use sweetened or unsweetened coconut — the choice is yours.

Although recipes usually call for an electric mixer to blend ingredients, you can almost always use a wooden spoon when making cookies. It just takes more physical effort. With either method, it usually takes about 3 minutes to get a butter-and-sugar mixture light and creamy.

- **Preheat oven to 375°F (190°C)**
- **Cookie sheet, ungreased**

3 cups	all-purpose flour	750 mL
½ cup	quick-cooking rolled oats	125 mL
1 tsp	baking soda	5 mL
¼ tsp	salt	1 mL
1 cup	butter, softened	250 mL
1 cup	packed brown sugar	250 mL
⅔ cup	granulated sugar	150 mL
2	eggs	2
½ cup	water	125 mL
1 tsp	almond extract	5 mL
2 cups	sweetened flaked coconut	500 mL
⅓ cup	raspberry jam	75 mL

1. On a sheet of waxed paper or in a bowl, combine flour, oats, baking soda and salt. Set aside.

2. In a large bowl, using an electric mixer on medium speed, beat butter and brown and granulated sugars until blended. Add eggs, water and almond extract, beating until light and creamy, about 3 minutes. On low speed, gradually add flour mixture and coconut, beating until blended.

3. Set aside about ¾ cup (175 mL) of the dough. Drop remaining dough by tablespoonfuls (15 mL) about 2 inches (5 cm) apart on cookie sheet. Make a small cavity in each cookie using a floured finger. Place ¼ tsp (1 mL) jam in cavity. Put ½ tsp (2 mL) of reserved dough on top of jam, not quite covering it. Bake in preheated oven for 10 to 14 minutes or until golden. Cool for 5 minutes on sheet, then transfer to a rack and cool completely.

Variation

Try other jams, such as blackberry, strawberry or apricot.

Tropical Fruit Macaroons

The combination of crushed pineapple and coconut gives these cookies a taste of the tropics.

MAKES ABOUT 4 DOZEN COOKIES

- **Preparation: 20 minutes**
- **Baking: 20 minutes**
- **Freezing: excellent**

TIPS

Both flaked and shredded coconut work well in macaroons.

If you prefer, use unsweetened coconut. The sweetened variety is usually easier to find in regular grocery stores, but unsweetened is always available in stores that sell bulk products.

- **Preheat oven to 350°F (180°C)**
- **Cookie sheet, lined with parchment paper**

1 cup	all-purpose flour	250 mL
1 tsp	baking powder	5 mL
2/3 cup	drained crushed pineapple	150 mL
1	can (14 oz or 300 mL) sweetened condensed milk	1
1/2 cup	butter, melted	125 mL
2 1/2 cups	sweetened flaked coconut	625 mL
1 cup	chopped almonds	250 mL
2 tsp	grated lemon zest	10 mL

1. On a sheet of waxed paper or in a bowl, combine flour and baking powder. Set aside.
2. In a large bowl, using a wooden spoon, combine pineapple, sweetened condensed milk, melted butter, coconut, almonds and lemon zest, stirring until thoroughly blended. Add flour mixture, mixing until blended.
3. Drop dough by tablespoonfuls (15 mL) about 1 inch (2.5 cm) apart on prepared cookie sheet. Bake in preheated oven for 15 to 20 minutes or until golden around edges. Cool for 5 minutes on sheet, then transfer to a rack and cool completely.

Variations

Replace lemon zest with lime, orange or grapefruit zest.

Omit lemon zest and stir in 1/2 tsp (2 mL) almond extract.

Hermits

I'm not sure where the name originated, but these heritage cookies, which usually contain raisins and walnuts, have been around for a long time. They were my grandmother's favorite.

MAKES ABOUT 4 DOZEN COOKIES

- **Preparation: 25 minutes**
- **Baking: 13 minutes**
- **Freezing: excellent**

TIPS

I like the flavor of Medjool dates or honey dates, especially when they are soft and fresh. They're wonderful for snacking on as well, so be sure to buy more than your recipe calls for.

Buy dates already pitted. It makes preparation quicker and easier.

- **Preheat oven to 375°F (190°C)**
- **Cookie sheet, greased or lined with parchment paper**

1¾ cups	all-purpose flour	425 mL
½ tsp	baking soda	2 mL
¼ tsp	salt	1 mL
1 tsp	ground cinnamon	5 mL
½ tsp	ground nutmeg	2 mL
¼ tsp	ground cloves	1 mL
⅔ cup	butter, softened	150 mL
¾ cup	packed brown sugar	175 mL
½ cup	granulated sugar	125 mL
1	egg	1
¼ cup	cold strong coffee	60 mL
1 cup	raisins	250 mL
1 cup	chopped dates	250 mL
¾ cup	coarsely chopped walnuts	175 mL

1. On a sheet of waxed paper or in a bowl, combine flour, baking soda, salt, cinnamon, nutmeg and cloves. Set aside.

2. In a large bowl, using an electric mixer on medium speed, beat butter, brown and granulated sugars, egg and coffee until light and creamy, about 3 minutes. On low speed, gradually add flour mixture, beating until blended. With a wooden spoon, stir in raisins, dates and walnuts.

3. Drop dough by tablespoonfuls (15 mL) about 2 inches (5 cm) apart on prepared cookie sheet. Bake in preheated oven for 9 to 13 minutes or until lightly browned. Cool for 5 minutes on sheet, then transfer to a rack and cool completely.

Variations

Use all dates or all raisins to suit your preference.

Omit nuts.

Fruit and Nut Overload

These cookies are so full of fruit and nuts they are almost like a power bar.

MAKES ABOUT 5 DOZEN COOKIES

- **Preparation: 30 minutes**
- **Baking: 13 minutes**
- **Freezing: excellent**

TIPS

The amount of dough may seem inadequate for all the fruit and nuts, but it works. If you're having trouble keeping the dough together, squeeze each mound with moistened fingertips after you drop it on the sheet. It will meld during baking.

These cookies keep well and are nice to ship as they are not fragile.

- **Preheat oven to 350°F (180°C)**
- **Cookie sheet, greased or lined with parchment paper**

1 1/2 cups	coarsely chopped Brazil nuts	375 mL
3/4 cup	coarsely chopped hazelnuts	175 mL
1/2 cup	chopped pecans	125 mL
1 1/4 cups	chopped dried apricots	300 mL
3/4 cup	chopped dried cranberries	175 mL
1/2 cup	chopped dates	125 mL
2 slices	dried pineapple, chopped	2 slices
1 1/4 cups	all-purpose flour, divided	300 mL
1/2 tsp	baking powder	2 mL
1/2 tsp	baking soda	2 mL
1/4 tsp	salt	1 mL
1/2 tsp	ground cinnamon	2 mL
1/2 cup	butter, softened	125 mL
3/4 cup	packed brown sugar	175 mL
1	egg	1

1. In a large bowl, combine Brazil nuts, hazelnuts, pecans, apricots, cranberries, dates and pineapple. Add 1/4 cup (60 mL) of the flour and mix until fruit and nuts are coated with flour. Set aside.

2. On a sheet of waxed paper or in a bowl, combine remaining 1 cup (250 mL) flour, baking powder, baking soda, salt and cinnamon. Set aside.

3. In a bowl, using an electric mixer on medium speed, beat butter, sugar and egg until light and creamy, about 3 minutes. On low speed, gradually add flour mixture, beating until blended. With a wooden spoon, stir in fruit mixture.

4. Drop dough by tablespoonfuls (15 mL) about 2 inches (5 cm) apart on prepared cookie sheet. Bake in preheated oven for 9 to 13 minutes or until light golden. Cool for 5 minutes on sheet, then transfer to a rack and cool completely.

Variations

Omit pineapple. The dough will hold together better.

Try other combinations of nuts and fruit, keeping the quantities the same as in the original recipe.

Chocolate Peanut Butter Oatmeal Cookies

The three most popular cookies — chocolate chip, oatmeal and peanut butter — combine in one sumptuous cookie.

MAKES ABOUT 4 DOZEN COOKIES

- **Preparation: 25 minutes**
- **Baking: 13 minutes**
- **Freezing: excellent**

TIPS

Buy light-colored cookie sheets with low or no sides for even baking. The darker nonstick ones absorb more heat, causing cookies to brown on the bottoms before the tops are cooked.

These cookies are perfect for a lunch box or as an after-school snack with a glass of cold milk or a mug of hot chocolate.

- **Preheat oven to 375°F (190°C)**
- **Cookie sheet, ungreased**

1 1/4 cups	all-purpose flour	300 mL
1 tsp	baking powder	5 mL
1/2 tsp	baking soda	2 mL
1/4 tsp	salt	1 mL
3/4 cup	butter, softened	175 mL
1/2 cup	creamy peanut butter	125 mL
3/4 cup	granulated sugar	175 mL
3/4 cup	packed brown sugar	175 mL
2	eggs	2
1 tsp	vanilla	5 mL
2 cups	quick-cooking rolled oats	500 mL
1 1/2 cups	chocolate-covered peanuts, chopped	375 mL
1/2 cup	crisp rice cereal	125 mL

1. On a sheet of waxed paper or in a bowl, combine flour, baking powder, baking soda and salt. Set aside.

2. In a large bowl, using an electric mixer on medium speed, beat butter, peanut butter and granulated and brown sugars until smooth and creamy, about 3 minutes. Add eggs, one at a time, beating well after each addition. Add vanilla. On low speed, gradually add flour mixture, beating until blended. With a wooden spoon, stir in oats, chocolate peanuts and cereal.

3. Drop dough by tablespoonfuls (15 mL) about 2 inches (5 cm) apart on cookie sheet. Press flat with a fork dipped in flour. Bake in preheated oven for 9 to 13 minutes or until crisp and golden. Cool for 5 minutes on sheet, then transfer to a rack and cool completely.

Variation

Replace chocolate-covered peanuts with 1 cup (250 mL) semisweet or milk chocolate chips and 1/2 cup (125 mL) chopped peanuts.

Key Lime Coconut Macaroons

These easy-to-make cookies will be particularly appealing to coconut-lovers.

MAKES ABOUT 2½ DOZEN COOKIES

- **Preparation: 15 minutes**
- **Baking: 25 minutes**
- **Freezing: excellent**

TIPS

When zesting and juicing a lime, remove lime zest first, then warm the fruit in a microwave oven for 5 seconds to obtain the most juice.

Drizzle melted chocolate over top of cookies for an attractive finish.

- **Preheat oven to 350°F (180°C)**
- **Cookie sheet, lined with parchment paper**

1	can (14 oz or 300 mL) sweetened condensed milk	1
⅓ cup	freshly squeezed key lime juice	75 mL
⅓ cup	all-purpose flour	75 mL
2⅔ cups	sweetened shredded coconut	650 mL
1 tbsp	grated key lime zest	15 mL

1. In a large bowl, combine sweetened condensed milk and lime juice, whisking until blended. With a wooden spoon, stir in flour, mixing until thoroughly blended. Stir in coconut and zest.
2. Drop dough by tablespoonfuls (15 mL) about 1 inch (2.5 cm) apart on prepared cookie sheet. Bake in preheated oven for 20 to 25 minutes or until golden around edges. Cool for 15 minutes on sheet, then transfer to a rack and cool completely.

Variations

Substitute Persian limes for the key limes.

Chocolate Toffee Cranberry Crunchies

These cookies are crisp on the outside, chewy on the inside and have a great butter and caramel flavor throughout.

MAKES ABOUT 5 DOZEN COOKIES

- **Preparation: 20 minutes**
- **Baking: 15 minutes**
- **Freezing: excellent**

TIPS

Parchment paper always makes cleanup easy, but it's practically mandatory when baking with sticky ingredients such as toffee. It solves the problem of cookies sticking to the pan.

I usually use Skor bars, but Heath bars also make great cookies with a similar taste.

Although recipes usually call for an electric mixer to blend ingredients, you can almost always use a wooden spoon when making cookies. It just takes more physical effort. With either method, it usually takes about 3 minutes to get a butter-and-sugar mixture light and creamy.

- **Preheat oven to 350°F (180°C)**
- **Cookie sheet, lined with parchment paper**

2 cups	all-purpose flour	500 mL
1 1/2 cups	quick-cooking rolled oats	375 mL
1 tsp	baking soda	5 mL
1/4 tsp	salt	1 mL
1 cup	butter, softened	250 mL
3/4 cup	granulated sugar	175 mL
3/4 cup	packed brown sugar	175 mL
2	eggs	2
1 1/2 cups	dried cranberries	375 mL
5	(1.4 oz/39 g each) crunchy chocolate-covered toffee bars, chopped	5

1. On a sheet of waxed paper or in a bowl, combine flour, oats, baking soda and salt. Set aside.

2. In a large bowl, using an electric mixer on medium speed, beat butter and granulated and brown sugars until smooth and creamy, about 3 minutes. Add eggs, one at a time, beating well after each addition. On low speed, gradually add flour mixture, beating until blended. With a wooden spoon, stir in cranberries and chopped chocolate bars.

3. Drop dough by tablespoonfuls (15 mL) about 2 inches (5 cm) apart on prepared cookie sheet. Bake in preheated oven for 11 to 15 minutes or until light golden. Cool for 5 minutes on sheet, then transfer to a rack and cool completely.

Variation

Replace chopped chocolate bars with 3/4 cup (175 mL) toffee bits and 1 cup (250 mL) miniature semisweet chocolate chips.

Toffee Crisp Oatmeal Cookies

Surprisingly for an oatmeal cookie, these have a candy bar–like taste.

MAKES ABOUT 5 DOZEN COOKIES

- **Preparation: 25 minutes**
- **Baking: 13 minutes**
- **Freezing: excellent**

TIPS

I prefer combining the dry ingredients on a piece of waxed paper instead of dirtying a bowl. Then I use the paper as a funnel when adding them to the butter mixture.

Make large cookies using a ⅓ cup (75 mL) dry measure or ice cream scoop to form balls of dough. Place about 4 inches (10 cm) apart on cookie sheet. Bake for 10 to 14 minutes or until golden around edges.

- **Preheat oven to 350°F (180°)**
- **Cookie sheet, lined with parchment paper**

1 cup	all-purpose flour	250 mL
¾ cup	wheat germ	175 mL
1 tsp	baking powder	5 mL
1 tsp	baking soda	5 mL
¼ tsp	salt	1 mL
2 cups	butter, softened	500 mL
1 cup	granulated sugar	250 mL
1 cup	packed brown sugar	250 mL
2	eggs	2
1 tsp	vanilla	5 mL
3¼ cups	quick-cooking rolled oats	800 mL
1 cup	toffee bits	250 mL
1 cup	semisweet chocolate chips	250 mL

1. On a sheet of waxed paper or in a bowl, combine flour, wheat germ, baking powder, baking soda and salt. Set aside.

2. In a large bowl, using an electric mixer on medium speed, beat butter and granulated and brown sugars until smooth and creamy, about 3 minutes. Add eggs, one at a time, beating well after each addition. Add vanilla. On low speed, gradually add flour mixture, beating until blended. With a wooden spoon, stir in oats, toffee bits and chocolate chips.

3. Drop dough by tablespoonfuls (15 mL) about 2 inches (5 cm) apart on prepared cookie sheet. Bake in preheated oven for 9 to 13 minutes or until golden. Cool for 5 minutes on sheet, then transfer to a rack and cool completely.

Variations

Replace toffee bits with raisins or dried cranberries.

For an all-chocolate cookie, omit toffee bits and use 1½ cups (375 mL) semisweet or milk chocolate chips.

Butterscotch Coconut Oatmeal Cookies

Whenever my niece's husband goes on a fishing trip, she bakes a batch of these for him to take along.

MAKES ABOUT 5 DOZEN COOKIES

- **Preparation: 25 minutes**
- **Baking: 11 minutes**
- **Freezing: excellent**

TIPS

I prefer combining the dry ingredients on a piece of waxed paper instead of dirtying a bowl. Then I use the paper as a funnel when adding them to the butter mixture.

For chewy cookies, bake 7 to 9 minutes or just until lightly browned around edges. If you prefer a crispier cookie, bake 9 to 11 minutes or until lightly browned overall.

There are no nuts in these, so they're perfect to send to school with your children.

- **Preheat oven to 375°F (190°C)**
- **Cookie sheet, ungreased**

1 ¼ cups	all-purpose flour	300 mL
1 tsp	baking soda	5 mL
¼ tsp	salt	1 mL
½ tsp	ground cinnamon	2 mL
1 cup	butter, softened	250 mL
¾ cup	granulated sugar	175 mL
¾ cup	packed brown sugar	175 mL
2	eggs	2
1 tsp	vanilla	5 mL
3 cups	quick-cooking rolled oats	750 mL
2 cups	butterscotch chips	500 mL
½ cup	sweetened flaked coconut	125 mL

1. On a sheet of waxed paper or in a bowl, combine flour, baking soda, salt and cinnamon. Set aside.

2. In a large bowl, using an electric mixer on medium speed, beat butter and granulated and brown sugars until blended. Add eggs, one a time, beating well after each addition. Add vanilla. On low speed, gradually add flour mixture, beating until blended. With a wooden spoon, stir in oats, butterscotch chips and coconut.

3. Drop dough by tablespoonfuls (15 mL) about 2 inches (5 cm) apart on cookie sheet. Bake in preheated oven for 7 to 11 minutes or until lightly browned around edges. Cool for 5 minutes on sheet, then transfer to a rack and cool completely.

Variation

Omit coconut.

Honey Cranberry Oat Cookies

Here's a healthy, tasty cookie the whole family will enjoy.

MAKES ABOUT 5 DOZEN COOKIES

- **Preparation: 25 minutes**
- **Baking: 12 minutes**
- **Freezing: excellent**

TIPS

For a more "oaty" taste and slightly drier texture, use large-flake old-fashioned rolled oats.

Cookies made with honey usually have a dense, moist, slightly chewy texture and a unique flavor. They usually keep well, too.

Although recipes usually call for an electric mixer to blend ingredients, you can almost always use a wooden spoon when making cookies. It just takes more physical effort. With either method, it usually takes about 3 minutes to get a butter-and-sugar mixture light and creamy.

- **Preheat oven to 375°F (190°C)**
- **Cookie sheet, greased or lined with parchment paper**

2 cups	all-purpose flour	500 mL
1 tsp	baking soda	5 mL
¼ tsp	salt	1 mL
1 cup	butter, softened	250 mL
1 cup	packed brown sugar	250 mL
1 cup	liquid honey	250 mL
2	eggs	2
1½ cups	quick-cooking rolled oats	375 mL
1½ cups	dried cranberries	375 mL
1 cup	slivered almonds	250 mL
1 cup	sunflower seeds	250 mL

1. On a sheet of waxed paper or in a bowl, combine flour, baking soda and salt. Set aside.

2. In a large bowl, using an electric mixer on medium speed, beat butter, brown sugar, honey and eggs until smooth and creamy, about 3 minutes. On low speed, gradually add flour mixture, beating until blended. With a wooden spoon, stir in oats, cranberries, almonds and sunflower seeds.

3. Drop dough by tablespoonfuls (15 mL) about 2 inches (5 cm) apart on prepared cookie sheet. Bake in preheated oven for 8 to 12 minutes or until golden. Cool for 5 minutes on sheet, then transfer to a rack and cool completely.

Variation

Add 1 tbsp (15 mL) grated orange zest along with the honey.

Black Forest Cookies

These scrumptious cookies have all the flavors of Black Forest cake, but in bite-size form.

MAKES ABOUT 5 DOZEN COOKIES

- **Preparation: 25 minutes**
- **Baking: 13 minutes**
- **Freezing: excellent**

TIPS

Dried fruits such as apricots, raisins, cranberries and cherries should be soft when they are fresh. Store them in the freezer to retain their freshness. If they seem hard, pour boiling water over them and let stand for 5 minutes to soften. Drain well and pat dry with paper towel.

The tartness of the dried cherries nicely complements the creamy sweetness of white chocolate, with just a touch of semisweet chocolate. But if you prefer, use all semisweet chocolate chips.

- **Preheat oven to 350°F (180°C)**
- **Cookie sheet, ungreased**

1⅔ cups	all-purpose flour	400 mL
1 tsp	baking powder	5 mL
1 tsp	baking soda	5 mL
¼ tsp	salt	1 mL
1 cup	butter, softened	250 mL
¾ cup	packed brown sugar	175 mL
½ cup	granulated sugar	125 mL
2	eggs	2
1 tsp	vanilla	5 mL
2 cups	quick-cooking rolled oats	500 mL
1¼ cups	white chocolate chips	300 mL
1 cup	semisweet chocolate chips	250 mL
1 cup	dried cherries, coarsely chopped	250 mL
¾ cup	slivered almonds	175 mL

1. On a sheet of waxed paper or in a bowl, combine flour, baking powder, baking soda and salt. Set aside.

2. In a large bowl, using an electric mixer on medium speed, beat butter and brown and granulated sugars until light and creamy, about 3 minutes. Add eggs, one at a time, beating well after each addition. Add vanilla. On low speed, gradually add flour mixture, beating until blended. With a wooden spoon, stir in oats, white and semisweet chocolate chips, cherries and almonds.

3. Drop dough by tablespoonfuls (15 mL) about 2 inches (5 cm) apart on cookie sheet. Bake in preheated oven for 9 to 13 minutes or until golden. Cool for 5 minutes on sheet, then transfer to a rack and cool completely.

Variations

Substitute dried cranberries for the cherries. There is no need to chop the cranberries as they are smaller.

For a very different taste, use maraschino cherries, chopped and patted dry with paper towel.

Cranberry Pecan Oatmeal Cookies

Depending upon how you bake them, these cookies can be soft and chewy or crispy. They are delicious either way, so the choice is yours.

MAKES ABOUT 4 DOZEN COOKIES

- **Preparation: 25 minutes**
- **Baking: 15 minutes**
- **Freezing: excellent**

TIP

Bake the minimum time for chewy cookies. They will look like they are not quite done when you take them out of the oven, but they will continue to cook on the sheet. Bake longer, until golden, if you prefer crisp cookies.

- **Preheat oven to 350°F (180°C)**
- **Cookie sheet, greased or lined with parchment paper**

³⁄₄ cup	all-purpose flour	175 mL
³⁄₄ tsp	baking soda	3 mL
¹⁄₄ tsp	salt	1 mL
1 tsp	ground cinnamon	5 mL
³⁄₄ cup	butter, softened	175 mL
³⁄₄ cup	packed brown sugar	175 mL
¹⁄₂ cup	granulated sugar	125 mL
1	egg	1
2 tbsp	milk	30 mL
3 cups	quick-cooking rolled oats	750 mL
1 cup	dried cranberries	250 mL
³⁄₄ cup	chopped pecans	175 mL
¹⁄₃ cup	sunflower seeds	75 mL

1. On a sheet of waxed paper or in a bowl, combine flour, baking soda, salt and cinnamon. Set aside.

2. In a large bowl, using an electric mixer on medium speed, beat butter, brown and granulated sugars, egg and milk until light and creamy, about 3 minutes. On low speed, gradually add flour mixture, beating until blended. With a wooden spoon, stir in oats, cranberries, pecans and sunflower seeds.

3. Drop dough by tablespoonfuls (15 mL) about 2 inches (5 cm) apart on prepared cookie sheet. Press flat with a fork dipped in flour. Bake in preheated oven for 11 to 15 minutes (see Tips, left). Cool for 5 minutes on sheet, then transfer to a rack and cool completely.

Variation

Omit cinnamon. Replace milk with orange juice and 1 tbsp (15 mL) grated orange zest.

Frosted Cashew Drops

An optional browned butter frosting transforms these simple cashew cookies into a special treat.

MAKES ABOUT 3 DOZEN COOKIES

- **Preparation: 35 minutes**
- **Baking: 14 minutes**
- **Cooking (Frosting): 4 minutes**
- **Freezing: excellent**

TIPS

I prefer combining the dry ingredients on a piece of waxed paper instead of dirtying a bowl. Then I use the paper as a funnel when adding them to the butter mixture.

Confectioners' sugar clumps during storage. Measure, then sift before using. If you don't have a sifter, a fine sieve works well.

- **Preheat oven to 350°F (180°C)**
- **Cookie sheet, ungreased**

COOKIE

2¼ cups	all-purpose flour	550 mL
1 tsp	baking soda	5 mL
¼ tsp	salt	1 mL
1 cup	butter, softened	250 mL
1 cup	packed brown sugar	250 mL
½ cup	granulated sugar	125 mL
1	egg	1
1 tsp	vanilla	5 mL
1½ cups	coarsely chopped cashews	375 mL

FROSTING, OPTIONAL

½ cup	butter	125 mL
3 cups	confectioners' (icing) sugar, sifted	750 mL
3 tbsp	milk (approx.)	45 mL
1 tsp	vanilla	5 mL
½ cup	finely chopped cashews	125 mL

1. *Cookie:* On a sheet of waxed paper or in a bowl, combine flour, baking soda and salt. Set aside.

2. In a large bowl, using an electric mixer on medium speed, beat butter, brown and granulated sugars, egg and vanilla until light and creamy, about 3 minutes. On low speed, gradually add flour mixture, beating until blended. With a wooden spoon, stir in cashews.

3. Drop dough by tablespoonfuls (15 mL) about 2 inches (5 cm) apart on cookie sheet. Bake in preheated oven for 10 to 14 minutes or until golden. Cool for 5 minutes on sheet, then transfer to rack and cool completely.

4. *Frosting, optional:* In a small saucepan, over medium heat, cook butter until it foams and starts to turn golden, about 4 minutes. Remove from heat. Pour into a bowl and let cool for 10 minutes. Using an electric mixer on low speed, gradually add confectioners' sugar, milk and vanilla, beating until blended. If necessary, add a little more milk to make a spreadable consistency.

5. Spread frosting on top of cooled cookies. Sprinkle with chopped cashews, pressing lightly into frosting. Let frosting set, about 1 hour.

White Chocolate Cashew Cookies

Crunchy cereal adds a pleasant texture to these and other cookies. It stays crisp during baking.

MAKES ABOUT 3½ DOZEN COOKIES

- **Preparation: 25 minutes**
- **Baking: 14 minutes**
- **Freezing: excellent**

TIPS

These cookies don't seem to be baked when they actually are. They firm up on cooling.

When storing cookies, be sure they are completely cool before packing. Otherwise, they will become soft.

- **Preheat oven to 375°F (190°C)**
- **Cookie sheet, ungreased**

½ cup	semisweet chocolate chips	125 mL
1⅓ cups	all-purpose flour	325 mL
1 tsp	baking soda	5 mL
¼ tsp	salt	1 mL
½ cup	butter, softened	125 mL
⅓ cup	granulated sugar	75 mL
⅓ cup	packed brown sugar	75 mL
1	egg	1
1½ cups	slightly crushed corn flakes cereal	375 mL
1 cup	white chocolate chips	250 mL
¾ cup	coarsely chopped cashews	175 mL

1. In a small saucepan over low heat, melt semisweet chocolate chips, stirring constantly, until smooth. Set aside to cool.

2. Meanwhile, on a sheet of waxed paper or in a bowl, combine flour, baking soda and salt. Set aside.

3. In a large bowl, using an electric mixer on medium speed, beat butter, granulated and brown sugars and egg until light and creamy, about 3 minutes. Add melted chocolate, mixing until blended. On low speed, gradually add flour mixture, beating until blended. With a wooden spoon, stir in cereal, white chocolate chips and cashews.

4. Drop dough by tablespoonfuls (15 mL) about 2 inches (5 cm) apart on cookie sheet. Flatten slightly with a fork dipped in granulated sugar. Bake in preheated oven for 10 to 14 minutes or until just set but still soft in the center. Cool for 5 minutes on sheet, then transfer to a rack and cool completely.

Variations

Replace corn flakes cereal with crisp rice cereal.

Replace cashews with dried cranberries.

Hawaiian Chews

Crispy outside and chewy inside, these cookies have great flavor and texture. I love the combination of crunchy nuts and chewy coconut and pineapple.

MAKES ABOUT 4½ DOZEN COOKIES

- **Preparation: 25 minutes**
- **Baking: 12 minutes**
- **Freezing: excellent**

TIPS

Brazil nuts have an earthy flavor and unique texture similar to macadamia nuts. They are one of my favorites.

Don't over-bake these cookies, as they'll get too crunchy.

- **Preheat oven to 350°F (180°C)**
- **Cookie sheet, greased or lined with parchment paper**

2 cups	all-purpose flour	500 mL
1 tsp	baking powder	5 mL
½ tsp	baking soda	2 mL
¼ tsp	salt	1 mL
1 tsp	ground cinnamon	5 mL
½ tsp	ground nutmeg	2 mL
½ cup	butter, softened	125 mL
1½ cups	packed brown sugar	375 mL
2	eggs	2
1 tsp	vanilla	5 mL
1½ cups	sweetened flaked coconut	375 mL
1 cup	coarsely chopped Brazil nuts	250 mL
¾ cup	chopped dried pineapple	175 mL

1. On a sheet of waxed paper or in a bowl, combine flour, baking powder, baking soda, salt, cinnamon and nutmeg. Set aside.

2. In a large bowl, using an electric mixer on medium speed, beat butter, brown sugar, eggs and vanilla until light and creamy, about 3 minutes. On low speed, gradually add flour mixture, beating until blended. With a wooden spoon, stir in coconut, nuts and pineapple.

3. Drop dough by tablespoonfuls (15 mL) about 2 inches (5 cm) apart on prepared cookie sheet. Flatten slightly with floured offset spatula or the palm of your hand. Bake in preheated oven for 8 to 12 minutes or until lightly browned around edges. Cool for 5 minutes on sheet, then transfer to a rack and cool completely.

Variation
Replace pineapple with dried mango.

White Chocolate Fruit and Nut Cookies

Crisp around the edges and chewy inside, these cookies taste every bit as good as they look.

MAKES ABOUT 6 DOZEN COOKIES

- **Preparation: 30 minutes**
- **Baking: 12 minutes**
- **Freezing: excellent**

TIPS

Most baked cookies freeze well. Store them frozen in airtight containers or freezer bags for up to 6 months.

To grate citrus zest, use a fine-hole, sharp-toothed grater or Microplane made for zesting. Use only the colored outer portion of the rind, not the white inner portion, which is quite bitter.

You should get about 4 tsp (20 mL) zest from 1 orange.

- **Preheat oven to 375°F (190°C)**
- **Cookie sheet, greased or lined with parchment paper**

2¼ cups	all-purpose flour	550 mL
1 tsp	baking soda	5 mL
½ tsp	salt	2 mL
1 cup	butter, softened	250 mL
¾ cup	packed brown sugar	175 mL
½ cup	granulated sugar	125 mL
2	eggs	2
1 tbsp	grated orange zest	15 mL
8	squares (1 oz/28 g each) white chocolate, cut in chunks	8
1¼ cups	coarsely chopped cashews	300 mL
¾ cup	dried cranberries	175 mL
½ cup	chopped dried mango	125 mL

1. On a sheet of waxed paper or in a bowl, combine flour, baking soda and salt. Set aside.

2. In a large bowl, using an electric mixer on medium speed, beat butter and brown and granulated sugars until light and creamy, about 3 minutes. Add eggs, one at a time, beating well after each addition. Add orange zest. On low speed, gradually add flour mixture, beating until blended. With a wooden spoon, stir in white chocolate, cashews, cranberries and mango.

3. Drop dough by heaping tablespoonfuls (20 mL) about 2 inches (5 cm) apart on prepared cookie sheet. Bake in preheated oven for 8 to 12 minutes or until golden around edges. Cool for 5 minutes on sheet, then transfer to a rack and cool completely.

Variations

Add ½ cup (125 mL) flaked coconut along with the mango.

Replace cashews with macadamia nuts or almonds.

Replace mango with chopped dried apricot.

Date 'n' Nut Meringues

This is a nice light cookie, perfect for those times when you need a little "lift."

**MAKES ABOUT
3 DOZEN COOKIES**

- **Preparation: 20 minutes**
- **Baking: 12 minutes**
- **Freezing: not recommended**

TIP

Unlike most meringues, these contain flour, which gives a more cookie-like texture.

- **Preheat oven to 350°F (180°C)**
- **Cookie sheet, greased or lined with parchment paper**

3	egg whites	3
1/4 tsp	salt	1 mL
1 tsp	vanilla	5 mL
1 cup	granulated sugar	250 mL
1 cup	all-purpose flour	250 mL
1 cup	chopped dates	250 mL
1 cup	chopped pecans	250 mL

1. In a bowl, using an electric mixer on medium speed, beat egg whites, salt and vanilla to soft peaks. Gradually add sugar, 2 tbsp (30 mL) at a time, beating until stiff peaks form. With a wooden spoon, stir in flour, dates and pecans. Mix well.

2. Drop by scant tablespoonfuls (10 mL) about 2 inches (5 cm) apart on prepared cookie sheet. Bake in preheated oven for 8 to 12 minutes or until lightly browned around edges. Cool for 5 minutes on sheet, then transfer to a rack and cool completely.

Lacy Pecan Thins

These cookies are like candy "brittle" in texture and taste. For a special treat, serve them with ice cream or fresh berries.

**MAKES ABOUT
3 1/2 DOZEN COOKIES**

- **Preparation: 15 minutes**
- **Cooking: 4 minutes**
- **Baking: 13 minutes**
- **Freezing: not recommended**

- **Preheat oven to 325°F (160°C)**
- **Cookie sheet, lined with parchment paper**

2/3 cup	packed brown sugar	150 mL
1/2 cup	butter	125 mL
1/2 cup	corn syrup	125 mL
1 cup	all-purpose flour	250 mL
1/2 cup	finely chopped pecans	125 mL
1/2 cup	unsweetened flaked coconut	125 mL

1. In a large saucepan, over medium-high heat, combine brown sugar, butter and corn syrup, stirring until melted and smooth. Remove from heat. Stir in flour, pecans and coconut.

2. Drop mixture by slightly rounded teaspoonfuls (7 mL) about 2 inches (5 cm) apart on prepared cookie sheet. Bake in preheated oven for 9 to 13 minutes or until golden. Cool for 5 minutes on sheet, then transfer to a rack and cool completely.

Almond and Pine Nut Macaroons

These cookies may not have many ingredients, but they sure have a lot of flavor.

MAKES ABOUT 2 DOZEN COOKIES

- Preparation: 15 minutes
- Baking: 25 minutes
- Freezing: not recommended

- **Preheat oven to 350°F (180°C)**
- **Cookie sheet, lined with parchment paper**

8 oz	almond paste, broken into pieces	250 g
1/2 cup	granulated sugar	125 mL
1/4 cup	confectioners' (icing) sugar, sifted	60 mL
1/4 tsp	salt	1 mL
3	egg whites	3
2/3 cup	pine nuts	150 mL

1. In a food processor, process almond paste into fine pieces. Add granulated and confectioners' sugars and salt and process until blended. Add egg whites and process until smoothly blended. Transfer to a bowl. Stir in pine nuts.
2. Drop dough by scant tablespoonfuls (10 mL) about 2 inches (5 cm) apart on prepared cookie sheet. Bake in preheated oven for 20 to 25 minutes or until golden. Cool completely on sheet.

Mixed Nut Macaroons

Not only are these cookies easy to make, but the blend of sweet and salty flavors is particularly delicious.

MAKES ABOUT 3 1/2 DOZEN COOKIES

- Preparation: 20 minutes
- Baking: 25 minutes
- Freezing: not recommended

TIP

Have egg whites at room temperature to obtain the best volume.

- **Preheat oven to 325°F (160°C)**
- **Cookie sheet, lined with parchment paper**

2 cups	sweetened flaked coconut	500 mL
2/3 cup	granulated sugar	150 mL
1/4 cup	all-purpose flour	60 mL
4	egg whites	4
1/2 tsp	almond extract	2 mL
1 1/2 cups	chopped deluxe salted mixed nuts (no peanuts)	375 mL

1. In a small bowl, combine coconut, sugar and flour. Mix well. Set aside.
2. In a large bowl, whisk egg whites and almond extract until foamy. With a wooden spoon, stir in coconut mixture and nuts, mixing until all ingredients are moistened.
3. Drop mixture by tablespoonfuls (15 mL) about 2 inches (5 cm) apart on prepared cookie sheet. Bake in preheated oven for 20 to 25 minutes or until golden. Cool completely on sheet.

Butterscotch Cashew Cookies

Refrigerator Cookies

Refrigerator cookies, sometimes called icebox cookies or slice-and-bake cookies, are perfect for busy people. They offer old-fashioned homemade goodness and the convenience of ready-made dough. Here's the secret: you make your own dough in advance, shape it into a roll, wrap and refrigerate or freeze. The dough is ready to slice and bake as required. I've noted the minimum chilling time required in all the recipes, but usually it's most convenient for people to prepare dough a day ahead of baking and refrigerate overnight.

Cookie dough, wrapped in plastic wrap, can be refrigerated for up to 2 weeks or frozen for up to 3 months. When freezing, freeze until firm, then wrap the dough again in heavy foil or place it in freezer bags. When you're getting ready to bake, thaw the dough at room temperature for about an hour, or in the refrigerator overnight, until it can be sliced easily.

The most common shape for refrigerator cookies is 2-inch (5 cm) rounds, cut from simple rolls that width in diameter. However, you can also make square cookies by packing the dough into square boxes such as those containing waxed paper or aluminum foil. Whatever their eventual shape, with just one afternoon of preparation, you can make enough cookie dough to last for months. And, if you're prone to over-indulging in freshly baked cookies, refrigerator cookies can help you keep your Cookie Monster appetite in check. You can portion the dough into several smaller rolls, then bake a few cookies at a time rather than a large batch, and savor every little bite.

Butterscotch Cashew Cookies

These chewy cookies are a great choice for school lunches. You can bake them as you need them, so they're always fresh.

MAKES ABOUT 4½ DOZEN COOKIES

- **Preparation: 25 minutes**
- **Chilling: 4 hours**
- **Baking: 14 minutes**
- **Freezing: excellent**

TIPS

I prefer combining the dry ingredients on a piece of waxed paper instead of dirtying a bowl. Then I use the paper as a funnel when adding them to the butter mixture.

Chips harden during chilling, which makes it difficult to slice the rolls. That's why these slices are thicker than usual, but they flatten and spread during baking.

For a chewy texture, bake cookies just until golden around the edges. For crisp cookies, bake for the maximum time or until golden overall.

- **Cookie sheet, greased or lined with parchment paper**

2½ cups	all-purpose flour	625 mL
1 tsp	baking soda	5 mL
¼ tsp	salt	1 mL
1 cup	butter, softened	250 mL
1½ cups	packed brown sugar	375 mL
2	eggs	2
1 tsp	vanilla	5 mL
2 cups	butterscotch chips	500 mL
1 cup	chopped cashews	250 mL

1. On a sheet of waxed paper or in a bowl, combine flour, baking soda and salt. Set aside.

2. In a large bowl, using an electric mixer on medium speed, beat butter and brown sugar until light and creamy, about 3 minutes. Add eggs, one at a time, beating well after each addition. Stir in vanilla. On low speed, gradually add flour mixture, beating until blended. With a wooden spoon, stir in butterscotch chips and cashews. Divide dough into halves. Shape each into a roll 13 inches (33 cm) long. Wrap and chill until firm, at least 4 hours.

3. Fifteen minutes before you're ready to bake, preheat oven to 350°F (180°C). Cut rolls into ½-inch (1 cm) slices. Place about 2 inches (5 cm) apart on prepared cookie sheet. Bake in preheated oven for 10 to 14 minutes or until edges are golden and tops are just starting to brown. Cool for 5 minutes on sheet, then transfer to a rack and cool completely.

Variations

Add ½ cup (125 mL) unsweetened flaked coconut along with the chips and nuts.

Substitute peanuts for the cashews.

Peanut Butter Icebox Cookies

Keep a roll of this dough in your refrigerator so you can serve freshly made warm cookies and milk at the drop of a hat. When making refrigerator cookies, I usually chill the dough overnight and bake the following day.

MAKES ABOUT 8 DOZEN COOKIES

- **Preparation: 25 minutes**
- **Chilling: 4 hours**
- **Baking: 11 minutes**
- **Freezing: excellent**

TIPS

If you prefer, use a wooden spoon instead of a mixer.

When cutting dough, ensure that your knife is sharp. I prefer to use a serrated knife for this dough, as it contains nuts.

Be sure your peanut butter is fresh. Its high fat content makes it susceptible to rancidity.

When wrapping dough for freezing or storage, wrap tightly in plastic wrap. If you plan to use the dough in the immediate future, waxed paper will do. See page 11 for instructions on freezing dough.

- **Cookie sheet, ungreased**

2 1/4 cups	all-purpose flour	550 mL
3/4 tsp	baking powder	3 mL
3/4 tsp	baking soda	3 mL
1/4 tsp	salt	1 mL
1/2 cup	butter, softened	125 mL
1/2 cup	creamy peanut butter	125 mL
3/4 cup	packed brown sugar	175 mL
2	eggs	2
1 tsp	vanilla	5 mL
1 cup	finely chopped peanuts	250 mL

1. On a sheet of waxed paper or in a bowl, combine flour, baking powder, baking soda and salt. Set aside.

2. In a large bowl, using an electric mixer on medium speed, beat butter, peanut butter, brown sugar, eggs and vanilla until light and creamy, about 3 minutes. On low speed, gradually add flour mixture, beating until blended. With a wooden spoon, stir in peanuts. Divide dough into halves. Shape each into a roll 12 inches (30 cm) long. Wrap and chill until firm, at least 4 hours.

3. Fifteen minutes before you're ready to bake, preheat oven to 375°F (190°C). Cut rolls into 1/4-inch (0.5 cm) slices. Place about 2 inches (5 cm) apart on cookie sheet. Bake in preheated oven for 7 to 11 minutes or until golden. Cool for 5 minutes on sheet, then transfer to a rack and cool completely.

Variations

Add 1/2 cup (125 mL) miniature chocolate chips and reduce peanuts to 1/2 cup (125 mL). The chips are a bit harder to cut, but the taste is great.

Instead of adding the peanuts to the dough, spread them on a sheet of waxed paper and roll the logs in them, pressing lightly into the dough. This gives the cookies a different look.

Seeds and Coconut Refrigerator Cookies

Crunchy with nuts and seeds, the wonderful taste of coconut and, of course, butter — these cookies are simply delightful. This is a big batch recipe — you may want to freeze one or two of the rolls for longer storage.

**MAKES ABOUT
13 DOZEN COOKIES**

- **Preparation: 25 minutes**
- **Chilling: 3 hours**
- **Baking: 24 minutes**
- **Freezing: excellent**

TIPS

For a different look, roll the logs of dough in finely chopped nuts, colored sugar or chocolate sprinkles before chilling.

When cutting dough, always ensure that your knife is sharp. I prefer to use a serrated knife for this dough, as it contains seeds and nuts.

If you like crispy cookies, bake them a little longer, until golden overall. Or try cutting the slices a little thinner. The thinner the cookie, the crispier the texture.

• **Cookie sheet, greased or lined with parchment paper**

2 cups	butter, softened	500 mL
1½ cups	granulated sugar	375 mL
½ tsp	salt	2 mL
3 cups	all-purpose flour	750 mL
2 cups	sweetened shredded coconut	500 mL
½ cup	finely chopped pecans	125 mL
½ cup	sesame seeds	125 mL
¼ cup	flax seeds	60 mL
¼ cup	sunflower seeds	60 mL

1. In a large bowl, using an electric mixer on medium speed, beat butter and sugar until light and creamy, about 3 minutes. On low speed, add salt, then gradually add flour, beating until dough becomes too stiff for the mixer, then finish mixing with a wooden spoon. Stir in coconut, pecans, sesame seeds, flax seeds and sunflower seeds. Using your hands, knead to form a smooth dough. Divide dough into thirds. Shape each into a roll 13 inches (33 cm) long. Wrap and chill until firm, at least 3 hours.

2. Fifteen minutes before you're ready to bake, preheat oven to 300°F (150°C). Cut rolls into ¼-inch (0.5 cm) slices. Place about 1 inch (2.5 cm) apart on prepared cookie sheet. Bake in preheated oven for 19 to 24 minutes or until golden. Cool for 5 minutes on sheet, then transfer to a rack and cool completely.

Variations

Vary the seeds to suit your taste. Pumpkin seeds are a nice addition, or use only two kinds of seeds — just make sure the quantity of seeds totals 1 cup (250 mL).

Omit pecans.

Lemon Cranberry Pistachio Wafers

This cookie has a tender, buttery, shortbread-like texture and colorful red and green flecks scattered throughout.

MAKES ABOUT 4 DOZEN COOKIES

- **Preparation: 25 minutes**
- **Chilling: 3 hours**
- **Baking: 12 minutes**
- **Freezing: excellent**

TIPS

In refrigerator rolls, ingredients like nuts and fruit are much easier to slice if they are chopped fairly fine.

When cutting dough, always ensure that your knife is sharp. I prefer to use a serrated knife for this dough as it contains nuts.

- **Cookie sheet, ungreased**

1 3/4 cups	all-purpose flour	425 mL
1/4 tsp	baking powder	1 mL
1/4 tsp	salt	1 mL
3/4 cup	butter, softened	175 mL
1/2 cup	confectioners' (icing) sugar, sifted	125 mL
1	egg	1
1 tbsp	grated lemon zest	15 mL
1/3 cup	finely chopped pistachios	75 mL
1/4 cup	chopped dried cranberries	60 mL

1. On a sheet of waxed paper or in a bowl, combine flour, baking powder and salt. Set aside.

2. In a large bowl, using an electric mixer on medium speed, beat butter, confectioners' sugar, egg and lemon zest until light and creamy, about 3 minutes. On low speed, gradually add flour mixture, beating until blended. With a wooden spoon, stir in pistachios and cranberries. Shape into a roll 12 inches (30 cm) long. Wrap and chill until firm, at least 3 hours.

3. Fifteen minutes before you're ready to bake, preheat oven to 375°F (190°C). Cut roll into 1/4-inch (0.5 cm) slices. Place about 1 inch (2.5 cm) apart on cookie sheet. Bake in preheated oven for 8 to 12 minutes or until golden. Cool for 5 minutes on sheet, then transfer to a rack and cool completely.

Variations

Replace lemon zest with orange zest.

Replace dried cranberries with dried cherries.

Dip half of each cookie in melted white or dark chocolate.

Lemon Lime Slices

These small, delicate cookies are incredibly tender and have a wonderful burst of citrus flavor. They're nice with a cup of tea or dish of sherbet.

MAKES ABOUT 6 DOZEN COOKIES

- **Preparation: 25 minutes**
- **Chilling: 3 hours**
- **Baking: 12 minutes**
- **Freezing: excellent**

TIPS

I recommend using a sharp serrated knife to slice these cookies. When slicing, rotate the roll frequently to avoid flattening one side and to ensure evenly shaped cookies that are round.

A reliable oven thermometer is a good investment. It will tell you whether your oven heat is aligned with the setting. If not, you can adjust it accordingly.

- **Cookie sheet, greased or lined with parchment paper**

1¾ cups	all-purpose flour	425 mL
¼ cup	cornstarch	60 mL
¼ tsp	salt	1 mL
¾ cup	butter, softened	175 mL
⅓ cup	confectioners' (icing) sugar, sifted	75 mL
1 tbsp	grated lemon zest	15 mL
1 tbsp	grated lime zest	15 mL
2 tbsp	freshly squeezed lemon juice	30 mL
2 tbsp	freshly squeezed lime juice	30 mL
⅔ cup	colored coarse sugar	150 mL

1. On a sheet of waxed paper or in a bowl, combine flour, cornstarch and salt. Set aside.

2. In a large bowl, using an electric mixer on medium speed, beat butter, confectioners' sugar, lemon and lime zests, and lemon and lime juices until light and creamy. On low speed, gradually add flour mixture until dough becomes too stiff for the mixer, then finish mixing with a wooden spoon until smooth. Divide dough into halves. Shape each into a roll 9 inches (23 cm) long. Spread colored sugar on a sheet of waxed paper and roll logs in it until nicely coated. Wrap and chill until firm, at least 3 hours.

3. Fifteen minutes before you're ready to bake, preheat oven to 350°F (180°C). Cut rolls into ¼-inch (0.5 cm) slices. Place about 1 inch (2.5 cm) apart on prepared cookie sheet. Bake in preheated oven for 8 to 12 minutes or until golden around edges. Cool for 10 minutes on sheet.

Variations

If you like lemon, substitute additional lemon zest and juice for the lime. Or omit lime zest and juice and add, if desired, ¼ cup (60 mL) poppy seeds with the dry ingredients.

For a different finish, place ⅔ cup (150 mL) confectioners' sugar in a plastic bag. Add warm cookies in batches and toss until coated. Transfer to a rack and cool completely, then place in bag with remaining sugar and shake again.

These make nice sandwich cookies. Spread a little lemon curd between two cookies.

Chocolate-Dipped Cinnamon Hazelnut Rounds

Keep dough for these cookies on hand if your family or friends love eating nuts. You'll be able to bake them as an unexpected treat in a matter of minutes.

MAKES ABOUT 3½ DOZEN COOKIES

- **Preparation: 35 minutes**
- **Chilling: 3 hours**
- **Baking: 22 minutes**
- **Cooking (Glaze): 4 minutes**
- **Freezing: excellent**

TIPS

This dough can be mixed in a food processor. Cut cold butter into chunks before using.

To toast hazelnuts, place them in a shallow pan and bake, stirring occasionally, at 350°F (180°C) for 8 to 10 minutes or until fragrant and starting to turn golden. Cool completely before using.

When grinding nuts in a food processor, add a bit of the flour or sugar from the recipe to prevent clumping.

- **Cookie sheet, greased or lined with parchment paper**

COOKIE

1 cup	all-purpose flour	250 mL
½ cup	hazelnuts, toasted and ground (see Tips, left)	125 mL
½ tsp	ground cinnamon	2 mL
¼ tsp	salt	1 mL
½ cup	butter, softened	125 mL
½ cup	confectioners' (icing) sugar, sifted	125 mL
1	egg white	1
½ tsp	vanilla	2 mL

GLAZE

5	squares (1 oz/28 g each) semisweet chocolate, chopped	5
1 tsp	vegetable oil	5 mL

1. *Cookie:* On a sheet of waxed paper or in a bowl, combine flour, hazelnuts, cinnamon and salt. Set aside.

2. In a large bowl, using an electric mixer on medium speed, beat butter, confectioners' sugar, egg white and vanilla until light and creamy, about 3 minutes. On low speed, gradually add flour mixture, mixing until blended. Shape dough into a roll 11 inches (28 cm) long. Wrap and chill until firm, at least 3 hours.

3. Fifteen minutes before you're ready to bake, preheat oven to 325°F (160°C). Cut roll into ¼-inch (0.5 cm) slices. Place about 1 inch (2.5 cm) apart on prepared cookie sheet. Bake in preheated oven for 18 to 22 minutes or until golden around edges. Let cool for 5 minutes on sheet, then transfer to a rack and cool completely.

4. *Glaze:* In a small saucepan over low heat, heat chocolate and oil, stirring until chocolate is melted and mixture is smooth. Dip half of each cookie in chocolate mixture. Place on rack over a piece of waxed paper. Set aside until chocolate hardens, about 1 hour.

Variations

Replace hazelnuts with unblanched almonds or pecans.

Add a pinch each of ground nutmeg and ground cloves.

Ginger Orange Almond Crisps

◆

These cookies are a good choice for ginger fans. This is a big-batch recipe. You may want to freeze one of the rolls for future use.

MAKES ABOUT 14½ DOZEN COOKIES

- **Preparation: 25 minutes**
- **Chilling: 4 hours**
- **Baking: 12 minutes**
- **Freezing: excellent**

TIPS

Turbinado is a raw sugar that is golden in color. It is available in most large grocery stores, bulk stores and natural foods stores. Demerara, muscovado or other raw sugars work equally well on these cookies. You can also use coarse or regular granulated sugar.

Instead of sprinkling sugar on top of the cookies, you can roll the logs in sugar to coat the edges. You'll need about ¾ cup (175 mL) sugar for 2 rolls.

Crystallized ginger is sold in small rounds and chunks. I find the rounds easier to cut.

- **Cookie sheet, ungreased**

1 cup	butter, softened	250 mL
1 cup	confectioners' (icing) sugar, sifted	250 mL
1	egg	1
1 tbsp	grated orange zest	15 mL
¼ tsp	salt	1 mL
2¼ cups	all-purpose flour	550 mL
¾ cup	coarsely chopped almonds	175 mL
¾ cup	finely chopped crystallized ginger	175 mL
⅓ cup	turbinado or other raw cane sugar (see Tips, left)	75 mL

1. In a large bowl, using an electric mixer on medium speed, beat butter and confectioners' sugar until light and creamy, about 3 minutes. Add egg and orange zest, mixing until smooth. On low speed, add salt, then gradually add flour, beating until dough becomes too stiff for the mixer, then finish mixing with a wooden spoon. Stir in almonds and ginger. Divide dough into halves. Shape each into a roll 11 inches (28 cm) long. Wrap and chill until firm, at least 4 hours.

2. Fifteen minutes before you're ready to bake, preheat oven to 375°F (190°C). Cut rolls into ⅛-inch (3 mm) slices. Place about 1 inch (2.5 cm) apart on cookie sheet. Sprinkle sugar over tops. Bake in preheated oven for 8 to 12 minutes or until golden around edges. Cool for 5 minutes on sheet, then transfer to a rack and cool completely.

Variation
Omit orange zest.

Brazil Nut Squares

These squares work on the same principle as refrigerator rolls, but they are a different shape.

MAKES ABOUT 4 DOZEN COOKIES

- **Preparation: 25 minutes**
- **Chilling: 4 hours**
- **Baking: 12 minutes**
- **Freezing: excellent**

TIPS

Use a small, empty waxed paper, plastic wrap or aluminum foil box.

For fancier presentation, dip half of each cookie, on the diagonal, in melted chocolate.

For a crispier cookie, bake a little longer until golden overall, not just around the edges.

Brazil nuts have a buttery flavor that is quite different from other nuts. With their golden color and traces of dark skin, they give a nice rustic look to the cookies, too.

- **Cookie sheet, ungreased**

1¾ cups	all-purpose flour	425 mL
¼ tsp	baking powder	1 mL
¼ tsp	baking soda	1 mL
¼ tsp	salt	1 mL
¾ cup	butter, softened	175 mL
½ cup	packed brown sugar	125 mL
1	egg	1
1 tsp	vanilla	5 mL
1 cup	finely chopped Brazil nuts	250 mL

1. On a sheet of waxed paper or in a bowl, combine flour, baking powder, baking soda and salt. Set aside.

2. In a large bowl, using an electric mixer on medium speed, beat butter, brown sugar, egg and vanilla until light and creamy, about 3 minutes. On low speed, gradually add flour mixture, beating until blended. With a wooden spoon, stir in nuts.

3. Line a 12- by 2- by 2-inch (30 cm by 5 cm by 5 cm) box with plastic wrap (see Tips, left). Pack dough into box firmly and evenly. Cover and chill until firm, at least 4 hours.

4. Fifteen minutes before you're ready to bake, preheat oven to 375°F (190°C). Cut bar into ¼-inch (0.5 cm) slices. Place 1 inch (2.5 cm) apart on cookie sheet. Bake in preheated oven for 8 to 12 minutes or until golden around edges. Cool for 5 minutes on sheet, then transfer to a rack and cool completely.

Variations

Replace Brazil nuts with cashews, pecans or hazelnuts.

Shape the dough into a roll for round cookies.

Oatmeal Raisin Rounds

Here's an old-fashioned favorite in an easy-to-bake form.

**MAKES ABOUT
5 DOZEN COOKIES**

- **Preparation: 25 minutes**
- **Chilling: 4 hours**
- **Baking: 12 minutes**
- **Freezing: excellent**

TIPS

There are a lot of raisins in this dough, which gives the cookies a nice flavor and appearance. Chop them very finely to make slicing easy.

If your dough doesn't cut nicely, simply reshape the cookies as you put them on the cookie sheet, using your fingers to stick the dough together.

A reliable oven thermometer is a good investment. It will tell you whether your oven heat is aligned with the setting. If not, you can adjust it accordingly.

- **Cookie sheet, ungreased**

1 cup	all-purpose flour	250 mL
1/2 tsp	baking soda	2 mL
1/4 tsp	salt	1 mL
1 tsp	ground cinnamon	5 mL
1/2 cup	butter, softened	125 mL
1/2 cup	granulated sugar	125 mL
1/2 cup	packed brown sugar	125 mL
1	egg	1
2 tbsp	light (fancy) molasses	30 mL
1 1/2 cups	quick-cooking rolled oats	375 mL
1 cup	raisins, finely chopped	250 mL

1. On a sheet of waxed paper or in a small bowl, combine flour, baking soda, salt and cinnamon. Set aside.

2. In a large bowl, using an electric mixer on medium speed, beat butter, granulated and brown sugars, egg and molasses until light and creamy, about 3 minutes. On low speed, gradually add flour mixture, beating until blended. With a wooden spoon, stir in oats and raisins. Divide dough into halves. Shape each into a roll 8 inches (20 cm) long. Wrap and chill until firm, at least 4 hours.

3. Fifteen minutes before you're ready to bake, preheat oven to 375°F (190°C). Cut rolls into 1/4-inch (0.5 cm) slices. Place about 2 inches (5 cm) apart on cookie sheet. Bake in preheated oven for 8 to 12 minutes or until golden. Cool for 5 minutes on sheet, then transfer to a rack and cool completely.

Variations

Replace raisins with dates or dried cranberries.

The hint of molasses is nice, but it can be omitted if you prefer.

Add 1 tbsp (15 mL) grated orange or lemon zest along with the egg.

Roll logs in finely chopped walnuts before chilling.

Apricot Fig Pinwheels

I speak from experience when I say that even people who claim they don't like figs love these cookies.

MAKES ABOUT 4 DOZEN COOKIES

- **Preparation: 40 minutes**
- **Chilling: 4 hours**
- **Baking: 16 minutes**
- **Freezing: excellent**

TIPS

Use whatever variety of fig you prefer. Golden Calimyrna figs look the best with apricot jam. If you're using Black Mission figs, substitute an equal quantity of raspberry jam for the apricot.

Be sure to cut the woody stems off the figs before chopping.

Use thick jam, not light, sugar-reduced spread, which is too soft to work in these cookies.

- **Cookie sheet, greased or lined with parchment paper**

1¾ cups	all-purpose flour	425 mL
2 tsp	baking powder	10 mL
¼ tsp	salt	1 mL
½ cup	butter, softened	125 mL
1 cup	granulated sugar	250 mL
1	egg	1
1 tsp	vanilla	5 mL
¾ cup	finely chopped dried figs	175 mL
⅓ cup	sweetened flaked coconut	75 mL
½ cup	apricot jam	125 mL

1. On a sheet of waxed paper or in a bowl, combine flour, baking powder and salt. Set aside.

2. In a large bowl, using an electric mixer on medium speed, beat butter, sugar, egg and vanilla until light and creamy, about 3 minutes. On low speed, gradually add flour mixture, beating until dough becomes too stiff for the mixer, then finish mixing with a wooden spoon. Using your hands, knead to form a smooth dough. Between two sheets of waxed paper, roll out dough into a 12- by 9-inch (30 cm by 23 cm) rectangle.

3. In a small bowl, combine figs, coconut and jam. Mix well. Remove top sheet of waxed paper from dough. Spread jam mixture evenly over dough, leaving a ½-inch (1 cm) border along one long side. Starting with the opposite long side and using the bottom sheet of waxed paper to help you, roll up the dough tightly jelly-roll fashion. Press edge to seal and, using your hands, mold roll into nicely rounded shape. Wrap and chill until firm, at least 4 hours.

4. Fifteen minutes before you're ready to bake, preheat oven to 375°F (190°C). Cut roll into ¼-inch (0.5 cm) slices. Place about 2 inches (5 cm) apart on prepared cookie sheet. Bake in preheated oven for 12 to 16 minutes or until golden around edges. Cool for 5 minutes on sheet, then transfer to a rack and cool completely.

Variations

Replace figs with dried apricots or chopped nuts.

Use marmalade or peach jam and golden Calimyrna figs.

Thin Oatmeal Crisps

These cookies are great on their own and, with a date or raspberry jam filling, they also make delicious sandwich cookies.

**MAKES ABOUT
14 DOZEN COOKIES**

- **Preparation: 20 minutes**
- **Chilling: 4 hours**
- **Baking: 12 minutes**
- **Freezing: excellent**

TIPS

This is a big-batch recipe — you may want to freeze one or two of the rolls for longer storage.

Although recipes usually call for an electric mixer to blend ingredients, you can almost always use a wooden spoon when making cookies. It just takes more physical effort. With either method, it usually takes about 3 minutes to get a butter-and-sugar mixture light and creamy.

A thin, sharp serrated knife, like a bread knife, works well for cutting this dough into thin slices.

- **Cookie sheet, greased or lined with parchment paper**

2 cups	all-purpose flour	500 mL
1 tsp	baking soda	5 mL
½ tsp	salt	2 mL
1 cup	butter, softened	250 mL
1 cup	packed brown sugar	250 mL
½ cup	water	125 mL
3 cups	quick-cooking rolled oats	750 mL

1. On a sheet of waxed paper or in a bowl, combine flour, baking soda and salt. Set aside.

2. In a large bowl, using an electric mixer on medium speed, beat butter and brown sugar until smooth and creamy, about 3 minutes. On low speed, add water and oats. Gradually add flour mixture, beating until blended. Divide dough into halves. Shape each into a roll 11 inches (28 cm) long. Wrap and chill until firm, at least 4 hours.

3. Fifteen minutes before you're ready to bake, preheat oven to 375°F (190°C). Cut rolls into ⅛-inch (3 mm) slices. Place about 1 inch (2.5 cm) apart on prepared cookie sheet. Bake in preheated oven for 8 to 12 minutes or until golden. Cool for 5 minutes on sheet, then transfer to a rack and cool completely.

Variations

Add 1½ tsp (7 mL) ground cinnamon to the dry ingredients.

Add 1 tbsp (15 mL) grated orange zest to the butter mixture.

Fruit and Spice Rounds

These cookies have a crispy texture and the blend of spices nicely complements the abundance of fruit and nuts. This is a big-batch recipe — you may want to freeze one or two of the rolls for longer storage.

MAKES ABOUT 13 DOZEN COOKIES

- **Preparation: 25 minutes**
- **Chilling: 4 hours**
- **Baking: 12 minutes**
- **Freezing: excellent**

TIPS

Use a food processor to easily chop the dates, raisins and nuts.

When wrapping dough for freezing or storage, wrap tightly in plastic wrap. If you're using the dough in the immediate future, waxed paper will do.

- **Cookie sheet, greased or lined with parchment paper**

3¼ cups	all-purpose flour	800 mL
1 tsp	baking soda	5 mL
2 tsp	ground cinnamon	10 mL
½ tsp	ground cloves	2 mL
½ tsp	ground nutmeg	2 mL
1 cup	butter, softened	250 mL
1½ cups	granulated sugar	375 mL
3	eggs	3
1 cup	chopped dates	250 mL
1 cup	chopped raisins	250 mL
1 cup	finely chopped walnuts	250 mL

1. On a sheet of waxed paper or in a bowl, combine flour, baking soda, cinnamon, cloves and nutmeg. Set aside.

2. In a large bowl, using an electric mixer on medium speed, beat butter and sugar until light and creamy, about 3 minutes. Add eggs, one at a time, beating well after each addition. On low speed, gradually add flour mixture, beating until blended. With a wooden spoon, stir in dates, raisins and walnuts. Divide dough into thirds. Shape each into a roll 13 inches (33 cm) long. Wrap and chill until firm, at least 4 hours.

3. Fifteen minutes before you're ready to bake, preheat oven to 375°F (190°C). Cut rolls into ¼-inch (0.5 cm) slices. Place about 2 inches (5 cm) apart on prepared cookie sheet. Bake in preheated oven for 8 to 12 minutes or until lightly browned. Cool for 5 minutes on sheet, then transfer to a rack and cool completely.

Variations

Replace raisins with dried cranberries or apricots.

Omit walnuts or use your favorite nut.

To dress up these cookies, add a lemon glaze. Mix 2 cups (500 mL) confectioners' (icing) sugar, sifted, with ¼ cup (60 mL) lemon juice. Spread evenly over tops.

Apricot Almond Refrigerator Cookies

You can't go wrong with a few rolls of these tasty cookies tucked away in your freezer.

MAKES ABOUT 9 DOZEN COOKIES

- **Preparation: 25 minutes**
- **Chilling: 4 hours**
- **Baking: 12 minutes**
- **Freezing: excellent**

TIPS

The dough for refrigerator cookies is often soft when you shape it, but it firms up with chilling. I prefer to leave it overnight to make sure it is firm enough for easy cutting.

I prefer combining the dry ingredients on a piece of waxed paper instead of dirtying a bowl. Then I use the paper as a funnel when adding them to the butter mixture.

Check your cookie sheets. Dark nonstick ones bake cookies faster, so it's wise to set your timer for the minimum time. You can always bake longer, but you can't change overbaked cookies.

- **Cookie sheet, ungreased**

2¾ cups	all-purpose flour	675 mL
1 tsp	baking powder	5 mL
½ tsp	baking soda	2 mL
¼ tsp	salt	1 mL
1 cup	butter, softened	250 mL
1 cup	granulated sugar	250 mL
2	eggs	2
1 tsp	vanilla	5 mL
¾ cup	finely chopped almonds	175 mL
¾ cup	finely chopped dried apricots	175 mL

1. On a sheet of waxed paper or in a bowl, combine flour, baking powder, baking soda and salt. Set aside.

2. In a large bowl, using an electric mixer on medium speed, beat butter, sugar, eggs and vanilla until light and creamy, about 3 minutes. On low speed, gradually add flour mixture, beating until blended. With a wooden spoon, stir in almonds and apricots. Divide dough into halves. Shape each into a roll 14 inches (35 cm) long. Wrap and chill until firm, at least 4 hours.

3. Fifteen minutes before you're ready to bake, preheat oven to 375°F (190°C). Cut rolls into ¼-inch (0.5 cm) slices. Place about 2 inches (5 cm) apart on cookie sheet. Bake in preheated oven for 8 to 12 minutes or until golden. Cool for 5 minutes on sheet, then transfer to a rack and cool completely.

Chocolate Orange Almond Slices

Although these cookies look like they would be difficult to make, they are actually quite easy. The checkerboard appearance is achieved by cutting the dough in half, flavoring it differently, then assembling it before baking.

MAKES ABOUT 8 DOZEN COOKIES

- **Preparation: 40 minutes**
- **Chilling: 6 hours, divided**
- **Baking: 12 minutes**
- **Freezing: excellent**

TIPS

The same 2 doughs can be used to make several different looks. You can simply make 2 layers or 4 layers for striped cookies in a square bar.

Dough for refrigerator cookies is often soft when you shape it, but it firms up with chilling. I prefer to leave it overnight to make sure it is firm enough for easy cutting.

When cutting dough, always ensure that your knife is sharp.

- **Cookie sheet, ungreased**

2 1/2 cups	all-purpose flour	625 mL
1 1/2 tsp	baking powder	7 mL
1/4 tsp	salt	1 mL
1 cup	butter, softened	250 mL
1 cup	granulated sugar	250 mL
1/2 cup	packed brown sugar	125 mL
1	egg	1
1 tbsp	grated orange zest	15 mL
1/3 cup	ground almonds	75 mL
2	squares (1 oz/28 g each) semisweet chocolate, melted and cooled	2

1. On a sheet of waxed paper or in a bowl, combine flour, baking powder and salt. Set aside.

2. In a large bowl, using an electric mixer on medium speed, beat butter, granulated and brown sugars and egg until light and creamy, about 3 minutes. On low speed, gradually add flour mixture, beating until blended. Divide dough into halves. With a wooden spoon, stir orange zest and almonds into 1 portion. Stir melted chocolate into the other portion. Shape each into a roll 12 inches (30 cm) long. Chill until firm, about 2 hours.

3. Cut each roll lengthwise into quarters. Reassemble 2 rolls, alternating chocolate and orange sections. Wrap and chill until firm, at least 4 hours.

4. Fifteen minutes before you're ready to bake, preheat oven to 375°F (190°C). Cut rolls into 1/4-inch (0.5 cm) slices. Place about 1 inch (2.5 cm) apart on cookie sheet. Bake in preheated oven for 8 to 12 minutes or until golden around the edges. Cool for 5 minutes on sheet, then transfer to a rack and cool completely.

Spumoni Slices

These cookies have the appearance and flavor of the popular Italian ice cream. Their colorful layers are sure to be a hit.

MAKES ABOUT 4 DOZEN COOKIES

- **Preparation: 35 minutes**
- **Chilling: 3 hours**
- **Baking: 11 minutes**
- **Freezing: excellent**

TIPS

The amount of food coloring you'll need depends upon the kind you're using. Paste colors are much stronger than liquid ones, so judge accordingly. Add just enough to make a pleasant color.

To distribute food coloring evenly, knead it into the dough using the palm of your hand. Add a little at a time until the right shade is reached. Keep in mind that color lightens slightly during baking.

- **Cookie sheet, ungreased**

2¼ cups	all-purpose flour	550 mL
¼ tsp	baking soda	1 mL
¼ tsp	salt	1 mL
1 cup	butter, softened	250 mL
⅔ cup	granulated sugar	150 mL
1	egg	1
1	square (1 oz/28 g) semisweet chocolate, melted and cooled	1
⅓ cup	finely chopped pistachios	75 mL
	Green food coloring	
⅓ cup	finely chopped red candied (glacé) cherries	75 mL
¼ tsp	almond extract	1 mL
	Red food coloring	

1. On a sheet of waxed paper or in a bowl, combine flour, baking soda and salt. Set aside.

2. In a large bowl, using an electric mixer on medium speed, beat butter, sugar and egg until light and creamy, about 3 minutes. On low speed, gradually add flour mixture, mixing until smooth. Divide dough into thirds. With a wooden spoon, stir melted chocolate into 1 portion. Stir pistachios and enough green food coloring to make a pastel dough into the second portion (see Tips, left). Stir cherries, almond extract and enough red coloring to make a pink dough into the third portion. Line an empty 12- by 2- by 2-inch (30 cm by 5 cm by 5 cm) waxed paper box with waxed paper or plastic wrap. Press pink dough evenly into box. Cover with chocolate dough, then green dough. Press down firmly to make even layers. Cover and chill until firm, at least 3 hours.

3. Fifteen minutes before you're ready to bake, preheat oven to 375°F (190°C). Cut roll into ¼-inch (0.5 cm) slices. Place about 2 inches (5 cm) apart on cookie sheet. Bake in preheated oven for 7 to 11 minutes or until set and lightly browned around edges. Cool for 5 minutes on sheet, then transfer to a rack and cool completely.

Chocolate Chip Refrigerator Cookies

Once you've tried these, you'll never buy another roll of slice 'n' bake chocolate chip cookies. They are delicious and very easy to make.

MAKES ABOUT 8 DOZEN COOKIES

- **Preparation: 30 minutes**
- **Chilling: 4 hours**
- **Baking: 12 minutes**
- **Freezing: excellent**

TIPS

When chilling, wrap dough in waxed paper or plastic wrap.

The chocolate chips make cutting a bit difficult, but not to worry. If the rounds aren't even, reshape them on the cookie sheet with your fingers. The cookies will look great when baked and taste even better.

Rolls of cookie dough can also be frozen. Thaw for about an hour at room temperature or in the refrigerator overnight, until the dough can be sliced easily.

- **Cookie sheet, ungreased**

2¾ cups	all-purpose flour	675 mL
1 tsp	baking soda	5 mL
¼ tsp	baking powder	1 mL
¼ tsp	salt	1 mL
1 cup	butter, softened	250 mL
1 cup	packed brown sugar	250 mL
½ cup	granulated sugar	125 mL
2	eggs	2
1 tsp	vanilla	5 mL
1 cup	semisweet chocolate chips	250 mL
½ cup	finely chopped pecans	125 mL

1. On a sheet of waxed paper or in a bowl, combine flour, baking soda, baking powder and salt. Set aside.

2. In a large bowl, using an electric mixer on medium speed, beat butter and brown and granulated sugars until light and creamy, about 3 minutes. Add eggs, one at a time, beating well after each addition. Add vanilla. On low speed, gradually add flour mixture, beating until blended. With a wooden spoon, stir in chocolate chips and pecans. Divide dough into halves. Shape each into a roll 12 inches (30 cm) long. Wrap and chill until firm, at least 4 hours.

3. Fifteen minutes before you're ready to bake, preheat oven to 350°F (180°C). Cut rolls into ¼-inch (0.5 cm) slices. Place about 2 inches (5 cm) apart on cookie sheet. Bake in preheated oven for 8 to 12 minutes or until light golden. Cool for 5 minutes on sheet, then transfer to a rack and cool completely.

Variations

Use milk chocolate chips or miniature semisweet chocolate chips.

Omit nuts or replace pecans with your favorite nut.

Slice 'n' Bake Brownie Cookies

These yummy cookies remind me of bite-size brownies.

MAKES ABOUT 5 1/2 DOZEN COOKIES

- **Preparation: 30 minutes**
- **Chilling: 2 hours**
- **Baking: 12 minutes**
- **Freezing: excellent**

TIPS

I prefer combining the dry ingredients on a piece of waxed paper instead of dirtying a bowl. Then I use the paper as a funnel when adding them to the butter mixture.

As you cut the roll, rotate it frequently to avoid flattening one side.

If a recipe makes more than one roll, remove only one at a time from the refrigerator for slicing.

- **Cookie sheet, ungreased**

2 1/2 cups	all-purpose flour	625 mL
1 tsp	baking powder	5 mL
1/2 tsp	baking soda	2 mL
1/4 tsp	salt	1 mL
1 cup	butter, softened	250 mL
1 1/2 cups	granulated sugar	375 mL
1	egg	1
1 cup	milk chocolate chips, melted and cooled	250 mL
3/4 cup	miniature semisweet chocolate chips	175 mL
3/4 cup	finely chopped pecans	175 mL
1/3 cup	coarse granulated sugar	75 mL

1. On a sheet of waxed paper or in a bowl, combine flour, baking powder, baking soda and salt. Set aside.

2. In a large bowl, using an electric mixer on medium speed, beat butter, granulated sugar and egg until light and creamy, about 3 minutes. On low speed, beat in melted chocolate. Gradually add flour mixture, beating until blended. With a wooden spoon, stir in chocolate chips and pecans. Divide dough into halves. Shape each into a roll 13 inches (33 cm) long. Wrap and chill until firm, at least 2 hours.

3. Fifteen minutes before you're ready to bake, preheat oven to 375°F (190°C). Cut rolls into 3/8-inch (9 mm) slices. Place about 2 inches (5 cm) apart on cookie sheet. Sprinkle coarse sugar evenly over tops. Bake in preheated oven for 8 to 12 minutes or until golden around edges. Cool for 5 minutes on sheet, then transfer to a rack and cool completely.

Variations

For a stronger chocolate flavor, replace milk chocolate chips with semisweet chocolate chips.

The coarse sugar on top adds a nice finishing touch, but it can be omitted. Look for it in bulk or at cake decorating stores.

Sugar Cookies

Pressed, Cutout and Sandwich Cookies

Pressed cookies result when relatively soft dough is pushed through a pastry bag or a cookie press. A cookie press is a device that comes with a variety of design plates. It is easy to operate — all you do is choose your design, pack the dough into the tube and press it through onto the cookie sheet. Using this device, anyone can produce perfectly shaped cookies with relatively intricate designs. When using a cookie press, follow the manufacturer's instructions. Be sure to pack the dough tightly to ensure there are no air holes, otherwise you won't get smooth shapes.

Cutout or rolled cookies are another example of cookie artistry at work. Sometimes the cookies are sprinkled with plain or colored sugar, frosted or embellished with decorations, such as chocolate sprinkles or candies. There are so many interesting cookie cutters available that making cutout cookies can be a terrific project that's fun for all family members. I've suggested specific cutters in my recipes, but you can substitute the shapes you prefer.

Sandwich cookies, as the name implies, are two cookies sandwiched together with filling in the middle. They come in a variety of shapes, sizes and flavors. Virtually any kind of cookie can be used and the filling can be very simple or more elaborate. The combination of cookies and filling really expands the possibilities for making something unique, with unusual flavors and textures.

Sugar Cookies

There are many variations of sugar cookies, each slightly different in flavor and texture. This is my favorite recipe. Not only does it taste great, but the dough is easy to work with.

MAKES ABOUT 5 DOZEN COOKIES

- **Preparation: 30 minutes**
- **Baking: 15 minutes**
- **Freezing: excellent**

TIPS

Use different-sized cookie cutters, if you prefer. The size noted refers to the longest measurement. Bake larger shapes for a longer time than smaller ones.

Dip your cookie cutters in flour between each cut to prevent them from sticking to the dough.

Roll dough ¼ inch (0.5 cm) thick if you prefer a softer cookie. Bake for 13 to 18 minutes. Baking time will depend on size and thickness of cookies. They should just be starting to brown around the edges.

- **Preheat oven to 325°F (160°C)**
- **2½-inch (6 cm) cookie cutters (see Tips)**
- **Cookie sheet, ungreased**

4 cups	all-purpose flour	1 L
1 tsp	baking powder	5 mL
¼ tsp	salt	1 mL
1 cup	butter, softened	250 mL
2 cups	granulated sugar	500 mL
2	eggs	2
2 tbsp	grated lemon zest	30 mL
2 tbsp	freshly squeezed lemon juice	30 mL
	Coarse or granulated sugar	

1. On a sheet of waxed paper or in a bowl, combine flour, baking powder and salt. Set aside.

2. In a large bowl, using an electric mixer on medium speed, beat butter and sugar until light and creamy, about 3 minutes. Add eggs, one at a time, beating well after each addition. Add lemon zest and juice. On low speed, gradually add flour mixture, beating until dough becomes too stiff for the mixer, then finish mixing with a wooden spoon to form a smooth dough.

3. On a floured surface, roll out dough to ⅛-inch (3 mm) thickness. Cut into desired shapes using floured cookie cutters. Place about 1 inch (2.5 cm) apart on cookie sheet. Bake in preheated oven for 10 to 15 minutes or until light golden around edges. Cool for 5 minutes on sheet, then transfer to a rack and cool completely.

Variations

Change the cookie shape to match the occasion. Cut out bunnies and eggs for Easter, hearts for Valentine's Day, and trees, stars and bells for Christmas.

Sprinkle regular or colored sugar on cookies before baking, or leave them plain and decorate with icing and sprinkles later. Royal Icing (see page 422) looks particularly nice on these cookies.

Spritz Cookies

Spritz cookies are a bit like shortbread because they contain a large amount of butter. A Scandinavian specialty, they are tender, crisp and buttery-tasting. Pushed through a press into pretty designs, they add a festive note to any occasion.

**MAKES ABOUT
5 DOZEN COOKIES**

- **Preparation: 25 minutes**
- **Baking: 10 minutes**
- **Freezing: excellent**

TIPS

Baking time will depend upon the size and shape of your cookies.

The dough should be soft enough so it can be pushed through a press easily. If it is too soft, add a little flour. If it's too stiff, mix in a little more softened butter.

- **Preheat oven to 375°F (190°C)**
- **Cookie press, fitted with design plate of your choice**
- **Cookie sheet, ungreased**

1 cup	butter, softened	250 mL
1 cup	confectioners' (icing) sugar, sifted	250 mL
2	egg yolks	2
1/2 tsp	vanilla	2 mL
1/4 tsp	almond extract	1 mL
1/4 tsp	salt	1 mL
2 cups	all-purpose flour	500 mL
	Colored sugar, optional	

1. In a large bowl, using an electric mixer on medium speed, beat butter and confectioners' sugar until light and creamy, about 3 minutes. Add egg yolks, beating until well blended. Add vanilla and almond extract. On low speed, add salt, then gradually add flour, beating until dough becomes too stiff for the mixer, then finish mixing with a wooden spoon until smooth.

2. Pack dough into fitted cookie press and press onto cookie sheet, about 1 inch (2.5 cm) apart. Sprinkle with colored sugar, if using. Bake in preheated oven for 6 to 10 minutes or until just starting to brown around edges. Cool for 5 minutes on sheet, then transfer to a rack and cool completely.

Variation

Spritz dough can be colored with food coloring. For instance, if you're using a wreath design, color the dough green. Try yellow if you are making flowers, and place a small piece of candied (glacé) cherry in the center before baking.

Almond Paste Macaroons

Most people associate macaroons with coconut, but ground almonds are actually the key ingredient. These cookies have amazing taste and are easy to make.

MAKES ABOUT 4 DOZEN COOKIES

- **Preparation: 15 minutes**
- **Baking: 20 minutes**
- **Freezing: excellent**

- **Pastry bag, fitted with ½-inch (1 cm) star tube**
- **Cookie sheet, lined with parchment paper**

8 oz	almond paste	250 g
¾ cup	confectioners' (icing) sugar, sifted	175 mL
¼ cup	granulated sugar	60 mL
2	egg whites	2
48	slivered almond pieces	48

1. In a food processor, combine almond paste and confectioners' and granulated sugars. Process until blended. Add egg whites and process until smooth, scraping down the sides of the bowl.

2. Pack dough into fitted pastry bag. Pipe 1-inch (2.5 cm) rosettes about 1 inch (2.5 cm) apart on prepared cookie sheet. Press an almond sliver on top of each. Bake in preheated oven for 15 to 20 minutes or until firm and golden. Cool for 10 minutes on sheet, then transfer to a rack and cool completely.

Red Raspberry Meringues

These tasty cookies are a colorful addition to a cookie box or tray. They also make a nice accompaniment for raspberry sherbet or a bowl of fresh berries.

MAKES ABOUT 4½ DOZEN COOKIES

- **Preparation: 15 minutes**
- **Baking: 2 hours**
- **Freezing: not recommended**

- **Preheat oven to 225°F (110°C)**
- **Pastry bag fitted with a ½-inch (1 cm) star tube**
- **Cookie sheet, lined with parchment paper**

3	egg whites	3
¼ tsp	cream of tartar	1 mL
Pinch	salt	Pinch
¾ cup	granulated sugar	175 mL
¼ cup	raspberry jam	60 mL
6 to 10	drops red food coloring	6 to 10

1. Using an electric mixer on high speed, beat egg whites, cream of tartar and salt until soft peaks form. Add sugar, 2 tbsp (30 mL) at a time, beating until stiff peaks form, about 10 minutes. Add jam and food coloring. Beat 1 minute.

2. Spoon meringue into fitted pastry bag. Pipe 1-inch (2.5 cm) rosettes about 1 inch (2.5 cm) apart on prepared cookie sheet. Bake in preheated oven for 1¾ to 2 hours or until crisp and dry. Cool completely on sheet.

Empire Cookies

I'm not sure where the name originated, but these have always been a favorite in my family, as well as with anyone else who has tasted this recipe.

MAKES ABOUT 2 DOZEN SANDWICH COOKIES

- **Preparation: 45 minutes**
- **Baking: 12 minutes**
- **Freezing: excellent**

TIPS

It takes about 3 minutes of beating to get a butter, sugar and egg mixture light and creamy.

The frosting will be soft and spreadable. It will spread out smoothly and dry nicely.

Use a small offset spatula for the frosting, spreading it as close to the edges as you can.

- **Preheat oven to 350°F (180°C)**
- **2-inch (5 cm) round cookie cutter**
- **Cookie sheet, greased or lined with parchment paper**

COOKIE

1 2/3 cups	all-purpose flour	400 mL
1/2 tsp	baking powder	2 mL
Pinch	salt	Pinch
1/2 cup	butter, softened	125 mL
1/2 cup	granulated sugar	125 mL
1	egg	1
1 tsp	vanilla	5 mL

FROSTING

1 1/2 cups	confectioners' (icing) sugar, sifted	375 mL
6 to 7 tsp	boiling water	30 to 35 mL
2 tsp	corn syrup	10 mL
1/4 tsp	almond extract	2 mL

GARNISH AND FILLING

7	red candied (glacé) cherries, quartered	7
1/3 cup	raspberry jam	75 mL

1. *Cookie:* Combine flour, baking powder and salt. Set aside.
2. In a large bowl, using an electric mixer on medium speed, beat butter, sugar, egg and vanilla until light and creamy. On low speed, gradually add flour mixture, beating until blended. Using your hands, knead to form a smooth dough.
3. Divide dough into halves. On a floured surface, roll out 1 portion at a time to 1/8-inch (3 mm) thickness. Dip cutter in flour and cut into rounds. Place about 1 inch (2.5 cm) apart on prepared cookie sheet. Bake in preheated oven for 8 to 12 minutes or until golden around the edges. Cool for 5 minutes on sheet, then transfer to a rack and cool completely.
4. *Frosting:* Beat confectioners' sugar, 6 tsp (30 mL) boiling water, corn syrup and almond extract until smooth. If necessary, add more water, 1/2 tsp (2 mL) at a time, to make a spreadable consistency.
5. Divide cookies into 2 batches. Spread frosting over top side of 1 batch. Place a piece of cherry in center of each frosted cookie. Let stand until frosting hardens, about 1 hour.
6. *Assembly:* Spread about 1/2 tsp (2 mL) jam on flat side of unfrosted cookies. Top with frosted cookies.

Viewnese Fingers

These luscious treats are a sandwich cookie, shaped like fingers and filled with a coffee filling. When my niece got married, she requested a huge box of these cookies for a wedding present. When I bake my Christmas cookies, they are a staple.

MAKES ABOUT 3½ DOZEN SANDWICH COOKIES

- **Preparation: 30 minutes**
- **Baking: 7 minutes**
- **Freezing: excellent**

TIPS

The dough should be slightly soft so it can be pushed through a cookie press easily. If it is too stiff to press easily, mix in another tablespoon (15 mL) of softened butter. If it is too soft, add a little flour.

These cookies will have slightly different lengths. Pair them up during assembly.

You can make these any length you like. Short ones are nice for a cookie tray but longer ones (about 3 inches/7.5 cm) make a nice hostess gift.

- **Preheat oven to 375°F (190°C)**
- **Cookie press with ½-inch (1 cm) star-shaped nozzle**
- **Cookie sheet, ungreased**

COOKIE

2 cups	all-purpose flour	500 mL
¼ tsp	baking powder	1 mL
1 cup	butter, softened	250 mL
½ cup	confectioners' (icing) sugar, sifted	125 mL
½ tsp	vanilla	2 mL

FILLING

3 tbsp	butter, softened	45 mL
1 cup	confectioners' (icing) sugar, sifted	250 mL
1½ tsp	instant coffee powder	7 mL
1½ tsp	hot water	7 mL

1. *Cookie:* On a sheet of waxed paper or in a bowl, combine flour and baking powder. Set aside.

2. In a large bowl, using an electric mixer on medium speed, beat butter, confectioners' sugar and vanilla until light and creamy, about 3 minutes. On low speed, gradually add flour mixture, beating until smooth (see Tips, left). Pack dough into fitted cookie press and press into strips about 1½ inches (4 cm) long, about 1 inch (2.5 cm) apart on cookie sheet. Bake in preheated oven for 5 to 7 minutes or until starting to brown around edges. Cool for 5 minutes on sheet, then transfer to a rack and cool completely.

3. *Filling:* In a small bowl, using a wooden spoon, combine butter and confectioners' sugar. Combine coffee powder and hot water; stir into butter mixture until smooth. If necessary, add a little milk or water to make a spreadable consistency.

4. *Assembly:* Divide cookies into 2 batches. Spread about 2 tsp (10 mL) filling over flat side of 1 batch. Place remainder on top, flat side down. Press lightly together.

Variation

Dip ends in melted chocolate for a fancier presentation.

Apricot Date Oatmeal Turnovers

Here's an old-fashioned favorite — a date square in cookie form.

MAKES ABOUT 3½ DOZEN COOKIES

- **Preparation: 45 minutes**
- **Chilling: 2 hours**
- **Cooking (Filling): 5 minutes**
- **Baking: 17 minutes**
- **Freezing: excellent**

TIPS

For convenience, use a food processor to chop the dates and apricots.

Try not to use too much flour when rolling. It will toughen any dough. You need just enough on the surface of the dough, your hands and the rolling pin to prevent sticking. If you use a pastry cloth and rolling pin cover, you'll have no problems with the dough sticking.

- **2½-inch (6 cm) round cookie cutter**
- **Cookie sheet, greased or lined with parchment paper**

DOUGH

2 cups	all-purpose flour	500 mL
½ tsp	baking soda	2 mL
¼ tsp	salt	1 mL
¾ tsp	ground cinnamon	3 mL
1 cup	butter, softened	250 mL
1 cup	granulated sugar	250 mL
1	egg	1
¼ cup	milk	60 mL
2½ cups	quick-cooking rolled oats	625 mL
½ cup	sweetened flaked coconut	125 mL

FILLING

1½ cups	chopped dates	375 mL
½ cup	chopped dried apricots	125 mL
½ cup	granulated sugar	125 mL
⅔ cup	hot water	150 mL
1 tbsp	butter	15 mL

1. *Cookie:* Combine flour, baking soda, salt and cinnamon. Set aside.

2. Using an electric mixer on medium speed, beat butter and sugar until light and creamy. Add egg and milk, beating until smooth. On low speed, gradually add flour mixture, beating until blended. With a wooden spoon, stir in oats and coconut. Divide dough into thirds. Cover and chill for at least 2 hours.

3. *Filling:* In a saucepan, over medium heat, bring dates, apricots, sugar, water and butter to a boil. Reduce heat and simmer until thick, stirring frequently. Set aside to cool.

4. Fifteen minutes before you are ready to bake, preheat oven to 350°F (180°C). On a floured surface, roll out 1 portion of dough to ⅛-inch (3 mm) thickness. Dip cutter in flour and cut into rounds. Spread 1 tsp (5 mL) filling in center, leaving edges clean. Top with a second round. Using a fork dipped in flour, lightly press edges together to seal. Prick top with fork to let steam escape. Repeat with remaining dough. Place on prepared cookie sheet, about 1 inch (2.5 cm) apart. Bake in preheated oven for 13 to 17 minutes or until golden. Cool for 5 minutes on sheet, then transfer to a rack and cool completely.

Raspberry Jam Tarts

These cookies are full of possibilities. Change the flavor with different jams. Change the look by using different cutters for the tops.

MAKES ABOUT 2 DOZEN COOKIES

- **Preparation: 35 minutes**
- **Baking: 15 minutes**
- **Freezing: excellent**

TIPS

Aspic cutters are great for making the small cutouts or you can use the tip of a sharp knife.

Dip your cookie cutters in flour between each cut to prevent them from sticking to the dough.

You can re-roll the scraps that are left over when you cut out the rounds. Cut shapes as closely together as possible to minimize the scraps.

- **Preheat oven to 350°F (180°C)**
- **2½-inch (6 cm) round cookie cutter**
- **¾-inch (1.5 cm) round cookie cutter (see Tips, left)**
- **Cookie sheet, ungreased**

2½ cups	all-purpose flour	625 mL
1 tsp	baking powder	5 mL
¼ tsp	salt	1 mL
1 cup	butter, softened	250 mL
1 cup	granulated sugar	250 mL
1	egg	1
2 tbsp	freshly squeezed lemon juice	30 mL
¾ cup	raspberry jam	175 mL

1. On a sheet of waxed paper or in a bowl, combine flour, baking powder and salt. Set aside.

2. In a large bowl, using an electric mixer on medium speed, beat butter and sugar until blended, about 1 minute. Add egg and lemon juice, beating until smooth. On low speed, gradually add flour mixture, beating until blended.

3. Divide dough into halves. On a floured surface, roll out 1 portion to ⅛-inch (3 mm) thickness. Dip 2½-inch (6 cm) cutter in flour and cut into rounds. Place about 1 inch (2.5 cm) apart on cookie sheet and place 1 tsp (5 mL) jam in center of each. Roll out remaining dough and cut into 2½-inch (6 cm) rounds then, using the small cutter, make a cutout in center. Place over filled cookies. Press around edges with floured fork to seal. Bake in preheated oven for 11 to 15 minutes or until golden around edges. Cool for 5 minutes on sheet, then transfer to a rack and cool completely.

Variations

Replace the raspberry jam with apricot, peach or pineapple.

Sprinkle coarse or granulated sugar on top of cookies before baking.

Glazed Lemon Poppy Seed Flowers

These cookies are very tender and practically melt in your mouth. The tart lemon glaze with the crunchy poppy seeds is irresistible.

MAKES ABOUT 5 DOZEN COOKIES

- **Preparation: 30 minutes**
- **Chilling: 1 hour**
- **Baking: 14 minutes**
- **Freezing: excellent**

TIPS

Cut other shapes, such as hearts, circles and bells — just be sure your cutters are the same size at their longest measurement or adjust the baking time accordingly.

Dip your cookie cutters in flour between each cut to prevent them from sticking to the dough.

This dough can be prepared and refrigerated for up to 3 days. Let stand at room temperature just long enough to make rolling easy.

- **2½-inch (6 cm) daisy-shaped cookie cutter (see Tips, left)**
- **Cookie sheet, greased or lined with parchment paper**

COOKIE

2 cups	all-purpose flour	500 mL
¼ cup	poppy seeds	60 mL
¼ tsp	salt	1 mL
1 cup	butter, softened	250 mL
½ cup	granulated sugar	125 mL
1	egg yolk	1
1 tbsp	grated lemon zest	15 mL
1 tsp	lemon extract	5 mL

GLAZE

1 cup	confectioners' (icing) sugar, sifted	250 mL
1 tbsp	butter, softened	15 mL
3 tbsp	whipping (35%) cream	45 mL
1 tsp	freshly squeezed lemon juice	5 mL

1. *Cookie:* On a sheet of waxed paper or in a bowl, combine flour, poppy seeds and salt. Set aside.

2. In a large bowl, using an electric mixer on medium speed, beat butter, sugar, egg yolk, lemon zest and lemon extract until light and creamy, about 3 minutes. On low speed, gradually add flour mixture, beating until blended. Cover and chill dough for at least 1 hour for easy rolling.

3. Fifteen minutes before you're ready to bake, preheat oven to 350°F (180°C). On a floured surface, roll out dough to ¼-inch (0.5 cm) thickness. Dip cutter in flour and cut out daisies. Place about 1 inch (2.5 cm) apart on prepared cookie sheet. Bake in preheated oven for 10 to 14 minutes or until golden around edges. Cool for 5 minutes on sheet, then transfer to a rack and cool for 15 minutes before glazing.

4. *Glaze:* In a small bowl, using an electric mixer on low speed, beat confectioners' sugar, butter, cream and lemon juice until smooth. If necessary, add a little more lemon juice to make a spreadable consistency. Using a small offset spatula, spread glaze over top of cookies. Cool completely on rack.

Hazelnut Layer Cookies

These cookies are an Austrian specialty. They are one of my favorites — once you've tried them, you'll understand why.

MAKES ABOUT 3 DOZEN SANDWICH COOKIES

- **Preparation: 30 minutes**
- **Baking: 11 minutes**
- **Freezing: excellent (unfilled)**

TIPS

You can use regular (not seedless) raspberry jam, but the flavor is not as good.

The dusting of confectioners' (icing) sugar is a nice touch, but it won't last. Dust the cookies when you're ready to serve them.

You'll need about 2 1/2 cups (625 mL) whole hazelnuts to get this quantity of ground.

Before grinding hazelnuts, toast them in a 350°F (180°C) oven for about 10 minutes, then rub them in a tea towel to remove as much of the skin as possible. It won't all come off, but what remains adds a nice color to the dough.

- **Preheat oven to 375°F (190°C)**
- **2-inch (5 cm) round cookie cutter**
- **1/2-inch (1 cm) round cookie cutter**
- **Cookie sheet, ungreased**

COOKIE

1 cup	butter, softened	250 mL
3/4 cup	granulated sugar	175 mL
1	egg	1
2 1/4 cups	all-purpose flour	550 mL
2 cups	ground toasted hazelnuts (see Tips, left)	500 mL

FILLING

2/3 cup	seedless raspberry jam	150 mL
	Confectioners' (icing) sugar, sifted	

1. *Cookie:* In a large bowl, using an electric mixer on medium speed, beat butter, sugar and egg until light and creamy, about 3 minutes. On low speed, gradually add flour, beating until blended. With a wooden spoon, stir in hazelnuts. Using your hands, knead to form a smooth dough.

2. On a floured surface, roll out dough to 1/8-inch (3 mm) thickness. Dip cutter in flour and cut out 2-inch (5 cm) rounds. With a 1/2-inch (1 cm) cutter, cut centers out of half of the cookies. Re-roll scraps for more cookies. Place about 1 inch (2.5 cm) apart on cookie sheet. Bake in preheated oven for 7 to 11 minutes or until golden around edges. Cool for 5 minutes on sheet, then transfer to a rack to cool completely.

3. *Assembly:* Spread about 1 tsp (5 mL) jam over flat side of whole cookies. Top with cutout cookies, flat side down. Press gently together. Before serving, dust tops lightly with confectioners' sugar.

Variations

Substitute pecans or almonds for the hazelnuts.
Substitute apricot jam in place of the raspberry.

Chocolate Caramel Pecan Rounds

These will remind you of the famous Turtles chocolates.

MAKES ABOUT 2¹/₂ DOZEN COOKIES

- **Preparation: 35 minutes**
- **Baking: 14 minutes**
- **Cooking (Topping): 8 minutes**
- **Standing: 1 hour**
- **Freezing: not recommended**

TIPS

Dip your cookie cutters in flour between each cut to prevent them from sticking to the dough.

You can re-roll the scraps that are left over when you cut out the rounds. Cut shapes as closely together as possible to minimize scraps.

- **Preheat oven to 350°F (180°C)**
- **2-inch (5 cm) round cookie cutter**
- **Cookie sheet, ungreased**

COOKIE

1 cup	butter, softened	250 mL
¹/₃ cup	granulated sugar	75 mL
¹/₂ tsp	vanilla	2 mL
¹/₄ tsp	salt	1 mL
2 cups	all-purpose flour	500 mL

TOPPING

12	vanilla caramels	12
1¹/₂ tsp	half-and-half (10%) cream	7 mL
¹/₂ cup	chopped pecans	125 mL
1	square (1 oz/28 g) semisweet chocolate, chopped and melted	1

1. *Cookie:* In a large bowl, using a wooden spoon, beat butter, sugar and vanilla until blended, about 3 minutes. Gradually add salt and flour. Mix well. Using your hands, knead to form a smooth dough.

2. On a lightly floured surface, roll out dough to ¹/₄-inch (0.5 cm) thickness. Using a cookie cutter dipped in flour, cut into rounds. Place on cookie sheet about 1 inch (2.5 cm) apart. Bake in preheated oven for 10 to 14 minutes or until golden around edges. Cool for 10 minutes on sheet, then transfer to a rack and cool completely.

3. *Topping:* In a small saucepan, over low heat, combine caramels and cream, stirring until melted and smooth. Dip one side of each cookie (about ¹/₃ of the surface) in caramel mixture, then into pecans. Place on a sheet of waxed paper and drizzle melted chocolate over top. Set aside until set, about 1 hour.

Variations

Place a pecan half on top of cookie before drizzling with chocolate.

Substitute peanuts or cashews for the pecans.

Chocolate Peppermint Patties

These cookies remind me of those classic chocolate mint candies, but in a softer form. They don't seem quite as decadent, meaning you can probably eat more.

MAKES ABOUT 2 DOZEN SANDWICH COOKIES

- **Preparation: 35 minutes**
- **Baking: 12 minutes**
- **Freezing: excellent (filled)**

TIPS

If you're not a big mint fan, decrease the peppermint extract to $1/8$ tsp (0.5 mL).

If any cookie dough that requires shaping or rolling seems soft, chill it for about 30 minutes for easier handling. This is better than adding more flour, which can toughen a cookie.

- **Preheat oven to 350°F (180°C)**
- **Cookie sheet, greased or lined with parchment paper**

COOKIE

1 1/4 cups	all-purpose flour	300 mL
1/2 tsp	baking powder	2 mL
1/4 tsp	salt	1 mL
1/4 cup	unsweetened cocoa powder, sifted	60 mL
1/2 cup	butter, softened	125 mL
1 cup	packed brown sugar	250 mL
1	egg	1
1 tsp	vanilla	5 mL

FILLING

2 tbsp	butter, softened	30 mL
1 2/3 cups	confectioners' (icing) sugar, sifted	400 mL
2 to 3 tbsp	half-and-half (10%) cream	30 to 45 mL
1/4 tsp	peppermint extract	1 mL

1. *Cookie:* On a sheet of waxed paper or in a bowl, combine flour, baking powder, salt and cocoa. Set aside.

2. In a bowl, using an electric mixer on medium speed, beat butter, brown sugar, egg and vanilla until light and creamy. On low speed, gradually add flour mixture, beating until blended.

3. Shape dough into $3/4$-inch (2 cm) balls. Place about 2 inches (5 cm) apart on prepared cookie sheet. Flatten with the palm of your hand to a $1\frac{1}{4}$-inch (3 cm) circle. Bake in preheated oven for 8 to 12 minutes or until set. Cool for 5 minutes on sheet, then transfer to a rack and cool completely.

4. *Filling:* In a small bowl, using an electric mixer on medium speed (or a wooden spoon, if you prefer), beat butter until creamy. On low speed, add confectioners' sugar, cream and peppermint extract, using just enough cream to make a spreadable consistency.

5. *Assembly:* Divide cookies into 2 batches. Spread about 1 tbsp (15 mL) filling on flat side of 1 batch. Place remaining cookies on top, flat side down. Press gently together.

Variation
Add green food coloring to the filling.

Oatmeal Date Sandwich Cookies

These are like old-fashioned date turnovers in cookie form. I prefer the cookie version since you get a lot more filling.

MAKES ABOUT 2½ DOZEN SANDWICH COOKIES

- **Preparation: 35 minutes**
- **Cooking (Filling): 5 minutes**
- **Cooling (Filling): 2 hours**
- **Baking: 14 minutes**
- **Freezing: excellent (filled)**

TIPS

Prepare the filling up to 2 days ahead.

A food processor makes chopping dates an easy chore.

Make bite-size cookies if you prefer. Drop by scant tablespoonfuls (10 mL) and bake for 8 to 12 minutes.

Once filled, these cookies quickly become soft and chewy. I actually like them this way, but if you prefer a crisp cookie, make the parts beforehand but assemble no earlier than a day ahead.

- **Preheat oven to 350°F (180°C)**
- **Cookie sheet, greased or lined with parchment paper**

COOKIE

⅔ cup	all-purpose flour	150 mL
¼ tsp	baking soda	1 mL
¼ tsp	salt	1 mL
¾ cup	butter, softened	175 mL
1 cup	packed brown sugar	250 mL
½ cup	granulated sugar	125 mL
1	egg	1
1 tbsp	grated orange zest	15 mL
2 tbsp	freshly squeezed orange juice	30 mL
3 cups	quick-cooking rolled oats	750 mL

FILLING

1 lb	chopped pitted dates	500 g
1 cup	granulated sugar	250 mL
1 cup	water	250 mL
2 tbsp	freshly squeezed lemon juice	30 mL

1. *Cookie:* On a sheet of waxed paper or in a bowl, combine flour, baking soda and salt. Set aside.

2. In a large bowl, using an electric mixer on medium speed, beat butter, brown and granulated sugars, egg, and orange zest and juice until light and creamy, about 3 minutes. On low speed, gradually add flour mixture, beating until blended. With a wooden spoon, stir in oats.

3. Drop dough by heaping tablespoonfuls (20 mL) about 2 inches (5 cm) apart on prepared cookie sheet. Using a fork dipped in flour, press down lightly to flatten. Bake in preheated oven for 10 to 14 minutes or until light golden. Cool for 5 minutes on sheet, then transfer to a rack and cool completely.

4. *Filling:* In a large saucepan over medium heat, combine dates, sugar, water and lemon juice. Bring to a boil, reduce heat and simmer, stirring occasionally, until thickened, about 5 minutes. Remove from heat. Cool for 2 hours.

5. *Assembly:* Divide cookies into 2 batches. Spread about 1 tbsp (15 mL) filling over flat side of 1 batch. Place remaining cookies on top, flat side down. Press gently together.

Chocolate Ginger Sandwiches

A crisp oatmeal cookie with a hint of ginger is twice as good when two of them are joined with melted chocolate.

MAKES ABOUT 2½ DOZEN SANDWICH COOKIES

- **Preparation: 35 minutes**
- **Baking: 12 minutes**
- **Cooking (Filling): 4 minutes**
- **Chilling: 30 minutes**
- **Freezing: not recommended**

TIPS

Parchment paper always makes cleanup easy, but it's practically mandatory when baking with sticky ingredients such as corn syrup or honey. It solves the problem of cookies sticking to the pan. Washable silicone sheets also work well.

Serve these with a dish of ice cream or a latte.

Use a level teaspoonful (5 mL) of dough for each cookie. These cookies will really spread and flatten during baking, which gives them a nice lacy look, brittle texture and caramel flavor.

- **Preheat oven to 375°F (190°C)**
- **Cookie sheet, lined with parchment paper**

COOKIE

2 cups	quick-cooking rolled oats	500 mL
1 cup	granulated sugar	250 mL
⅔ cup	all-purpose flour	150 mL
½ tsp	ground ginger	2 mL
⅔ cup	butter, melted	150 mL
¼ cup	corn syrup	60 mL
¼ cup	milk	60 mL

FILLING

6	squares (1 oz/28 g each) semisweet chocolate, chopped	6
6	squares (1 oz/28 g each) white chocolate, chopped	6

1. *Cookie:* On a sheet of waxed paper or in a bowl, combine oats, sugar, flour and ginger. Set aside.

2. In a large bowl, combine melted butter, corn syrup and milk. With a wooden spoon, stir until smooth. Add flour mixture, mixing until blended.

3. Drop dough by teaspoonfuls (5 mL) about 3 inches (7.5 cm) apart on prepared cookie sheet. With a wet offset spatula or your finger, press flat. Bake in preheated oven for 8 to 12 minutes or until light golden. Cool completely on sheet.

4. *Filling:* In separate small saucepans over low heat, melt semisweet and white chocolate, stirring until smooth. Remove from heat and set aside to cool slightly, until chocolate is a soft spreading consistency.

5. *Assembly:* Divide cookies into 4 batches. Spread semisweet chocolate over flat side of 1 batch. Top with second batch, flat side down. Repeat with remainder using white chocolate. Set on a sheet of waxed paper on a cookie sheet. Chill to harden chocolate, about 30 minutes.

Variation

These cookies are also great plain or with a chocolate drizzle on top.

Chocolate Oat Sandwich Bites

Chocolate and peanut butter make a great filling for small oatmeal cookies. They taste like a chocolate-covered granola bar, only better.

MAKES ABOUT 16 SANDWICH COOKIES

- **Preparation: 35 minutes**
- **Baking: 10 minutes**
- **Cooking (Filling): 4 minutes**
- **Chilling: 30 minutes**
- **Freezing: excellent (filled)**

TIPS

Your peanut butter should be soft and creamy. Some peanut butters settle, leaving an oil layer on top. If this happens, stir well before using.

Quick-cooking oats are the most common variety used for cookies. Old-fashioned or large-flake are specified when a more "oaty" taste and appearance is desired.

- **Preheat oven to 350°F (180°C)**
- **Cookie sheet, greased or lined with parchment paper**

COOKIE

⅔ cup	butter	150 mL
1 cup	all-purpose flour	250 mL
1 cup	quick-cooking rolled oats	250 mL
½ cup	packed brown sugar	125 mL
1 tbsp	liquid honey	15 mL
½ tsp	baking soda	2 mL
1	egg	1
¼ cup	finely chopped peanuts	60 mL

FILLING

¾ cup	semisweet chocolate chips	175 mL
3 tbsp	creamy peanut butter	45 mL

1. *Cookie:* In a large saucepan over medium heat, melt butter. Remove from heat. With a wooden spoon, stir in flour, oats, brown sugar, honey, baking soda, egg and peanuts, mixing until smooth.

2. Shape dough into ¾-inch (2 cm) balls. Place about 2 inches (5 cm) apart on prepared cookie sheet. Using an offset spatula or your fingers, press flat to 1¼-inch (3 cm) rounds. Bake in preheated oven for 6 to 10 minutes or until golden. Cool for 5 minutes on sheet, then transfer to a rack and cool completely.

3. *Filling:* In a small saucepan over low heat, melt chocolate, stirring until smooth. Remove from heat. With a wooden spoon, stir in peanut butter until smooth. Cool slightly, about 2 minutes.

4. *Assembly:* Divide cookies into 2 batches. Spread a scant tablespoonful (10 mL) filling over flat side of 1 batch. Place remaining cookies on top, flat side down. Chill to set filling, about 30 minutes.

Variations

Omit peanut butter in filling.

Replace semisweet chocolate chips with milk chocolate chips.

Cinnamon Raspberry Stacks

The extra time it takes to make these cookies is well spent as they are very attractive and the combination of differently flavored dough is quite delectable.

MAKES ABOUT 22 SANDWICH COOKIES

- **Preparation: 45 minutes**
- **Cooking: 12 minutes**
- **Chilling: 1 hour**
- **Baking: 12 minutes**
- **Freezing: excellent (unfilled)**

TIPS

Aspic or canapé cutters, which come in a variety of shapes (such as triangle, star, circle or heart) are perfect for making the center cutouts. They are available at kitchen stores.

A small offset spatula works well for spreading small amounts of filling on cookies.

If you're planning to freeze these cookies, do so before you fill them. You can thaw as many as you want when you're ready to fill.

After cutting, re-roll scraps of dough to make more cookies.

- **Preheat oven to 375°F (190°C)**
- **2¹⁄₂-inch (6 cm) and ¹⁄₂-inch (1 cm) cookie cutter (see Tips, left)**
- **Cookie sheet, ungreased**

CINNAMON DOUGH

¹⁄₂ cup	butter	125 mL
¹⁄₂ cup	confectioners' (icing) sugar, sifted	125 mL
1	egg yolk	1
1¹⁄₂ tsp	ground cinnamon	7 mL
1 cup	all-purpose flour	250 mL

PLAIN DOUGH

¹⁄₂ cup	butter, softened	125 mL
¹⁄₂ cup	confectioners' (icing) sugar sifted	125 mL
1	egg yolk	1
1 tsp	vanilla	5 mL
1¹⁄₄ cups	all-purpose flour	300 mL

FILLING

²⁄₃ cup	seedless raspberry jam	150 mL
	Confectioners' (icing) sugar, sifted	

1. *Cinnamon Dough:* In a saucepan over medium heat, heat butter until it melts and turns golden, about 12 minutes. Transfer to a bowl and chill until hard, then beat until softened. Add sugar, egg yolk and cinnamon, beating until light and creamy. Gradually beat in flour. Knead to form a smooth dough. Cover and chill for 1 hour.

2. *Plain Dough:* In a bowl, beat butter, sugar, egg yolk and vanilla until light and creamy. Gradually beat in flour. Knead to form a smooth dough. Cover and chill for 30 minutes.

3. On a floured surface, roll out cinnamon dough to ¹⁄₈-inch (3 mm) thickness. Cut into 2¹⁄₂-inch (6 cm) rounds. Place about 1 inch (2.5 cm) apart on cookie sheet. Repeat with plain dough, then, using ¹⁄₂-inch (1 cm) cutter, cut the center out of the plain circles. Place on cookie sheet. Bake in preheated oven for 8 to 12 minutes or until just golden around edges. Cool for 5 minutes on sheet, then transfer to a rack and cool completely.

4. *Assembly:* Spread 1 tsp (5 mL) jam over flat side of cinnamon cookies. Top with plain cookies, bottom sides down. Press together gently. Just before serving, sprinkle with sugar.

Coconut Cream Macaroon Sandwiches

These chewy macaroon cookies with a creamy coconut filling are, as my niece says, "awesome."

**MAKES ABOUT
1 ½ DOZEN SANDWICH
COOKIES**

- Preparation: 30 minutes
- Baking: 15 minutes
- Freezing: excellent (filled)

TIPS

Coconut extract gives baked goods containing coconut a more intense coconut flavor.

Coconut milk is sold in cans. It is available in Oriental stores or grocery stores, and can be found near the evaporated milk.

- Preheat oven to 350°F (180°C)
- Cookie sheet, greased or lined with parchment paper

COOKIE

2	eggs, separated	2
Pinch	salt	Pinch
¾ cup	granulated sugar	175 mL
½ tsp	coconut extract	2 mL
1 ½ cups	sweetened flaked coconut	375 mL
¾ cup	all-purpose flour	175 mL

FILLING

1 tbsp	butter, softened	15 mL
1 ¼ cups	confectioners' (icing) sugar, sifted	300 mL
1 ½ tbsp	coconut milk	22 mL
½ tsp	coconut extract	2 mL

1. *Cookie:* In a small bowl, using an electric mixer on high speed, beat egg whites and salt until foamy. Gradually add sugar, 2 tbsp (30 mL) at a time, beating until very stiff, about 4 minutes. Set aside.

2. In a large bowl, using a wooden spoon, mix egg yolks, coconut extract, coconut and flour until blended. Add egg white mixture, mixing until thoroughly moistened.

3. Drop dough by scant tablespoonfuls (10 mL) about 2 inches (5 cm) apart on prepared cookie sheet. With a wet spatula or finger, flatten mounds slightly. Bake in preheated oven for 10 to 15 minutes or until golden. Cool for 10 minutes on sheet, then transfer to a rack and cool completely.

4. *Filling:* In a small bowl, beat butter, confectioners' sugar, coconut milk and coconut extract until smooth.

5. *Assembly:* Divide cookies into 2 batches. Spread about 1 tbsp (15 mL) filling over flat side of 1 batch. Place remaining cookies on top, flat side down. Press gently together.

Variation
Add ½ cup (125 mL) finely chopped almonds along with the coconut.

Chocolate-Filled Cashew Cookies

These cookies provide a good hit of chocolate nestled between two tender, nutty cashew cookies. Yum.

MAKES ABOUT 4 DOZEN SANDWICH COOKIES

- **Preparation: 35 minutes**
- **Baking: 14 minutes**
- **Cooking (Filling): 4 minutes**
- **Chilling: 30 minutes**
- **Freezing: excellent (filled)**

TIPS

Use a small offset spatula for spreading fillings on sandwich cookies. This will become one of your favorite baking tools.

Try not to use too much flour when rolling. It will toughen any dough. You need just enough on the surface of the dough, your hands and the rolling pin to prevent sticking. If you use a pastry cloth and rolling pin cover, you'll have no problems with the dough sticking.

- **Preheat oven to 350°F (180°C)**
- **2-inch (5 cm) round cookie cutter**
- **Cookie sheet, ungreased**

COOKIE

1 cup	butter, softened	250 mL
¾ cup	packed brown sugar	175 mL
1	egg	1
½ cup	sour cream	125 mL
1 tsp	vanilla	5 mL
3 cups	all-purpose flour	750 mL

FILLING

1½ cups	semisweet chocolate chips	375 mL
6 tbsp	butter	90 mL
1⅔ cups	finely chopped cashews	400 mL

1. *Cookie:* In a large bowl, using an electric mixer on medium speed, beat butter, brown sugar, egg, sour cream and vanilla until smooth. On low speed, gradually add flour, beating until dough becomes too stiff for the mixer, then finish mixing with a wooden spoon to form a smooth, soft dough. If necessary, cover and chill 1 hour for easy rolling.

2. Divide dough into halves. On floured surface, roll out 1 portion at a time to ⅛-inch (3 mm) thickness. Dip cutter in flour and cut into rounds. Place about 1 inch (2.5 cm) apart on prepared cookie sheet. Bake in preheated oven for 10 to 14 minutes or until golden around edges. Cool for 5 minutes on sheet, then transfer to a rack and cool completely.

3. *Filling:* In a saucepan over low heat, melt chocolate chips and butter, stirring until smooth. Remove from heat. Stir in cashews.

4. *Assembly:* Divide cookies into 2 batches. Spread about 1 tbsp (15 mL) filling over flat side of 1 batch. Place remaining cookies on top, flat side down. Chill to set filling, about 30 minutes.

Variations

Use peanuts or hazelnuts in place of the cashews.

Substitute white, milk chocolate or peanut butter chips for the semisweet.

Raspberry Pecan Ribbons

Shaped Cookies and Biscotti

Many all-time favorite cookies like biscotti, peanut butter cookies and shortbread are shaped by hand. The shapes can vary from sticks and crescents to balls and wedges, and the cookies can be left plain, dipped in chocolate, sprinkled with sugar or frosted. The dough is often chilled before shaping to make it easier to handle.

Some, like biscotti, can be quickly shaped because the dough bakes in a large portion, while others are more time-consuming because the cookies need to be shaped individually. But all are easy to make. Biscotti, unlike most cookies, require two bakings. This gives them their hard, crunchy texture, which makes them ideal for dunking. You'll discover many different flavors, textures and looks in this section, so you're bound to find some favorites.

Raspberry Pecan Ribbons

◆

These are an easy-to-make version of the ever-popular thumbprint cookie. Change the look and taste with different jams.

MAKES ABOUT 4 DOZEN COOKIES

- **Preparation: 25 minutes**
- **Baking: 19 minutes**
- **Freezing: excellent**

TIPS

A white icing drizzle can dress these cookies up. In a bowl, combine $\frac{1}{4}$ cup (60 mL) confectioners' (icing) sugar and 1 tsp (5 mL) water, adding more water, if necessary, to make a drizzling consistency.

Use a food processor to chop nuts finely.

Toast nuts for the best flavor. Be sure to cool them completely before chopping.

Pecans and walnuts can always be interchanged in recipes. It is simply a matter of taste.

- **Preheat oven to 325°F (160°C)**
- **Cookie sheet, ungreased**

1 $\frac{1}{2}$ cups	all-purpose flour	375 mL
1 tsp	baking powder	5 mL
$\frac{1}{4}$ tsp	salt	1 mL
$\frac{1}{2}$ cup	butter, softened	125 mL
$\frac{1}{2}$ cup	granulated sugar	125 mL
1	egg	1
1 tbsp	grated lemon zest	15 mL
$\frac{3}{4}$ cup	finely chopped pecans	175 mL
$\frac{1}{3}$ cup	raspberry jam	75 mL

1. On a sheet of waxed paper or in a bowl, combine flour, baking powder and salt. Set aside.

2. In a large bowl, using a wooden spoon, beat butter, sugar, egg and lemon zest until light and creamy, about 3 minutes. Gradually add flour mixture, beating until blended.

3. Divide dough into thirds. Shape each into a roll 10 inches (25 cm) long. Spread pecans on a sheet of waxed paper and roll each log in the nuts until evenly coated. Place logs about 4 inches (10 cm) apart on cookie sheet. Flatten to 1$\frac{1}{2}$-inch (4 cm) width. Make a $\frac{1}{2}$-inch (1 cm) indentation down center of each strip using a floured finger or the back of a wooden spoon. Bake in preheated oven for 15 to 19 minutes or until lightly browned around edges. Press indentation again. Cool for 15 minutes on sheet, then transfer to a rack and cool completely.

4. When cooled, fill each indentation with 2 tablespoons (30 mL) of jam, spreading along the length of the rolls to completely fill the indentations. Cut each roll into 12 or 16 pieces.

Variation

Use other soft spreads such as marmalade, or blueberry, peach, strawberry or apricot jam.

Macadamia Ginger Macaroons

◆

If you love coconut, you'll love these macaroons. They also contain yummy macadamia nuts and ginger.

**MAKES ABOUT
3 DOZEN COOKIES**

- **Preparation: 35 minutes**
- **Baking: 15 minutes**
- **Chilling: 10 minutes**
- **Freezing: excellent (without melted chocolate dip)**

TIPS

This dough is quite sticky. Moisten your hands to keep it from sticking to your fingers.

To keep coconut soft and moist, store it in the freezer.

I prefer cookie sheets without sides because I can place unbaked cookies on a piece of parchment paper and slide the paper on and off the sheet easily. While one sheet is baking, I'm putting cookies on the next piece of parchment.

- **Preheat oven to 350°F (180°C)**
- **Cookie sheet, greased or lined with parchment paper**

3 cups	sweetened flaked coconut	750 mL
½ cup	granulated sugar	125 mL
6 tbsp	all-purpose flour	90 mL
¾ tsp	ground ginger	3 mL
4	egg whites	4
⅔ cup	finely chopped macadamia nuts	150 mL
⅓ cup	finely chopped crystallized ginger	75 mL
2	squares (1 oz/28 g each) semisweet chocolate, chopped and melted	2

1. In a large bowl, using a wooden spoon, combine coconut, sugar, flour and ground ginger. Mix well. Add egg whites, mixing until ingredients are thoroughly moistened. Stir in nuts and crystallized ginger.

2. Shape heaping tablespoonfuls (20 mL) of mixture into rolls and place about 2 inches (5 cm) apart on prepared cookie sheet. Bake in preheated oven for 10 to 15 minutes or until golden around edges. Cool completely on sheets.

3. Dip both ends of cooled cookies in melted chocolate. Place on waxed paper. Chill until chocolate is set, about 10 minutes.

Variation

Replace macadamia nuts with an equal quantity of chopped almonds.

Gingersnaps

This spicy cookie has definitely withstood the test of time. This variation is crisp and thin with a pleasantly mild ginger flavor.

MAKES ABOUT 6½ DOZEN COOKIES

- **Preparation: 25 minutes**
- **Chilling: 2 hours**
- **Baking: 14 minutes**
- **Freezing: excellent**

TIPS

Turbinado sugar is a coarse raw sugar. It is available in many grocery stores, bulk stores and natural foods stores. You can substitute coarse white sugar for sprinkling over cookies.

If ground white pepper isn't available, use ¼ tsp (1 mL) freshly ground black pepper. You will notice black specks in the dough.

- **Preheat oven to 350°F (180°C)**
- **Cookie sheet, ungreased**

3¾ cups	all-purpose flour	925 mL
1¼ tsp	baking powder	6 mL
¼ tsp	salt	1 mL
2 tbsp	ground ginger	30 mL
1 tbsp	ground cinnamon	15 mL
½ tsp	ground white pepper	2 mL
¼ tsp	ground cloves	1 mL
1½ cups	butter, softened	375 mL
1¾ cups	packed brown sugar	425 mL
1	egg	1
1 tbsp	grated fresh gingerroot	15 mL
2 tsp	grated lemon zest	10 mL
¼ cup	turbinado sugar	60 mL

1. On a sheet of waxed paper or in a bowl, combine flour, baking powder, salt, ginger, cinnamon, pepper and cloves. Set aside.

2. In a large bowl, using an electric mixer on medium speed, beat butter, brown sugar, egg, gingerroot and lemon zest until smooth and creamy. On low speed, gradually add flour mixture, beating until dough becomes too stiff for the mixer, then finish mixing with a wooden spoon until smooth. Cover and chill dough for 2 hours for easy handling.

3. Shape teaspoonfuls (5 mL) of dough into balls. Place about 1 inch (2.5 cm) apart on cookie sheet. With the bottom of a glass dipped in flour, press down firmly on each to form thin rounds. Sprinkle turbinado sugar evenly over tops. Bake in preheated oven for 10 to 14 minutes or until crisp and golden. Cool for 5 minutes on sheet, then transfer to a rack and cool completely.

Variation

If you are a fan of the chocolate-ginger combo, omit the turbinado sugar and instead sandwich 2 cookies together with melted chocolate.

Hazelnut Stacks

These cookies are crisp on the outside but chewy on the inside, and rich with the luscious buttery flavor of hazelnuts.

MAKES ABOUT 20 COOKIES

- **Preparation: 30 minutes**
- **Baking: 19 minutes**
- **Freezing: excellent**

TIPS

Hazelnuts are also known as filberts.

To toast hazelnuts, preheat oven to 350°F (180°C) and place nuts on rimmed baking sheet. Bake, stirring occasionally, until golden, 8 to 10 minutes. Place in a towel and rub to remove as much of the skins as possible. Cool completely.

Store these cookies in an airtight container at room temperature for up to 5 days.

A reliable oven thermometer is a good investment. It will tell you whether your oven heat is aligned with the setting. If not, you can adjust it accordingly.

- **Preheat oven to 375°F (190°C)**
- **Cookie sheet, greased or lined with parchment paper**

1 1/3 cups	hazelnuts, toasted (see Tips, left) and cooled	325 mL
3/4 cup	granulated sugar, divided	175 mL
2	egg whites	2
1/4 tsp	salt	1 mL
1/2 cup	all-purpose flour	125 mL

1. In a food processor, combine cooled toasted nuts and 1/4 cup (60 mL) of the sugar. Process until very finely chopped. Set aside.

2. In a small bowl, using an electric mixer on high speed, beat egg whites and salt to soft peaks. Gradually add remaining 1/2 cup (125 mL) sugar, 2 tbsp (30 mL) at a time, beating to stiff peaks. With a wooden spoon, stir flour and nut mixture into egg whites, mixing just to blend.

3. With moistened fingers, shape tablespoonfuls (15 mL) of dough into pyramid-shaped mounds and place about 2 inches (5 cm) apart on prepared cookie sheet. Bake in preheated oven for 15 to 19 minutes or until lightly browned. Cool completely on sheet.

Variations

Replace hazelnuts with unblanched almonds.

Dress these up with a drizzle of melted chocolate or by dipping the bottoms in melted chocolate. You can also dust them lightly with confectioners' (icing) sugar just before serving.

Crunchy Almond Crescents

Almond paste may seem expensive, but one bite of these easy-to-make cookies will reassure you that it's well worth the price.

MAKES ABOUT 2½ DOZEN COOKIES

- **Preparation: 25 minutes**
- **Baking: 14 minutes**
- **Freezing: excellent**

TIPS

Parchment paper makes cleanup easy. It also solves the problem of cookies sticking to the pan. Washable silicone sheets also work well.

Store these in an airtight container between layers of waxed paper for up to 4 days.

These are a great accompaniment to a bowl of fresh fruit or sherbet.

◆

- **Preheat oven to 375°F (190°C)**
- **Cookie sheet, greased or lined with parchment paper**

7 oz	almond paste	210 g
1 cup	granulated sugar	250 mL
2	egg whites	2
1 cup	finely chopped almonds	250 mL

1. Break almond paste into pieces. In a food processor, process almond paste and sugar until paste is pulverized. Add egg whites and process until blended.

2. Spread almonds on a sheet of waxed paper. Drop scant tablespoonfuls (10 mL) of dough onto almonds and roll until evenly coated. Shape into crescents and place about 2 inches (5 cm) apart on prepared cookie sheet. Bake in preheated oven for 10 to 14 minutes or until golden. Cool completely on sheet.

Variations

To dress up these cookies, drizzle melted chocolate on top or dip both ends in melted chocolate.

Sprinkle with confectioners' (icing) sugar just before serving.

Nutty Apricot Macaroons

If you love nuts, one taste of these cookies will transport you to heaven. They are not too sweet. Enjoy them with a dish of ice cream or sherbet, or a cup of espresso.

**MAKES ABOUT
1 ½ DOZEN COOKIES**

- **Preparation: 30 minutes**
- **Cooking: 5 minutes**
- **Baking: 19 minutes**
- **Freezing: excellent**

TIPS

To toast ingredients such as coconut, almonds and pine nuts, spread in a shallow baking pan and bake at 350°F (180°C) for 5 to 10 minutes, stirring occasionally, until golden and fragrant.

For a non-alcoholic cookie, use orange juice in place of the liqueur.

Always use large eggs when baking.

- **Preheat oven to 350°F (180°C)**
- **Cookie sheet, greased or lined with parchment paper**

¼ cup	finely chopped dried apricots	60 mL
¼ cup	almond liqueur	60 mL
¾ cup	toasted slivered almonds (see Tips, left)	175 mL
½ cup	toasted pine nuts	125 mL
⅔ cup	granulated sugar	150 mL
1 tbsp	all-purpose flour	15 mL
1	egg white	1
½ tsp	vanilla	2 mL
½ cup	finely chopped almonds	125 mL

1. In a small saucepan over medium heat, combine apricots and liqueur. Bring to a boil and cook, stirring occasionally, until liquid evaporates, about 5 minutes. Remove from heat. Set aside to cool.

2. In a food processor, process slivered almonds, pine nuts, sugar and flour until nuts are finely ground. Add egg white and vanilla. Process until dough forms a ball. Transfer to a bowl. With a wooden spoon, stir in reserved apricot mixture.

3. Spread finely chopped almonds in a small shallow dish. With moistened hands, shape dough into ¾-inch (2 cm) balls. Roll balls in almonds until evenly coated. Place about 2 inches (5 cm) apart on prepared cookie sheet. Using a moistened offset spatula, flatten each to a 1½-inch (4 cm) round. Bake in preheated oven for 15 to 19 minutes or until golden. Cool completely on sheet.

Variation
Replace the finely chopped almonds with finely chopped pine nuts.

Chocolate Crinkles

The distinct cracked top makes these cookies stand out. It just happens naturally during baking — you don't have to do anything special to achieve it.

MAKES ABOUT 3 DOZEN COOKIES

- **Preparation: 20 minutes**
- **Chilling: 2 hours**
- **Baking: 12 minutes**
- **Freezing: excellent**

TIPS

Confectioners' (icing) sugar will clump during storage. Before using, be sure to sift it (after measuring). This is especially important when it is used as a coating or in a frosting.

Use a lightly flavored oil, such as canola, in baking. Avoid strongly flavored oils, such as peanut and olive, unless specified in the recipe.

These cookies keep well and the recipe can easily be doubled to have extra on hand.

- **Preheat oven to 350°F (180°C)**
- **Cookie sheet, ungreased**

1 cup	all-purpose flour	250 mL
1 tsp	baking powder	5 mL
¼ tsp	salt	1 mL
1 cup	packed brown sugar	250 mL
¼ cup	vegetable oil	60 mL
2	squares (1 oz/28 g each) unsweetened chocolate, chopped, melted and cooled	2
2	eggs	2
½ tsp	vanilla	2 mL
¾ cup	confectioners' (icing) sugar, sifted	175 mL

1. On a sheet of waxed paper or in a bowl, combine flour, baking powder and salt. Set aside.

2. In a large bowl, whisk together brown sugar, oil, melted chocolate, eggs and vanilla until smoothly blended. With a wooden spoon, gradually stir in flour mixture, mixing until smooth. Cover and freeze for 30 minutes or refrigerate for 2 hours for easy handling.

3. Put confectioners' sugar in a small shallow dish. Shape dough into 1-inch (2.5 cm) balls. Roll balls in confectioners' sugar until evenly coated. Place about 2 inches (5 cm) apart on cookie sheet. Bake in preheated oven for 8 to 12 minutes or until set and tops are cracked and dry. Cool for 5 minutes on sheet, then transfer to a rack and cool completely.

Brandy Lemon Lace Rolls

Similar to brandy snaps, these candy-like cookies can be left flat or shaped into rolls while they're still warm.

MAKES ABOUT 3 DOZEN COOKIES

- **Preparation: 25 minutes**
- **Cooking: 4 minutes**
- **Baking: 7 minutes**
- **Freezing: not recommended**

TIPS

Baking just 6 cookies at a time gives you enough time to shape them before they become too cool.

Filling: Just before serving, beat 1 cup (250 mL) whipping (35%) cream with 3 tbsp (45 mL) confectioners' (icing) sugar and 1 tbsp (15 mL) brandy to stiff peaks. Pack into a pastry bag fitted with a plain nozzle and fill rolls.

If cookies cool and become too stiff to roll, warm them slightly in the oven.

These cookies are quite fragile and will crumble easily. That's okay — the crumbs are delicious sprinkled over or stirred into ice cream.

- **Preheat oven to 350°F (180°C)**
- **Cookie sheet, lined with parchment paper**

¼ cup	granulated sugar	60 mL
¼ cup	butter	60 mL
¼ cup	corn syrup	60 mL
⅓ cup	all-purpose flour	75 mL
1 tbsp	brandy	15 mL
2 tsp	grated lemon zest	10 mL
¼ tsp	ground cinnamon	1 mL

1. In a small saucepan over medium heat, bring sugar, butter and corn syrup to a boil. Remove from heat. Whisk in flour, brandy, lemon zest and cinnamon.

2. Making 6 cookies at a time, drop scant teaspoonfuls (4 mL) of batter on prepared cookie sheet. Bake in preheated oven for 5 to 7 minutes or until golden. Let stand on sheet for 1 minute or until slightly set but still soft. If you prefer flat cookies, let cool completely on sheet. To make rolls, quickly shape the soft, warm cookie around the handle of a thick wooden spoon. Let cool completely, then remove and fill (see Tips, left).

Variation

Omit lemon zest and/or cinnamon for a plain brandy snap.

Coffee Hazelnut Crescents

These cookies are similar to Crunchy Almond Crescents but with different flavoring. They are more shortbread-like in texture, but are equally loaded with nuts.

MAKES ABOUT 4 DOZEN COOKIES

- **Preparation: 20 minutes**
- **Baking: 19 minutes**
- **Freezing: excellent**

TIPS

Crescents will flatten slightly during baking.

Butter is a must for shortbread-like cookies. The flavor and texture it provides are unbeatable.

Instant espresso coffee powder is available in many Italian grocery stores as well as specialty coffee stores. It's a wonderful staple to have on hand for adding flavor to baked goods, as a little goes a long way.

To dip ends in chocolate, melt 3 oz (84 g) chopped semisweet chocolate with 1 tbsp (15 mL) butter.

- **Preheat oven to 300°F (150°C)**
- **Cookie sheet, ungreased**

1 cup	butter, softened	250 mL
½ cup	granulated sugar	125 mL
2 cups	all-purpose flour	500 mL
¼ tsp	salt	1 mL
2 tsp	instant espresso coffee powder	10 mL
1 cup	finely chopped hazelnuts	250 mL

1. In a large bowl, using an electric mixer on medium speed, beat butter and sugar until light and creamy, about 3 minutes. On low speed, gradually add flour, beating until dough becomes too stiff for the mixer, then finish mixing with a wooden spoon until smooth. Stir in salt, coffee powder and hazelnuts. Using your hands, knead to form a stiff dough.

2. Shape tablespoonfuls (15 mL) of dough into small rolls with tapered ends. Bend to form crescents. Place about 1 inch (2.5 cm) apart on cookie sheet. Bake in preheated oven for 15 to 19 minutes or until golden around edges. Cool for 5 minutes on sheet, then transfer to a rack and cool completely.

Variations

Replace hazelnuts with pecans or almonds.

Spread a coffee frosting (see filling on page 310) on top of these. Using tines of a fork, run lines down the frosting to resemble bark.

Omit the coffee powder for a plain nutty cookie.

Substitute almonds for the hazelnuts. Shape into balls rather than crescents and press an almond on top before baking.

Sesame Thins

Fantastic is the best word to describe these cookies, which can easily become addictive.

MAKES ABOUT 3 DOZEN COOKIES

- **Preparation: 25 minutes**
- **Baking: 13 minutes**
- **Freezing: not recommended**

TIPS

Be sure not to put more than 6 cookies on each sheet, because they spread considerably during baking.

The dough is quite sticky. Be prepared to wash your hands often while making these cookies.

- **Preheat oven to 350°F (180°C)**
- **Cookie sheet, greased or lined with parchment paper**

½ cup	butter, softened	125 mL
¾ cup	granulated sugar	175 mL
1 tbsp	grated lemon zest	15 mL
1	egg white	1
½ tsp	vanilla	2 mL
3 tbsp	all-purpose flour	45 mL
Pinch	salt	Pinch
1½ cups	sesame seeds	375 mL

1. In a large bowl, using a wooden spoon, beat butter and sugar until light and creamy, about 3 minutes. Add lemon zest, egg white and vanilla. Mix well. Add flour, salt and sesame seeds, mixing until ingredients are well moistened.

2. Shape dough into ¾-inch (2 cm) balls. Place about 3 inches (7.5 cm) apart on prepared cookie sheet (see Tips). Press each ball flat using a wet offset spatula or fingers. Bake in preheated oven for 9 to 13 minutes or until golden. Cool completely on cookie sheet.

Variation

Substitute ¼ cup (60 mL) black sesame seeds for an equal quantity of the white sesame seeds. They are sold in Oriental supermarkets.

Cherry Almond Butterballs

◆

The subtle flavor of nutmeg in the coating enhances the almond flavor in the cookie.

MAKES ABOUT 4½ DOZEN COOKIES

- **Preparation: 25 minutes**
- **Baking: 20 minutes**
- **Freezing: excellent**

TIPS

Although recipes usually call for an electric mixer to blend ingredients, you can almost always use a wooden spoon when making cookies. It just takes more physical effort. With either method, it usually takes about 3 minutes to get a butter-and-sugar mixture light and creamy.

Stiff dough, like that for shortbread and shaped cookies, is best kneaded with your hands to get it smooth. If it seems too soft or sticky, add a little flour. If crumbly, add a bit more butter.

- **Preheat oven to 300°F (150°C)**
- **Cookie sheet, ungreased**

2 cups	all-purpose flour	500 mL
¼ tsp	salt	1 mL
1¼ cups	ground blanched almonds	300 mL
1 cup	butter, softened	250 mL
½ cup	granulated sugar	125 mL
½ tsp	almond extract	2 mL
27	red candied (glacé) cherries, halved	27
½ cup	superfine granulated sugar	125 mL
1 tsp	ground nutmeg	5 mL

1. On a sheet of waxed paper or in a bowl, combine flour, salt and almonds. Set aside.

2. In a large bowl, using an electric mixer on medium speed, beat butter, sugar and almond extract until light and creamy, about 3 minutes. On low speed, gradually add flour mixture, beating until dough becomes too stiff for the mixer, then finish mixing with a wooden spoon until smooth. Using your hands, knead to form a smooth dough.

3. Shape tablespoonfuls (15 mL) of dough into balls. Press a cherry half into the center. Fold dough around cherry to enclose it. Place about 1 inch (2.5 cm) apart on cookie sheet. Bake in preheated oven for 16 to 20 minutes or until set and lightly golden. Cool for 5 minutes on sheet, then transfer to a rack placed over a sheet of waxed paper.

4. Combine superfine sugar and nutmeg in a small shallow dish. Roll warm balls in sugar mixture. Place on a rack and cool completely.

Variations

Replace nutmeg with cinnamon.

Roll cookies in plain confectioners' (icing) sugar for a different look.

Lemon Almond Balls

These are definitely one of my favorites, chewy and very nutty.

**MAKES ABOUT
4 DOZEN COOKIES**

- **Preparation: 20 minutes**
- **Baking: 17 minutes**
- **Freezing: excellent**

TIPS

If you prefer, decorate these balls. Place an almond half or candied (glacé) cherry half on top of cookie before baking.

These cookies tend to stick, so parchment paper or silicone baking sheets, if you have them, are an especially good choice when making this recipe.

- **Preheat oven to 350°F (180°C)**
- **Cookie sheet, lined with parchment paper**

2²/₃ cups	unblanched almonds	650 mL
1²/₃ cups	granulated sugar, divided	400 mL
1 tbsp	grated lemon zest	15 mL
¹/₄ tsp	salt	1 mL
2	eggs, beaten	2
¹/₂ tsp	almond extract	2 mL

1. In a food processor, process almonds and 1¹/₃ cups (325 mL) of the sugar until finely ground. Transfer to a large bowl. With a wooden spoon, stir in lemon zest, salt, eggs and almond extract, mixing until well blended.

2. Put remaining ¹/₃ cup (75 mL) sugar in a small shallow dish. With moistened hands, shape dough into 1-inch (2.5 cm) balls. Roll balls in sugar until evenly coated. Place about 2 inches (5 cm) apart on prepared cookie sheet. Bake in preheated oven for 13 to 17 minutes or until golden around edges. Cool completely on sheet.

Variation

Replace almonds with hazelnuts.

Classic Peanut Butter Cookies

No cookie book is complete without this classic. There are many versions of it, but this is the one I was brought up on and is still my favorite. The cinnamon is my mother's creative touch.

MAKES ABOUT 5 DOZEN COOKIES

- **Preparation: 25 minutes**
- **Baking: 16 minutes**
- **Freezing: excellent**

TIPS

Use creamy rather than crunchy peanut butter for these cookies. There's lots of crunch from the added peanuts.

A reliable oven thermometer is a good investment. It will tell you whether your oven heat is aligned with the setting. If not, you can adjust it accordingly.

- **Preheat oven to 375°F (190°C)**
- **Cookie sheet, ungreased**

2⅓ cups	all-purpose flour	575 mL
1 tsp	baking soda	5 mL
¼ tsp	salt	1 mL
½ tsp	ground cinnamon	2 mL
1 cup	butter, softened	250 mL
1 cup	creamy peanut butter	250 mL
1 cup	granulated sugar	250 mL
1 cup	packed brown sugar	250 mL
2	eggs	2
¾ cup	chopped dry-roasted peanuts	175 mL

1. On a sheet of waxed paper or in a bowl, combine flour, baking soda, salt and cinnamon. Set aside.

2. In a large bowl, using an electric mixer on medium speed, beat butter, peanut butter, and granulated and brown sugars until blended. Add eggs, one at a time, mixing well after each addition, and beat until mixture is light and creamy, about 3 minutes. On low speed, gradually add flour mixture, beating until blended. With a wooden spoon, stir in peanuts.

3. Shape dough into 1-inch (2.5 cm) balls. Place about 2 inches (5 cm) apart on cookie sheet. Using a fork dipped in sugar or flour, press flat, forming a crisscross pattern. Bake in preheated oven for 12 to 16 minutes or until set and golden. Cool for 5 minutes on sheet, then transfer to a rack and cool completely.

Variations

Omit the peanuts for a plain peanut butter cookie.

Substitute honey-roasted peanuts for the regular ones. They add a nice flavor to these cookies.

Try these as sandwich cookies, filled with banana ice cream or strawberry jam.

Pineapple Macadamia Wedges

Not only do these taste good, their different shape makes them a particularly nice addition to cookie trays.

**MAKES ABOUT
4 DOZEN COOKIES**

- **Preparation: 25 minutes**
- **Baking: 19 minutes**
- **Freezing: excellent**

TIPS

The macadamia nuts can be replaced with almonds or Brazil nuts, but the flavor of the cookies will be quite different.

Dried pineapple is often sold in bulk in the snack food section.

- **Preheat oven to 350°F (180°C)**
- **Cookie sheet, greased or lined with parchment paper**

COOKIE

1 cup	butter, softened	250 mL
2/3 cup	granulated sugar	150 mL
1 tsp	vanilla	5 mL
2 cups	all-purpose flour	500 mL
1/4 tsp	salt	1 mL
1 cup	finely chopped macadamia nuts	250 mL
3/4 cup	chopped dried pineapple	175 mL

DRIZZLE, OPTIONAL

3/4 cup	confectioners' (icing) sugar, sifted	175 mL
1 tbsp	pineapple juice	15 mL

1. *Cookie:* In a large bowl, using an electric mixer on medium speed, beat butter, sugar and vanilla until light and creamy, about 3 minutes. On low speed, gradually add flour and salt, beating until dough becomes too stiff for the mixer, then finish mixing with a wooden spoon until smooth. Stir in nuts and pineapple. Using your hands, knead to form a smooth dough.

2. Divide dough into sixths. Shape each into a ball. Place 3 balls on prepared cookie sheet. Flatten each to a 5-inch (12.5 cm) round. Smooth the edge, then, using a fork dipped in flour, press around edge to make a pattern. Cut each round into 8 wedges (like cutting a pie), leaving the circle intact. Repeat with remaining dough. Bake in preheated oven for 15 to 19 minutes or until light golden. Cool for 5 minutes on sheet. Re-cut rounds into wedges. Transfer to a rack and cool completely.

3. *Drizzle, optional:* In a bowl, combine confectioners' sugar and juice to make a drizzling consistency. Drizzle over cooled cookie wedges. Let drizzle set, about 30 minutes.

Variation

Replace pineapple with dried cranberries. Use orange juice in the drizzle.

Four-Nut Biscotti

Enjoy several looks from one recipe. Leave these plain, drizzle chocolate over the top or dip the ends in melted semisweet or white chocolate.

MAKES ABOUT 4½ DOZEN BISCOTTI

- **Preparation: 25 minutes**
- **Baking: 1 hour**
- **Cooling: 15 minutes**
- **Freezing: excellent**

TIPS

This dough is quite soft and a bit sticky, hence the floured hands and use of a spoon instead of an electric mixer.

A sharp serrated knife works best for cutting biscotti.

The glaze gives the biscotti nice appearance and taste, but it can be omitted.

Use any combination of nuts you like, keeping the total amount to 2 cups (500 mL).

- **Preheat oven to 350°F (180°C)**
- **Cookie sheet, greased or lined with parchment paper**

BISCOTTI

3½ cups	all-purpose flour	875 mL
½ tsp	baking powder	2 mL
½ tsp	salt	2 mL
1 cup	butter, softened	250 mL
1 cup	granulated sugar	250 mL
⅔ cup	packed brown sugar	150 mL
3	eggs	3
1 tsp	almond extract	5 mL
½ cup	each coarsely chopped hazelnuts, pecans, pistachios and slivered almonds	125 mL

GLAZE

1	egg	1
2 tbsp	water	30 mL
¼ cup	turbinado or coarse sugar	60 mL

1. *Biscotti:* On a sheet of waxed paper or in a bowl, combine flour, baking powder and salt. Set aside.

2. In a large bowl, using a wooden spoon, beat butter and granulated and brown sugars until blended. Add eggs, one at a time, beating well after each addition. Mix in almond extract. Gradually add flour mixture, mixing until smooth. Stir in nuts.

3. Spoon mixture into 2 lengths on prepared cookie sheet. With floured hands, shape each into a roll about 14 inches (35 cm) long. Flatten rolls to 4 inches (10 cm) wide, leaving top slightly rounded.

4. *Glaze:* In a small bowl, beat egg and water until blended. Brush over top of rolls. Sprinkle with sugar. Bake in preheated oven for 25 to 30 minutes or until lightly browned around edges. Cool for 15 minutes on sheet, then transfer to a cutting board. Cut into ½-inch (1 cm) slices. Place upright about ½ inch (1 cm) apart on cookie sheet. Return to oven. Turn off oven and leave 30 minutes to dry. Cool for 5 minutes on sheet, then transfer to a rack and cool completely.

Crunchy Date and Nut Balls

These small, bite-size cookies have a tender yet crunchy texture.

MAKES ABOUT 3½ DOZEN COOKIES

- **Preparation: 25 minutes**
- **Chilling: 30 minutes**
- **Baking: 12 minutes**
- **Freezing: excellent**

TIPS

These cookies retain their ball shape during baking rather than spreading and flattening.

Dates keep cookies moist and chewy, in addition to adding sweetness and delicious flavor.

When chopping dates, spray the blade of your knife with cooking spray to prevent sticking.

- **Preheat oven to 375°F (190°C)**
- **Cookie sheet, ungreased**

1¼ cups	all-purpose flour	300 mL
½ tsp	baking powder	2 mL
½ tsp	baking soda	2 mL
¼ tsp	salt	1 mL
½ cup	butter, softened	125 mL
¾ cup	packed brown sugar	175 mL
1	egg	1
1 tsp	vanilla	5 mL
2 cups	corn flakes cereal, slightly crushed	500 mL
1 cup	chopped dates	250 mL
½ cup	chopped walnuts	125 mL

1. On a sheet of waxed paper or in a bowl, combine flour, baking powder, baking soda and salt. Set aside.

2. In a large bowl, using an electric mixer on medium speed, beat butter, brown sugar, egg and vanilla until light and creamy, about 3 minutes. On low speed, gradually add flour mixture, beating until blended. With a wooden spoon, stir in cereal, dates and walnuts. Cover and chill for 30 minutes for easy handling.

3. Shape dough into 1-inch (2.5 cm) balls. Place about 2 inches (5 cm) apart on cookie sheet. Bake in preheated oven for 8 to 12 minutes or until set and golden around edges. Cool for 5 minutes on sheet, then transfer to a rack and cool completely.

Variation

Replace ¼ cup (60 mL) dates with dried cranberries or chopped dried apricots.

Mini Cranberry Cookie Cakes

These have a soft cake-like texture and look like mini muffins. The cranberries give them a pleasant tart flavor.

**MAKES ABOUT
20 COOKIES**

- **Preparation: 25 minutes**
- **Baking: 20 minutes**
- **Freezing: excellent**

TIPS

For best results, use light-colored muffin pans. The darker ones cook more quickly. If your pans are nonstick black, check the cakes after 12 minutes or decrease the temperature to 325°F (160°C).

If you're putting these in a box for gift giving or on a cookie tray after baking, place them in small festive paper cups.

- **Preheat oven to 350°F (180°C)**
- **Mini muffin pans, greased and floured**

COOKIE

1/2 cup	butter, softened	125 mL
1/2 cup	granulated sugar	125 mL
2	eggs	2
1 tsp	grated lemon zest	5 mL
2/3 cup	all-purpose flour	150 mL
1/2 cup	dried cranberries	125 mL

TOPPING

2 tbsp	sliced almonds	30 mL
1 tbsp	granulated sugar	15 mL

1. *Cookie:* In a large bowl, using an electric mixer on medium speed, beat butter and sugar until light and creamy, about 3 minutes. Add eggs, one at a time, beating well after each addition. Add lemon zest. On low speed, gradually add flour, beating until blended. With a wooden spoon, stir in cranberries. Spoon dough into prepared muffin pan, pressing into pan.

2. *Topping:* In a small bowl, combine almonds and sugar. Sprinkle about 1/2 tsp (2 mL) over each cookie. Using your finger, press in lightly so mixture sticks to the dough. Bake in preheated oven for 15 to 20 minutes or until golden around edges. Cool for 15 minutes in pan, then transfer to a rack and cool completely.

Variations

Replace lemon zest with 1/4 tsp (1 mL) almond extract.
Substitute sliced unblanched hazelnuts for the almonds.

Cranberry Almond Biscotti

These biscotti are not too sweet and not too hard. The crisp, tender texture makes them enjoyable without needing to be dunked.

**MAKES ABOUT
4 DOZEN BISCOTTI**

- **Preparation: 25 minutes**
- **Baking: 58 minutes**
- **Cooling: 15 minutes**
- **Freezing: excellent**

TIPS

A sharp serrated knife works best for cutting biscotti.

These biscotti look and taste great with the ends dipped in white chocolate.

Although these biscotti don't need to be dunked, they are nice served in the Italian fashion, with a glass of sweet wine.

- **Preheat oven to 325°F (160°C)**
- **Cookie sheet, greased or lined with parchment paper**

2¼ cups	all-purpose flour	550 mL
1½ tsp	baking powder	7 mL
¼ tsp	salt	1 mL
½ cup	butter, softened	125 mL
¾ cup	granulated sugar	175 mL
2	eggs	2
1 tbsp	grated orange zest	15 mL
1 tbsp	freshly squeezed orange juice	15 mL
1 cup	dried cranberries	250 mL
½ cup	slivered almonds	125 mL

1. On a sheet of waxed paper or in a bowl, combine flour, baking powder and salt. Set aside.

2. In a large bowl, using an electric mixer on medium speed, beat butter and sugar until blended. Add eggs, one at a time, beating well after each addition. Beat in orange zest and juice. On low speed, gradually add flour mixture, beating until dough becomes too stiff for the mixer, then finish mixing with a wooden spoon until smooth. Stir in cranberries and almonds.

3. Divide dough into halves. Shape each into a roll 12 inches (30 cm) long. Place about 4 inches (10 cm) apart on prepared cookie sheet. Flatten rolls to 2½ inches (6 cm) wide, leaving top slightly rounded. Bake in preheated oven for 35 to 40 minutes or until firm and golden around edges. Cool for 15 minutes on sheet, then transfer to a cutting board. Cut into ½-inch (1 cm) slices. Place cut side down on cookie sheet. Bake for 8 minutes. Turn slices over and bake for 5 to 10 minutes or until crisp and golden. Cool for 5 minutes on sheet, then transfer to a rack and cool completely.

Variations

Replace cranberries with chopped dried apricots.

Replace almonds with chopped hazelnuts or pistachios.

Replace orange zest and juice with lemon.

Lemon Poppy Seed Biscotti

A real digression from traditional nutty biscotti, these tender, crisp sticks are delicious with afternoon tea.

**MAKES ABOUT
2½ DOZEN BISCOTTI**

- **Preparation: 20 minutes**
- **Baking: 50 minutes**
- **Cooling: 15 minutes**
- **Freezing: excellent**

TIPS

Store poppy seeds in the freezer to retain their freshness. They develop an unpleasant rancid flavor with age.

Some people prefer thicker slices, about ¾-inch (2 cm). The choice is yours. Thick ones will take a little longer to dry in the second baking.

- **Preheat oven to 350°F (180°C)**
- **Cookie sheet, greased or lined with parchment paper**

2 cups	all-purpose flour	500 mL
1½ tsp	baking powder	7 mL
¼ tsp	salt	1 mL
½ cup	butter, softened	125 mL
¾ cup	granulated sugar	175 mL
2	eggs	2
2 tbsp	grated lemon zest	30 mL
1 tbsp	freshly squeezed lemon juice	15 mL
⅓ cup	poppy seeds	75 mL

1. On a sheet of waxed paper or in a bowl, combine flour, baking powder and salt. Set aside.

2. In a large bowl, using an electric mixer on medium speed, beat butter and sugar until light and creamy, about 3 minutes. Add eggs, one at a time, beating well after each addition. Add lemon zest and juice. On low speed, gradually add flour mixture, beating until blended. With a wooden spoon, stir in poppy seeds.

3. Divide dough into halves. Shape each into a roll 7 inches (18 cm) long. Place about 4 inches (10 cm) apart on prepared cookie sheet. Flatten rolls to 3 inches (7.5 cm) wide, leaving top slightly rounded. Bake in preheated oven for 25 to 30 minutes or until lightly browned. Cool for 15 minutes on sheet, then transfer to a cutting board. Cut into ½-inch (1 cm) slices. Place upright on cookie sheet. Bake for 15 to 20 minutes or until crisp and golden. Cool for 5 minutes on sheet, then transfer to a rack and cool completely.

Variation
Replace lemon zest and juice with orange or lime.

Chocolate-Wrapped Ginger Biscotti

A dark chocolate dough wraps around a lighter ginger dough to form an attractive two-toned biscotti.

MAKES ABOUT 2½ DOZEN BISCOTTI

- **Preparation: 40 minutes**
- **Baking: 55 minutes**
- **Cooling: 15 minutes**
- **Freezing: excellent**

TIPS

To distribute cocoa evenly and avoid streaks in a dough, knead the dough with your hands on a lightly floured surface.

Cocoa tends to lump during storage. Before mixing, even the smallest amount should be sifted to remove the lumps, as they won't disappear during baking.

A sharp serrated knife works best for cutting biscotti.

- **Preheat oven to 375°F (190°C)**
- **Cookie sheet, greased or lined with parchment paper**

2 cups	all-purpose flour	500 mL
2 tsp	baking powder	10 mL
¼ tsp	salt	1 mL
⅓ cup	butter, softened	75 mL
⅔ cup	granulated sugar	150 mL
2	eggs	2
2 tbsp	unsweetened cocoa powder, sifted	30 mL
¼ cup	finely chopped crystallized ginger	60 mL
½ cup	miniature semisweet chocolate chips	125 mL
¼ tsp	ground ginger	1 mL

1. On a sheet of waxed paper or in a bowl, combine flour, baking powder and salt. Set aside.

2. In a large bowl, using an electric mixer on medium speed, beat butter and sugar until light and creamy, about 3 minutes. Add eggs, one at a time, beating well after each addition. On low speed, gradually add flour mixture, beating until blended. Divide dough into halves. With a wooden spoon, stir cocoa powder and crystallized ginger into 1 portion and, using your hands, knead until thoroughly integrated. Add mini chocolate chips and ground ginger to the other portion and, using your hands, knead until thoroughly integrated.

3. Divide each portion into halves to make 4 portions. Between two sheets of waxed paper, roll 1 portion of chocolate dough into an 8- by 6-inch (20 by 15 cm) rectangle. Remove top sheet of waxed paper. Shape 1 portion of light dough into a roll 8 inches (20 cm) long. Place roll in the center of chocolate dough and wrap chocolate dough around it. Repeat with remaining dough and place the 2 rolls about 4 inches (10 cm) apart on prepared cookie sheet. Flatten slightly, leaving top slightly rounded.

4. Bake in preheated oven for 35 to 40 minutes or until set. Cool for 15 minutes on sheet, then transfer to a cutting board. Reduce oven temperature to 325°F (160°C). Cut rolls into ½-inch (1 cm) slices. Place upright on cookie sheet. Bake for 10 to 15 minutes or until crisp and center is light golden. Cool for 5 minutes on sheet, then transfer to a rack and cool completely.

Maple Walnut Biscotti

Maple extract has a wonderful real maple flavor that is ideal for baking. Because cookies don't require much liquid, you can't use maple syrup to provide that taste.

MAKES ABOUT 2½ DOZEN BISCOTTI

- **Preparation: 20 minutes**
- **Baking: 50 minutes**
- **Cooling: 15 minutes**
- **Freezing: excellent**

TIPS

When grinding nuts in a food processor, add a little flour or sugar from your recipe to keep them from clumping.

Be sure biscotti are thoroughly dry and cool before packing or they will soften during storage.

- **Preheat oven to 350°F (180°C)**
- **Cookie sheet, greased or lined with parchment paper**

2 cups	all-purpose flour	500 mL
⅓ cup	ground walnuts	75 mL
1¼ tsp	baking powder	6 mL
¼ tsp	salt	1 mL
2	eggs	2
½ cup	packed brown sugar	125 mL
¼ cup	granulated sugar	60 mL
½ cup	vegetable oil	125 mL
1 tsp	maple extract	5 mL
1 cup	coarsely chopped walnuts	250 mL

1. On a sheet of waxed paper or in a bowl, combine flour, ground walnuts, baking powder and salt. Set aside.

2. In a large bowl, using a wooden spoon, beat eggs, brown and granulated sugars, oil and maple extract until smoothly blended. Add flour mixture, stirring until smooth. Add walnuts. Using your hands, knead to form a smooth dough.

3. Divide dough into halves. Shape each into a roll 8 inches (20 cm) long. Place about 4 inches (10 cm) apart on prepared cookie sheet. Flatten rolls to 3 inches (7.5 cm) wide, leaving top slightly rounded. Bake in preheated oven for 25 to 30 minutes or until light golden. Cool for 15 minutes on sheet, then transfer to a cutting board. Cut into ½-inch (1 cm) slices. Place cut side down on cookie sheet. Bake for 10 minutes. Turn slices over and bake for 5 to 10 minutes or until crisp and golden. Cool for 5 minutes on sheet, then transfer to a rack and cool completely.

Variations

Replace walnuts with pecans.

Omit maple extract. Add 1 tbsp (15 mL) instant espresso coffee powder along with the flour mixture.

Chocolate Cappuccino Biscotti

◆

Now you can eat your cappuccino and drink it, too. In fact, these biscotti go very well with cappuccino. These are a little smaller than some biscotti, but that makes them a particularly nice afternoon pick-me-up.

**MAKES ABOUT
4 DOZEN BISCOTTI**

- **Preparation: 30 minutes**
- **Baking: 35 minutes**
- **Cooling: 15 minutes**
- **Freezing: excellent**

TIP

Turbinado is a raw cane sugar. If you don't have it, use another coarse-textured brown sugar, such as Demerara or muscovado.

- **Preheat oven to 375°F (190°C)**
- **Cookie sheet, greased or lined with parchment paper**

BISCOTTI

2 ½ cups	all-purpose flour	625 mL
1 ½ tsp	baking powder	7 mL
¼ tsp	salt	1 mL
2 tbsp	instant espresso coffee powder	30 mL
1 tsp	ground cinnamon	5 mL
½ cup	butter, softened	125 mL
1 cup	granulated sugar	250 mL
2	eggs	2
2 tbsp	coffee liqueur	30 mL
3	squares (1 oz/28 g each) semisweet chocolate, finely chopped	3

GLAZE

1	egg, lightly beaten	1
2 tbsp	turbinado sugar	30 mL

1. *Biscotti:* On a sheet of waxed paper or in a bowl, combine flour, baking powder, salt, espresso powder and cinnamon. Set aside.

2. In a large bowl, using an electric mixer on medium speed, beat butter and granulated sugar until light and creamy, about 3 minutes. Add eggs, one at a time, beating well after each addition. Add liqueur. On low speed, gradually add flour mixture, beating until dough becomes too stiff for the mixer, then finish mixing with a wooden spoon until smooth. Stir in chopped chocolate. Using your hands, knead to form a smooth dough.

3. Divide dough into halves. Shape each into a roll 12 inches (30 cm) long. Place about 4 inches (10 cm) apart on prepared cookie sheet. Flatten rolls to 2 inches (5 cm) wide, leaving top slightly rounded.

4. *Glaze:* Brush top of rolls with beaten egg. Sprinkle turbinado sugar evenly over top. Bake in preheated oven for 20 minutes or until set and lightly browned around edges. Cool for 15 minutes on sheet, then transfer to a cutting board. Cut into ½-inch (1 cm) slices. Stand upright on cookie sheet. Bake for 10 to 15 minutes or until crisp and golden. Cool for 5 minutes on sheet, then transfer to a rack and cool completely.

Chocolate Chunk Pecan Cookies
and Toffee Chocolate Almond Chippers

Chocolate Cookies

Chocolate is such a popular ingredient, it deserves a section of its own. You'll find cookies containing chocolate in other chapters of this book, but there the luscious chocolate flavor is secondary. Here, chocolate dominates. Some of the cookies are downright decadent and will satisfy even the most committed chocoholic.

I guarantee there's a cookie in this chapter for every chocolate-lover you know. They range from plain and simple to those loaded with chocolate-compatible ingredients, such as nuts, cereals, caramels and dried fruits, which add texture and taste. The chocolate flavors run the gamut from deep dark to creamy milk and, from time to time, are accented with buttery white chocolate.

Different flavors will suit different preferences, but all are delicious. Packaged in a fancy box or tin, they make a welcome gift with the personal touch you just don't get from a box of store-bought chocolates. The hardest part of this chapter was eliminating some of my many favorites that I just couldn't fit in.

Chocolate Chunk Pecan Cookies

Chocolate has to be a cookie's best friend. This rich, buttery dough, studded with chocolate and pecans, bakes into a delicious cookie with a soft, chewy texture.

MAKES ABOUT 5 DOZEN COOKIES

- **Preparation: 25 minutes**
- **Baking: 12 minutes**
- **Freezing: excellent**

TIPS

Don't overbake chocolate chip cookies if you like them chewy. With longer baking, they are still very edible but they have a crispier texture.

Although recipes usually call for an electric mixer to blend ingredients, you can almost always use a wooden spoon when making cookies. It just takes more physical effort. With either method, it usually takes about 3 minutes to get a butter-and-sugar mixture light and creamy.

- **Preheat oven to 375°F (190°C)**
- **Cookie sheet, ungreased**

2¼ cups	all-purpose flour	550 mL
1 tsp	baking soda	5 mL
½ tsp	salt	2 mL
1 cup	butter, softened	250 mL
¾ cup	granulated sugar	175 mL
¾ cup	packed brown sugar	175 mL
2	eggs	2
1 tsp	vanilla	5 mL
15	squares (1 oz/28 g each) semisweet chocolate, coarsely chopped	15
1 cup	coarsely chopped pecans	250 mL

1. On a sheet of waxed paper or in a bowl, combine flour, baking soda and salt. Set aside.

2. In a large bowl, using an electric mixer on medium speed, beat butter and granulated and brown sugars until light and creamy, about 3 minutes. Add eggs, one at a time, beating well after each addition. Beat in vanilla. On low speed, gradually add flour mixture, beating until blended. With a wooden spoon, stir in chocolate and pecans.

3. Drop dough by tablespoonfuls (15 mL) about 2 inches (5 cm) apart on cookie sheet. Bake in preheated oven for 8 to 12 minutes or until golden around edges. Cool for 5 minutes on sheet, then transfer to a rack and cool completely.

Variations

Omit the pecans for a version that doesn't contain nuts.

Replace chopped chocolate with 2½ cups (625 mL) chocolate chips.

Toffee Chocolate Almond Chippers

When you have a craving for something sweet and you can't decide between a cookie and a candy bar, these cookies fit the bill.

MAKES ABOUT 3 DOZEN COOKIES

- **Preparation: 25 minutes**
- **Baking: 16 minutes**
- **Freezing: excellent**

TIPS

I like to use Skor bars, which are available in bulk. Heath bars are another good choice for this recipe.

If you bake most chocolate chip cookies until they are golden around the edges but still pale in the center, they will be soft and chewy. Bake until they are a light golden color overall, and they will be crisp. Try some both ways the next time you make a batch and decide your preference.

Chill the chocolate bars for easy chopping. You can also put them in a heavy plastic bag and smash them with a meat mallet.

- **Preheat oven to 350°F (180°C)**
- **Cookie sheet, lined with parchment paper**

1 ½ cups	all-purpose flour	375 mL
¾ tsp	baking soda	3 mL
¼ tsp	salt	1 mL
½ cup	butter, softened	125 mL
½ cup	packed brown sugar	125 mL
¼ cup	granulated sugar	60 mL
1	egg	1
2 tbsp	milk	30 mL
½ tsp	almond extract	2 mL
4	(1.4 oz/39 g each) chocolate-covered toffee bars, chopped	4
1 cup	semisweet chocolate chips	250 mL
1 cup	slivered almonds	250 mL

1. On a sheet of waxed paper or in a bowl, combine flour, baking soda and salt. Set aside.

2. In a large bowl, using an electric mixer on medium speed, beat butter, brown and granulated sugars, egg, milk and almond extract until light and creamy, about 3 minutes. On low speed, gradually add flour mixture, beating until blended. With a wooden spoon, stir in toffee bars, chocolate chips and almonds.

3. Drop dough by tablespoonfuls (15 mL) about 2 inches (5 cm) apart on prepared cookie sheet. Bake in preheated oven for 12 to 16 minutes or until golden. Cool for 5 minutes on sheet, then transfer to a rack and cool completely.

Variations

Substitute chopped pecans or cashews for the almonds.

For a milder chocolate taste, use milk chocolate chips.

If you prefer a deeper chocolate flavor, add 2 tbsp (30 mL) cocoa powder to the dry ingredients.

Turn these into sandwich cookies with a filling of chocolate or butterscotch ripple ice cream.

Double Chocolate Chunk Cookies

These are so good warm you should be prepared to make a double batch if you serve them that way. The chocolate flavor permeates the dough and the chunks provide a great finish.

MAKES ABOUT 4 DOZEN COOKIES

- **Preparation: 25 minutes**
- **Baking: 12 minutes**
- **Freezing: excellent**

TIPS

Cocoa tends to clump in storage. Before using, sift it with other dry ingredients.

You can use brown and granulated sugar interchangeably. Brown sugar contains molasses, so it is moist and has a slight caramel flavor. Because it is moister, brown sugar will clump and dry out, while granulated sugar will stay granular, which makes it easier to mix.

- **Preheat oven to 375°F (190°C)**
- **Cookie sheet, greased or lined with parchment paper**

1 ½ cups	all-purpose flour	375 mL
½ cup	unsweetened cocoa powder, sifted	125 mL
1 tsp	baking soda	5 mL
¼ tsp	salt	1 mL
1 cup	butter, softened	250 mL
¾ cup	packed brown sugar	175 mL
⅔ cup	granulated sugar	150 mL
1	egg	1
1 tsp	vanilla	5 mL
6	squares (1 oz/28 g each) bittersweet chocolate, cut in chunks	6
6	squares (1 oz/28 g each) semisweet chocolate, cut in chunks	6
1 cup	coarsely chopped pecans	250 mL

1. On a sheet of waxed paper or in a bowl, combine flour, cocoa, baking soda and salt. Set aside.

2. In a large bowl, using an electric mixer on medium speed, beat butter and brown and granulated sugars until light and creamy, about 3 minutes. Add egg and vanilla, beating until blended. On low speed, gradually add flour mixture, beating until blended. With a wooden spoon, stir in bittersweet and semi-sweet chocolate and pecans.

3. Drop dough by tablespoonfuls (15 mL) about 2 inches (5 cm) apart on prepared cookie sheet. Bake in preheated oven for 8 to 12 minutes or until set. Cool for 5 minutes on sheet, then transfer to a rack and cool completely.

Variations

Use all semisweet chocolate.

Replace half of the chocolate with white chocolate.

Use 1 cup (250 mL) semi- sweet chocolate chips in place of the chunks.

Judie's Chocolate Chip Cookies

Many, many people in her hometown love my sister's chocolate chip cookies. And I have to admit, they are pretty darn good.

**MAKES ABOUT
5 DOZEN COOKIES**

- **Preparation: 25 minutes**
- **Baking: 12 minutes**
- **Freezing: excellent**

TIPS

I usually bake with butter because I like its flavor and because shortening usually contains unhealthy trans fats. However, my niece's kids have difficulty digesting butter, so I've included her mother's recipe for these delicious cookies. Make them using shortening that doesn't contain hydrogenated oils.

Remember, cookies continue to bake when they come out of the oven. If you aren't sure, bake them for a little less time than you think is right.

Nuts are always an option in chocolate chip cookies. Sometimes I use half the batter, then add nuts to the remaining half.

If you do omit the nuts, you can replace them with more chocolate chips.

- **Preheat oven to 375°F (190°C)**
- **Cookie sheet, ungreased**

1¾ cups	all-purpose flour	425 mL
½ cup	quick-cooking rolled oats	125 mL
1 tsp	baking soda	5 mL
½ tsp	salt	2 mL
1 cup	non-hydrogenated shortening (see Tips, left)	250 mL
1¼ cups	packed brown sugar	300 mL
2	eggs	2
2½ cups	semisweet chocolate chips	625 mL
1 cup	chopped pecans, optional	250 mL

1. On a sheet of waxed paper or in a bowl, combine flour, oats, baking soda and salt. Set aside.

2. In a large bowl, using an electric mixer on medium speed, beat shortening, brown sugar and eggs until light and creamy, about 3 minutes. On low speed, gradually add flour mixture, beating until blended. With a wooden spoon, stir in chocolate chips and pecans, if using.

3. Drop dough by tablespoonfuls (15 mL) about 2 inches (5 cm) apart on cookie sheet. Bake in preheated oven for 8 to 12 minutes or until golden around edges. Cool for 5 minutes on sheet, then transfer to a rack and cool completely.

Variations

Replace chocolate chips with 10 squares (1 oz/28 g each) chocolate, chopped.

Replace pecans with slivered almonds.

Peanut Fudgies

These cookies are like a chewy brownie that's loaded with chips and peanuts.

MAKES ABOUT 3½ DOZEN COOKIES

- **Preparation: 30 minutes**
- **Cooking: 4 minutes**
- **Baking: 13 minutes**
- **Freezing: excellent**

TIPS

Use a sharp chef's knife to chop nuts, and do it on a wooden board, or pulse them in a food processor. If you prefer, look for nuts that are already chopped.

If you're not using nuts soon after purchase, store them in the freezer to prevent rancidity.

- **Preheat oven to 350°F (180°C)**
- **Cookie sheet, greased or lined with parchment paper**

2¼ cups	semisweet chocolate chips, divided	550 mL
½ cup	butter	125 mL
⅔ cup	all-purpose flour	150 mL
½ tsp	baking soda	2 mL
2	eggs	2
¾ cup	packed brown sugar	175 mL
1¼ cups	chopped honey-roasted peanuts	300 mL
1 cup	peanut butter chips	250 mL

1. In a small saucepan, over low heat, melt 1¼ cups (300 mL) chocolate chips and butter, stirring until smooth. Remove from heat. Set aside to cool.

2. On a sheet of waxed paper or in a bowl, combine flour and baking soda. Set aside.

3. In a large bowl, using a wooden spoon, beat eggs and brown sugar until well blended. Stir in cooled chocolate mixture. Gradually add flour mixture, mixing until smooth. Stir in peanuts, peanut butter chips and remaining 1 cup (250 mL) chocolate chips.

4. Drop dough by tablespoonfuls (15 mL) about 2 inches (5 cm) apart on prepared cookie sheet. Bake in preheated oven for 9 to 13 minutes or until set around edges but slightly soft in the center. Cool for 5 minutes on sheet, then transfer to a rack and cool completely.

Variation

Other nuts, like cashews, pecans or hazelnuts, are also great in this recipe.

Chocolate Cherry Mounds

These luscious mounds are a slightly firmer version of melted chocolate with nuts and cherries. They're rich and delicious.

MAKES ABOUT 4½ DOZEN COOKIES

- **Preparation: 30 minutes**
- **Cooking: 4 minutes**
- **Baking: 15 minutes**
- **Freezing: excellent**

TIP

Toasting nuts before baking improves their flavor. Spread them out on a rimmed baking sheet and bake at 350°F (180°C) for about 10 minutes or until fragrant and lightly browned. If nuts are chopped, they'll take less time. Cool before using.

- **Preheat oven to 325°F (160°C)**
- **Cookie sheet, ungreased**

1 cup	all-purpose flour	250 mL
1 tsp	baking powder	5 mL
¼ tsp	salt	1 mL
12	squares (1 oz/28 g each) semisweet chocolate, divided into 2 groups of 6 and chopped	12
4	squares (1 oz/28 g each) unsweetened chocolate, chopped	4
6 tbsp	butter	90 mL
1 cup	granulated sugar	250 mL
3	eggs	3
1½ tsp	vanilla	7 mL
1½ cups	coarsely chopped pecans	375 mL
¾ cup	chopped dried cherries	175 mL

1. On a sheet of waxed paper or in a bowl, combine flour, baking powder and salt. Set aside.

2. In a large saucepan over low heat, combine 6 squares worth of the semisweet chocolate, the unsweetened chocolate and butter, stirring until melted and smooth. Remove from heat. With a wooden spoon, stir in sugar. Add eggs, one at a time, beating well after each addition. Stir in vanilla. Gradually add flour mixture, stirring until smooth. Add pecans, cherries and remaining chopped semisweet chocolate, mixing until thoroughly blended.

3. Drop by tablespoonfuls (15 mL) about 2 inches (5 cm) apart on cookie sheet. Bake in preheated oven for 11 to 15 minutes or until set. Cool for 5 minutes on sheet, then transfer to a rack and cool completely.

Variations

Any kind of nut works well in these cookies.

Replace cherries with dried cranberries. There's no need to chop cranberries because they are smaller.

Omit cherries and add 1 tbsp (15 mL) instant espresso coffee powder to the dough along with the flour.

Nutty Chocolate Candy Cookies

No flour and no eggs! These cookies are chewy, chocolaty and nutty — halfway between a cookie and a candy. However you describe them, they certainly are delicious.

MAKES ABOUT 3½ DOZEN COOKIES

- **Preparation: 30 minutes**
- **Cooking: 5 minutes**
- **Baking: 12 minutes**
- **Freezing: excellent**

TIPS

It's hard to tell when chocolate cookies are done because there's no golden color to give you a clue. If you touch the top lightly, they will feel set. Remember, cookies will continue to cook after being removed from the oven.

A reliable oven thermometer is a good investment. It will tell you whether your oven heat is aligned with the setting. If not, you can adjust it accordingly.

- **Preheat oven to 350°F (180°C)**
- **Cookie sheet, greased or lined with parchment paper**

1	can (14 oz or 300 mL) sweetened condensed milk	1
2	squares (1 oz/28 g each) unsweetened chocolate, chopped	2
2	squares (1 oz/28 g each) bittersweet chocolate, chopped	2
1 tbsp	butter	15 mL
½ tsp	almond extract	2 mL
1 cup	unsweetened flaked coconut	250 mL
¾ cup	slivered almonds	175 mL
½ cup	coarsely chopped hazelnuts	125 mL
½ cup	coarsely chopped pecans	125 mL

1. In a large saucepan over low heat, heat condensed milk, unsweetened and bittersweet chocolate and butter, stirring until chocolate is melted and mixture is smooth. Remove from heat. With a wooden spoon, stir in almond extract, coconut, almonds, hazelnuts and pecans.

2. Drop dough by tablespoonfuls (15 mL) about 2 inches (5 cm) apart on prepared cookie sheet. Bake in preheated oven for 8 to 12 minutes or until set. Cool completely on sheet.

Variations

Replace one of the nuts, or the coconut, with dried cranberries or chopped dried apricots.

Use your favorite kinds of nuts. I like a mixture, but you can also use 1¾ cups (425 mL) of a single variety.

Triple Chocolate Fudge Cookies

These cookies are soft and almost fudge-like. Chocolate-lovers will thoroughly enjoy the intense chocolate flavor.

MAKES ABOUT 5 DOZEN COOKIES

- **Preparation: 25 minutes**
- **Baking: 11 minutes**
- **Freezing: excellent**

TIPS

When storing soft cookies, be sure they have cooled completely. Separate each layer with waxed paper and store in airtight containers.

Don't store soft cookies with crisp cookies, as neither will retain their desired texture.

- **Preheat oven to 375°F (190°C)**
- **Cookie sheet, ungreased**

2¼ cups	all-purpose flour	550 mL
½ cup	unsweetened cocoa powder, sifted	125 mL
1 tsp	baking soda	5 mL
¼ tsp	salt	1 mL
1 cup	butter, softened	250 mL
¾ cup	packed brown sugar	175 mL
¾ cup	granulated sugar	175 mL
2	eggs	2
1 tsp	vanilla	5 mL
1 cup	semisweet chocolate chips	250 mL
1 cup	white chocolate chips	250 mL
1 cup	milk chocolate chips	250 mL

1. On a sheet of waxed paper or in a bowl, combine flour, cocoa, baking soda and salt. Set aside.

2. In a large bowl, using an electric mixer on medium speed, beat butter and brown and granulated sugars until light and creamy, about 3 minutes. Add eggs, one at a time, beating well after each addition. Beat in vanilla. On low speed, gradually add flour mixture, beating until blended. With a wooden spoon, stir in semisweet, white and milk chocolate chips.

3. Drop dough by tablespoonfuls (15 mL) about 2 inches (5 cm) apart on cookie sheet. Bake in preheated oven for 7 to 11 minutes or until puffed and set around edges but slightly soft in center. Cool for 5 minutes on sheet, then transfer to a rack and cool completely.

Variation

Vary the kind of chocolate chips, keeping total amount to 3 cups (750 mL).

Marbled Chocolate Puffs

These are light, puffy meringues with a great hit of chocolate. The cooked meringue is well worth the extra preparation time because it allows you to use melted chocolate in a meringue cookie, which is delicious and unusual.

MAKES ABOUT 3½ DOZEN COOKIES

- **Preparation: 20 minutes**
- **Cooking: 4 minutes**
- **Baking: 40 minutes**
- **Freezing: not recommended**

TIPS

Don't fold the chocolate and meringue too much. It will marble more as you spoon it out.

If you don't have a double boiler, look for a metal bowl that will fit inside a pot and extend about halfway down into the pot.

These meringues will be crispy outside but chewy inside.

- **Preheat oven to 275°F (140°C)**
- **Cookie sheet greased or lined with parchment paper**

3	squares (1 oz/28 g each) bittersweet chocolate, chopped	3
4	egg whites	4
1 cup	granulated sugar	250 mL
½ tsp	vanilla	2 mL

1. In a small saucepan, over low heat, melt chocolate, stirring until smooth. Remove from heat. Set aside to cool slightly.

2. In a metal bowl or the top of a double boiler, combine egg whites and sugar. Place bowl over a pot of simmering (not boiling) water so the bowl is just above, not touching, the water. Whisk egg white mixture until it is translucent and hot, about 4 minutes. Transfer to a large bowl. Using an electric mixer on high speed, beat until stiff, shiny peaks form, about 4 minutes. Beat in vanilla. Drizzle with melted chocolate and, with a spatula, gently fold chocolate into the meringue just until slightly marbled.

3. Drop meringue in large mounds about 2 inches (5 cm) apart on prepared cookie sheet. Bake in preheated oven for 35 to 40 minutes or until outside is crisp and dry. Cool completely on sheet.

Soft and Chewy Chocolate Indulgences

These decadent cookies are loaded with chocolate flavor and are simply irresistible while still warm.

MAKES ABOUT 3 DOZEN COOKIES

- **Preparation: 25 minutes**
- **Baking: 12 minutes**
- **Freezing: excellent**

TIPS

Cookies should be set around the edges but a little soft in the center when you take them out of the oven. They continue to cook while cooling on the cookie sheet.

Use real vanilla for baking. It has a wonderful true flavor you don't get in artificial versions.

- **Preheat oven to 350°F (180°C)**
- **Cookie sheet, greased or lined with parchment paper**

1 1/2 cups	all-purpose flour	375 mL
3/4 cup	unsweetened cocoa powder, sifted	175 mL
1/2 tsp	baking soda	2 mL
1/2 tsp	salt	2 mL
1 cup	butter, softened	250 mL
1 cup	packed brown sugar	250 mL
1/2 cup	granulated sugar	125 mL
2	eggs	2
1 1/2 tsp	vanilla	7 mL
2 cups	semisweet chocolate chips	500 mL

1. On a sheet of waxed paper or in a bowl, combine flour, cocoa, baking soda and salt. Set aside.

2. In a large bowl, using an electric mixer on medium speed, beat butter and brown and granulated sugars until light and creamy, about 3 minutes. Add eggs, one at a time, beating well after each addition. Beat in vanilla. On low speed, gradually add flour mixture, beating until blended. With a wooden spoon, stir in chocolate chips.

3. Drop dough by heaping tablespoonfuls (20 mL) about 2 inches (5 cm) apart on prepared cookie sheet. Bake in preheated oven for 8 to 12 minutes or just until set. Cool for 5 minutes on sheet, then transfer to a rack and cool completely.

Variation

Replace semisweet chocolate chips with milk chocolate chips.

Chocolate Chunk Walnut Oat Cookies

Ground oats give these cookies a taste and texture unlike any others. They are thicker than most, with a great "oaty" taste. Not really crisp or chewy, they are soft but not cakey.

MAKES ABOUT 4 DOZEN COOKIES

- **Preparation: 25 minutes**
- **Baking: 12 minutes**
- **Freezing: excellent**

TIPS

Use quick-cooking or large-flake old-fashioned rolled oats, as you prefer.

To freeze these cookies to bake later, drop the dough on sheet as described and freeze until firm. Transfer to a freezer bag. When ready to bake, place on cookie sheet. Let thaw for about 10 minutes, then bake 15 to 20 minutes.

- **Preheat oven to 375°F (190°C)**
- **Cookie sheet, ungreased**

2 cups	rolled oats (see Tips, left)	500 mL
2 1/2 cups	semisweet chocolate chips, divided	625 mL
2 cups	all-purpose flour	500 mL
1 tsp	baking powder	5 mL
1 tsp	baking soda	5 mL
1/2 tsp	salt	2 mL
1 cup	butter, softened	250 mL
1 cup	granulated sugar	250 mL
1 cup	packed brown sugar	250 mL
2	eggs	2
1 tsp	vanilla	5 mL
1 cup	chopped walnuts	250 mL

1. In a food processor or blender, process oats and 1/2 cup (125 mL) of the chocolate chips until ground to a fine powder. Place on a sheet of waxed paper or in a bowl. Add flour, baking powder, baking soda and salt, and mix to blend. Set aside.

2. In a large bowl, using an electric mixer on medium speed, beat butter and granulated and brown sugars until light and creamy, about 3 minutes. Add eggs, one at a time, beating well after each addition. Beat in vanilla. On low speed, gradually add flour mixture, beating until blended. With a wooden spoon, stir in remaining 2 cups (500 mL) chocolate chips and walnuts.

3. Drop dough by tablespoonfuls (15 mL) about 2 inches (5 cm) apart on cookie sheet. Bake in preheated oven for 8 to 12 minutes or until golden. Cool for 5 minutes on sheet, then transfer to a rack and cool completely.

Variations

Any nut is great in this cookie. Try almonds, pecans or cashews.

Add 1 tsp (5 mL) ground cinnamon to the flour mixture.

Chocolate Peanut Butter Cashew Crisps

Awesome! What more is there to say?

MAKES ABOUT 3 DOZEN COOKIES

- **Preparation: 25 minutes**
- **Baking: 14 minutes**
- **Freezing: excellent**

TIPS

I prefer combining the dry ingredients on a piece of waxed paper instead of dirtying a bowl. Then I use the paper as a funnel when adding them to the butter mixture.

Nuts have a high fat content, which can cause them to become rancid fairly quickly. Store them in the freezer to keep them fresh.

Don't overbeat cookie dough. The more air you incorporate into the dough, the lighter and more cake-like the texture will become. Cookies should be chewy or crisp.

- **Preheat oven to 350°F (180°C)**
- **Cookie sheet, ungreased**

1¾ cups	all-purpose flour	425 mL
½ tsp	baking soda	2 mL
¼ tsp	salt	1 mL
½ cup	butter, softened	125 mL
½ cup	crunchy peanut butter	125 mL
½ cup	granulated sugar	125 mL
½ cup	packed brown sugar	125 mL
1	egg	1
¼ cup	corn syrup	60 mL
1½ cups	semisweet chocolate chips	375 mL
1 cup	crisp rice cereal	250 mL
½ cup	coarsely chopped cashews	125 mL

1. On a sheet of waxed paper or in a bowl, combine flour, baking soda and salt. Set aside.

2. In a large bowl, using an electric mixer on medium speed, beat butter, peanut butter, granulated and brown sugars, egg and corn syrup until light and creamy, about 3 minutes. On low speed, gradually add flour mixture, beating until blended. With a wooden spoon, stir in chocolate chips, cereal and cashews.

3. Drop dough by heaping tablespoonfuls (20 mL) about 2 inches (5 cm) apart on cookie sheet. Bake in preheated oven for 10 to 14 minutes or until golden. Cool for 5 minutes on sheet, then transfer to a rack and cool completely.

Variations

Substitute any kind of nut for the cashews.

Replace cashews with flaked coconut.

Chewy Chocolate Walnut Strips

This easy-to-make cookie doesn't require much time for shaping. The dough is shaped into large logs, then cut into strips when cool.

MAKES ABOUT 4 DOZEN COOKIES

- **Preparation: 30 minutes**
- **Baking: 18 minutes**
- **Freezing: excellent**

TIP

Baking powder and baking soda don't last forever. Check the expiry date. If they haven't been used within the past 6 months, replace them. It's disappointing to bake cookies that don't rise because of old leavening.

- **Preheat oven to 350°F (180°C)**
- **Cookie sheet, greased or lined with parchment paper**

2 cups	all-purpose flour	500 mL
1/2 cup	unsweetened cocoa powder, sifted	125 mL
1/2 tsp	baking soda	2 mL
1/4 tsp	salt	1 mL
3/4 cup	butter, softened	175 mL
3/4 cup	granulated sugar	175 mL
1/2 cup	packed brown sugar	125 mL
2	eggs	2
2 cups	semisweet chocolate chips	500 mL
3/4 cup	chopped walnuts	175 mL
4	squares (1 oz/28 g each) semisweet chocolate, chopped, melted and cooled	4

1. On a sheet of waxed paper or in a bowl, combine flour, cocoa, baking soda and salt. Set aside.

2. In a large bowl, using an electric mixer on medium speed, beat butter and granulated and brown sugars until light and creamy, about 3 minutes. Add eggs, one at a time, beating well after each addition. On low speed, gradually add flour mixture, beating until blended. With a wooden spoon, stir in chocolate chips and walnuts.

3. Divide dough into quarters. Shape each into a strip about 12 inches (30 cm) long. Place about 4 inches (10 cm) apart on prepared cookie sheet. Bake in preheated oven for 14 to 18 minutes or until set. Cool for 5 minutes on sheet, then transfer to a rack and cool completely.

4. Drizzle melted chocolate on top of cookie strips. Set aside until chocolate is set, about 30 minutes, then with a sharp knife cut into 1-inch (2.5 cm) slices.

Variations

Use white chocolate for the drizzle, or do half with white and half with semisweet.

Omit the nuts or use your favorite.

Chocolate Rum Balls

This recipe is a must for your collection of no-bakes.

MAKES ABOUT 3 DOZEN COOKIES

- **Preparation: 20 minutes**
- **Standing: 1 hour**
- **Ripening: 1 day**
- **Freezing: excellent**

TIPS

Chocolate shot is also called chocolate vermicelli or chocolate sprinkles. It is available where cake decorating supplies are sold and in bulk stores.

Let balls ripen for at least 1 day before eating. They will improve with standing.

- **Cookie sheet lined with waxed paper**

2¼ cups	chocolate wafer crumbs	550 mL
1 cup	confectioners' (icing) sugar, sifted	250 mL
¾ cup	finely chopped walnuts	175 mL
2 tbsp	unsweetened cocoa powder, sifted	30 mL
¼ cup	butter, melted	60 mL
¼ cup	dark rum	60 mL
3 tbsp	corn syrup	45 mL
¾ cup	chocolate shot (see Tips)	175 mL

1. In a large bowl, combine wafer crumbs, confectioners' sugar, walnuts and cocoa. Mix well.

2. In a small bowl, using a wooden spoon, combine melted butter, rum and corn syrup. Mix well. Add to crumb mixture. Mix, then, using your hands, knead until mixture holds together.

3. Spread chocolate shot in a small shallow dish. Shape dough into 1-inch (2.5 cm) balls. Roll in chocolate shot to cover thoroughly. Place on waxed paper. Set aside until dry, about 1 hour. Store in an airtight container in the refrigerator for at least 1 day before eating.

Variations

Replace rum with brandy.

Replace rum with 1 tbsp (15 mL) rum extract.

Roll balls in toasted or plain medium flaked or shredded coconut or finely chopped nuts. It's nice to do a variety of coatings for the one batch.

Chocolate-Dipped Brownie Mounds

Bite-size brownies dipped in chocolate are easy to make from a roll of refrigerator chocolate cookie dough.

MAKES ABOUT 4 DOZEN COOKIES

- **Preparation: 35 minutes**
- **Chilling: 2 hours**
- **Baking: 14 minutes**
- **Freezing: excellent (not dipped)**

TIPS

If chocolate mixture thickens before you have all the cookies dipped, rewarm it slightly to soften.

You can buy coating chocolate, which hardens quickly, in small wafer shapes. They make dipping easy. Look for them in bulk and cake decorating stores.

If freezing, do not dip the cookies in chocolate until you're ready to serve.

To get perfectly round cookies, pack the dough into an appropriate-size used roll from waxed paper, plastic wrap or aluminum foil. Once chilled, simply cut tube open.

- **Cookie sheet, greased or lined with parchment paper**

COOKIE

1 1/2 cups	all-purpose flour	375 mL
1/3 cup	unsweetened cocoa powder, sifted	75 mL
1/2 tsp	baking powder	2 mL
1/2 tsp	baking soda	2 mL
1/4 tsp	salt	1 mL
1/2 cup	butter, softened	125 mL
3/4 cup	granulated sugar	175 mL
1	egg	1

CHOCOLATE DIP

5	squares (1 oz/28 g each) semisweet chocolate, chopped	5
1 tsp	vegetable oil	5 mL

1. *Cookie:* On a sheet of waxed paper or in a bowl, combine flour, cocoa, baking powder, baking soda and salt. Set aside.

2. In a large bowl, using an electric mixer on medium speed, beat butter, sugar and egg until light and creamy, about 3 minutes. On low speed, gradually add flour mixture, beating until blended. Divide dough into thirds. Shape each into a roll 12 inches (30 cm) long. Wrap and chill until firm, at least 2 hours.

3. When you're ready to bake, preheat oven to 350°F (180°C). Cut rolls into 3/4-inch (2 cm) slices. Place cut side down about 1 inch (2.5 cm) apart on prepared cookie sheet. Bake in preheated oven for 10 to 14 minutes or until set around edges but still soft in the center. Cool for 5 minutes on sheet, then transfer to a rack and cool completely.

4. *Chocolate Dip:* In a small saucepan over low heat, melt chocolate and oil, stirring until smooth. Remove from heat. Transfer to a small bowl for easy dipping. Dip side of each cookie into chocolate, covering half the cookie. Set on a rack placed over a sheet of waxed paper. Chill 20 minutes to set chocolate.

Variation

Dip some of the cookies in melted white chocolate.

Chocolate Chunk Oatmeal Cookies

These cookies are particularly good for after-school snacks and lunch-box treats.

MAKES ABOUT 5 DOZEN COOKIES

- **Preparation: 25 minutes**
- **Baking: 14 minutes**
- **Freezing: excellent**

TIPS

Always check cookies halfway through the baking time to see how they are browning. If they are browning faster at the back of the oven, turn the cookie sheet around.

When using an electric mixer, scrape down the sides of the bowl often so all the ingredients are properly blended.

- **Preheat oven to 325°F (160°C)**
- **Cookie sheet, ungreased**

1³⁄₄ cups	all-purpose flour	425 mL
1¹⁄₂ tsp	baking powder	7 mL
1 tsp	baking soda	5 mL
¹⁄₂ tsp	salt	2 mL
1 tsp	ground cinnamon	5 mL
³⁄₄ cup	butter, softened	175 mL
1³⁄₄ cups	packed brown sugar	425 mL
2	eggs	2
3 tbsp	milk	45 mL
1¹⁄₂ tsp	vanilla	7 mL
2 cups	quick-cooking rolled oats	500 mL
10	squares (1 oz/28 g each) semisweet chocolate, chopped	10
1¹⁄₂ cups	coarsely chopped pecans	375 mL
1 cup	sweetened flaked coconut	250 mL

1. On a sheet of waxed paper or in a bowl, combine flour, baking powder, baking soda, salt and cinnamon. Set aside.

2. In a large bowl, using an electric mixer on medium speed, beat butter and brown sugar until light and creamy, about 3 minutes. Add eggs, one at a time, beating well after each addition. Beat in milk and vanilla. On low speed, gradually add flour mixture, beating until blended. With a wooden spoon, stir in oats, chocolate, pecans and coconut.

3. Drop dough by tablespoonfuls (15 mL) about 2 inches (5 cm) apart on cookie sheet. Bake in preheated oven for 10 to 14 minutes or until golden around edges. Cool for 5 minutes on sheet, then transfer to a rack and cool completely.

Variation

Substitute large-flake old-fashioned oats for the quick-cooking. They will provide a more homey appearance and a slightly drier, but oatier, taste.

Chocolate Chip Oatmeal Toffee Cookies

◆

With their deep chocolate flavor, these cookies remind me of a candy bar disguised as a cookie.

MAKES ABOUT 5 DOZEN COOKIES

- **Preparation: 25 minutes**
- **Baking: 12 minutes**
- **Freezing: excellent**

TIPS

For a crisp cookie, bake 10 to 14 minutes.

Toffee bits don't keep very well. They soften and lose their crunchiness with age, so don't stock up on them.

Skor toffee bits are available in bulk and in packages where the chocolate chips are displayed. Heath is another well-known brand.

- **Preheat oven to 375°F (190°C)**
- **Cookie sheet, greased or lined with parchment paper**

1¾ cups	all-purpose flour	425 mL
1 tsp	baking soda	5 mL
¼ tsp	salt	1 mL
½ tsp	ground cinnamon	2 mL
1¼ cups	butter, softened	300 mL
1 cup	packed brown sugar	250 mL
½ cup	granulated sugar	125 mL
2	eggs	2
2 tbsp	milk	30 mL
2½ cups	quick-cooking rolled oats	625 mL
1½ cups	semisweet chocolate chips	375 mL
1 cup	milk chocolate chips	250 mL
¾ cup	toffee bits	175 mL

1. On a sheet of waxed paper or in a bowl, combine flour, baking soda, salt and cinnamon. Set aside.

2. In a large bowl, using an electric mixer on medium speed, beat butter and brown and granulated sugars until light and creamy, about 3 minutes. Add eggs, one at a time, beating well after each addition. Beat in milk. On low speed, gradually add flour mixture, beating until blended. With a wooden spoon, stir in oats, semisweet and milk chocolate chips and toffee bits.

3. Drop dough by tablespoonfuls (15 mL) about 2 inches (5 cm) apart on prepared cookie sheet. Bake in preheated oven for 8 to 12 minutes or until golden. Cool for 5 minutes on sheet, then transfer to a rack and cool completely.

Variations

Replace toffee bits with chopped nuts.

Replace milk chocolate chips with semisweet or white chocolate chips, or butterscotch chips.

Chocolate Orange Oatmeal Cookies

Here's a sweet, crisp, chocolaty cookie with a hint of orange. It makes a great ice cream sandwich with orange or chocolate ice cream.

MAKES ABOUT 4 DOZEN COOKIES

- **Preparation: 25 minutes**
- **Baking: 12 minutes**
- **Freezing: excellent**

TIPS

Although recipes usually call for an electric mixer to blend ingredients, you can almost always use a wooden spoon when making cookies. It just takes more physical effort. With either method, it usually takes about 3 minutes to get a butter-and-sugar mixture light and creamy.

When baking, always set your timer for the minimum time recommended. You can always bake a little longer, but you can't fix an overbaked product.

- **Preheat oven to 375°F (190°C)**
- **Cookie sheet, ungreased**

¾ cup	all-purpose flour	175 mL
½ tsp	baking soda	2 mL
¼ tsp	salt	1 mL
½ cup	butter, softened	125 mL
¾ cup	granulated sugar	175 mL
½ cup	packed brown sugar	125 mL
1	egg	1
1 tbsp	grated orange zest	15 mL
1¼ cups	quick-cooking rolled oats	300 mL
1 cup	semisweet chocolate chips	250 mL
1 cup	white chocolate chips	250 mL
1 cup	slivered almonds	250 mL

1. On a sheet of waxed paper or in a bowl, combine flour, baking soda and salt. Set aside.

2. In a large bowl, using an electric mixer on medium speed, beat butter, granulated and brown sugars, egg and orange zest until light and creamy, about 3 minutes. On low speed, gradually add flour mixture, beating until blended. With a wooden spoon, stir in oats, semisweet and white chocolate chips and almonds.

3. Drop dough by tablespoonfuls (15 mL) about 2 inches (5 cm) apart on cookie sheet. Bake in preheated oven for 8 to 12 minutes or until golden. Cool for 5 minutes on sheet, then transfer to a rack and cool completely.

Variations

Replace almonds with dried cranberries.

Replace both kinds of chocolate chips with 2 cups (500 mL) chopped bittersweet chocolate.

If you prefer, make this recipe into bars. Press the dough into a greased 13- by 9-inch (3 L) cake pan and bake at 350°F (180°C) for 30 to 35 minutes or until golden.

Milk Chocolate Peanut Butter Cookies

These cookies have a mild peanut butter taste with lots of chocolate. They're perfect with a glass of milk for an after-school treat.

MAKES ABOUT 5 DOZEN COOKIES

- **Preparation: 20 minutes**
- **Baking: 15 minutes**
- **Freezing: excellent**

TIP

Check the best-before date on peanut butter. It can go rancid quickly if not properly stored.

- **Preheat oven to 350°F (180°C)**
- **Cookie sheet, ungreased**

2 1/2 cups	all-purpose flour	625 mL
1 tsp	baking soda	5 mL
1 cup	butter, softened	250 mL
3/4 cup	creamy peanut butter	175 mL
1 cup	granulated sugar	250 mL
1 cup	packed brown sugar	250 mL
2	eggs	2
3 cups	milk chocolate chips	750 mL

1. On a sheet of waxed paper or in a bowl, combine flour and baking soda. Set aside.

2. In a large bowl, using an electric mixer on medium speed, beat butter, peanut butter and granulated and brown sugars until light and creamy, about 3 minutes. Add eggs, one at a time, beating well after each addition. On low speed, gradually add flour mixture, beating until blended. With a wooden spoon, stir in chocolate chips.

3. Drop dough by tablespoonfuls (15 mL) about 2 inches (5 cm) apart on cookie sheet. Bake in preheated oven for 11 to 15 minutes or until light golden. Cool for 5 minutes on sheet, then transfer to a rack and cool completely.

Variation

Add 1 cup (250 mL) peanuts along with the chocolate chips.

Fabulous Florentines

Florentines, a chewy cookie made with almonds and candied citrus peel, are one of my favorite cookies, so I worked hard to come up with the best recipe. The blend of dark chocolate and orange with crunchy almonds is amazing. I enjoyed these so much, I lost count of the number of times I tested them.

MAKES ABOUT 4 DOZEN COOKIES

- **Preparation: 35 minutes**
- **Baking: 11 minutes**
- **Freezing: not recommended**

TIPS

These are delicious served in, with or as a garnish for a scoop of orange sherbet or ice cream. They actually make great ice cream sandwiches as well.

Caution — these spread considerably during baking, so keep the amount of dough per cookie small and leave ample room between the cookies. Bake only 6 cookies per sheet.

- **Preheat oven to 350°F (180°C)**
- **Cookie sheet, greased or lined with parchment paper**

6 tbsp	butter	90 mL
¼ cup	whipping (35%) cream	60 mL
1 tbsp	corn syrup	15 mL
½ cup	granulated sugar	125 mL
2 tbsp	all-purpose flour	30 mL
1 tsp	grated orange zest	5 mL
1 cup	slivered almonds, finely chopped	250 mL
½ cup	finely chopped candied orange peel	125 mL
8	squares (1 oz/28 g each) bittersweet chocolate, chopped, melted and cooled	8

1. In a medium saucepan, combine butter, whipping cream and corn syrup. With a wooden spoon, stir in sugar, flour and orange zest, mixing until smooth. Over medium-high heat, bring mixture to a boil, stirring frequently. Remove from heat. Stir in almonds and candied orange peel.

2. Drop dough by 1½ teaspoonfuls (7 mL) about 3 inches (7.5 cm) apart on prepared cookie sheet. Flatten slightly with the back of a spoon or an offset spatula. Bake in preheated oven for 9 to 11 minutes or just until set and light golden. Cool for 1 minute on sheet then, with a wide spatula, transfer to a rack and cool completely.

3. When cool, using a small offset spatula, spread melted chocolate over the flat side of each cookie. Return to rack, chocolate side up, and leave until chocolate sets, about 1 hour.

Variations

Replace candied orange peel with mixed candied peel.

Try white chocolate on some of the cookies. Some of each looks nice in a box or on a tray.

Chocolate Toffee Nut Cookies

This crisp cookie is loaded with chocolate and toffee bits.

**MAKES ABOUT
5 DOZEN COOKIES**

- **Preparation: 30 minutes**
- **Baking: 15 minutes**
- **Freezing: excellent**

TIPS

Whenever a dough contains caramel, it's a good idea to use parchment paper, or another nonstick surface such as silicone sheets, because caramel is very sticky.

You can replace all or part of the all-purpose flour called for in any cookie recipe with an equal quantity of whole wheat flour.

Unbleached and regular all-purpose flours are interchangeable. What you use depends on your preference.

- **Preheat oven to 350°F (180°C)**
- **Cookie sheet, greased or lined with parchment paper**

2¾ cups	all-purpose flour	675 mL
1 tsp	baking soda	5 mL
¼ tsp	salt	1 mL
1½ cups	butter, melted and cooled slightly	375 mL
1 cup	packed brown sugar	250 mL
½ cup	granulated sugar	125 mL
2	eggs	2
1½ tsp	vanilla	7 mL
2¼ cups	semisweet chocolate chips	550 mL
6	squares (1 oz/28 g each) bittersweet chocolate, chopped	6
¾ cup	chopped pecans	175 mL
¾ cup	toffee bits	175 mL

1. On a sheet of waxed paper or in a bowl, combine flour, baking soda and salt. Set aside.

2. In a large bowl, using an electric mixer on medium speed, beat melted butter and brown and granulated sugars until light and creamy, about 3 minutes. Add eggs, one at a time, beating well after each addition. Beat in vanilla. On low speed, gradually add flour mixture, beating until blended. With a wooden spoon, stir in chocolate chips, chocolate chunks, pecans and toffee bits.

3. Drop dough by tablespoonfuls (15 mL) about 2 inches (5 cm) apart on prepared cookie sheet. Bake in preheated oven for 11 to 15 minutes or until light golden. Cool for 5 minutes on sheet, then transfer to a rack and cool completely.

Variation

Replace some or all of the semisweet chocolate chips with milk chocolate chips or white chocolate chips.

Chocolate Cinnamon Wheels

These are pretty to look at and fun to eat. In this refrigerator cookie, which slices into attractive spirals, a chocolate walnut filling is rolled inside a shortbread dough.

**MAKES ABOUT
2 DOZEN COOKIES**

- **Preparation: 35 minutes**
- **Chilling: 4 hours**
- **Baking: 18 minutes**
- **Freezing: excellent**

TIPS

If you prefer, use a wooden spoon because the small amount of dough is easily mixed.

Slice this roll using a sharp, thin, non-serrated knife. The slices are a bit thicker than most refrigerator cookies because of the filling.

- **Cookie sheet, greased or lined with parchment paper**

DOUGH

1/3 cup	butter, softened	75 mL
1/2 cup	granulated sugar	125 mL
1	egg	1
1/4 tsp	salt	1 mL
1 1/2 cups	all-purpose flour	375 mL

FILLING

1 1/4 cups	miniature semisweet chocolate chips	300 mL
3/4 cup	finely chopped walnuts	175 mL
1/4 cup	packed brown sugar	60 mL
2 tsp	ground cinnamon	10 mL
3 tbsp	butter, melted	45 mL

1. *Dough:* In a large bowl, using an electric mixer on medium speed, beat butter, sugar and egg until light and creamy, about 3 minutes. On low speed, gradually add salt and flour, mixing until blended. Using your hands, knead to form a smooth dough. Between 2 sheets of waxed paper, roll out dough to a 12- by 10-inch (30 cm by 25 cm) rectangle.

2. *Filling:* In a bowl, combine chocolate chips, walnuts, brown sugar, cinnamon and melted butter. Mix well. Chips should melt slightly from the warm butter. If they don't, microwave the mixture on High for 10 seconds to soften.

3. Remove top sheet of waxed paper from dough. With an offset spatula, spread filling evenly over dough, leaving a 1/2-inch (1 cm) border on one long side. Starting with the opposite long side and using the bottom sheet of waxed paper to help you, roll up the dough jelly-roll fashion. Press edge to seal and, using your hands, mold roll into nicely rounded shape. Wrap and chill until firm, at least 4 hours.

4. Fifteen minutes before you're ready to bake, preheat oven to 350°F (180°C). Cut roll into 1/2-inch (1 cm) slices. Place about 2 inches (5 cm) apart on prepared cookie sheet. Bake in preheated oven for 14 to 18 minutes or until light golden. Cool for 5 minutes on sheet, then transfer to a rack and cool completely.

Mini Chocolate Hazelnut Biscotti

These small, crunchy chocolate biscotti with an abundance of hazelnuts are perfect dippers for a cup of steaming coffee or hot chocolate.

MAKES ABOUT 10 DOZEN BISCOTTI

- **Preparation: 30 minutes**
- **Baking: 1 hour**
- **Cooling: 10 minutes**
- **Freezing: excellent**

TIP

Because biscotti have a hard, dry texture, they store particularly well. Be sure to bake them thoroughly. If they aren't dry enough, they will soften and become chewy when stored.

- **Preheat oven to 325°F (160°C)**
- **Cookie sheet, greased or lined with parchment paper**

2¾ cups	all-purpose flour	675 mL
2½ tsp	baking powder	12 mL
¼ tsp	salt	1 mL
⅔ cup	butter, softened	150 mL
1 cup	granulated sugar	250 mL
3	eggs	3
2 cups	semisweet chocolate chips, melted and cooled	500 mL
1 cup	finely chopped hazelnuts	250 mL
4	squares (1 oz/28 g each) semisweet chocolate, chopped	4

1. On a sheet of waxed paper or in a bowl, combine flour, baking powder and salt. Set aside.

2. In a large bowl, using an electric mixer on medium speed, beat butter and sugar until light and creamy, about 3 minutes. Add eggs, one at a time, beating well after each addition. On low speed, beat in melted chocolate until blended. Gradually add flour mixture, beating until blended. With a wooden spoon, stir in hazelnuts and chopped chocolate.

3. Divide dough into quarters. Shape each into a roll about 15 inches (37.5 cm) long. Place about 4 inches (10 cm) apart on prepared cookie sheet. Flatten rolls to 1½ inch (4 cm) wide, leaving top slightly rounded. Bake in preheated oven for 25 to 30 minutes or until set. Cool for 10 minutes on cookie sheet. Transfer rolls to a cutting board. Cut warm biscotti into ½-inch (1 cm) slices. Stand upright about ½ inch (1 cm) apart on cookie sheet. Return to oven and bake 25 to 30 minutes or until dry and crisp and hazelnuts just start to turn golden. Cool for 5 minutes on sheet, then transfer to a rack and cool completely.

Variations

Dip the ends in melted chocolate for a fancier look.

Substitute pecans or almonds for the hazelnuts.

Chocolate Chip Almond Crisps

Ground rice cereal gives these cookies an interesting taste and texture that will keep people guessing about what they contain. A ground chocolate candy bar adds to the mystery.

MAKES ABOUT 7 DOZEN COOKIES

- **Preparation: 30 minutes**
- **Baking: 14 minutes**
- **Freezing: excellent**

TIPS

For soft cookies, don't flatten the dough balls.

This dough has a texture similar to that of a stiff shortbread dough, which is why it's easier to work it with your hands than to continue mixing with the mixer.

- **Preheat oven to 375°F (190°C)**
- **Cookie sheet, greased or lined with parchment paper**

4 cups	crisp rice cereal	1 L
3	(1.4 oz/39 g each) crunchy chocolate-covered toffee bars, chopped	3
2 cups	all-purpose flour	500 mL
1 tsp	baking powder	5 mL
1 tsp	baking soda	5 mL
1/4 tsp	salt	1 mL
1 cup	butter, softened	250 mL
1 cup	packed brown sugar	250 mL
3/4 cup	granulated sugar	175 mL
2	eggs	2
2 cups	semisweet chocolate chips	500 mL
1 1/2 cups	finely chopped almonds	375 mL

1. In a food processor, process cereal until ground. Add toffee bars and process until ground. Add flour, baking powder, baking soda and salt. Process to blend. Transfer to a sheet of waxed paper or a bowl. Set aside.

2. In a large bowl, using an electric mixer on medium speed, beat butter and brown and granulated sugars until light and creamy, about 3 minutes. Add eggs, one at a time, beating well after each addition. On low speed, gradually add flour mixture, beating until blended. Using your hands, knead to form a smooth dough. With a wooden spoon, stir in chocolate chips and almonds.

3. Shape dough into 1-inch (2.5 cm) balls. Place about 2 inches (5 cm) apart on prepared cookie sheet. With a floured fork, press balls to flatten. Bake in preheated oven for 10 to 14 minutes or until golden around edges. Cool for 5 minutes on sheet, then transfer to a rack and cool completely.

Variation

Use your favorite chips to replace the semisweet chocolate. Milk, white or a mixture of chocolate chips is nice.

Fudge Drops

These yummy drops are crisp on the outside with a chewy middle. They have lots of chocolate, nuts and coconut throughout.

MAKES ABOUT 2½ DOZEN COOKIES

- **Preparation: 25 minutes**
- **Cooking: 4 minutes**
- **Baking: 16 minutes**
- **Freezing: not recommended**

TIPS

For a marbled appearance, fold mixture just slightly. It will blend more when dropped on the cookie sheet. If you prefer a chocolate look, blend in the chocolate more thoroughly.

These cookies will flatten slightly while they bake, which gives them their unique texture.

- **Preheat oven to 350°F (180°C)**
- **Cookie sheet, greased or lined with parchment paper**

1 cup	semisweet chocolate chips	250 mL
2	egg whites	2
Pinch	salt	Pinch
½ tsp	white vinegar	2 mL
½ tsp	vanilla	2 mL
½ cup	granulated sugar	125 mL
½ cup	unsweetened flaked coconut	125 mL
½ cup	chopped pecans	125 mL

1. In a small saucepan over low heat, melt chocolate chips, stirring until smooth. Set aside to cool.

2. In a small bowl, using an electric mixer on high speed, beat egg whites, salt, vinegar and vanilla until frothy. Gradually add sugar, 2 tbsp (30 mL) at a time, beating until stiff, shiny peaks form. With a spatula, fold in coconut and nuts gently but thoroughly. Fold in melted chocolate just until mixture is lightly marbled (see Tips, left).

3. Drop mixture by tablespoonfuls (15 mL) about 2 inches (5 cm) apart on prepared cookie sheet. Bake in preheated oven for 12 to 16 minutes or until dry on top. Cool completely on sheet.

Variation

Replace semisweet chocolate chips with milk chocolate chips for a milder chocolate taste.

Chocolate Toffee Peanut Mounds

These cookies couldn't be easier to make or more delicious.

**MAKES ABOUT
2 DOZEN COOKIES**

- **Preparation: 15 minutes**
- **Cooking: 4 minutes**
- **Chilling: 1 hour**
- **Freezing: not recommended**

- **Cookie sheet lined with waxed paper**

6	squares (1 oz/28 g each) semisweet chocolate, chopped	6
1 cup	coarsely chopped toffee-coated peanuts	250 mL
½ cup	dried cranberries	125 mL

1. In a medium saucepan over low heat, melt chocolate, stirring constantly. Remove from heat. With a wooden spoon, stir in peanuts and cranberries until all ingredients are coated.
2. Drop mixture by tablespoonfuls (15 mL) about 1 inch (2.5 cm) apart on waxed paper. Chill until chocolate is set, about 1 hour.

Chocolate Cashew Crunchies

The combination of sweet and salty in these no-bake treats is irresistible.

**MAKES ABOUT
4 DOZEN COOKIES**

- **Preparation: 15 minutes**
- **Cooking: 4 minutes**
- **Chilling: 1 hour**
- **Standing: 2 hours**
- **Freezing: not recommended**

TIPS

Once the chocolate is firm, store cookies in airtight container with waxed paper between layers. They may develop a whitish coating when cold. It will disappear at room temperature.

Use the thinner pretzel sticks. If using knots, break them into smaller pieces.

- **Cookie sheet lined with waxed paper**

12	squares (1 oz/28 g each) bittersweet chocolate, chopped	12
2 tbsp	butter	30 mL
1½ cups	coarsely chopped cashews	375 mL
1½ cups	salted pretzel sticks, broken into ¾-inch (2 cm) pieces	375 mL
2	squares (1 oz/28 g each) white chocolate, chopped and melted	2

1. In a large saucepan over low heat, melt bittersweet chocolate and butter, stirring until smooth. Remove from heat and let cool for 10 minutes. With a wooden spoon, stir in cashews and pretzels until all ingredients are coated.
2. Drop mixture by tablespoonfuls (15 mL) about 1 inch (2.5 cm) apart on waxed paper. Chill until chocolate is set, about 1 hour.
3. Drizzle white chocolate over cookies. Let stand until chocolate is set, about 2 hours.

Variation
Use white chocolate in place of bittersweet for the mounds, and drizzle with dark chocolate.

Crunchy Chocolate Nut Cookies

These cookies are similar to macaroons, but made with nuts rather than the usual coconut. They make a great Valentine's gift, one that is much more personal than a store-bought box of chocolates.

MAKES ABOUT 2½ DOZEN COOKIES

- **Preparation: 35 minutes**
- **Baking: 19 minutes**
- **Cooking: 4 minutes**
- **Standing: 2 hours**
- **Freezing: excellent (not dipped)**

TIPS

Instead of using a pastry bag, you can drop the mixture from a spoon onto the cookie sheet. With moistened fingers, shape top of cookie into a teardrop.

If you're freezing these cookies, leave them plain, then dip them in chocolate just before using.

- **Preheat oven to 325°F (160°C)**
- **Cookie sheet, lined with parchment paper**
- **Pastry bag with ½-inch (1 cm) round tip**

2	egg whites	2
Pinch	cream of tartar	Pinch
Pinch	salt	Pinch
1 cup	granulated sugar	250 mL
⅓ cup	unsweetened cocoa powder, sifted	75 mL
¾ cup	ground hazelnuts	175 mL
¾ cup	ground unblanched almonds	175 mL
4	squares (1 oz/28 g each) white chocolate, chopped	4

1. In a small bowl, using an electric mixer on high speed, beat egg whites, cream of tartar and salt to soft peaks. Gradually add sugar, 2 tbsp (30 mL) at a time, beating until stiff, shiny peaks form. On low speed, beat in cocoa just until combined. With a wooden spoon, stir in hazelnuts and almonds.

2. Place mixture in pastry bag. Pipe small kisses, about 2 teaspoonfuls (10 mL) each, about 1 inch (2.5 cm) apart on prepared cookie sheet. Bake in preheated oven for 15 to 19 minutes or until set and surface seems dry. Cool for 5 minutes on sheet, then transfer to a rack and cool completely.

3. In a small saucepan over low heat, melt white chocolate, stirring until smooth. Transfer mixture to a small bowl for easy dipping. Dip bottom third of each cookie in melted chocolate. Place on sheet of waxed paper and leave until chocolate is set, about 2 hours.

Variations

To make "snowcaps," dip top of cookie, rather than bottom, in melted white chocolate.

Use semisweet rather than white chocolate for dipping.

Mom's Fancy Pressed Shortbread

Shortbread and Holiday Cookies

Shortbread originated in Scotland, where it was originally served during the Christmas season. "Short" means crumbly, which refers to its characteristic texture. Shortbread has three basic ingredients — butter, flour and sugar. However, the kinds of sugar and flour, as well as the method of mixing and baking, differ among recipes, resulting in an amazing range of tastes and textures.

Shortbread is easy to make. It can be mixed with an electric mixer or a wooden spoon, in a food processor or using a pastry blender. It can also be kneaded by hand. Most dough requires some kneading to become smooth since the batter doesn't contain liquid or eggs. Since shortbreads are easy to make, keep well and require no special ingredients, there's no reason not to enjoy them year-round.

Shortbread is a holiday favorite in the British Isles, but I've also included some time-honored recipes from around the world. There are also recipes for cookies that are colorful or filled with holiday ingredients, which make a much-appreciated gift. You'll even find some cookies that travel well.

Mom's Fancy Pressed Shortbread

♦

These tiny, fragile, buttery cookies were my mother's specialty. Only she (not me) would have the patience to cut tiny pieces of red and green cherries to decorate her cookie wreaths. Use the holiday design you prefer in your cookie press — star, bell, tree, wreath or whatever you have — all work well.

MAKES ABOUT 10 DOZEN SMALL COOKIES

- **Preparation: 25 minutes**
- **Baking: 10 minutes**
- **Freezing: excellent**

TIPS

To color sugar, add a few drops of food coloring to granulated sugar. Mix well with the back of a spoon or a spatula until color is evenly distributed. Transfer to a saltshaker to sprinkle evenly over cookies.

There's no substitute for butter when making shortbread.

- **Preheat oven to 350°F (180°C)**
- **Cookie press fitted with holiday-design nozzle**
- **Cookie sheet, ungreased**

1 cup + 2 tbsp	butter, softened	275 mL
½ cup	confectioners' (icing) sugar, sifted	125 mL
¼ tsp	salt	1 mL
2 cups	all-purpose flour	500 mL
	Colored sugar or candied cherries	

1. In a large bowl, using an electric mixer on medium speed, beat butter and confectioners' sugar until light and creamy, about 3 minutes. On low speed, gradually add salt and flour, beating until blended.

2. Pack dough into fitted cookie press and press about 1 inch (2.5 cm) apart on cookie sheet. Sprinkle with colored sugar and/or decorate with pieces of cherry, as desired. Bake in preheated oven for 5 to 10 minutes or until light golden around edges. Cool for 5 minutes on sheet, then transfer to a rack and cool completely.

Whipped Shortbread

This cookie has the same tender, melt-in-your-mouth texture and flavor as rolled shortbread, but with much less effort.

MAKES ABOUT 3 DOZEN COOKIES

- **Preparation: 15 minutes**
- **Baking: 25 minutes**
- **Freezing: excellent**

TIPS

If you don't have superfine sugar, whirl regular granulated sugar in a blender or food processor until fine.

Unsalted and salted butter are interchangeable. The difference is in the taste. The sweet, delicate flavor of unsalted butter really comes through in shortbread, where butter is the main ingredient.

- **Preheat oven to 300°F (150°C)**
- **Cookie sheet, ungreased**

1 ½ cups	all-purpose flour	375 mL
¼ cup	cornstarch	60 mL
1 cup	butter, softened	250 mL
½ cup	superfine granulated sugar (see Tips, left)	125 mL
1 tsp	vanilla	5 mL
	Candied (glacé) cherries, halved, or pecan halves, optional	

1. On a sheet of waxed paper or in a bowl, combine flour and cornstarch. Set aside.

2. In a large bowl, using an electric mixer on medium speed, beat butter, sugar and vanilla until light and creamy, about 3 minutes. On low speed, gradually add flour mixture, beating until blended.

3. Drop dough by tablespoonfuls (15 mL) about 1 inch (2.5 cm) apart on cookie sheet. If desired, decorate top with a cherry half or pecan half. Bake in preheated oven for 20 to 25 minutes or until light golden around edges. Cool for 5 minutes on sheet, then transfer to a rack and cool completely.

Oatmeal Pecan Shortbread

Brown sugar gives this shortbread a nice caramel flavor and crisp texture.

**MAKES ABOUT
4 DOZEN COOKIES**

- **Preparation: 25 minutes**
- **Baking: 20 minutes**
- **Freezing: excellent**

TIPS

Use quick-cooking oats, not instant or large-flake old-fashioned oats, in this recipe.

Use an offset spatula to transfer cookies that are more fragile, such as these, to and from cookie sheets.

- **Preheat oven to 300°F (150°C)**
- **2-inch (5 cm) cookie cutters**
- **Cookie sheet, ungreased**

1 1/2 cups	all-purpose flour	375 mL
2/3 cup	quick-cooking rolled oats	150 mL
1/2 cup	packed brown sugar	125 mL
1/4 cup	finely chopped pecans	60 mL
1/2 tsp	ground cinnamon	2 mL
3/4 cup	butter, softened	175 mL

1. In a large bowl, combine flour, oats, brown sugar, pecans and cinnamon. Mix well. With a wooden spoon, blend in butter until mixture is crumbly. Using your hands, knead to form a soft, smooth dough. If necessary, cover and chill for 30 minutes for easy rolling.

2. Divide dough into halves. On floured surface, roll out 1 portion at a time to 1/4-inch (0.5 cm) thickness. Dip cutters in flour and cut into desired shapes. Place on cookie sheet about 1 inch (2.5 cm) apart. Bake in preheated oven for 15 to 20 minutes or until light golden. Cool for 5 minutes on sheet, then transfer to a rack and cool completely.

Variation

Divide dough into halves. Press each into a 5 1/2-inch (13.5 cm) round on cookie sheet. Mark into wedges and crimp the edges with a fork. Bake for 35 to 40 minutes.

Citrus Refrigerator Shortbread

A light sprinkling of granulated sugar before baking or confectioners' (icing) sugar after the cookies have cooled finishes these off nicely.

MAKES ABOUT 9 DOZEN COOKIES

- **Preparation: 25 minutes**
- **Chilling: 3 hours**
- **Baking: 15 minutes**
- **Freezing: excellent**

TIPS

If you don't have superfine sugar, whirl regular granulated sugar in a blender or food processor until fine.

You should get 1 tsp (5 mL) zest from a lime, 1 tbsp (15 mL) from a lemon and 4 tsp (20 mL) from an orange. Remove only the outer colored part. The white layer underneath, which is known as the pith, is bitter.

Use a sharp straight-edged knife to cut this dough.

- **Cookie sheet, ungreased**

1 ½ cups	all-purpose flour	375 mL
¾ cup	cornstarch	175 mL
¼ tsp	salt	1 mL
1 cup	butter, softened	250 mL
½ cup	superfine granulated sugar (see Tips, left)	125 mL
1 ½ tsp	grated lemon zest	7 mL
1 ½ tsp	grated lime zest	7 mL
1 ½ tsp	grated orange zest	7 mL
1 tbsp	freshly squeezed lemon, lime or orange juice	15 mL

1. On a sheet of waxed paper or in a bowl, combine flour, cornstarch and salt. Set aside.

2. In a large bowl, using an electric mixer on medium speed, beat butter and sugar until light and creamy, about 3 minutes. Beat in lemon, lime and orange zests and juice until smooth. On low speed, gradually add flour mixture, beating until blended. Using your hands, knead to form a smooth dough. Divide dough into thirds. Shape each into a roll 9 inches (23 cm) long. Wrap and chill until firm, at least 3 hours.

3. Fifteen minutes before you're ready to bake, preheat oven to 350°F (180°C). Cut rolls into ¼-inch (0.5 cm) slices. Place about 1 inch (2.5 cm) apart on cookie sheet. Bake in preheated oven for 10 to 15 minutes or until golden around edges. Cool for 5 minutes on sheet, then transfer to a rack and cool completely.

Variation

Use 4½ tsp (22 mL) of only one kind of zest rather than a mixture.

Cherry Pistachio Shortbreads

These colorful cookies are particularly nice for the festive season. They also make a great treat year-round.

MAKES ABOUT 40 COOKIES

- **Preparation: 20 minutes**
- **Baking: 25 minutes**
- **Freezing: excellent**

TIPS

If you use unsalted butter for shortbread, add a pinch of salt along with the flour.

These cookies can also be shaped into 1-inch (2.5 cm) balls and flattened with a fork dipped in sugar. Same taste with a different look.

- **Preheat oven to 300°F (150°C)**
- **Cookie sheet, ungreased**

1 cup	butter, softened	250 mL
½ cup	confectioners' (icing) sugar, sifted	125 mL
1 tsp	vanilla	5 mL
1¾ cups	all-purpose flour	425 mL
¾ cup	coarsely chopped pistachios	175 mL
½ cup	chopped dried cherries	125 mL
2 tbsp	granulated sugar	30 mL

1. In a large bowl, using an electric mixer on medium speed, beat butter, confectioners' sugar and vanilla until light and creamy, about 3 minutes. With a wooden spoon, stir in flour, pistachios and cherries, mixing until thoroughly blended. Using your hands, knead to form a smooth dough.

2. Drop dough by tablespoonfuls (15 mL) about 1 inch (2.5 cm) apart on cookie sheet. Sprinkle tops evenly with granulated sugar. Bake in preheated oven for 20 to 25 minutes or until golden around edges. Cool for 5 minutes on sheet, then transfer to a rack and cool completely.

Variations

Replace cherries with dried cranberries. Try using cranberries flavored with cherry or orange for something different.

Replace pistachios with almonds or pecans.

Frosted Lemon Poppy Seed Shortbread Cookies

Poppy seeds give these cookies an interesting taste and appearance. The lemon frosting, which is a bit tart, adds a nice touch.

MAKES ABOUT 8 DOZEN COOKIES

- **Preparation: 35 minutes**
- **Chilling: 2 hours**
- **Baking: 15 minutes**
- **Freezing: excellent**

TIPS

Shortbreads are best stored at room temperature in a cool, dry place rather than in the refrigerator.

Store poppy seeds in the freezer so they don't develop a rancid flavor.

- **Cookie sheet, ungreased**

COOKIE

1¼ cups	all-purpose flour	300 mL
½ cup	cornstarch	125 mL
1 tbsp	poppy seeds	15 mL
¾ cup	butter, softened	175 mL
½ cup	confectioners' (icing) sugar, sifted	125 mL
1 tbsp	grated lemon zest	15 mL
1 tbsp	freshly squeezed lemon juice	15 mL

FROSTING

¾ cup	confectioners' (icing) sugar, sifted	175 mL
¼ cup	butter, softened	60 mL
1 tsp	grated lemon zest	5 mL
1 tsp	freshly squeezed lemon juice	5 mL

1. *Cookie:* On a sheet of waxed paper or in a bowl, combine flour, cornstarch and poppy seeds. Set aside.

2. In a large bowl, using an electric mixer on medium speed, beat butter, confectioners' sugar and lemon zest and juice until light and creamy, about 3 minutes. On low speed, gradually add flour mixture, beating until blended. Using your hands, knead to form a smooth dough. Divide dough into halves. Shape each into a roll 12 inches (30 cm) long. Wrap and chill until firm, at least 2 hours.

3. Fifteen minutes before you're ready to bake, preheat oven to 350°F (180°C). Cut rolls into ¼-inch (0.5 cm) slices. Place about 1 inch (2.5 cm) apart on cookie sheet. Bake in preheated oven for 11 to 15 minutes or until golden around edges. Cool for 5 minutes on sheet, then transfer to a rack and cool completely.

4. *Frosting:* In a small bowl, combine confectioners' sugar, butter and lemon zest and juice. Beat with an electric mixer on low speed or a wooden spoon until smooth. Spread over cooled cookies.

Variation

These cookies are also delicious without the frosting.

Nutty and Nice Shortbreads

I'm not sure which is better, the flavor of these cookies or their appearance. The sprinkling of sliced hazelnuts makes them particularly attractive. They are definitely a favorite at my house.

MAKES ABOUT 4 DOZEN COOKIES

- **Preparation: 25 minutes**
- **Baking: 20 minutes**
- **Freezing: excellent**

TIPS
You can buy thinly sliced unblanched hazelnuts, which look very attractive, in most grocery stores and bulk stores.

I recommend using parchment paper when baking these cookies because the egg white drips onto the cookie sheet and tends to stick.

- **Preheat oven to 325°F (160°C)**
- **2-inch (5 cm) round cookie cutter**
- **Cookie sheet, lined with parchment paper**

1 cup	butter, softened	250 mL
⅓ cup	granulated sugar	75 mL
2 tbsp	cornstarch	30 mL
1 tsp	vanilla	5 mL
2 cups	all-purpose flour	500 mL
⅓ cup	finely chopped walnuts	75 mL
⅓ cup	finely chopped pecans	75 mL
⅓ cup	finely chopped hazelnuts	75 mL
1	egg white, lightly beaten	1
½ cup	sliced unblanched hazelnuts	125 mL

1. In a large bowl, using an electric mixer on medium speed, beat butter, sugar, cornstarch and vanilla until light and creamy, about 3 minutes. With wooden spoon, stir in flour, walnuts, pecans and chopped hazelnuts, mixing until thoroughly blended. Using your hands, knead to form a smooth dough.

2. On floured surface, roll out dough to ¼-inch (0.5 cm) thickness. Dip cutter in flour and cut into rounds. Place about 1 inch (2.5 cm) apart on prepared cookie sheet. Brush tops with beaten egg white. Sprinkle with sliced hazelnuts. Bake in preheated oven for 15 to 20 minutes or until golden around edges. Cool for 5 minutes on sheet, then transfer to a rack and cool completely.

Variation
For a glistening top, mix 1 tbsp (15 mL) granulated sugar with the sliced hazelnuts.

Bittersweet Cashew Rounds

Lots of chocolate and nuts make these hearty shortbreads hard to resist.

**MAKES ABOUT
3½ DOZEN COOKIES**

- **Preparation: 25 minutes**
- **Baking: 20 minutes**
- **Freezing: excellent**

TIPS

When you flatten the balls with a fork, it leaves interesting lines on top. The bottom of a glass leaves a flat surface. Try both ways for different looks.

A sprinkle of granulated sugar is always a nice finish on any shortbread cookie.

These cookies travel well, so they are a good choice for holiday care packages.

- **Preheat oven to 350°F (180°C)**
- **Cookie sheet, ungreased**

1¾ cups	all-purpose flour	425 mL
¼ cup	cornstarch	60 mL
1 cup	butter, softened	250 mL
½ cup	confectioners' (icing) sugar, sifted	125 mL
3	squares (1 oz/28 g each) bittersweet chocolate, chopped	3
½ cup	chopped cashews	125 mL

1. On a sheet of waxed paper or in a bowl, combine flour and cornstarch. Set aside.

2. In a large bowl, using an electric mixer on medium speed, beat butter and confectioners' sugar until light and creamy, about 3 minutes. On low speed, gradually add flour mixture, beating until blended. With a wooden spoon, stir in chocolate and cashews. Using your hands, knead to form a smooth dough.

3. Shape dough into 1-inch (2.5 cm) balls. Place about 2 inches (5 cm) apart on cookie sheet. Flatten slightly with a fork or the bottom of a glass dipped in granulated sugar. Bake in preheated oven or 15 to 20 minutes or until golden around edges. Cool for 5 minutes on sheet, then transfer to a rack and cool completely.

Variations

Substitute semisweet or milk chocolate for the bittersweet. Peanuts work well in place of the cashews.

Toffee Crunch Almond Shortbread

Pack some of these in a small, colorful cookie tin for a great holiday gift.

MAKES ABOUT 5 DOZEN COOKIES

- **Preparation: 25 minutes**
- **Baking: 30 minutes**
- **Freezing: excellent**

TIPS

I recommend using parchment paper when baking these cookies because the toffee is very sticky.

If you don't have superfine sugar, whirl regular granulated sugar in a blender or food processor until fine.

These shortbreads taste great with a bit of chocolate. You can drizzle melted chocolate over the tops, or dip half of the entire cookie in melted chocolate. If you choose to dip, you'll need about 8 oz (250 g) of chocolate.

Because shortbread recipes use no eggs, they can easily be halved or doubled. I usually make larger batches since the cookies keep well and disappear quickly.

- **Preheat oven to 300°F (150°C)**
- **Cookie sheet, lined with parchment paper**

3 cups	all-purpose flour	750 mL
1 cup	rice flour	250 mL
¼ tsp	salt	1 mL
2 cups	butter, softened	500 mL
1 cup	superfine granulated sugar (see Tip, left)	250 mL
1 cup	chopped unblanched almonds	250 mL
1 cup	toffee bits	250 mL

1. On a sheet of waxed paper or in a bowl, combine all-purpose and rice flours and salt. Set aside.

2. In a large bowl, using an electric mixer on medium speed, beat butter and sugar until light and creamy, about 3 minutes. On low speed, gradually add flour mixture, beating until blended. With a wooden spoon, stir in almonds and toffee bits. Using your hands, knead to form a smooth dough.

3. Shape dough into 1-inch (2.5 cm) balls. Place about 2 inches (5 cm) apart on prepared cookie sheet. Flatten to about ¼-inch (0.5 cm) thickness with the bottom of a glass dipped in granulated sugar or flour. Bake in preheated oven for 25 to 30 minutes or until lightly browned around edges. Cool for 5 minutes on sheet, then transfer to a rack and cool completely.

Mocha Java Shortbread Logs

◆

A great choice for coffee-lovers. Enjoy them with an espresso coffee for a double dose of caffeine.

**MAKES ABOUT
4 DOZEN COOKIES**

- **Preparation: 25 minutes**
- **Baking: 20 minutes**
- **Freezing: excellent**

TIPS

These have a great coffee impact. For a milder flavor, decrease espresso to 1 tbsp (15 mL).

Roll warm cookies in confectioners' (icing) sugar.

- **Preheat oven to 350°F (180°C)**
- **Cookie sheet, ungreased**

2 cups	all-purpose flour	500 mL
2 tbsp	cornstarch	30 mL
2 tbsp	instant espresso coffee powder	30 mL
2	squares (1 oz/28 g each) semisweet chocolate, finely chopped	2
1 cup	butter, softened	250 mL
½ cup	granulated sugar	125 mL

1. On a sheet of waxed paper or in a bowl, combine flour, cornstarch, coffee powder and chocolate. Set aside.
2. In a large bowl, using an electric mixer on medium speed, beat butter and sugar until light and creamy, about 3 minutes. With a wooden spoon, stir in flour mixture, mixing until thoroughly blended. Using your hands, knead to form a smooth dough.
3. Shape into small logs, each about 2- by ½-inch (5 cm by 1 cm). Place about 1 inch (2.5 cm) apart on cookie sheet. Bake in preheated oven for 15 to 20 minutes or until lightly browned around edges. Cool for 5 minutes on sheet, then transfer to a rack and cool completely.

Variations

Drizzle the logs with melted chocolate or omit the chocolate in the recipe for a true coffee flavor.

For an interesting crunch, replace the instant espresso coffee powder with 3 tbsp (45 mL) finely crushed espresso or mocha java coffee beans.

Chocolate Ginger Shortbread Cookies

These look and taste great plain, but you can dress them up with a sprinkle of confectioners' (icing) sugar or a chocolate drizzle. Chocolate-lovers may want to dip the entire bottom in melted chocolate.

MAKES ABOUT 40 COOKIES

- **Preparation: 20 minutes**
- **Baking: 23 minutes**
- **Freezing: excellent**

TIPS

When creaming butter, it's important to have it at the right temperature. It should be a spreadable consistency. If it's too hard, it won't beat to a creamy texture; if it's too soft, the dough will be too soft to handle and your cookies won't hold their shape.

When wrapping dough for freezing or storage, wrap tightly in plastic wrap. If you plan to use it in the immediate future, waxed paper will do.

- **Preheat oven to 325°F (160°C)**
- **Cookie sheet, ungreased**

1 cup	butter, softened	250 mL
½ cup	granulated sugar	125 mL
2 cups	all-purpose flour	500 mL
¼ tsp	ground ginger	1 mL
½ cup	finely chopped crystallized ginger	125 mL
½ cup	chopped milk chocolate	125 mL

1. In a large bowl, using an electric mixer on medium speed, beat butter and sugar until light and creamy, about 3 minutes. With a wooden spoon, stir in flour, ground ginger, crystallized ginger and chocolate, mixing until thoroughly blended. Using your hands, knead to form a smooth dough.

2. Drop dough by tablespoonfuls (15 mL) about 2 inches (5 cm) apart on cookie sheet. Bake in preheated oven for 18 to 23 minutes or until lightly browned around edges. Cool for 5 minutes on sheet, then transfer to a rack and cool completely.

Variations

Omit ground ginger if you prefer a milder ginger flavor.

If you love dark chocolate, replace the milk chocolate with bittersweet.

Tropical Shortbread

These cookies are like a trip to the tropics without the flight.

**MAKES ABOUT
6½ DOZEN COOKIES**

- **Preparation: 25 minutes**
- **Chilling: 2 hours**
- **Baking: 15 minutes**
- **Freezing: excellent**

TIPS

Coconut extract is not as common as other extracts, such as vanilla. However, it has become one of my favorite ingredients for cookies that contain coconut. It adds a wonderful burst of coconut flavor.

Use a sharp serrated knife to cut this dough.

- **Cookie sheet, ungreased**

1 cup	butter, softened	250 mL
⅓ cup	granulated sugar	75 mL
1 tsp	coconut extract	5 mL
1¾ cups	all-purpose flour	425 mL
¼ tsp	salt	1 mL
1 cup	sweetened flaked coconut	250 mL
¾ cup	chopped macadamia nuts	175 mL
½ cup	chopped candied pineapple	125 mL

1. In a large bowl, using an electric mixer on medium speed, beat butter, sugar and coconut extract until light and creamy, about 3 minutes. On low speed, gradually add flour and salt, beating until blended. With a wooden spoon, stir in coconut, nuts and pineapple. Using your hands, knead to form a smooth dough. Divide dough into halves. Shape each into a roll 10 inches (25 cm) long. Wrap and chill until firm, at least 2 hours.

2. Fifteen minutes before you're ready to bake, preheat oven to 350°F (180°C). Cut rolls into ¼-inch (0.5 cm) slices. Place about 2 inches (5 cm) apart on cookie sheet. Bake in preheated oven for 10 to 15 minutes or until golden around edges. Cool for 5 minutes on sheet, then transfer to a rack and cool completely.

Variations

Replace macadamia nuts with almonds.

Omit candied pineapple or replace with candied (glacé) cherries.

Slice-and-Bake Cherry Pecan Shortbread

Freeze a few of these rolls and get a head start on your holiday baking.

MAKES ABOUT 5 DOZEN COOKIES

- **Preparation: 25 minutes**
- **Chilling: 3 hours**
- **Baking: 25 minutes**
- **Freezing: excellent**

TIPS

These cookies are delicious two ways. You can bake them like most shortbreads, until they are lightly browned around the edges (20 minutes), which gives them a slightly softer texture than when they are baked until the tops, too, are lightly browned. The longer baking time (25 minutes) produces a crispier result, more like a tender sugar cookie.

Use a sharp serrated knife to cut this dough as it will easily cut through the nuts and cherries.

For make-ahead baking, you may want to double this recipe.

- **Cookie sheet, ungreased**

1¾ cups	all-purpose flour	425 mL
¼ cup	cornstarch	60 mL
Pinch	salt	Pinch
1 cup	butter, softened	250 mL
½ cup	confectioners' (icing) sugar, sifted	125 mL
1 tbsp	grated lemon zest	15 mL
½ cup	chopped red candied (glacé) cherries	125 mL
½ cup	chopped green candied (glacé) cherries	125 mL
½ cup	finely chopped pecans	125 mL

1. On a sheet of waxed paper or in a bowl, combine flour, cornstarch and salt. Set aside.

2. In a large bowl, using an electric mixer on medium speed, beat butter, confectioners' sugar and lemon zest until light and creamy, about 3 minutes. On low speed, gradually add flour mixture, beating until blended. With a wooden spoon, stir in red and green cherries and pecans. Using your hands, knead to form a smooth dough. Divide dough into halves. Shape each into a roll 8 inches (20 cm) long. Wrap and chill until firm, at least 3 hours.

3. Fifteen minutes before you're ready to bake, preheat oven to 300°F (150°C). Cut rolls into ¼-inch (0.5 cm) slices. Place about 2 inches (5 cm) apart on cookie sheet. Bake in preheated oven for 20 to 25 minutes or until lightly browned around edges. Cool for 5 minutes on sheet, then transfer to a rack and cool completely.

Variations

Omit green cherries and use twice the quantity of red cherries only.

Substitute walnuts for the pecans.

Replace the cherries with chopped mixed candied fruit.

Chocolate Caramel Shortbread

◆

The best of both worlds — a melt-in-your-mouth shortbread cookie combined with a favorite crunchy toffee chocolate bar.

MAKES ABOUT 3 DOZEN COOKIES

- **Preparation: 25 minutes**
- **Baking: 25 minutes**
- **Freezing: excellent**

TIPS

A common brand of chocolate toffee bar is Toblerone Milk Chocolate with Almond Honey Nougat. Many store-brand bars are also available. For a stronger chocolate taste, buy the dark chocolate version. You should have about 1$\frac{1}{3}$ cups (325 mL) chopped chocolate bar.

Be sure to use parchment paper when baking these cookies, as the toffee is sticky.

- **Preheat oven to 325°F (160°C)**
- **Cookie sheet, lined with parchment paper**

1 cup	butter, softened	250 mL
$\frac{1}{2}$ cup	granulated sugar	125 mL
2 cups	all-purpose flour	500 mL
2 tbsp	cornstarch	30 mL
1	milk chocolate toffee bar (6 oz/175 g), coarsely chopped	1

1. In a large bowl, using an electric mixer on medium speed, beat butter and sugar until light and creamy, about 3 minutes. With a wooden spoon, stir in flour and cornstarch, mixing until thoroughly blended. Using your hands, knead to form a smooth dough.

2. Reserve 36 large pieces of the chocolate bar. Work remainder into dough, using your hands or a wooden spoon. Drop dough by tablespoonfuls (15 mL) about 1 inch (2.5 cm) apart on prepared cookie sheet. Press a reserved chunk of chocolate bar on top of each cookie. Bake in preheated oven for 20 to 25 minutes or until lightly browned around edges. Cool for 5 minutes on sheet, then transfer to a rack and cool completely.

Variation

Dust these cookies with confectioners' (icing) sugar before serving.

Halloween Pumpkin Cookies

I'm always looking for new ways to use pumpkin at Halloween, and this combination with white chocolate and macadamia nuts is a real keeper. It will extend far beyond my Halloween cookie baking.

MAKES ABOUT 5 DOZEN COOKIES

- **Preparation: 25 minutes**
- **Baking: 15 minutes**
- **Freezing: excellent**

TIPS

Be sure to buy pure pumpkin. The pumpkin pie filling has sugar and spices already added to it.

Soft cookies like these should be stored in an airtight container at room temperature. They also freeze well.

When measuring brown sugar, press it firmly into a dry measuring cup. When turned out on a flat surface it should hold its shape.

- **Preheat oven to 350°F (180°C)**
- **Cookie sheet, greased or lined with parchment paper**

2 cups	all-purpose flour	500 mL
1 tsp	baking soda	5 mL
¼ tsp	salt	1 mL
2 tsp	ground cinnamon	10 mL
¼ tsp	ground nutmeg	1 mL
¼ tsp	ground cloves	1 mL
1 cup	butter, softened	250 mL
1 cup	packed brown sugar	250 mL
1 cup	pumpkin purée (not pie filling)	250 mL
1	egg	1
2 cups	white chocolate chips	500 mL
1 cup	coarsely chopped macadamia nuts	250 mL
½ cup	pumpkin seeds	125 mL

1. On a sheet of waxed paper or in a bowl, combine flour, baking soda, salt, cinnamon, nutmeg and cloves. Set aside.

2. In a large bowl, using an electric mixer on medium speed, beat butter, brown sugar, pumpkin and egg until smooth, about 3 minutes. On low speed, gradually add flour mixture, beating until blended. With a wooden spoon, stir in white chocolate chips, macadamia nuts and pumpkin seeds.

3. Drop by tablespoonfuls (15 mL) about 2 inches (5 cm) apart on prepared cookie sheet. Bake in preheated oven for 11 to 15 minutes or until set. Cool for 5 minutes on sheet, then transfer to a rack and cool completely.

Variations

Replace pumpkin seeds with sunflower seeds or omit completely.

Replace macadamia nuts with almonds.

Shortbread Cutouts

Cut out these cookies into holiday shapes, such as trees or Santas, or turn them into personalized place cards for a special dinner or name tags for gifts.

MAKES ABOUT 3 DOZEN COOKIES

- **Preparation: 20 minutes**
- **Baking: 25 minutes**
- **Freezing: excellent**

TIPS

To use these as gift tags, make a hole in the end or the top of each cookie with a straw before baking. Re-cut the hole as soon as cookies come out of the oven. After decorating, put a thin ribbon or string through the hole. To decorate as place or name cards, use tubes of prepared icing or gel to write out the names. For decorating with candies, use icing as glue.

Icings and gels are available in many colors. They are ideal for writing on and decorating cookies and cakes. Kids can be very creative with these as tools.

- **Preheat oven to 300°F (150°C)**
- **Holiday or rectangular cookie cutters**
- **Cookie sheet, ungreased**

1 ½ cups	all-purpose flour	375 mL
¾ cup	cornstarch	175 mL
½ cup	superfine granulated sugar (see Tips, page 393)	125 mL
¼ tsp	salt	1 mL
1 cup	butter, softened	250 mL

DECORATIONS, OPTIONAL

Colored sugars, candies and frosting

1. In a large bowl, combine flour, cornstarch, sugar and salt. Add butter. With a wooden spoon, mix until blended, then, using your hands, knead to form a smooth dough.

2. Divide dough into halves. On a floured surface, roll out each to ¼-inch (0.5 cm) thickness. Dip cutters in flour and cut into desired shapes. Place about 1 inch (2.5 cm) apart on cookie sheet. If desired, sprinkle with colored sugar. Bake in preheated oven for 15 to 25 minutes or until golden around edges. (Time will depend on the size of the cookies.) Cool for 5 minutes on sheet, then transfer to a rack and cool completely.

Variation

Shape into 1-inch (2.5 cm) balls, flatten slightly and sprinkle with colored sugar.

Raspberry Almond Shortbread Wreaths

These pretty cutout cookies make an attractive addition to your holiday cookie tray.

MAKES ABOUT 40 COOKIES

- **Preparation: 40 minutes**
- **Baking: 9 minutes**
- **Freezing: not recommended**

TIPS

Use different shapes for the center cutout. Stars and hearts are attractive.

Aspic or canapé cutters are great for cutting out the centers.

After you have removed the centers from the second batch of dough, piece them together and roll out again to make more cookies.

- **Preheat oven to 350°F (180°C)**
- **2-inch (5 cm) round cookie cutter**
- **¾-inch (2 cm) round cookie cutter (see Tips, left)**
- **Cookie sheet, ungreased**

1 cup	butter, softened	250 mL
⅔ cup	granulated sugar	150 mL
½ tsp	almond extract	2 mL
2 cups	all-purpose flour	500 mL
¾ cup	ground almonds	175 mL
½ cup	seedless raspberry jam	125 mL
	Confectioners' (icing) sugar	

1. In a large bowl, using an electric mixer on medium speed, beat butter, granulated sugar and almond extract until light and creamy, about 3 minutes. On low speed, gradually add flour, beating until smooth. With a wooden spoon, stir in almonds until blended, then, using your hands, knead to form a smooth dough.

2. Divide dough into halves. On a floured surface, roll out 1 portion to ⅛-inch (3 mm) thickness. Dip 2-inch (5 cm) cutter in flour and cut into rounds. Place about 1 inch (2.5 cm) apart on cookie sheet. Roll out remaining dough to ⅛-inch (3 mm) thickness and cut into 2-inch (5 cm) rounds, then, using the ¾-inch (2 cm) cutter, cut the centers from this batch of cookies. Place about 1 inch (2.5 cm) apart on cookie sheet. Bake in preheated oven for 5 to 9 minutes or until lightly browned around edges. Cool for 5 minutes on sheet, then transfer to a rack and cool completely.

3. *Assembly:* Spread about ½ tsp (2 mL) jam over flat side of cookies without holes. Dust confectioners' sugar over top of the cookies with center holes. Place cookies, sugar side up, over jam.

Variations

Replace almonds with hazelnuts or pecans.

Replace raspberry jam with apricot.

Mincemeat Pillows

This tender cream cheese pastry is nice to work with and it tastes great, too. Prepared mincemeat makes an easy filling.

MAKES ABOUT 4 DOZEN SANDWICH COOKIES

- **Preparation: 35 minutes**
- **Baking: 18 minutes**
- **Freezing: excellent (filled)**

TIP

Coarse sugar is available in bulk stores and cake supply stores. You can also use regular granulated sugar, turbinado sugar or Demerara sugar.

- **Preheat oven to 375°F (190°C)**
- **3-inch (7.5 cm) round cookie cutter**
- **Cookie sheet, greased or lined with parchment paper**

PASTRY

1 cup	butter, softened	250 mL
1	package (8 oz/250 g) cream cheese, softened	1
1/4 cup	granulated sugar	60 mL
2 cups	all-purpose flour	500 mL
1/2 tsp	ground cinnamon	2 mL

FILLING

1 1/2 cups	prepared mincemeat	375 mL
2 tsp	ground cinnamon	10 mL

GLAZE

1	egg, beaten	1
1/4 cup	coarse sugar	60 mL

1. *Pastry:* In a large bowl, using an electric mixer on medium speed, beat butter and cream cheese until smooth. On low speed, gradually add sugar, flour and cinnamon, beating until blended. On a floured surface, roll out dough to 1/8-inch (3 mm) thickness. Dip cutter in flour and cut into rounds.

2. *Filling:* In a small bowl, combine mincemeat and cinnamon. Mix well. Place about 1 tsp (5 mL) mincemeat in center of each cookie. Fold to form a half-moon. With a floured fork, seal edges together. Place about 1 inch (2.5 cm) apart on prepared cookie sheet.

3. *Glaze:* Brush top of cookies with beaten egg. Sprinkle sugar over top. Bake in preheated oven for 13 to 18 minutes or until golden around the edges. Cool for 5 minutes on sheet, then transfer to a rack and cool completely.

Variation

Replace mincemeat with an equal quantity of whole-berry cranberry sauce or a thick red jam.

White Chocolate Cranberry Drops

Sweet, creamy white chocolate blends beautifully with tart cranberries in a rich shortbread dough. These are so easy to make, there's no excuse for not baking.

MAKES ABOUT 4 DOZEN COOKIES

- **Preparation: 25 minutes**
- **Baking: 18 minutes**
- **Freezing: excellent**

TIPS

If you don't have superfine sugar, whirl regular granulated sugar in a food processor or blender until fine.

I recommend using parchment paper when baking these cookies, as the white chocolate is likely to stick.

- **Preheat oven to 350°F (180°C)**
- **Cookie sheet, lined with parchment paper**

2 cups	all-purpose flour	500 mL
¼ cup	cornstarch	60 mL
1 cup	butter, softened	250 mL
½ cup	superfine granulated sugar (see Tips, left)	125 mL
1 tsp	vanilla	5 mL
1 cup	chopped dried cranberries	250 mL
¾ cup	white chocolate chips	175 mL

1. On a sheet of waxed paper or in a bowl, combine flour and cornstarch. Set aside.

2. In a large bowl, using an electric mixer on medium speed, beat butter, sugar and vanilla until light and creamy, about 3 minutes. On low speed, gradually add flour mixture, beating until blended. Using your hands, knead to form a smooth dough. Add cranberries and white chocolate chips. Knead well.

3. Drop dough by tablespoonfuls (15 mL) about 2 inches (5 cm) apart on prepared cookie sheet. Bake in preheated oven for 13 to 18 minutes or until lightly browned around edges. Cool for 5 minutes on sheet, then transfer to a rack and cool completely.

Variations

Add a drizzle of white chocolate over tops of cookies.

Replace white chocolate chips with semisweet chocolate chips.

Replace cranberries with dried cherries or dried blueberries.

Candy Cane Twists

Kids will enjoy making these cookies and leaving them for Santa as much as Santa will enjoy receiving them.

MAKES ABOUT 4 DOZEN COOKIES

- **Preparation: 25 minutes**
- **Baking: 11 minutes**
- **Freezing: excellent**

TIP

If you like peppermint, increase the extract to ¾ tsp (3 mL).

- **Preheat oven to 375°F (190°C)**
- **Cookie sheet, ungreased**

2½ cups	all-purpose flour	625 mL
1 tsp	baking powder	5 mL
1 cup	butter, softened	250 mL
¾ cup	granulated sugar	175 mL
1	egg	1
½ tsp	peppermint extract	2 mL
½ tsp	red food coloring	2 mL
¼ cup	crushed red and white peppermints or candy canes, optional	60 mL

1. On a sheet of waxed paper or in a bowl, combine flour and baking powder. Set aside.

2. In a large bowl, using an electric mixer on medium speed, beat butter, sugar, egg and peppermint extract until light and creamy, about 3 minutes. On low speed, gradually add flour mixture, beating until blended. Divide dough into halves. Add food coloring to 1 portion and, using your hands, knead until thoroughly mixed in. If using, knead crushed candies into other portion.

3. For each candy cane, roll 1 tsp (5 mL) of each kind of dough into a rope 5 inches (12.5 cm) long. Place 2 ropes side by side and twist together, then gently roll to meld. Place about 2 inches (5 cm) apart on cookie sheet. Curve one end to form handle of cane. Bake in preheated oven for 7 to 11 minutes or until light golden around edges. Cool for 5 minutes on sheet, then transfer to a rack and cool completely.

Variation

Use green food coloring, mints or candy canes that have green stripes on them.

Cherry Almond Coconut Macaroons

These colorful, candy-like cookies are always a hit with coconut fans. These are a particularly easy-to-make version of macaroons.

MAKES ABOUT 5 DOZEN COOKIES

- **Preparation: 20 minutes**
- **Baking: 15 minutes**
- **Freezing: excellent**

TIP

Use sweetened coconut if you prefer. Both work well — it's simply a matter of taste.

- **Preheat oven to 350°F (180°C)**
- **Cookie sheet, greased or lined with parchment paper**

5½ cups	unsweetened flaked coconut	1.375 L
1	can (14 oz or 300 mL) sweetened condensed milk	1
½ tsp	almond extract	2 mL
½ tsp	coconut extract	2 mL
1 cup	chopped red candied (glacé) cherries	250 mL
¾ cup	slivered almonds	175 mL

1. In a large bowl, combine coconut, sweetened condensed milk and almond and coconut extracts. Using a wooden spoon, mix well until all ingredients are thoroughly moistened. Stir in cherries and almonds.

2. Drop mixture by tablespoonfuls (15 mL) about 2 inches (5 cm) apart on prepared cookie sheet. Bake in preheated oven for 10 to 15 minutes or until light golden. Cool for 10 minutes on sheet, then transfer to a rack and cool completely.

Variations

Decorate the tops with a cherry half before baking.

Replace cherries with regular or miniature chocolate chips. Semisweet, milk or white chocolate chips would work well in this recipe.

Omit cherries. Increase almonds to 1 cup (250 mL).

Holiday Haystacks

This creamy, crunchy confection demonstrates that cookies don't need to be difficult to make to taste superb.

MAKES ABOUT 3 DOZEN COOKIES

- **Preparation: 15 minutes**
- **Cooking: 4 minutes**
- **Chilling: 1 hour**
- **Freezing: not recommended**

- **Cookie sheet, lined with waxed paper**

12	squares (1 oz/28 g each) white chocolate, chopped	12
1 cup	sliced almonds, toasted (see Tips, page 334)	250 mL
1 cup	sweetened flaked coconut, toasted	250 mL
1 cup	quartered red candied (glacé) cherries	250 mL

1. In a saucepan over low heat, melt white chocolate, stirring until smooth. Remove from heat. Stir in almonds, coconut and cherries. Mix until evenly coated with chocolate.

2. Drop mixture by tablespoonfuls (15 mL) on waxed paper. Chill until firm, about 1 hour. Store in a cool, dry place in an airtight container with waxed paper between layers.

Almond Pine Nut Drops

If you enjoy marzipan, you'll love these Italian specialties, which are served during the holidays.

MAKES ABOUT 3 DOZEN COOKIES

- **Preparation: 15 minutes**
- **Baking: 18 minutes**
- **Freezing: excellent**

TIP

Store these in an airtight container in layers separated with waxed paper. Store at room temperature for up to 5 days or freeze for up to 6 months.

- **Preheat oven to 350°F (180°C)**
- **Cookie sheet, lined with parchment paper**

12 oz	almond paste, broken into small pieces	375 g
¾ cup	superfine granulated sugar (see Tips, page 411)	175 mL
½ cup	confectioners' (icing) sugar, sifted	125 mL
2	egg whites	2
1¼ cups	pine nuts, coarsely chopped	300 mL

1. In a large bowl, using an electric mixer on low speed, beat almond paste, granulated sugar, confectioners' sugar and egg whites until blended, then increase speed to medium and beat for 2 minutes. With a wooden spoon, stir in pine nuts.

2. Drop mixture by tablespoonfuls (15 mL) about 2 inches (5 cm) apart on prepared cookie sheet. Bake in preheated oven for 13 to 18 minutes or until lightly browned. Cool completely on sheet.

Variation

Replace half or all of the pine nuts with chopped blanched almonds.

Cranberry Walnut Icebox Cookies

Cranberries, which are so much a part of the holiday season, have a wonderful tart flavor. They work well in these cookies, giving them not only great taste but a terrific appearance as well.

MAKES ABOUT 7 DOZEN COOKIES

- **Preparation: 25 minutes**
- **Chilling: 4 hours**
- **Baking: 15 minutes**
- **Freezing: excellent**

TIPS

Fresh cranberries work best in these cookies, but if you're using frozen ones, chop them frozen and add them to the batter in that state. If they have thawed, pat them dry with paper towels and mix them into the dough after you have mixed in the walnuts, to prevent the dough from turning pink.

Check the expiry date on your baking powder to ensure it is fresh. Nothing is more disappointing than making cookies and ending up with poor results because your baking powder did not work. Your cookies will be tough and won't rise during baking.

- **Cookie sheet, greased or lined with parchment paper**

3 1/2 cups	all-purpose flour	875 mL
1 tsp	baking powder	5 mL
1/4 tsp	baking soda	1 mL
1/4 tsp	salt	1 mL
1 1/4 cups	butter, softened	300 mL
1 cup	packed brown sugar	250 mL
2/3 cup	granulated sugar	150 mL
2	eggs	2
1 tbsp	orange zest	15 mL
1 cup	chopped walnuts	250 mL
2 cups	chopped cranberries	500 mL

1. On a sheet of waxed paper or in a bowl, combine flour, baking powder, baking soda and salt. Set aside.

2. In a large bowl, using an electric mixer on medium speed, beat butter and brown and granulated sugars until light and creamy, about 3 minutes. Add eggs, one at a time, beating well after each addition. Beat in orange zest. On low speed, gradually add flour mixture, beating until blended. With a wooden spoon, carefully stir in walnuts and cranberries. Divide dough into thirds. Shape each into a roll 7 inches (18 cm) long. Wrap and chill until firm, at least 4 hours.

3. Fifteen minutes before you're ready to bake, preheat oven to 375°F (190°C). Cut rolls into 1/4-inch (0.5 cm) slices. Place about 2 inches (5 cm) apart on prepared cookie sheet. Bake in preheated oven for 11 to 15 minutes or until lightly browned around edges. Cool for 5 minutes on sheet, then transfer to a rack and cool completely.

Variations

Replace walnuts with pecans.

Replace orange zest with lemon zest or with 1/2 tsp (2 mL) almond extract or 1 tsp (5 mL) vanilla.

Danish Hazelnut Spice Cookies

◆

These cookies are similar in flavor to gingerbread, with the addition of crunchy hazelnuts. They can be rolled and cut out with cookie cutters (see Tips) or shaped into rolls and chilled, ready to bake when you need them.

MAKES ABOUT 9 DOZEN COOKIES

- **Preparation: 25 minutes**
- **Chilling: 4 hours**
- **Baking: 14 minutes**
- **Freezing: excellent**

TIPS

To make cutout cookies, divide dough into halves and, on a floured surface, roll each to $1/4$-inch (0.5 cm) thickness. Using a cookie cutter dipped in flour, cut out desired shapes. Bake as above.

These rolls can be frozen for up to 3 months. Thaw before slicing. (See page 11 for instructions on freezing and thawing dough.)

Because the recipe uses no eggs, it can easily be halved.

- **Cookie sheet, greased or lined with parchment paper**

2$3/4$ cups	all-purpose flour	675 mL
1 cup	finely chopped hazelnuts	250 mL
1 tsp	baking soda	5 mL
$1/4$ tsp	salt	1 mL
1 tbsp	ground cinnamon	15 mL
2 tsp	ground ginger	10 mL
1 tsp	ground cloves	5 mL
$1/2$ tsp	ground nutmeg	2 mL
1 cup	butter, softened	250 mL
1 cup	packed brown sugar	250 mL
$1/2$ cup	corn syrup	125 mL

1. On a sheet of waxed paper or in a bowl, combine flour, hazelnuts, baking soda, salt, cinnamon, ginger, cloves and nutmeg. Set aside.

2. In a large bowl, using an electric mixer on medium speed, beat butter, brown sugar and corn syrup until smooth. Gradually add flour mixture, beating until blended, then, using your hands, knead to form a smooth dough. Divide dough into halves. Shape each into a roll 14 inches (35 cm) long. Wrap and chill until firm, at least 4 hours.

3. Fifteen minutes before you're ready to bake, preheat oven to 375°F (190°C). Cut rolls into $1/4$-inch (0.5 cm) slices. Place about 1 inch (2.5 cm) apart on prepared cookie sheet. Bake in preheated oven for 10 to 14 minutes or until golden. Cool for 5 minutes on sheet, then transfer to a rack and cool completely.

Variation

Replace hazelnuts with unblanched almonds or Brazil nuts.

Apricot Pecan Rugelach

These cookies, which are Jewish in origin, are a traditional favorite during the holiday season.

MAKES ABOUT 4 DOZEN COOKIES

- **Preparation: 40 minutes**
- **Chilling: 2½ hours**
- **Baking: 29 minutes**
- **Freezing: excellent**

TIPS

The flavor of these cookies depends on the jam. Choose a thick, tart jam with a nice fruit flavor. Be sure to chop any large pieces of fruit before combining with the lemon juice, and mix well.

The cream cheese should be soft for mixing. If it's too hard, place on a piece of waxed paper and soften in a microwave oven on High for about 10 seconds.

I recommend using parchment paper as the jam tends to stick.

- **Cookie sheet, lined with parchment paper**

DOUGH

8 oz	cream cheese, softened	250 g
1 cup	butter, softened	250 mL
3 tbsp	granulated sugar	45 mL
2 cups	all-purpose flour	500 mL

FILLING

1 cup	apricot jam (see Tips, left)	250 mL
1 tsp	freshly squeezed lemon juice	5 mL
1 cup	finely chopped pecans	250 mL
1 tsp	ground cinnamon	5 mL

TOPPING

1	egg	1
2 tbsp	coarse or regular granulated sugar	30 mL

1. *Dough:* In a large bowl, using an electric mixer on medium speed, beat cream cheese, butter and sugar until smooth. On low speed, gradually add flour, beating until dough becomes too stiff for the mixer, then finish mixing with a wooden spoon. Divide dough into quarters. Wrap and chill for 2 hours.

2. *Filling:* In a small bowl, combine jam and lemon juice. Set aside.

3. On lightly floured surface, roll out dough, 1 portion at a time, into an 11-inch (27.5 cm) circle. Using a small offset spatula, carefully spread with ¼ of the jam mixture. Sprinkle ¼ of the pecans and cinnamon over jam. Using a long, sharp knife, cut circle into 12 pie-shaped wedges. Starting from the wide end, tightly roll up each wedge to form a crescent. Place crescents on prepared cookie sheet about 2 inches (5 cm) apart. Repeat with remaining dough and filling. Chill for 30 minutes. Fifteen minutes before you are ready to bake, preheat oven to 350°F (180°C).

4. *Topping:* Beat egg lightly. Brush over surface of chilled cookies. Sprinkle sugar evenly over tops. Bake in preheated oven for 25 to 29 minutes or until golden. Cool for 15 minutes on sheet, then transfer to a rack and cool completely.

Variations

Replace pecans with almonds or hazelnuts.

Replace apricot jam with raspberry.

Honey Fruit Drops

These cookies taste like a light fruitcake in bite-size form. The honey gives them great flavor and a soft, moist texture.

MAKES ABOUT 4 DOZEN COOKIES

- **Preparation: 25 minutes**
- **Baking: 15 minutes**
- **Freezing: excellent**

TIP

Honey keeps cookies soft and moist during storage. Because they don't dry out, they are great to have on hand during the holidays.

- **Preheat oven to 350°F (180°C)**
- **Cookie sheet, greased or lined with parchment paper**

2 cups	all-purpose flour	500 mL
½ tsp	baking powder	2 mL
½ tsp	baking soda	2 mL
¼ tsp	salt	1 mL
½ cup	butter, softened	125 mL
½ cup	granulated sugar	125 mL
½ cup	liquid honey	125 mL
1	egg	1
1 tsp	lemon extract	5 mL
¾ cup	chopped pecans	175 mL
½ cup	chopped candied (glacé) cherries	125 mL
½ cup	chopped candied (glacé) pineapple	125 mL
½ cup	chopped dried cranberries	125 mL
½ cup	chopped dates	125 mL
½ cup	chopped dried apricots	125 mL

1. On a sheet of waxed paper or in a bowl, combine flour, baking powder, baking soda and salt. Set aside.

2. In a large bowl, using an electric mixer on medium speed, beat butter, sugar, honey, egg and lemon extract until smooth, about 3 minutes. On low speed, gradually add flour mixture, beating until blended. With a wooden spoon, stir in pecans, cherries, pineapple, cranberries, dates and apricots.

3. Drop dough by tablespoonfuls (15 mL) about 2 inches (5 cm) apart on prepared cookie sheet. Bake in preheated oven for 10 to 15 minutes or until golden. Cool for 5 minutes on sheet, then transfer to a rack and cool completely.

Variations

Vary the fruits to suit your taste, keeping the amounts the same as in the original recipe. Use candied peel, raisins, figs or dried cherries.

Replace lemon extract with an equal quantity of ground cinnamon or vanilla.

Cranberry Walnut Wheels

These attractive spirals take a little extra time to prepare, but the rolls can be made ahead and baked at a later date. The cranberries add special holiday appeal.

MAKES ABOUT 4 DOZEN COOKIES

- **Preparation: 35 minutes**
- **Chilling: 4½ hours**
- **Baking: 16 minutes**
- **Freezing: excellent**

TIPS

If you're using frozen cranberries in the filling, thaw them and pat dry with paper towels before blending.

When you need both the zest and juice from citrus fruit, you need to use fresh fruit. If you only need the juice, refrigerated or bottled juice works fine, although the taste of freshly squeezed juice is always preferable.

Make the bottom sheet of waxed paper long enough so you have a substantial overhang to help you roll up the dough.

Use a sharp serrated knife to cut this dough.

- **Cookie sheet, greased or lined with parchment paper**

DOUGH

1½ cups	all-purpose flour	375 mL
¼ tsp	baking powder	1 mL
¼ tsp	salt	1 mL
½ cup	butter, softened	125 mL
¾ cup	granulated sugar	175 mL
1	egg	1
1 tsp	vanilla	5 mL

FILLING

½ cup	cranberries, thawed if frozen (see Tips, left)	125 mL
½ cup	walnuts	125 mL
¼ cup	packed brown sugar	60 mL
1 tbsp	grated lemon zest	15 mL
2 tsp	freshly squeezed lemon juice	10 mL

1. *Dough:* On a sheet of waxed paper or in a bowl, combine flour, baking powder and salt. Set aside.

2. In a large bowl, using an electric mixer on medium speed, beat butter, sugar, egg and vanilla until light and creamy, about 3 minutes. On low speed, gradually add flour mixture, beating until blended. Using your hands, knead to form a smooth dough.

3. Between 2 sheets of waxed paper, roll out dough into a 12-inch (30 cm) square. Slide onto cookie sheet. Chill until starting to firm up, about 30 minutes.

4. *Filling:* In a food processor, combine cranberries, walnuts, brown sugar and lemon zest and juice. Process until finely chopped. Remove top sheet of waxed paper from dough and spread evenly with filling, leaving ½-inch (1 cm) border on 2 opposite edges. Starting with one of those edges and using the bottom sheet of waxed paper to help you, roll up the dough jelly-roll fashion. Press to firm up roll and seal edge. Wrap in waxed paper and chill until firm, at least 4 hours.

5. Fifteen minutes before you're ready to bake, preheat oven to 375°F (190°C). Cut roll into ¼-inch (0.5 cm) slices. Place about 2 inches (5 cm) apart on prepared cookie sheet. Bake in preheated oven for 12 to 16 minutes or until golden around edges. Cool for 5 minutes on sheet, then transfer to a rack and cool completely.

Gingerbread People

The holidays wouldn't be complete without making at least one batch of these traditional favorites for the kids to decorate.

- **Preparation: 25 minutes**
- **Chilling: 1 hour**
- **Baking: 20 minutes**
- **Standing: 1 hour**
- **Freezing: excellent (not decorated)**

TIPS

Don't limit gingerbread making to the holiday season. Let the cutters you use and how you decorate determine the theme. Pumpkins, bunnies, hearts, dogs, teddy bears and so on, all work well with the dough.

The baking time will depend upon the size of the cookies.

Royal Icing can also be made with meringue powder in place of the egg white. Just follow the package directions. It can be purchased in bulk stores and cake decorating supply stores.

- **Gingerbread people cookie cutters**
- **Cookie sheet, greased or lined with parchment paper**

COOKIE

2¼ cups	all-purpose flour	550 mL
¾ tsp	baking soda	3 mL
¼ tsp	salt	1 mL
1¼ tsp	ground ginger	6 mL
1 tsp	ground cinnamon	5 mL
½ tsp	ground cloves	2 mL
½ cup	butter, softened	125 mL
⅔ cup	packed brown sugar	150 mL
1	egg	1
¼ cup	light (fancy) molasses	60 mL

ROYAL ICING

1	egg white	1
Pinch	cream of tartar	Pinch
Approx 1½ cups	confectioners' (icing) sugar, sifted	375 mL

DECORATIONS

Colorful candies, raisins and sprinkles

1. *Cookie:* Combine flour, baking soda, salt, ginger, cinnamon and cloves. Set aside.

2. In a large bowl, using an electric mixer on medium speed, beat butter, brown sugar, egg and molasses until smooth. On low speed, gradually add flour mixture, beating until blended, then knead to form a smooth dough. Wrap and chill dough 1 hour.

3. Fifteen minutes before you're ready to bake, preheat oven to 350°F (180°C). Divide dough into halves. On a floured board, roll out each to ¼-inch (0.5 cm) thickness. Using cookie cutters dipped in flour, cut out cookies. Place about 2 inches (5 cm) apart on prepared cookie sheet. Bake in preheated oven for 15 to 20 minutes or until set. Cool for 5 minutes on sheet, then transfer to a rack and cool completely.

4. *Royal Icing:* In a bowl, beat egg white and cream of tartar until frothy. Gradually add confectioners' sugar, beating until stiff, shiny peaks form. Using a pastry bag fitted with a plain tube, pipe icing onto cookies to create faces and other features. Add candies, raisins and sprinkles to make buttons and eyes. Use the icing as a glue. Let stand until icing dries, about 1 hour.

Green Cherry Christmas Trees

These three-dimensional trees make great centerpieces for your festive holiday dinner table.

MAKES 6 TREES

- **Preparation: 45 minutes**
- **Baking: 20 minutes**
- **Freezing: not recommended**

TIPS

Edible glitter is great sprinkled on the melted chocolate while it is still wet.

Colored sugar also looks wonderful.

Omit the candied cherries. They add a nice flavor, but make the dough a bit more difficult to cut out.

Omit the food coloring and sprinkle plain cookies with green sugar sprinkles.

- **Preheat oven to 325°F (160°C)**
- **5 progressively larger star-shaped cookie cutters**
- **Cookie sheet, ungreased**

1 cup	butter, softened	250 mL
1/2 cup	granulated sugar	125 mL
2 1/4 cups	all-purpose flour	550 mL
	Green food coloring	
1/2 cup	finely chopped green candied (glacé) cherries	125 mL
6	squares (1 oz/28 g each) white chocolate, chopped	6
1 tsp	vegetable oil	5 mL

DECORATIONS

Colored sprinkles or candies

1. In a large bowl, using a wooden spoon, beat butter and sugar until smooth and creamy, about 3 minutes. Gradually add flour, mixing until blended, then, using your hands, knead to form a smooth dough. Add enough green coloring to make a green dough and knead until evenly colored. Knead in cherries.

2. Divide dough into sixths. On floured surface, roll out each portion to 1/4-inch (0.5 cm) thickness. Using 5 progressively larger star-shaped cookie cutters dipped in flour, cut out cookies. Use a 1-inch (2.5 cm) cutter for the top and 4 more that gradually increase in size from 2 1/2 inches (6 cm) to 4 inches (10 cm). Repeat with 5 remaining portions of dough. Place cookies about 1 inch (2.5 cm) apart on cookie sheet. Keep similar sizes on the same sheet for even baking. Bake in preheated oven for 15 to 20 minutes or until set. Cool for 5 minutes on sheet, then transfer to a rack and cool completely.

3. In a small saucepan on low heat, melt chocolate and oil, stirring until smooth.

4. *Assembly:* On a work surface, place a 4-inch (10 cm) star. Stack 4 stars in order of size, largest to smallest, on top, spreading a little melted chocolate between each layer and allowing it to drip down over the sides of the stars. Place a dollop of melted chocolate on top star and stand the smallest star on edge on top. Drizzle trees with melted chocolate and sprinkle with colored sprinkles or candies.

Cherry Mandelbrot

Good for You, Too

Just because they are loaded with nutritious ingredients doesn't mean you have to shop in natural foods stores to make the cookies in this chapter. With ingredients such as whole grain cereals, dried fruits and even vegetables, these cookies are definitely good for you. And although they aren't designed for specialty diets, you'll find some recipes that are free of ingredients people may find troublesome, such as eggs, nuts and lactose, the sugar found in dairy products that can cause digestive problems in sensitive individuals. To keep calories lower without sacrificing flavor, I've tried to reduce sugar and fat while increasing dietary fiber. In most cases, I've used unbleached rather than bleached flour and tried to include at least some whole wheat flour, for its pleasant nutty flavor, as well as its superior nutritional profile.

These cookies qualify as high-energy foods that will satisfy hearty appetites with a minimum of guilt. Most of the recipes are easy-to-make drop cookies, and they freeze and travel well. That means you can have them ready for your favorite outdoor activity — hiking, camping or biking. You can also serve them for an after-school or lunch-box treat or for a quick energy boost any time of the day.

Cherry Mandelbrot

Mandelbrot or almond bread is shaped and baked like a loaf. Similar to biscotti, it is then sliced and re-baked to make crisp cookies. This version is lower in fat and provides more dietary fiber than most.

MAKES ABOUT 3 DOZEN COOKIES

- **Preparation: 30 minutes**
- **Baking: 42 minutes**
- **Cooling: 10 minutes**
- **Oven cooling: 45 minutes**
- **Freezing: excellent**

TIPS

Use a sharp serrated knife to cut the semi-baked cookies.

Store mandelbrot in airtight container at room temperature for up to 1 month.

- **Preheat oven to 350°F (180°C)**
- **Two 9- by 5-inch (2 L) loaf pans, lined with parchment paper**
- **Cookie sheet, ungreased**

1 cup	unbleached all-purpose flour	250 mL
1 cup	whole wheat flour	250 mL
1/4 cup	wheat germ	60 mL
2 tsp	baking powder	10 mL
1/4 tsp	salt	1 mL
1/2 tsp	ground cinnamon	2 mL
2 tbsp	butter, softened	30 mL
3/4 cup	granulated sugar	175 mL
2 tbsp	vegetable oil	30 mL
2	eggs	2
1	egg white	1
1 tbsp	grated orange zest	15 mL
1/4 cup	freshly squeezed orange juice	60 mL
2 tbsp	lower-fat plain yogurt	30 mL
1/2 cup	sliced almonds	125 mL
1/2 cup	dried cherries	125 mL

1. On a sheet of waxed paper or in a bowl, combine all-purpose and whole wheat flours, wheat germ, baking powder, salt and cinnamon. Set aside.

2. In a large bowl, using a wooden spoon, beat butter, sugar, oil, eggs, egg white, orange zest, orange juice and yogurt until smooth. Gradually add flour mixture, beating until blended. Stir in almonds and cherries.

3. Divide dough into halves and place in prepared pans. Bake in preheated oven for 25 to 30 minutes or until tops are golden. Cool for 10 minutes in pan, then transfer to a cutting board. Cut into 1/2-inch (1 cm) slices. Place upright about 1 inch (2.5 cm) apart on cookie sheet. Bake for 8 to 12 minutes or until golden. Turn oven off and leave in oven for 40 to 45 minutes or until crisp.

Variation

Replace almonds with coarsely chopped hazelnuts or Brazil nuts and cherries with dried cranberries.

Cranberry Apricot Oat Cookies

Ground oats give these cookies a wonderful rich taste.

MAKES ABOUT 3 DOZEN COOKIES

- **Preparation: 25 minutes**
- **Baking: 15 minutes**
- **Freezing: excellent**

TIPS

You can successfully substitute a soft non-hydrogenated margarine for the butter in these cookies.

Substitute 1/2 cup (125 mL) whole wheat flour for the all-purpose for a slightly drier but nicely flavored cookie.

- **Preheat oven to 325°F (160°C)**
- **Cookie sheet, greased or lined with parchment paper**

1 1/2 cups	quick-cooking rolled oats	375 mL
1/2 cup	unbleached all-purpose flour	125 mL
1/2 cup	whole wheat flour	125 mL
1/2 tsp	baking powder	2 mL
1/2 tsp	baking soda	2 mL
1 1/2 tsp	ground cinnamon	7 mL
1/2 cup	butter, softened	125 mL
1 cup	packed brown sugar	250 mL
1	egg	1
3/4 cup	dried cranberries	175 mL
3/4 cup	chopped dried apricots	175 mL

1. In a food processor, process oats until they have the consistency of fine flour. On a sheet of waxed paper or in a bowl, combine ground oats, all-purpose and whole wheat flours, baking powder, baking soda and cinnamon. Set aside.

2. In a large bowl, using an electric mixer on medium speed, beat butter, brown sugar and egg until light and creamy, about 3 minutes. With a wooden spoon, stir in flour mixture, cranberries and apricots.

3. Drop dough by tablespoonfuls (15 mL) about 2 inches (5 cm) apart on prepared cookie sheet. Bake in preheated oven for 11 to 15 minutes or until lightly browned. Cool for 5 minutes on sheet, then transfer to a rack and cool completely.

Variation

Replace dried cranberries with an equal quantity of raisins or chopped dates.

Oatmeal Raisin Cookies

Here's a lighter, lower-fat version of a classic cookie.

MAKES ABOUT 4½ DOZEN COOKIES

- **Preparation: 25 minutes**
- **Baking: 11 minutes**
- **Freezing: excellent**

TIPS

Cookies that are low in fat don't keep as well as those containing more fat. These are best eaten within 2 days or frozen.

Apple butter replaces some of the fat and also gives these cookies a nice flavor. It is sold in the health food sections of grocery stores and in many European and Mennonite stores.

- **Preheat oven to 375°F (190°C)**
- **Large rimmed baking sheet**
- **Cookie sheet, greased or lined with parchment paper**

3 cups	quick-cooking rolled oats	750 mL
½ cup	chopped pecans	125 mL
2 cups	unbleached all-purpose flour	500 mL
1 tsp	baking soda	5 mL
½ tsp	baking powder	2 mL
¼ tsp	salt	1 mL
1 tsp	ground cinnamon	5 mL
½ tsp	ground cloves	2 mL
1½ cups	packed brown sugar	375 mL
½ cup	apple butter	125 mL
2	eggs	2
¼ cup	vegetable oil	60 mL
1½ cups	raisins	375 mL

1. On a large rimmed baking sheet, spread out oats and pecans. Bake in preheated oven, stirring occasionally, for 5 to 8 minutes or until lightly browned. Remove from oven. Set aside to cool.

2. On a sheet of waxed paper or in a bowl, combine flour, baking soda, baking powder, salt, cinnamon and cloves. Set aside.

3. In a large bowl, using an electric mixer on medium speed, beat brown sugar, apple butter, eggs and oil until very light and fluffy, about 5 minutes. On low speed, gradually add flour mixture, beating until blended. With a wooden spoon, stir in oat mixture and raisins.

4. Drop dough by tablespoonfuls (15 mL) about 2 inches (5 cm) apart on prepared cookie sheet. Press down with a floured fork. Bake in preheated oven for 7 to 11 minutes or until lightly browned. Cool for 5 minutes on sheet, then transfer to a rack and cool completely.

Variations

Replace raisins with dried cranberries.

Replace apple butter with plum butter.

Carrot Cake Cookies

You'll love this bite-size take on carrot cake.

- **Preparation: 30 minutes**
- **Baking: 13 minutes**
- **Freezing: excellent**

TIPS

Peel the carrots before grating. If peel is left on, it may react with the leavening and create green specks in the cookies.

Check your spices regularly as they don't last forever. I replace mine every 6 months. You can buy small amounts in bulk of those you don't use frequently.

- **Preheat oven to 350°F (180°C)**
- **Cookie sheet, greased or lined with parchment paper**

1 ¼ cups	unbleached all-purpose flour	300 mL
½ tsp	baking powder	2 mL
¼ tsp	salt	1 mL
¾ tsp	ground cinnamon	3 mL
¼ tsp	ground nutmeg	1 mL
½ cup	butter, softened	125 mL
½ cup	packed brown sugar	125 mL
1	egg	1
¾ cup	grated peeled carrot	175 mL
¾ cup	raisins	175 mL
¾ cup	chopped pecans	175 mL
½ cup	unsweetened flaked coconut	125 mL

1. On sheet of waxed paper or in a bowl, combine flour, baking powder, salt, cinnamon and nutmeg. Set aside.

2. In a large bowl, using an electric mixer on medium speed, beat butter, brown sugar and egg until light and creamy, about 3 minutes. On low speed, gradually add flour mixture, beating until blended. With a wooden spoon, stir in carrot, raisins, pecans and coconut.

3. Drop dough by tablespoonfuls (15 mL) about 2 inches (5 cm) apart on prepared cookie sheet. Bake in preheated oven for 9 to 13 minutes or until lightly browned. Cool for 5 minutes on sheet, then transfer to a rack and cool completely.

Variations

Replace raisins with dried cranberries.

Omit the nuts.

Replace carrot with grated zucchini.

Applesauce Hermits

Here's an old-fashioned favorite spice cookie made healthier with whole wheat flour and less sugar and fat than the traditional version.

**MAKES ABOUT
2½ DOZEN COOKIES**

- **Preparation: 25 minutes**
- **Baking: 17 minutes**
- **Freezing: excellent**

TIPS

If your raisins have dried out, pour boiling water over them and leave for 5 minutes to soften. Drain and pat dry with paper towels before using.

I like to line cookie sheets with parchment paper. You can easily slip it on and off a cookie sheet without sides. There's no need to wash the sheet and the cookies don't stick.

Replace the butter with a soft, non-hydrogenated margarine, if you prefer.

- **Preheat oven to 325°F (160°C)**
- **Cookie sheet, greased or lined with parchment paper**

¾ cup	whole wheat flour	175 mL
⅔ cup	unbleached all-purpose flour	150 mL
1½ tsp	baking powder	7 mL
1 tsp	ground cinnamon	5 mL
¼ tsp	ground cloves	1 mL
¼ tsp	ground nutmeg	1 mL
⅓ cup	butter, softened	75 mL
⅔ cup	packed brown sugar	150 mL
1	egg	1
¼ cup	unsweetened applesauce	60 mL
1 cup	raisins	250 mL

1. On a sheet of waxed paper or in a bowl, combine whole wheat and all-purpose flours, baking powder, cinnamon, cloves and nutmeg. Set aside.

2. In a large bowl, using an electric mixer on medium speed, beat butter, brown sugar, egg and applesauce until light and creamy, about 3 minutes. On low speed, gradually add flour mixture, beating until blended. With a wooden spoon, stir in raisins.

3. Drop dough by tablespoonfuls (15 mL) about 2 inches (5 cm) apart on prepared cookie sheet. Bake in preheated oven for 13 to 17 minutes or until lightly browned. Cool for 5 minutes on sheet, then transfer to a rack and cool completely.

Variations

Replace applesauce with an equal quantity of milk or yogurt.

Use any combination of chopped dried fruit, such as dates, apricots, cranberries or figs, in place of the raisins.

Spicy Zucchini Cookies

I guarantee that kids prefer their vegetables in cookies rather than cooked or in a salad.

MAKES ABOUT 3½ DOZEN COOKIES

- **Preparation: 30 minutes**
- **Baking: 16 minutes**
- **Freezing: excellent**

TIPS

These cookies are soft and cake-like. Store them in an airtight container.

Never store crisp cookies with soft ones. The crisp ones will soften and the soft ones will dry out.

It isn't necessary to peel the zucchini, unless you expect negative comments about the green flecks.

- **Preheat oven to 350°F (180°C)**
- **Cookie sheet, greased or lined with parchment paper**

1¾ cups	unbleached all-purpose flour	425 mL
2 tsp	baking powder	10 mL
¼ tsp	salt	1 mL
1 tsp	ground cinnamon	5 mL
¼ tsp	ground nutmeg	1 mL
½ cup	butter, softened	125 mL
1 cup	packed brown sugar	250 mL
1	egg	1
¼ cup	milk	60 mL
1½ cups	grated zucchini	375 mL
¾ cup	raisins	175 mL
½ cup	chopped walnuts	125 mL

1. On a sheet of waxed paper or in a bowl, combine flour, baking powder, salt, cinnamon and nutmeg. Set aside.

2. In a large bowl, using an electric mixer on medium speed, beat butter, brown sugar and egg until light and creamy, about 3 minutes. On low speed, add flour mixture alternately with milk, making 3 additions of flour and 2 of milk, beating until blended. With a wooden spoon, stir in zucchini, raisins and walnuts.

3. Drop dough by tablespoonfuls (15 mL) about 2 inches (5 cm) apart on prepared cookie sheet. Bake in preheated oven for 12 to 16 minutes or until lightly browned. Cool for 5 minutes on sheet, then transfer to a rack and cool completely.

Variations

Omit the nuts or replace them with an equal quantity of flaked coconut.

Add 1 tbsp (15 mL) grated orange zest and replace milk with an equal quantity of orange juice.

Crunchy Apricot Oat Drops

Not only are these cookies easy to make, but they are nutritious and delicious as well.

MAKES ABOUT 3 DOZEN COOKIES

- **Preparation: 30 minutes**
- **Baking: 12 minutes**
- **Freezing: excellent**

TIPS

Do not use light or whipped margarine when baking. These products are lower in fat and often contain water, which may result in baked goods that aren't acceptable.

When baking, always place cookie dough on a cool sheet. Cookies will spread too much if the sheet is warm.

Always set your timer for the minimum time suggested. You can always bake longer, if necessary.

- **Preheat oven to 350°F (180°C)**
- **Cookie sheet, greased or lined with parchment paper**

¾ cup	unbleached all-purpose flour	175 mL
½ tsp	baking soda	2 mL
¼ tsp	salt	1 mL
½ tsp	ground cinnamon	2 mL
½ cup	butter, softened	125 mL
¾ cup	packed brown sugar	175 mL
1	egg	1
¾ cup	quick-cooking rolled oats	175 mL
⅓ cup	wheat germ	75 mL
1 cup	crisp rice cereal	250 mL
¾ cup	chopped dried apricots	175 mL
⅓ cup	unsweetened flaked coconut	75 mL
¼ cup	sunflower seeds	60 mL

1. On a sheet of waxed paper or in a bowl, combine flour, baking soda, salt and cinnamon. Set aside.
2. In a large bowl, using an electric mixer on medium speed, beat butter, brown sugar and egg until light and creamy, about 3 minutes. On low speed, gradually add flour mixture, beating until blended. With a wooden spoon, stir in oats and wheat germ. Add cereal, apricots, coconut and sunflower seeds. Mix well.
3. Drop dough by tablespoonfuls (15 mL) about 2 inches (5 cm) apart on prepared cookie sheet. Bake in preheated oven for 8 to 12 minutes or until golden. Cool for 5 minutes on sheet, then transfer to a rack and cool completely.

Variation

Replace apricots with dried cranberries, raisins or chopped dates.

Multigrain Madness

◆

Crunchy grains and seeds give these hearty cookies great texture and taste.

MAKES ABOUT 2 DOZEN COOKIES

- **Preparation: 25 minutes**
- **Baking: 15 minutes**
- **Freezing: excellent**

TIPS

Use candy-coated chocolate pieces such as M&M's.

Store cookies in layers separated by waxed paper in airtight containers.

These cookies freeze well for up to 3 months.

To make small cookies, drop by tablespoonfuls (15 mL) and bake for 8 to 12 minutes.

- **Preheat oven to 350°F (180°C)**
- **Cookie sheet, greased or lined with parchment paper**

1¼ cups	unbleached all-purpose flour	300 mL
½ cup	wheat germ	125 mL
½ tsp	baking soda	2 mL
½ tsp	ground cinnamon	2 mL
⅔ cup	butter, softened	150 mL
½ cup	granulated sugar	125 mL
½ cup	packed brown sugar	125 mL
1	egg	1
⅓ cup	vegetable oil	75 mL
¼ cup	liquid honey	60 mL
2¼ cups	quick-cooking rolled oats	550 mL
1 cup	candy-coated chocolate pieces (see Tips, left)	250 mL
1 cup	raisins	250 mL
½ cup	sunflower seeds	125 mL

1. On a sheet of waxed paper or in a bowl, combine flour, wheat germ, baking soda and cinnamon. Set aside.

2. In a large bowl, using an electric mixer on medium speed, beat butter, granulated and brown sugars and egg until light and creamy, about 3 minutes. Add oil and honey, beating until blended. On low speed, gradually add flour mixture, beating until blended. With a wooden spoon, stir in oats, candy pieces, raisins and sunflower seeds.

3. Drop dough by ¼ cupfuls (60 mL) about 4 inches (10 cm) apart on prepared cookie sheet. Bake in preheated oven for 11 to 15 minutes or until lightly browned. Cool for 5 minutes on sheet, then transfer to a rack and cool completely.

Variations

Replace half of the sunflower seeds with flax seeds.

For an even healthier cookie, replace the candy pieces with dried fruits such as cranberries or chopped apricots or dates.

Refrigerator Spicy Almond Crisps

◆

There's no egg in these cookies and the honey gives them a great flavor.

MAKES ABOUT 9 DOZEN COOKIES

- **Preparation: 30 minutes**
- **Chilling: 4 hours**
- **Baking: 12 minutes**
- **Freezing: excellent**

TIPS

Bake longer if you like crisp cookies and for less time if you prefer them softer.

Store whole wheat flour in the freezer to retain its freshness. It doesn't keep as long as white flour. It has a shelf life of 6 months compared to 1 year for white flour.

Make sure you have at least 2 inches (5 cm) between your cookie sheet and the sides of your oven so the air can circulate properly to ensure even baking.

- **Cookie sheet, ungreased**

2 cups	unbleached all-purpose flour	500 mL
2 cups	whole wheat flour	500 mL
1 1/2 tsp	baking soda	7 mL
1/2 tsp	salt	2 mL
2 tsp	ground cinnamon	10 mL
2 tsp	ground cloves	10 mL
2 tsp	ground ginger	10 mL
1 cup	butter, softened	250 mL
1 cup	granulated sugar	250 mL
3/4 cup	liquid honey	175 mL
1 1/2 cups	finely chopped unblanched almonds	375 mL

1. On a sheet of waxed paper or in a bowl, combine all-purpose and whole wheat flours, baking soda, salt, cinnamon, cloves and ginger. Set aside.

2. In a large bowl, using an electric mixer on medium speed, beat butter, sugar and honey until smooth, about 3 minutes. On low speed, gradually add flour mixture, beating until blended. With a wooden spoon, stir in almonds. Divide dough into halves. Shape each into a roll 14 inches (35 cm) long. Wrap and chill until firm, at least 4 hours.

3. Fifteen minutes before you're ready to bake, preheat oven to 375°F (190°C). Cut rolls into 1/4-inch (0.5) slices. Place about 1 inch (2.5 cm) apart on cookie sheet. Bake in preheated oven for 8 to 12 minutes or until set and lightly browned. Cool for 5 minutes on sheet, then transfer to a rack and cool completely.

Variation
Substitute pecans, walnuts or hazelnuts for the almonds.

Mixed Seed and Fruit Spice Cookies

◆

Flax seeds give these cookies a wonderful crunch and unique flavor, while adding nutritional value.

MAKES ABOUT 3 DOZEN COOKIES

- **Preparation: 30 minutes**
- **Baking: 12 minutes**
- **Freezing: excellent**

TIPS

Store flax seeds in freezer to prevent rancidity.

Flax seeds are a good source of soluble fiber and omega-3 fatty acids. Consumption of omega-3 fatty acids has been linked with lower rates of heart disease and stroke.

- **Preheat oven to 350°F (180°C)**
- **Cookie sheet, greased or lined with parchment paper**

1 ¼ cups	unbleached all-purpose flour	300 mL
½ cup	ground flax seeds	125 mL
½ tsp	baking powder	2 mL
½ tsp	baking soda	2 mL
¼ tsp	salt	1 mL
½ tsp	ground cinnamon	2 mL
½ tsp	ground cloves	2 mL
½ tsp	ground nutmeg	2 mL
⅓ cup	butter, softened	75 mL
⅔ cup	packed brown sugar	150 mL
1	egg	1
⅓ cup	corn syrup	75 mL
2 tbsp	milk	30 mL
¾ cup	chopped dried apricots	175 mL
¾ cup	dried cranberries	175 mL
⅓ cup	sunflower seeds	75 mL
¼ cup	sesame seeds	60 mL
¼ cup	flax seeds	60 mL

1. Combine flour, ground flax seeds, baking powder, baking soda, salt, cinnamon, cloves and nutmeg. Set aside.

2. In a large bowl, using an electric mixer on medium speed, beat butter, brown sugar, egg, corn syrup and milk until smooth and creamy. On low speed, gradually add flour mixture, beating until blended. With a wooden spoon, stir in apricots, cranberries and sunflower, sesame and flax seeds.

3. Drop dough by tablespoonfuls (15 mL) about 2 inches (5 cm) apart on prepared cookie sheet. Bake in preheated oven for 8 to 12 minutes or until lightly browned. Cool for 5 minutes on sheet, then transfer to a rack and cool completely.

Variation

Substitute other dried fruit, such as raisins, or chopped dried mango or dates, for the apricots and cranberries.

Cherry Fruit Logs

Nicely spiced, these cookies are similar to gingerbread with the addition of dried fruits. They are easy to shape, too.

MAKES ABOUT 4 DOZEN COOKIES

- **Preparation: 30 minutes**
- **Chilling: 1 hour**
- **Baking: 15 minutes**
- **Freezing: excellent**

TIPS

Use a sharp serrated knife to cut these cookies.

Don't overbake or the cookies will be crisp rather than chewy.

The recipe makes a large quantity, but the cookies keep well and freeze well.

If you prefer, substitute soft, non-hydrogenated margarine for the butter.

- **Cookie sheet, greased or lined with parchment paper**

1 cup	unbleached all-purpose flour	250 mL
1 cup	whole wheat flour	250 mL
1 tsp	baking soda	5 mL
1/4 tsp	salt	1 mL
1 tsp	ground cinnamon	5 mL
1/2 tsp	ground ginger	2 mL
1/4 tsp	ground cloves	1 mL
1/2 cup	butter, softened	125 mL
1 cup	packed brown sugar	250 mL
1	egg	1
3 tbsp	light (fancy) molasses	45 mL
3 tbsp	cold strong coffee	45 mL
3/4 cup	chopped dried cherries	175 mL
1/2 cup	chopped dried apricots	125 mL
1/3 cup	chopped crystallized ginger	75 mL

1. On a sheet of waxed paper or in a bowl, combine all-purpose and whole wheat flours, baking soda, salt, cinnamon, ginger and cloves. Set aside.

2. In a large bowl, using an electric mixer on medium speed, beat butter, brown sugar, egg, molasses and coffee until smooth and creamy. On low speed, gradually add flour mixture, beating until blended. With a wooden spoon, stir in cherries, apricots and crystallized ginger. Cover and chill for 1 hour.

3. Fifteen minutes before you're ready to bake, preheat oven to 350°F (180°C). Divide dough into quarters. Shape each into a roll 12 inches (30 cm) long. Place 4 inches (10 cm) apart on prepared cookie sheet. Flatten to 2 inches (5 cm) wide. Bake in preheated oven for 10 to 15 minutes or until starting to brown around edges but still soft. Cool on sheets for 10 minutes, then transfer to a cutting board. Cut diagonally into 1-inch (2.5 cm) slices. Transfer to a rack and cool completely.

Variation

Substitute other dried fruits, such as raisins, cranberries or chopped dates or figs, for the cherries.

Mini Hazelnut Biscotti

The honey flavor is especially nice in these small crisp biscotti. They are lower in fat than most biscotti and perfect to dip in coffee or tea.

MAKES ABOUT 5 DOZEN BISCOTTI

- **Preparation: 20 minutes**
- **Baking: 45 minutes**
- **Cooling: 15 minutes**
- **Freezing: excellent**

TIPS

Be prepared — this dough is very stiff, so you will need to work it with your hands to get it smooth.

Use a sharp serrated knife to cut biscotti.

- **Preheat oven to 350°F (180°C)**
- **Cookie sheet, greased or lined with parchment paper**

2 cups	unbleached all-purpose flour	500 mL
2/3 cup	granulated sugar	150 mL
1/2 cup	ground hazelnuts	125 mL
1/2 tsp	baking powder	2 mL
1/2 tsp	baking soda	2 mL
1/4 tsp	salt	1 mL
1 tsp	ground cinnamon	5 mL
3/4 cup	whole hazelnuts	175 mL
1/3 cup	liquid honey	75 mL
2 tsp	grated orange zest	10 mL
1/3 cup	freshly squeezed orange juice	75 mL

1. In a large bowl, combine flour, sugar, ground hazelnuts, baking powder, baking soda, salt, cinnamon and whole hazelnuts. Mix to blend.

2. Add honey and orange zest and juice. With a wooden spoon, stir until blended, then, using your hands, knead to form a smooth, stiff dough.

3. Divide dough into halves. Shape each into a roll 15 inches (37.5 cm) long. Place about 2 inches (5 cm) apart on prepared cookie sheet. Bake in preheated oven for 25 to 30 minutes or until set and golden. Cool for 15 minutes on sheet, then transfer to a cutting board. Cut diagonally into 1/2-inch (1 cm) slices. Place upright about 1 inch (2.5 cm) apart on cookie sheet. Bake for 15 minutes until crisp and golden. Cool for 5 minutes on sheet, then transfer to a rack and cool completely.

Variation

Substitute almonds or Brazil nuts for the hazelnuts.

Chocolate Hazelnut Meringues

The brown sugar adds color and flavor to these chewy meringues. The chocolate and nut topping makes them very attractive — and tasty, too.

MAKES ABOUT 3½ DOZEN COOKIES

- **Preparation: 25 minutes**
- **Baking: 32 minutes**
- **Freezing: not recommended**

TIPS

If you prefer, grate the chocolate on a fine grater rather than chopping it.

Bake 25 to 30 minutes for chewy meringues or 30 to 35 minutes for crisp ones.

- **Preheat oven to 275°F (140°C)**
- **Cookie sheet, lined with parchment paper**

1¼ cups	finely chopped toasted hazelnuts, divided	300 mL
2 tbsp	all-purpose flour	30 mL
4	egg whites	4
¼ tsp	cream of tartar	1 mL
Pinch	salt	Pinch
1½ cups	packed brown sugar	375 mL
1½	squares (1 oz/28 g each) semisweet chocolate, finely chopped (see Tips, left)	1½

1. On a sheet of waxed paper or in a bowl, combine 1 cup (250 mL) of the hazelnuts and flour. Mix well. Set aside.

2. In a small bowl, using an electric mixer on high speed, beat egg whites, cream of tartar and salt until soft peaks form. Gradually add brown sugar, 2 tbsp (30 mL) at a time, beating until stiff peaks form. With a spatula, fold in nut mixture gently but thoroughly.

3. Drop batter by scant tablespoonfuls (10 mL) about 1 inch (2.5 cm) apart on prepared cookie sheet. Bake in preheated oven for 25 to 30 minutes or until firm. Remove from oven and sprinkle chocolate on top of cookies. Bake for 2 minutes to soften chocolate. Sprinkle remaining ¼ cup (60 mL) hazelnuts over chocolate. Cool completely on sheet.

Variations

Substitute an equal quantity of chopped pecans for the hazelnuts.

Add 2 tsp (10 mL) instant espresso coffee powder along with the brown sugar for a nice coffee meringue.

Chewy Cranberry Apricot Balls

If you like to snack on dried fruits and nuts, these are for you.

MAKES ABOUT 5 DOZEN COOKIES

- **Preparation: 20 minutes**
- **Cooking: 15 minutes**
- **Standing: 1 hour**
- **Freezing: excellent**

> **TIP**
>
> Store these and Coconut Apricot Balls in an airtight container in refrigerator.

- **Cookie sheet, lined with waxed paper**

1 1/4 cups	chopped dried apricots	300 mL
2/3 cup	dried cranberries	150 mL
3/4 cup	corn syrup	175 mL
2 1/2 cups	sweetened flaked coconut	625 mL
1 cup	finely chopped pecans	250 mL
3/4 cup	granulated sugar, optional	175 mL

1. Over medium heat, bring apricots, cranberries and corn syrup to a boil. Cover, reduce heat and simmer, stirring often, until thickened, 10 to 15 minutes. Remove from heat. Stir in coconut and pecans and mix well. Cool until easy to handle, about 30 minutes.
2. Shape into 3/4-inch (2 cm) balls. If using, spread sugar in a small shallow dish and roll balls in it until coated. Place on waxed paper. Let stand until dry, about 1 hour.

Coconut Apricot Balls

These balls make a nice dessert with ice cream or sherbet or a great snack because they aren't too sweet.

MAKES ABOUT 2 1/2 DOZEN COOKIES

- **Preparation: 20 minutes**
- **Standing: overnight**
- **Freezing: excellent**

> **TIP**
>
> It's easier to roll these balls if you moisten your hands.

- **Cookie sheet, lined with waxed paper**

1 cup	chopped dried apricots	250 mL
1/2 cup	chopped dates	125 mL
1/2 cup	dried cranberries	125 mL
1 tbsp	grated orange zest	15 mL
3 tbsp	freshly squeezed orange juice	45 mL
1 2/3 cups	sweetened flaked coconut, divided	400 mL
3/4 cup	finely chopped pecans	175 mL

1. In a bowl, combine apricots, dates, cranberries and orange zest and juice. Mix well. Cover and let stand for at least 1 hour.
2. Transfer mixture to a food processor and process until finely chopped. Return to bowl. Add 1 cup (250 mL) of the coconut and pecans. Mix until ingredients are thoroughly moistened.
3. Place remaining coconut in a small shallow dish. Shape mixture into 3/4-inch (2 cm) balls and roll in coconut, pressing firmly. Place on waxed paper. Let stand overnight to dry.

Peanut Butter and Banana Sandwich Cookies

Not Just for Kids

Kids enjoy making cookies that contain their favorite ingredients. That's why recipes in this section include different kinds of cereal, chocolate chips, marshmallows, caramels, potato chips and peanut butter. These cookies are relatively quick and easy to make so kids can quickly arrive at the best part — tasting. For many recipes, you don't even need to turn on the oven.

In addition to creating something delicious to eat, making cookies is a perfect opportunity to enjoy quality family time. It also helps to develop simple practical skills, such as measuring, counting, chopping and mixing, as well as personal qualities such as self-confidence and responsibility. Let your kids choose the recipes they want to make and help with the shopping. They will be thrilled to be able to prepare their own lunch-box treats and after-school snacks. The recipes are foolproof and guarantee results that kids can proudly share with their families and friends.

Peanut Butter and Banana Sandwich Cookies

This no-egg sandwich cookie is as much fun to make as it is to eat.

MAKES ABOUT 2 DOZEN COOKIES

- **Preparation: 35 minutes**
- **Baking: 14 minutes**
- **Freezing: not recommended**

TIPS

These cookies are also excellent left plain without a frosting.

The cookies are crisp and crunchy but will soften a little after they are filled. If you prefer a crisp cookie, fill them no more than a day ahead.

The riper the banana, the better the flavor. The banana should be soft and ripe for easy mixing. If it isn't, mash it with a fork before mixing.

- **Preheat oven to 350°F (180°C)**
- **Cookie sheet, greased or lined with parchment paper**

COOKIE

1 cup	butter, softened	250 mL
1 cup	granulated sugar	250 mL
1/2 cup	thinly sliced ripe banana (1 medium)	125 mL
2 1/3 cups	all-purpose flour	575 mL
1/2 tsp	baking soda	2 mL
1/4 tsp	salt	1 mL
1 cup	chopped peanuts	250 mL

FROSTING

1/4 cup	butter, softened	60 mL
3 tbsp	creamy peanut butter	45 mL
3 cups	confectioners' (icing) sugar, sifted	750 mL
1/4 cup	milk	60 mL

1. *Cookie:* In a large bowl, combine butter, sugar, banana, flour, baking soda and salt. Using an electric mixer on low speed, beat until smooth, scraping the bowl often. With a wooden spoon, stir in peanuts.

2. Drop dough by tablespoonfuls (15 mL) about 2 inches (5 cm) apart on prepared cookie sheet. Bake in preheated oven for 10 to 14 minutes or until golden around edges. Cool for 5 minutes on sheet, then transfer to a rack and cool completely.

3. *Frosting:* In a medium bowl, using an electric mixer on medium speed, beat butter and peanut butter until smooth, about 1 minute. Gradually add confectioners' sugar and milk, beating to a smooth, spreadable consistency. Spread about 1 tbsp (15 mL) frosting on flat side of half of the cookies. Place remaining cookies on top, flat side down. Press gently together.

Variation

If you prefer a non-peanut cookie, substitute pecans. Omit peanut butter in the frosting and increase the butter to 1/3 cup (75 mL).

Chocolate-Covered Raisin Crunchies

Try these cookies with kids who claim to not like raisins. The raisins are in disguise.

MAKES ABOUT 4 DOZEN COOKIES

- **Preparation: 25 minutes**
- **Baking: 13 minutes**
- **Freezing: excellent**

TIPS

To shape drop cookies, fill a tablespoon (15 mL) with dough, then push it off onto the cookie sheet using another spoon or small spatula.

Kids may like to make frozen cookie mounds. Drop the dough on the cookie sheet as above, then freeze until firm. Transfer the pucks to a freezer bag. When ready to use, place on the cookie sheet. Cover with waxed paper and thaw for 30 to 45 minutes at room temperature, then bake as directed.

- **Preheat oven to 350°F (180°C)**
- **Cookie sheet, greased or lined with parchment paper**

1 2/3 cups	all-purpose flour	400 mL
1 1/2 cups	quick-cooking rolled oats	375 mL
1 1/2 tsp	baking powder	7 mL
1/2 tsp	baking soda	2 mL
1/4 tsp	salt	1 mL
2/3 cup	butter, softened	150 mL
2/3 cup	granulated sugar	150 mL
2/3 cup	packed brown sugar	150 mL
2	eggs	2
1 1/2 cups	crisp rice cereal	375 mL
1 cup	chocolate-covered raisins	250 mL
1/2 cup	flaked coconut	125 mL

1. On a sheet of waxed paper or in a bowl, combine flour, oats, baking powder, baking soda and salt. Set aside.

2. In a large bowl, using an electric mixer on medium speed or a wooden spoon, beat butter and granulated and brown sugars until light and creamy, about 3 minutes. Add eggs, one at a time, beating well after each addition. Gradually add flour mixture, beating until blended. With a wooden spoon, stir in cereal, raisins and coconut, mixing until thoroughly blended.

3. Drop dough by tablespoonfuls (15 mL) about 2 inches (5 cm) apart on prepared cookie sheet. Bake in preheated oven for 9 to 13 minutes or until golden. Cool for 5 minutes on sheet, then transfer to a rack and cool completely.

Variations

Replace chocolate-covered raisins with chocolate-covered peanuts or chocolate chips.

Replace rice cereal with crushed corn flakes cereal.

No-Bake Chinese Noodle Crunchies

Children from preschool to teens will enjoy making these cookies.

MAKES ABOUT 3 DOZEN COOKIES

- **Preparation: 15 minutes**
- **Cooking: 4 minutes**
- **Chilling: 1 hour**
- **Freezing: not recommended**

TIPS

It's important to use low heat and stir constantly when melting chips to ensure they don't burn. You can also melt chocolate mixtures in a double boiler.

Be sure your chips are fresh. If they have a whitish coating on them they don't melt as easily.

- **Cookie sheet lined with waxed paper**

1 cup	butterscotch chips	250 mL
1/2 cup	creamy peanut butter	125 mL
2 cups	chopped chow mein noodles	500 mL
1 cup	peanuts	250 mL
1 cup	miniature marshmallows	250 mL

1. In a medium saucepan over low heat, melt butterscotch chips and peanut butter, stirring with a wooden spoon until smooth. Remove from heat. Add noodles and peanuts. Mix well. Add marshmallows, stirring until thoroughly coated.

2. Drop mixture by tablespoonfuls (15 mL) on waxed paper. Chill until set, about 1 hour.

Variation

Use your favorite chip. Chocolate is also great with the peanut butter.

No-Bake Chocolate Peanut Drops

It's hard to find a kid who doesn't like peanut butter and chocolate in any form — bars, candy, ice cream or cake. Add these scrumptious cookies to the list.

MAKES ABOUT 5 DOZEN COOKIES

- **Preparation: 15 minutes**
- **Cooking: 4 minutes**
- **Chilling: 2 hours**
- **Freezing: not recommended**

- **Cookie sheet lined with waxed paper**

1/2 cup	butter	125 mL
1/3 cup	unsweetened cocoa powder, sifted	75 mL
1	can (14 oz or 300 mL) sweetened condensed milk	1
1/2 cup	creamy peanut butter	125 mL
2 1/2 cups	quick-cooking rolled oats	625 mL
1 cup	coarsely chopped peanuts	250 mL
1/2 cup	sunflower seeds	125 mL
1/2 cup	dried cranberries	125 mL

1. In a large saucepan over low heat, cook butter, cocoa and condensed milk, stirring with a wooden spoon until smooth. Remove from heat. Stir in peanut butter until smooth. Add oats, peanuts, sunflower seeds and cranberries. Mix well.

2. Drop dough by tablespoonfuls (15 mL) on waxed paper. Refrigerate until firm, about 2 hours.

No-Bake Chewy Caramel Balls

You don't have to be a kid to love these chewy balls.

MAKES ABOUT 4 DOZEN BALLS

- **Preparation: 20 minutes**
- **Cooking: 8 minutes**
- **Standing: 1 hour**
- **Freezing: excellent**

TIP

When making these balls, lightly butter your hands to make rolling easier.

- **Cookie sheet lined with waxed paper**

9 oz	soft caramels, unwrapped (about 36)	270 g
3 tbsp	half-and-half (10%) cream	45 mL
1 1/2 cups	crisp rice cereal	375 mL
1 cup	corn flakes cereal	250 mL
3/4 cup	flaked coconut	175 mL
1/2 cup	dried cranberries	125 mL
1/3 cup	finely chopped walnuts	75 mL

1. In a small saucepan over low heat, cook caramels and cream, stirring with a wooden spoon until melted and smooth.

2. In a large bowl, combine rice cereal, corn flakes cereal, coconut, cranberries and walnuts. Add caramel mixture. With a wooden spoon, stir until all ingredients are coated. Shape mixture into 1-inch (2.5 cm) balls. Place on waxed paper. Let stand until set, about 1 hour.

No-Bake Strawberries

Here's a colorful cookie that kids can make.

MAKES ABOUT 3 DOZEN STRAWBERRIES

- **Preparation: 20 minutes**
- **Chilling: 2 hours**
- **Standing: 2 hours**
- **Freezing: not recommended**

TIPS

Use fine or medium desiccated coconut. Shredded or flaked is too stringy to shape.

Use a tube of prepared green frosting that comes with a leaf icing tip.

- **Cookie sheet lined with waxed paper**

1	can (14 oz or 300 mL) sweetened condensed milk	1
1	package (6 oz/170 g) strawberry gelatin powder, divided	1
1 tbsp	freshly squeezed lemon juice	15 mL
20 drops	red food coloring	20 drops
4½ cups	medium desiccated coconut (see Tips, left)	1.125 L
	Green frosting (see Tips, left)	

1. In a large bowl, using a wooden spoon, stir sweetened condensed milk, ⅔ cup (150 mL) of the gelatin powder, lemon juice and food coloring until blended. Add coconut, stirring until thoroughly blended. Cover and chill mixture until it is easy to shape, about 2 hours.

2. Shape tablespoonfuls (15 mL) into balls, slightly pointed at one end. Roll in remaining gelatin powder to coat. Put a dab of green frosting on the top to resemble leaves. Place on waxed paper. Let stand at room temperature until dry, about 2 hours. Store in airtight container in refrigerator.

No-Bake Chips 'n' Nut Treats

Potato chips make the special crunch in these candy-like balls.

MAKES ABOUT 40 BALLS

- **Preparation: 15 minutes**
- **Cooking: 8 minutes**
- **Chilling: 1 hour**
- **Freezing: not recommended**

- **Cookie sheet lined with waxed paper**

2 cups	semisweet chocolate chips	500 mL
2 cups	peanut butter chips	500 mL
2 cups	butterscotch chips	500 mL
1 cup	crushed regular potato chips	250 mL
1 cup	chopped peanuts	250 mL
¾ cup	miniature candy-coated chocolate pieces (such as M&M's)	175 mL

1. In a large saucepan over low heat, melt chocolate, peanut butter and butterscotch chips, stirring with a wooden spoon until smooth. Remove from heat. Add potato chips, peanuts and candy pieces. Mix well.

2. Drop by tablespoonfuls (15 mL) on waxed paper. Chill until firm, about 1 hour.

No-Bake Rocky Road Mounds

Kids know the ingredients for Rocky Road long before they are able to make the ice cream or the bars for which it is named, so it won't be hard to convince them to try this recipe.

**MAKES ABOUT
5 DOZEN COOKIES**

- **Preparation: 15 minutes**
- **Cooking: 4 minutes**
- **Chilling: 1 hour**
- **Freezing: not recommended**

- **Cookie sheet lined with waxed paper**

2 cups	semisweet chocolate chips	500 mL
1 cup	creamy peanut butter	250 mL
2 cups	coarsely chopped honey-roasted peanuts	500 mL
5 1/2 cups	miniature white marshmallows	1.375 L

1. In a large saucepan over low heat, melt chocolate chips and peanut butter, stirring with a wooden spoon until smooth. Remove from heat. Stir in peanuts. Mix well. Add marshmallows and stir just until they are coated with chocolate.
2. Drop mixture by tablespoonfuls (15 mL) on waxed paper. Chill until firm, about 1 hour.

Variation

Use milk chocolate chips if you prefer a milder chocolate and stronger peanut butter taste.

Crunchy Sweet and Salty Clusters

This combination of sweet chocolate and butterscotch with salty nuts and pretzels is outstanding.

**MAKES ABOUT
2 DOZEN COOKIES**

- **Preparation: 15 minutes**
- **Cooking: 4 minutes**
- **Chilling: 1 hour**
- **Freezing: not recommended**

- **Cookie sheet lined with waxed paper**

1 cup	milk chocolate chips	250 mL
1 cup	butterscotch chips	250 mL
1/2 cup	chopped cashews	125 mL
1/2 cup	chopped pretzels	125 mL
1/2 cup	miniature candy-coated chocolate pieces	125 mL

1. In a large saucepan over low heat, melt chocolate and butterscotch chips, stirring with a wooden spoon until smooth. Remove from heat. Stir in cashews, pretzels and candy pieces, mixing until all ingredients are coated.
2. Drop mixture by tablespoonfuls (15 mL) on waxed paper. Chill until firm, about 1 hour.

Chocolate Caramel Cereal Drops

If you plan to make these drops for a special occasion, I recommend making two batches. They won't last long.

**MAKES ABOUT
2 DOZEN COOKIES**

- **Preparation: 20 minutes**
- **Cooking: 8 minutes**
- **Standing: 1 hour**
- **Freezing: not recommended**

- **Cookie sheet lined with waxed paper**

4 oz	soft caramels, unwrapped (15)	125 g
2/3 cup	semisweet chocolate chips	150 mL
2 tbsp	water	30 mL
2 cups	corn flakes cereal, slightly crushed	500 mL
3/4 cup	peanuts	175 mL

1. In a medium saucepan over low heat, heat caramels, chocolate chips and water, stirring constantly with a wooden spoon, until melted and smooth. Remove from heat. Stir in cereal and peanuts, mixing until all ingredients are coated.
2. Drop mixture by teaspoonfuls (5 mL) on waxed paper. Let stand until firm, about 1 hour.

Potato Chip Crisps

Potato chips will always be a favorite of kids young and old. Let your kids make these for Dad on Father's Day.

**MAKES ABOUT
3 1/2 DOZEN COOKIES**

- **Preparation: 20 minutes**
- **Baking: 12 minutes**
- **Freezing: excellent**

TIPS

Use regular potato chips, not the flavored variety.

This is like a shortbread dough with lots of added crunch. Yes, there is no egg.

- **Preheat oven to 350°F (180°C)**
- **Cookie sheet, ungreased**

1 cup	butter, softened	250 mL
1/2 cup	packed brown sugar	125 mL
1 tsp	vanilla	5 mL
2 cups	all-purpose flour	500 mL
3/4 cup	crushed potato chips	175 mL
3/4 cup	chopped pecans	175 mL
1/2 cup	butterscotch chips	125 mL

1. In a large bowl, using a wooden spoon, beat butter, brown sugar and vanilla until light and creamy, about 3 minutes. Gradually add flour, stirring until smooth. Add potato chips, pecans and butterscotch chips, mixing until thoroughly blended.
2. Drop dough by tablespoonfuls (15 mL) about 2 inches (5 cm) apart on cookie sheet. Bake in preheated oven for 8 to 12 minutes or until golden around edges. Cool for 5 minutes on sheet, then transfer to a rack and cool completely.

Oatmeal Candy Cookies

Although moms prefer that their kids not eat candy, it's easier to justify when it's combined in an oatmeal cookie.

MAKES ABOUT 3½ DOZEN COOKIES

- **Preparation: 20 minutes**
- **Baking: 13 minutes**
- **Freezing: excellent**

TIPS

The most common brands of candy-coated chocolate pieces are M&M's and Smarties. They are available in bulk stores and stores that carry candies and snacks.

When baking cookies, if you like the nutty flavor of whole wheat flour, you can substitute an equal quantity of it for all-purpose flour. When trying the substitution for the first time, I prefer to use half and half to see if I like the flavor.

- **Preheat oven to 350°F (180°C)**
- **Cookie sheet, greased or lined with parchment paper**

1 cup	all-purpose flour	250 mL
1½ tsp	baking powder	7 mL
½ tsp	baking soda	2 mL
¼ tsp	salt	1 mL
½ cup	butter, softened	125 mL
½ cup	granulated sugar	125 mL
½ cup	packed brown sugar	125 mL
1	egg	1
1 tsp	vanilla	5 mL
1 cup	quick-cooking rolled oats	250 mL
1 cup	candy-coated chocolate pieces	250 mL
½ cup	unsweetened flaked coconut	125 mL

1. On a sheet of waxed paper or in a bowl, combine flour, baking powder, baking soda and salt. Set aside.

2. In a large bowl, using an electric mixer on medium speed, beat butter, granulated and brown sugars, egg and vanilla until light and creamy, about 3 minutes. On low speed, gradually add flour mixture, beating until smooth. With a wooden spoon, stir in oats, candy pieces and coconut.

3. Drop dough by tablespoonfuls (15 mL) on prepared cookie sheet. Bake in preheated oven for 9 to 13 minutes or until golden. Cool for 5 minutes on sheet, then transfer to a rack and cool completely.

Variation

Replace the candy pieces with chopped chocolate-covered nuts or halved baking gumdrops, which are available at bulk stores. They are smaller than regular gumdrops and don't melt when heated.

Banana Granola Cookies

What could be better than wholesome granola in a soft cake-like banana cookie? Dress up these cookies with a banana frosting or leave them plain to pack for lunch or snacking. Packed in a school lunch box, they make a great treat.

MAKES ABOUT 4 DOZEN COOKIES

- **Preparation: 25 minutes**
- **Baking: 13 minutes**
- **Freezing: excellent**

TIP

If you don't have an electric mixer, most drop cookies can be mixed with a wooden spoon. It takes a little more work to get the mixture light and creamy. The cookies will have a more homemade look. Kids usually prefer using a spoon and don't mind the extra effort. Plus they get to lick the spoon.

- **Preheat oven to 375°F (190°C)**
- **Cookie sheet, greased or lined with parchment paper**

COOKIE

1 1/2 cups	all-purpose flour	375 mL
1/2 tsp	baking soda	2 mL
1/4 tsp	salt	1 mL
1 tsp	ground cinnamon	5 mL
1/2 cup	butter, softened	125 mL
1 cup	packed brown sugar	250 mL
1	egg	1
1 cup	mashed ripe banana (2 medium)	250 mL
1 cup	granola cereal	250 mL
1/2 cup	unsweetened flaked coconut	125 mL
1/2 cup	raisins	125 mL
1/3 cup	sunflower seeds	75 mL

BANANA FROSTING, OPTIONAL

1/4 cup	butter, softened	60 mL
1/4 cup	mashed ripe banana (1/2 medium)	60 mL
2 cups	confectioners' (icing) sugar, sifted	500 mL
2 tsp	freshly squeezed lemon juice	10 mL

1. *Cookie:* On a sheet of waxed paper or in a bowl, combine flour, baking soda, salt and cinnamon. Set aside.

2. In a large bowl, using an electric mixer on medium speed or a wooden spoon, beat butter, brown sugar and egg until light and creamy, about 3 minutes. Beat in banana. Gradually add flour mixture, beating until blended. With a wooden spoon, stir in cereal, coconut, raisins and sunflower seeds, mixing until thoroughly blended.

3. Drop dough by tablespoonfuls (15 mL) about 2 inches (5 cm) apart on prepared cookie sheet. Bake in preheated oven for 9 to 13 minutes or until golden. Cool for 5 minutes on sheet, then transfer to a rack and cool completely.

4. *Banana Frosting, optional:* In a medium bowl, using an electric mixer on medium speed, beat butter and mashed banana until smooth. Gradually add confectioners' sugar and lemon juice, beating to a smooth, spreadable consistency. Spread frosting on top of cooled cookies.

Chocolate Marshmallow Sandwich Cookies

I had so much fun making these cookies, I can just imagine how much kids will enjoy the process.

**MAKES ABOUT
2 DOZEN SANDWICH
COOKIES**

- **Preparation: 25 minutes**
- **Baking: 12 minutes**
- **Freezing: not recommended**

TIPS

Use colored marshmallows for fun.

Don't worry — the tops of these cookies will have a crackled look.

Marshmallows don't freeze well. For longer storage, freeze the cookies and assemble the sandwiches when you're ready to eat them.

- **Preheat oven to 350°F (180°C)**
- **Cookie sheet, ungreased**

2 cups	all-purpose flour	500 mL
1/2 cup	unsweetened cocoa powder, sifted	125 mL
2 tsp	baking soda	10 mL
2/3 cup	butter	150 mL
1 1/2 cups	granulated sugar, divided	375 mL
1	egg	1
1/4 cup	corn syrup	60 mL
1/3 cup	miniature chocolate chips	75 mL
24	large marshmallows	24

1. On a sheet of waxed paper or in a bowl, combine flour, cocoa and baking soda. Set aside.
2. In a large bowl, using an electric mixer on medium speed, beat butter, 1 1/4 cups (300 mL) of the sugar, egg and corn syrup until light and creamy, about 3 minutes. On low speed, gradually add flour mixture, beating until smooth. With a wooden spoon, stir in chocolate chips.
3. Shape dough into 1-inch (2.5 cm) balls. Roll in remaining 1/4 cup (75 mL) sugar to coat well. Place about 2 inches (5 cm) apart on cookie sheet. Bake in preheated oven for 8 to 12 minutes or until set. Cool for 5 minutes on sheet, then transfer to a rack and cool completely.
4. *Assembly:* Place 1 marshmallow on the flat side of 1 cookie. Place on small paper plate. Microwave on High for 12 to 15 seconds or until marshmallow just starts to bulge and is hot. Immediately place another cookie, flat side down, on top of the marshmallow. Press gently so marshmallow spreads to outer edge of cookie. Repeat with remaining cookies and marshmallows.

Variation

Fill these cookies with a scoop of your favorite ice cream. Place in the freezer until you're ready to serve. For storage, wrap individually in plastic wrap.

Spicy Oatmeal Raisin Cookies

Cake Mix Cookies

The convenience of a cake mix gives you a jump-start on baking a batch of delicious cookies. The cake mix makes the batter hold even the crunchiest, chunkiest ingredients. Because many of the ingredients are pre-measured, it eliminates much of the need for measuring, which also saves on washing up. The pre-measured ingredients also reduce the room for error. I'm sure once you've tried a few of the cookie recipes made with a cake mix, you'll agree they're quick, easy and delicious — a perfect choice for spur-of-the-moment treats. Keep one chocolate and one white cake mix on hand for whenever you feel the urge to make homemade cookies.

Spicy Oatmeal Raisin Cookies

Once a favorite, always a favorite.

MAKES ABOUT 4 DOZEN COOKIES

- **Preparation: 15 minutes**
- **Baking: 12 minutes**
- **Freezing: excellent**

TIPS

Use quick-cooking oats to make cookies. You can use large-flake old-fashioned oats for a more "oaty" taste, but the texture will change slightly.

Don't let cookies remain on the baking sheet longer than 5 minutes. They will continue to cook and be more difficult to remove.

- **Preheat oven to 375°F (190°C)**
- **Cookie sheet, greased or lined with parchment paper**

1	package (18.25 oz/515 g) white cake mix	1
1 cup	quick-cooking rolled oats	250 mL
2 tsp	ground cinnamon	10 mL
1 tsp	ground nutmeg	5 mL
2	eggs	2
½ cup	vegetable oil	125 mL
1 cup	raisins	250 mL

1. In a large bowl, using an electric mixer on low speed, beat cake mix, oats, cinnamon, nutmeg, eggs and oil for 1 minute or just until blended. With a wooden spoon, stir in raisins.

2. Drop dough by tablespoonfuls (15 mL) about 2 inches (5 cm) apart on prepared cookie sheet. Flatten slightly with fingers or an offset spatula. Bake in preheated oven for 8 to 12 minutes or until lightly browned. Cool for 5 minutes on sheet, then transfer to a rack and cool completely.

Variation

Replace raisins with dried cranberries or a mixture of other dried fruits, such as chopped papaya, pineapple, mango and dates. Adjust spice to suit your own taste.

Gingerbread Shapes

Don't limit these to the festive season. With different cookie-cutter shapes and decorations, you can make gingerbread a year-round treat.

MAKES ABOUT 2 DOZEN COOKIES

- **Preparation: 30 minutes**
- **Chilling: 3 hours**
- **Baking: 12 minutes**
- **Freezing: excellent (not decorated)**

TIPS

Use Royal Icing (see recipe, page 422) or a prepared icing to frost these cookies.

If making gingerbread people cookies, press raisins for eyes and colorful candies for buttons in dough before baking.

If you're baking ahead, don't add the decorations. Cool and store the cookies in a container with a loose-fitting lid. They are ready to decorate when you are.

- **Preheat oven to 375°F (190°C)**
- **4-inch (10 cm) cookie cutter**
- **Cookie sheet, greased or lined with parchment paper**

1	package (18.25 oz/515 g) spice cake mix	1
3/4 cup	all-purpose flour	175 mL
2 tsp	ground ginger	10 mL
2	eggs	2
1/3 cup	vegetable oil	75 mL
1/3 cup	light (fancy) molasses	75 mL
	Vanilla frosting, optional (see Tips, left)	

1. In a large bowl, using a wooden spoon, combine cake mix, flour, ginger, eggs, oil and molasses, mixing until smooth (dough will be soft). Cover and refrigerate until firm enough to handle, about 3 hours.

2. On a lightly floured surface, roll out dough to 1/4-inch (0.5 cm) thickness. Cut with cookie cutter dipped in flour. Place on prepared cookie sheet (see Tips, left). Bake in preheated oven for 8 to 12 minutes or until edges start to brown. Cool for 5 minutes on sheet, then transfer to a rack and cool completely.

Variation

There are different sizes of gingerbread people cutters and various shapes of different sizes that you can use to make these cookies. Decrease baking time if you are using smaller cutters and increase time for larger ones.

Chocolate Macadamia Nut Oatmeal Cookies

Loaded with chocolate and luscious macadamia nuts, these cookies are a real treat.

MAKES ABOUT 5 DOZEN COOKIES

- **Preparation: 20 minutes**
- **Baking: 15 minutes**
- **Freezing: excellent**

TIP

Use large-flake old-fashioned oats for a more "oaty" taste. Be sure not to use instant oatmeal, which doesn't work in baking because it's too fine.

- **Preheat oven to 375°F (190°C)**
- **Cookie sheet, greased or lined with parchment paper**

1	package (18.25 oz/515 g) white cake mix	1
½ cup	quick-cooking rolled oats	125 mL
2	eggs	2
½ cup	butter, melted	125 mL
1 tsp	vanilla	5 mL
1½ cups	coarsely chopped macadamia nuts	375 mL
1½ cups	semisweet chocolate chunks or chips	375 mL

1. In a large bowl, using an electric mixer on low speed, beat cake mix, oats, eggs, melted butter and vanilla for 1 minute or just until smooth. With a wooden spoon, stir in nuts and chocolate chunks.

2. Drop dough by tablespoonfuls (15 mL) about 2 inches (5 cm) apart on prepared cookie sheet. Bake in preheated oven for 10 to 15 minutes or until light golden. Cool for 5 minutes on sheet, then transfer to a rack and cool completely.

Variation

Substitute pecans for macadamia nuts and white chocolate chunks for the semisweet.

Peanut Butter Cookies

An old-fashioned favorite that is easier to prepare with the use of a cake mix.

MAKES ABOUT 4 DOZEN COOKIES

- **Preparation: 20 minutes**
- **Baking: 14 minutes**
- **Freezing: excellent**

- **Preheat oven to 375°F (190°C)**
- **Cookie sheet, greased or lined with parchment paper**

1 cup	creamy peanut butter	250 mL
2	eggs	2
1 tbsp	milk	15 mL
1	package (18.25 oz/515 g) white cake mix	1
	Granulated sugar	

1. In a large bowl, combine peanut butter, eggs, milk and half of the cake mix, mixing well. Add remaining cake mix. Blend well, then use your hands to form a smooth dough.
2. Shape dough into 1-inch (2.5 cm) balls. Place about 2 inches (5 cm) apart on prepared cookie sheet. Press flat with a fork dipped in sugar. Bake in preheated oven for 10 to 14 minutes or until set. Cool for 5 minutes on sheet, then transfer to a rack and cool completely.

Cereal Crisps

Cereal never tasted so good. There's a lot of crunch packed into every bite of these delicious cookies. It won't be hard to convince kids to eat their breakfast cereal.

MAKES ABOUT 4 DOZEN COOKIES

- **Preparation: 20 minutes**
- **Baking: 12 minutes**
- **Freezing: excellent**

- **Preheat oven to 375°F (190°C)**
- **Cookie sheet, greased or lined with parchment paper**

1	package (18.25 oz/515 g) white cake mix	1
1	egg	1
½ cup	water	125 mL
½ cup	vegetable oil	125 mL
1¼ cups	crisp rice cereal	300 mL
¾ cup	corn flakes cereal	175 mL
½ cup	unsweetened flaked coconut	125 mL
½ cup	chopped walnuts	125 mL

1. In a large bowl, using an electric mixer on low speed, beat cake mix, egg, water and oil until smooth. Stir in rice cereal, corn flakes cereal, coconut and walnuts.
2. Drop dough by tablespoonfuls (15 mL) about 2 inches (5 cm) apart on prepared cookie sheet. Bake for 8 to 12 minutes or until lightly browned around edges. Cool for 5 minutes on sheet, then transfer to a rack and cool completely.

Lemon Crisps

Crisp and lemony —
this is a wonderful plain
cookie to enjoy with a cup
of tea.

**MAKES ABOUT
4 DOZEN COOKIES**

- **Preparation: 20 minutes**
- **Baking: 12 minutes**
- **Freezing: excellent**

TIPS

When grating the zest for
lemons and oranges, use
only the colored part. The
white pith underneath has
a bitter flavor.

You can also mix this
dough using an electric
mixer on low speed for
1 minute.

- **Preheat oven to 350°F (180°C)**
- **Cookie sheet, greased or lined with parchment paper**

1	package (18.25 oz/515 g) lemon cake mix	1
1	egg	1
½ cup	butter, melted	125 mL
1 tsp	grated lemon zest	5 mL
	Granulated sugar	

1. In a large bowl, using a wooden spoon, combine cake mix, egg, melted butter and lemon zest, mixing until well blended.

2. Place granulated sugar in small shallow dish. Shape dough into 1-inch (2.5 cm) balls. Roll balls in granulated sugar until evenly coated. Place about 2 inches (5 cm) apart on prepared cookie sheet. Press flat with bottom of a glass dipped in sugar. Bake in preheated oven for 8 to 12 minutes or until lightly browned around edges. Cool for 5 minutes on sheet, then transfer to a rack and cool completely.

Variation

Make these into sandwich cookies by putting 2 cookies together with lemon frosting or raspberry jam between.

Chunky Chocolate Pecan Cookies

A good choice for the cookie jar.

MAKES ABOUT 4½ DOZEN COOKIES

- **Preparation: 20 minutes**
- **Baking: 15 minutes**
- **Freezing: excellent**

- **Preheat oven to 375°F (190°C)**
- **Cookie sheet, greased or lined with parchment paper**

1	package (18.25 oz/515 g) white cake mix	1
2	eggs	2
½ cup	butter, melted	125 mL
1 tsp	vanilla	5 mL
1½ cups	semisweet chocolate chunks or chips	375 mL
1¼ cups	coarsely chopped pecans	300 mL

1. In a bowl, beat cake mix, eggs, melted butter and vanilla just until smooth. Stir in chocolate chunks and pecans.

2. Drop dough by tablespoonfuls (15 mL) about 2 inches (5 cm) apart on prepared cookie sheet. Bake in preheated oven for 10 to 15 minutes or until light golden. Cool for 5 minutes on sheet, then transfer to a rack and cool completely.

Refrigerator Nut Wafers

With a roll of dough in the refrigerator, fresh-baked cookies are only minutes away.

MAKES ABOUT 7 DOZEN COOKIES

- **Preparation: 20 minutes**
- **Chilling: 4 hours**
- **Baking: 11 minutes**
- **Freezing: excellent**

- **Cookie sheet, greased or lined with parchment paper**

1	package (18.25 oz/515 g) white cake mix	1
1	egg	1
½ cup	butter, melted	125 mL
1 tbsp	water	15 mL
1 tsp	vanilla	5 mL
1½ cups	chopped pecans or hazelnuts	375 mL

1. In a bowl, combine cake mix, egg, melted butter, water and vanilla. Add pecans and knead to form a smooth dough. Divide dough into halves. Shape each into a roll 2 inches (5 cm) in diameter. Wrap and chill until firm, about 4 hours.

2. Preheat oven to 375°F (190°C). Cut rolls into ⅛-inch (3 mm) slices. Place about 1 inch (2.5 cm) apart on prepared cookie sheet. Bake in preheated oven for 7 to 11 minutes or until lightly browned around the edges. Cool for 5 minutes on sheet, then transfer to a rack and cool completely.

Chocolate Caramel Pecan Cookies

Pecans and chocolate chips always go well together in cookies.

MAKES ABOUT 4 DOZEN COOKIES

- **Preparation: 20 minutes**
- **Baking: 12 minutes**
- **Freezing: excellent**

- **Preheat oven to 375°F (190°C)**
- **Cookie sheet, greased or lined with parchment paper**

1	package (18.25 oz/515 g) white cake mix	1
2	eggs	2
½ cup	butter, melted	125 mL
6	squares (1 oz/28 g each) semisweet chocolate, chopped	6
25	individual soft caramels, quartered	25
¾ cup	chopped pecans	175 mL

1. In a bowl, beat cake mix, eggs and melted butter for 1 minute or just until smooth. Stir in chocolate, caramels and pecans.

2. Drop dough by tablespoonfuls (15 mL) about 2 inches (5 cm) apart on prepared cookie sheet. Flatten slightly with fingers or an offset spatula. Bake in preheated oven for 8 to 12 minutes or until lightly browned. Cool for 5 minutes on sheet, then transfer to a rack and cool completely.

Double Chocolate Dreams

A chocoholic's dream. Try them warm from the oven, but be prepared to make a second batch.

MAKES ABOUT 4 DOZEN COOKIES

- **Preparation: 20 minutes**
- **Baking: 12 minutes**
- **Freezing: excellent**

- **Preheat oven to 375°F (190°C)**
- **Cookie sheet, greased or lined with parchment paper**

1	package (18.25 oz/515 g) devil's food cake mix	1
2	eggs	2
½ cup	vegetable oil	125 mL
2 cups	semisweet chocolate chips	500 mL
¾ cup	chopped nuts, your choice	175 mL

1. In a large bowl, using a wooden spoon, combine cake mix, eggs and oil, mixing until well blended. Dough will be stiff. Stir in chocolate chips and nuts.

2. Drop dough by tablespoonfuls (15 mL) about 2 inches (5 cm) apart on prepared cookie sheet. Bake in preheated oven for 8 to 12 minutes or just until set. Cool for 5 minutes on sheet, then transfer to a rack and cool completely.

Almond Crisps

This is a plain, crisp cookie with a delightful almond flavor.

MAKES ABOUT 4 DOZEN COOKIES

- **Preparation: 25 minutes**
- **Baking: 12 minutes**
- **Freezing: excellent**

TIPS

Although recipes usually call for an electric mixer to blend ingredients, you can almost always use a wooden spoon when making cookies. This batter can also be mixed using an electric mixer on low speed for 1 minute.

Use unblanched almonds for an attractive appearance. The flecks of brown skin add a nice flavor, too.

Cooled baked cookies can be frozen in airtight plastic bags for up to 6 months.

- **Preheat oven to 375°F (190°C)**
- **Cookie sheet, greased or lined with parchment paper**

1	package (18.25 oz/515 g) white cake mix	1
1 cup	very finely chopped or ground almonds	250 mL
1	egg	1
1/2 cup	butter, melted	125 mL
1 tbsp	water	15 mL
1 tsp	almond extract	5 mL
	Granulated sugar	
	Whole almonds, optional	

1. In a large bowl, using a wooden spoon, combine cake mix, almonds, egg, melted butter, water and almond extract until blended, about 1 minute.

2. Shape dough into 1-inch (2.5 cm) balls. Place about 2 inches (5 cm) apart on prepared cookie sheet. Press flat with bottom of glass dipped in sugar. If desired, press an almond on top of each cookie. Bake in preheated oven for 8 to 12 minutes or until lightly browned. Cool for 5 minutes on sheet, then transfer to a rack and cool completely.

Variations

Replace almonds with hazelnuts or pecans.

Replace almond extract with vanilla.

Hazelnut Biscotti

Double baking makes biscotti extra crunchy, so they are ideal for dunking into your favorite drink. Because they are very firm and dry, they stay fresh and are unlikely to break during shipping, which makes them a good choice if you want to mail a homemade gift.

MAKES ABOUT 3½ DOZEN BISCOTTI

- **Preparation: 15 minutes**
- **Baking: 35 minutes**
- **Cooling: 15 minutes**
- **Freezing: excellent**

TIPS

Use a sharp serrated knife for cutting biscotti.

Parchment paper makes easy work of transferring the biscotti to a cutting board.

Store biscotti in airtight containers for up to 3 weeks.

- **Preheat oven to 350°F (180°C)**
- **Cookie sheet, greased or lined with parchment paper**

1	package (18.25 oz/515 g) white cake mix	1
⅔ cup	all-purpose flour	150 mL
⅓ cup	ground hazelnuts	75 mL
2	eggs	2
½ cup	vegetable oil	125 mL
1 tbsp	grated lemon zest	15 mL
⅔ cup	coarsely chopped hazelnuts	150 mL

1. In a large bowl, using an electric mixer on low speed, beat cake mix, flour, ground hazelnuts, eggs, oil and lemon zest for 1 minute or until blended. With a wooden spoon, stir in chopped hazelnuts. Using your hands, knead to form a smooth dough.

2. Divide dough into halves. On a prepared cookie sheet, shape each into a 10- by 3-inch (25 cm by 7.5 cm) rectangle, approximately ½ inch (1 cm) thick. Bake in preheated oven for 15 minutes until firm and golden. Cool for 15 minutes on sheet, then transfer to a cutting board. Cut into ½-inch (1 cm) slices. Place cut side down on cookie sheet. Bake for 10 minutes. Turn slices over and bake for 5 to 10 minutes or until crisp and golden. Cool for 5 minutes on sheet, then transfer to a rack and cool completely.

Variations

Use your favorite nut. Pecans and almonds work well in these cookies.

Omit lemon zest.

Rum Balls

There are many recipes for this classic no-bake treat. It's nice to make while another recipe is in the oven — or in the summer, when you don't want to turn on the oven.

**MAKES ABOUT
5 DOZEN COOKIES**

- **Preparation: 20 minutes**
- **Standing: 1 hour**
- **Freezing: excellent**

TIPS

This is an excellent way to use leftover cake, if that ever happens. Keep this recipe in mind if you have the opportunity to bake an extra cake when preparing another cake recipe.

Prepare these balls several days ahead to let flavors develop.

Place in small paper cups for serving or gift giving.

◆

- **Cookie sheet lined with waxed paper**

1	package (18.25 oz/515 g) chocolate cake mix, baked and cooled	1
1 cup	finely chopped walnuts	250 mL
4 tsp	rum	20 mL
2 cups	confectioners' (icing) sugar, sifted	500 mL
1/4 cup	unsweetened cocoa powder, sifted	60 mL
	Finely chopped nuts or chocolate sprinkles	

1. In a large bowl, crumble cake. With a fork, stir cake until crumbs are fine and uniform in size. Add walnuts, rum, confectioners' sugar and cocoa. With a wooden spoon, stir until thoroughly blended.

2. Spread nuts or sprinkles in a small shallow dish. Shape heaping tablespoonfuls (20 mL) of dough into 1-inch (2.5 cm) balls. Roll balls in nuts or sprinkles, pressing firmly to adhere coating. Place on prepared cookie sheet. Let stand for about 1 hour, until set. Store in an airtight container in refrigerator.

Variations

Rum can be replaced with 1 tsp (5 mL) rum extract.

Use pecans or almonds in place of the walnuts.

Chocolate Peanut Butter Cookies

These cookies are just like peanuts — you can't stop at just one.

**MAKES ABOUT
4 DOZEN COOKIES**

- **Preparation: 20 minutes**
- **Baking: 12 minutes**
- **Freezing: excellent**

- **Preheat oven to 350°F (180°C)**
- **Cookie sheet, greased or lined with parchment paper**

1	package (18.25 oz/515 g) devil's food cake mix	1
1 cup	creamy peanut butter	250 mL
2	eggs	2
¼ cup	milk	60 mL
1 cup	peanut butter chips	250 mL
¾ cup	chopped peanuts	175 mL

1. In a large bowl, using a wooden spoon, combine cake mix, peanut butter, eggs and milk, mixing until blended. Stir in peanut butter chips and peanuts.

2. Drop dough by tablespoonfuls (15 mL) about 2 inches (5 cm) apart on prepared cookie sheet. Bake in preheated oven for 8 to 12 minutes or until set. Cool for 5 minutes on sheet, then transfer to a rack and cool completely.

Crispy Chocolate Chunk Cookies

The addition of crispy rice cereal gives these cookies a pleasingly chewy texture that complements the chocolate.

**MAKES ABOUT
4 DOZEN COOKIES**

- **Preparation: 20 minutes**
- **Baking: 12 minutes**
- **Freezing: excellent**

- **Preheat oven to 375°F (190°C)**
- **Cookie sheet, greased or lined with parchment paper**

1	package (18.25 oz/515 g) devil's food cake mix	1
2	eggs	2
½ cup	butter, melted	125 mL
6	squares (1 oz/28 g each) semisweet chocolate, coarsely chopped	6
1½ cups	crisp rice cereal	375 mL

1. In a large bowl, using an electric mixer on low speed, beat cake mix, eggs and melted butter for 1 minute or just until smooth. With a wooden spoon, stir in chocolate and cereal.

2. Drop dough by tablespoonfuls (15 mL) about 2 inches (5 cm) apart on prepared cookie sheet. Flatten slightly with fingers. Bake in preheated oven for 8 to 12 minutes or until set. Cool for 5 minutes on sheet, then transfer to a rack and cool completely.

Crunchy Chocolate Dreams

The taste of these rich, dark cookies resembles a chocolate bar.

MAKES ABOUT 4 DOZEN

- **Preparation: 20 minutes**
- **Baking: 12 minutes**
- **Freezing: excellent**

- **Preheat oven to 375°F (190°C)**
- **Cookie sheet, greased or lined with parchment paper**

1	package (18.25 oz/515 g) devil's food cake mix	1
2	eggs	2
½ cup	vegetable oil	125 mL
1 cup	semisweet chocolate chips	250 mL
¾ cup	chopped walnuts	175 mL
¾ cup	crunchy toffee bits	175 mL

1. In a large bowl, using a wooden spoon, combine cake mix, eggs and oil, mixing until well blended (dough will be stiff). Stir in chocolate chips, walnuts and toffee bits.

2. Drop dough by tablespoonfuls (15 mL) about 2 inches (5 cm) apart on prepared cookie sheet. Bake in preheated oven for 8 to 12 minutes or until firm around edges. Cool for 5 minutes on sheet, then transfer to a rack and cool completely.

Double Chocolate Chewies

This versatile chocolate cookie lends itself to a variety of additions, such as chips, nuts and dried fruit.

MAKES ABOUT 4 DOZEN COOKIES

- **Preparation: 20 minutes**
- **Baking: 12 minutes**
- **Freezing: excellent**

- **Preheat oven to 375°F (190°C)**
- **Cookie sheet, greased or lined with parchment paper**

1	package (18.25 oz/515 g) devil's food cake mix	1
1	egg	1
⅓ cup	water	75 mL
¼ cup	butter, melted	60 mL
1½ cups	white chocolate chips	375 mL
½ cup	dried cranberries	125 mL
½ cup	slivered almonds	125 mL

1. In a large bowl, using an electric mixer on low speed, beat cake mix, egg, water and melted butter for 1 minute or just until smooth. With a wooden spoon, stir in chocolate chips, cranberries and almonds.

2. Drop dough by tablespoonfuls (15 mL) about 2 inches (5 cm) apart on prepared cookie sheet. Bake in preheated oven for 8 to 12 minutes or just until softly set. Cool for 5 minutes on sheet, then transfer to a rack and cool completely.

Index

Library and Archives Canada Cataloguing in Publication

Snider, Jill, 1947–
  Bake something great! : 400 bars, squares & cookies / Jill Snider.

Includes index.
Compilation of two previous titles by author: Bars & squares, 2006, and Cookies, 2007.

ISBN 978-0-7788-0281-5

  1. Cookies. 2. Bars (Desserts). 3. Cookbooks. I. Title.

TX772.S635 2011   641.8'654   C2011-902994-4